Criminal Law in Russia

Criminal Law in Russia

Svetlana Paramonova

This book was originally published as a monograph in the International Encyclopaedia of Laws/Criminal Law.

Founding Editor: Roger Blanpain
General Editor: Frank Hendrickx
Volume Editors: Frank Verbruggen & Vanessa Franssen

Wolters Kluwer

Published by:
Kluwer Law International B.V.
PO Box 316
2400 AH Alphen aan den Rijn
The Netherlands
E-mail: international-sales@wolterskluwer.com
Website: lrus.wolterskluwer.com

Sold and distributed by:
Wolters Kluwer Legal & Regulatory U.S.
7201 McKinney Circle
Frederick, MD 21704
United States of America

ISBN 978-94-035-3120-5

e-Book: ISBN 978-94-035-3121-2
web-PDF: ISBN 978-94-035-3122-9

To my beloved Dad, Leonid

The Author

Dr. Svetlana Paramonova, Dipl. jur., L.L.M., Ph.D., is a professor at the Master Program on International Criminal Justice of the Rovira Virgili University (Tarragona, Spain) since 2019. From 2017 until 2018, Svetlana was a professor at the Department of European and International Law at the Free University of Brussels (Vesalius College), Belgium. Previously, she was a Robert Schuman Fellow at the Research Service for Members of the European Parliament in Brussels as well as a senior researcher (Marie-Curie Fellow) at the Faculty of Criminal Law of the University of Zagreb (Croatia). For seven years, until 2015, Dr. Svetlana Paramonova was a senior researcher at the Max Planck Institute for Foreign and International Law (Freiburg, Germany).

She obtained her law diploma at the Federal University of Siberia in Krasnoyarsk, Russia, in 2006. The same year, she was awarded "The Best Thesis of Law in 2006" in the International Law section, organized by the Association of Universities of Russian Law, Moscow University. During her studies, she received a scholarship to study at the University of Greifswald (Germany). At the Federal University of Siberia, she was responsible for international exchange programs at the Department of Comparative Law. From 2003 to 2006, she worked as a legal advisor to the law clinic and as a lawyer at the university's Institute of Law. In 2008, supported by a grant from the German Academic Exchange Service (DAAD), she completed her L.L.M. at the University of Passau (Germany). There, she was a research assistant at the Department of Criminal and Procedural Law and responsible for DAAD projects for Russia.

She received a Ph.D. from the University of Passau in 2013 for a dissertation on criminal jurisdiction in cyberspace. For her book "Internationales Strafrecht im Cyberspace," Svetlana received the "German-Russian Award for Lawyers 2014" organized by the German-Russian Lawyers Association (Deutsch-Russische Juristenvereinigung e.V.). Since 2014, Svetlana has been a reviewer of academic journals/books at the Higher School of Economics (HSE), Moscow (Russia). She is a member of the Petersburger Dialog, Berlin, as well as the German-Russian Forum "Potsdamer Begegnungen."

She has published widely on constitutional, criminal (comparative) law and on investment guarantees. Numerous publications focused on Russian law, particularly in the areas of jurisdictions in cyberspace, human rights, bioethical issues, and the death penalty. Svetlana is the author of more than fifty publications, including two books, chapters in collective volumes, articles, and conference papers.

Table of Contents

List of Abbreviations

APEC	Asia-Pacific Economic Cooperation
App. No.	Application Number
CAT	UN Committee Against Torture
CIS	Commonwealth of Independent States
CoE	Council of Europe
Const.	Конституция (Constitution of the Russian Federation)
CPT	European Committee for the Prevention of Torture and Inhuman and Degrading Treatment or Punishment
GDP	Gross Domestic Product
ECHR	European Convention on Human Rights
ECtHR	European Court of Human Rights
FKZ	Федеральный Конституционный Закон (Federal Constitutional Law)
FSSS	Федеральная служба государственной статистики Российской Федерации (Federal State Statistics Service of the Russian Federation)
FZ	Федеральный Закон (Federal Law)
GKR	Гражданский Кодекс РФ (Civil Code of the Russian Federation)
ICCPR	International Covenant on Civil and Political Rights
ICESCR	International Covenant on Economic, Social and Cultural Rights
KoAPR	Кодекс об административных нарушениях Российской Федерации (Administrative Code)
KritVj	Kritische Vierteljahresschrift für Gesetzgebung und Rechtswissenschaft (Legal journal)
MZMP	Moskovskij Zhurnal mezhdunarodnogo prava (Legal journal)
MINEC	Ministry of Economic Development of the Russian Federation
NKR	Налоговый Кодекс РФ (Tax Code of the Russian Federation)
NKVD	Народный Комиссариат Внутренних Дел (People's Commissariat of Internal Affairs)
OECD	Organisation for Economic Co-operation and Development

List of Abbreviations

OtP	Федеральный Закон «О полиции» (Federal Law On the Police)
para.	paragraph
RF	Российская Федерация (Russian Federation)
RSFSR	Российская Советская Федеративная Социалистическая Республика (Russian Soviet Federative Socialist Republic)
UIKR	Уголовно-исполнительный Кодекс Российской Федерации (Correctional Code of the Russian Federation)
UKR	Уголовный Кодекс Российской Федерации (Criminal Code of the Russian Federation)
UN	United Nations
UPKR	Уголовно-процессуальный Кодекс Российской Федерации (Code of Criminal Procedure of the Russian Federation)
USSR	Союз Советских Социалистических Республик (Union of Soviet Socialist Republics)
ZSP	Zhurnal zarubezhnogo zakonodatel´stva i sravnitel´nogo pravovedenija (Legal journal)
ZStW	Zeitschrift für die gesamte Strafrechtswissenschaft (Legal journal)

General Introduction

§1. The General Background of Russia

I. Geography and Climate

1. Russia is the largest country in the world, with Moscow as its capital city. Russia covers an area of 17,098,200 sq.km, over 45% of which are north of the Arctic Circle, where permafrost and polar nights reign. Russia covers Eastern Europe and Northern Asia. Its territory consists of 13% of cultivated land, 51% of forest land, 13% of surface water, including swamps.[1]

2. Russia's frontiers run to 58,222 km in length. Russia is bounded by Arctic Ocean seas (Barents, White, Kara Laptev, Eastern Siberian, Tchukotka seas), Pacific Ocean seas (Bering, Okhotsk, Japanese seas), and Atlantic Ocean seas (Baltic, Black, Azov seas). Kaliningrad oblast[2] is an exclave of Russia. It is surrounded by two States: Lithuania and Poland, and borders the Baltic Sea. The largest islands are Archipelago New Land (82.6 sq.km), Sakhalin (76.4 sq.km), Novosibirsk Archipelago (38 sq.km), Archipelago Northern Land (37 sq.km). Russia has borders with 14 sovereign States as well as South Ossetia and Abkhazia, which are both recognized as sovereign States by Russia. The borders are situated as follows: in the North West with Norway and Finland, in the West with Estonia, Latvia, Belarus, Lithuania and Poland (with the last two via Kaliningrad oblast), in the South West with Ukraine, in the South with Georgia, Azerbaijan and Kazakhstan, in the South East with China, Mongolia and the Korean People's Democratic Republic, and finally, in the East with USA (by the Bering Strait) and Japan (by the Sea of Okhotsk).[3]

3. At the southern-most border of Russia (Northern Caucasus), average temperatures reach 0°C–minus 5°C in January. In the northern-most part of Russia (East of the Republic of Sakha, Yakutia), average temperatures in January are minus 40°C–50°C. The lowest temperatures in this region reach minus 65°C–70°C. The world's lowest minimum January temperature (outside Antarctica) occurred in Oymyakon, southeast of Verkhoyansk (North Siberia), where a temperature of

1. MINEC, 2014.
2. 'Oblast' is a type of federal subject of the Russian Federation. For details on the administrative structure, *see* paras. 11–20.
3. Federal State Statistics Service of the Russian Federation (hereinafter FSSS).

minus 71°C was recorded.[4] In July, the average temperature ranges from 1°C on the northern coast of Siberia to 24°C to 25°C on the Caspian plain.[5]

II. Population

4. Russia is the tenth most populous nation in the world. According to the latest figures available, its population is ca. 146,748,600.[6] The sex ratio is 46% of men to 54% of women, which has remained stable for the last six years. 74% (ca. 108,590,000) of the entire population live in towns/cities, 26% (38,150,000) in rural areas. Though Russia's population is comparatively large, its density is low because of the enormous size of the country: ca. 11 persons per 1 sq.km.[7] The population is densest in European Russia, near the Ural Mountains, and in southwest Siberia. The number of emigrants to Russia more than doubled from 2009 (1,987,598) to 2013 (4,496,861).[8] The most populated cities in Russia are Moscow (counting temporary registrations but not illegal migrants) with 12,692,466 inhabitants (8.7% of the entire population) and St. Petersburg counting 5,392,992 inhabitants (3.6% of the entire population).[9]

5. Russia is a diverse, multiethnic society. Although almost 80% of Russian citizens identify themselves as ethnic Russians, there are other large ethnic and religious groups: Tatars 4%, Ukrainians 2%, Bashkir 1.2%, Chuvash 1.1%, Chechens 0.9%, Armenians 0.8%, others (including Koreans, Chinese, Vietnamese, Daghestani, Ingush, Byelorussians, Georgians, Moldavians, Gypsies, and Jews) 10.4%.[10]

6. According to Article 68 of the **Constitution of the Russian Federation** of 1993 (Const.),[11] Russian is the official state language. The Constitution, however, allows the existence of **co-official languages**. There are 27 co-official languages within Russia's various constituencies. Co-official languages are used in daily life as well as in all official procedures, for instance, in the criminal proceedings in those particular regions/republics. For instance, Kalmyk (Mongolic language family; in the Republic of Kalmykia) or Tuvan (Turkic language family; in the Tuva Republic). Co-official languages are under federal protection. The Federal Constitutional Law on the State Language[12] and the Federal Law on the Languages of the Ethnic Groups of the Russian Federation[13] contain further regulations on this matter.

---

4. North Siberia, http://www.excursion.siberia-eco.org/html/north_siberia.html, last accessed: May 13, 2016; Mayr, Spiegel N 8, 2006.
5. FSSS; *see* Paramonova, National characteristics, fundamental principles, and history of criminal law in Russia, 2014, pp. 175–178.
6. FSSS, state of 2020.
7. FSSS, state 2020.
8. FSSS, state 2013; *see also* "Russia cracking down on illegal migrants." International Herald Tribune, Jan. 15, 2007.
9. FSSS, state of 2009; for the figures of 2020, *see* World population review.
10. FSSS, state of 2020, *see* World population review; *see* Encyclopedia Britannica: Russia.
11. Constitution of the Russian Federation, Dec. 12, 1993.
12. Federal Constitutional Law "On the State Language," Jun. 1, 2005, N 53-FZ.
13. Federal Law "On the Languages of the Nations of the Russian Federation," Oct. 25, 1991, N 1807-I.

III. Economy

7. In 2019, the **gross domestic product (GDP)** of Russia was USD 1750 billion, the sixth largest in the world, with the GDP growing at 1.8% per year.[14] The GDP value of Russia represents 1.44% of the world economy.

8. In addition to being one of the world's leading producers of oil and natural gas, Russia is also a top exporter of metals, such as steel and primary aluminum.[15] A revival of Russian agriculture in recent years has led to Russia shifting from being a net grain importer to a net grain exporter. Since 2018, Russia is the world's top wheat exporter. Wheat production in 2020 is forecast at 73.5 million tonnes, up from 71.6 million the previous year. According to the preliminary data from the FSSS, the production of all grains in Russia in 2021 will be 121 million tonnes.[16] In 2018, the composition of the **GDP by sector** was as follows: agriculture 3.15%, industry 32.06.3%, and services 54.12%.[17]

9. The **GDP per capita** on a purchasing power parity basis divided by population for the year 2017 was USD 30,284.[18] Approximately 11% of Russians lived below the national poverty line in 2013, significantly down from 40% in 1998 at the worst of the post-Soviet collapse.[19] The dependence of the Russian economy on oil was exposed during the 2008–2009 global financial crisis and eventually again in 2014. The situation worsened with the imposition of sanctions by the West. The economy contracted by 0.2% in 2016; however, it rebounded with a 1.5% growth in 2017.[20] In 2018, the GDP Annual Growth Rate was already at 2.5%.[21] The unemployment rate in 2018 (4.8%) decreased by ca. 0.3% in comparison to the previous year's estimate (5.1%).[22]

10. The Russian Federation played a leading role in the economy of the Soviet Union by virtue of its great size and abundant natural resources. Under the Soviet regime, these resources made possible great economic advances, including the rapid development of mining, metallurgy, and heavy engineering, the expansion of the railway network, and a massive increase in the energy supply, especially in the production of oil, gas, and electricity.[23] Russia has, however, undergone significant changes since the dissolution of the Soviet Union, moving from a globally isolated, centrally planned economy to a more globally integrated, market-based economy. Economic reforms in the 1990s privatized most industries, with notable exceptions

14. CIA World Factbook, World Bank data (2019 est.).
15. CIA World Factbook.
16. FSSS, state of 2020.
17. CIA World Factbook (2019 est.).
18. International Monetary Fund, 2019; also *see* https://www.investopedia.com/insights/worlds-top-economies/.
19. "Russia's economy under Vladimir Putin": RIA Novosti.
20. International Monetary Fund, 2019; also *see* https://www.investopedia.com/insights/worlds-top-economies/.
21. FSSS, state 2019.
22. CIA World Factbook.
23. Encyclopedia Britannica: Russia.

in the energy and defense-related sectors. Nonetheless, the rapid privatization process, including a much-criticized "loans-for-shares" scheme that turned over major state-owned firms to politically connected "oligarchs," has left equity ownership highly concentrated.[24]

IV. Political and Administrative Structure

A. Contemporary System of the Russian Federation

11. According to Article 1 of the Constitution of the Russian Federation (approved by referendum on December 12, 1993), Russia is a democratic federal state with a **republican form of government**. There is a strong presidency, and the legal system is governed by the rule of law. The names "Russian Federation" ***(Российская Федерация)*** and "Russia" ***(Россия)*** are equipollent.

12. State power in the Russian Federation is vested in the President of the Russian Federation ***(Президент Российской Федерации)***, the Federal Assembly ***(Федеральное Собранце)*** the **Government of the Russian Federation** ***(Правительство Российской Федерации)***, and the courts of the Russian Federation ***(суды Российской Федерации)*** (Article 11 Const.).

13. The **President** of the Russian Federation is the head of state (Articles 80–93 Const.) and is elected by the voters under conditions of universal, equal, and direct suffrage (18 years old) by secret ballot. He or she cannot serve more than two consecutive terms. In 2008, an amendment to the Constitution, which took effect with the 2012 election, extended the presidential term from four to six years.[25] As Russia's head of state, the President is vested with significant powers. He or she determines the basic direction of Russia's domestic and foreign policy and appoints the chairman of the Government, key judges, as well as federal ministers. The President is also the commander in chief of the armed forces and can declare war or a state of emergency. He or she is entitled to issue decrees ***(указы)*** that basically have the force of law.

14. The **Federal Assembly** ***(Федеральное Собрание,*** Articles 94–110 Const.)—the Parliament of the Russian Federation—is a representative legislative body of the Russian Federation and is composed of two Houses: the **Council of the Federation** ***(Совет Федерации)*** and the **State Duma** ***(Государственная Дума)***

24. Paramonova, National characteristics, fundamental principles, and history of criminal law in Russia, 2014, pp. 180–182.
25. The Federal Constitutional Law "On the Change of the Presidential Term and of the Term of the State Duma," N 6-FKZ.

The Council of the Federation is the upper chamber of the Federal Assembly. It consists of 170 representatives: each of the 85 entities of the Federation sends two representatives to the Council. The State Duma—the lower chamber of the Federal Assembly—consists of 450 deputies who are elected for the term of four years (Articles 94, 95 Const.).

15. The power to initiate legislation in the Russian Federation belongs to the President, the Council of the Federation, the members of the Council of the Federation, the deputies of the State Duma, the Government, and the legislative (representative) bodies of the entities of the Federation. The Constitutional Court, the Supreme Court, and the Supreme Arbitration Court can initiate legislation within the scope of their authority.

16. The Federal Laws adopted by the State Duma (by a majority of votes of the total number of deputies) must be submitted within five days for consideration by the Council of the Federation. Bills are submitted to the State Duma (Article 104, paragraphs 1, 2 Const.). A Federal Law is considered to be approved by the Council of the Federation if over half of the total number of members of the chamber have voted for it or if the Council of the Federation does not consider it within fourteen days. If the Council of the Federation rejects a law, the two chambers may create a conciliatory commission for overcoming contradictions that arose, after which the Federal Law must be recognized by the State Duma. If the State Duma disagrees with the decision of the Council of the Federation, a Federal Law is considered adopted if, during a second vote, not less than two-thirds of the total number of deputies of the State Duma support it (Article 105 Const.). The adopted Federal Law must be submitted within five days to the President of the Russian Federation for signing and promulgation (Article 107 Const.).[26]

17. According to Article 1 of the Constitution, the Russian Federation is a **federal state** *(федеративное государство*, Article 1 Const.). In 1993, the number of **entities of the Federation** *(субъекты Российской Федерации)* reached 89. In recent years, several regions were merged, and the number of entities was reduced to 83.[27] Through the referendum held in Crimea in March 2014, two additional regions (Republic of Crimea and Sevastopol) were adjoined to Russia.[28] Currently, the Russian Federation has 85 "entities of the Federation": 22 **republics** *(республика)*, 9 **territories** *(край)* , 46 **regions** *(область),* 1 **autonomous region** *(автономная область),* 4 **autonomous districts** *(автономный округ),* and 3 **cities of federal importance** *(город федерального значения)* which are St. Petersburg, Moscow, and Sevastopol (Article 65 Const.).

26. *See* Paramonova, National characteristics, fundamental principles, and history of criminal law in Russia, 2014, pp. 182–184.
27. With the amendments introduced to the Constitution in the following Federal Constitutional Laws: Jul. 21, 2007 (2007 N 5-FKZ); Dec. 30, 2006 (2006 N 6-FKZ); Jul. 12, 2006 (2006 N 2-FKZ); Oct. 14, 2005 (2005 N 6-FKZ); Mar. 25, 2004 (2004 N 1-FKZ).
28. Mar. 21, 2014 (2014 N 6-FKZ) "On the admission of the Republic of Crimea into the Russian Federation."

18. The "entities of the Federation" are subdivided into 1864 districts, 1098 cities and towns, 333 urban districts and areas, 1850 urban settlements, 243,261 rural administrations.[29] Republics, autonomous districts, and autonomous regions are formed and named after the eponymous nationality (e.g., Tuva Republic). Those parts of Russia that do not form autonomous ethnic units are divided into various territories and regions (e.g., Krasnoyarskij kraj). Since the early 1990s, ethnicity has caused numerous conflicts (e.g., in Chechnya and Dagestan) within and between these units. Many national minorities have demanded more autonomy and, in a few cases, even complete independence.

B. USSR System

19. Previously, the Soviet governmental system was based on principles of centralized administration with the **General Secretary** *(генеральный секретарь)* as the head of the one-party system. The consecutive Constitutions promulgated in 1918, 1924, 1936, and 1977 did, in fact, not limit state power. The idea of separation of powers, as such, was regarded as deconstructive.[30] The **Supreme Council** *(Верховный Совет)* was the highest legislative body in the USSR and the only body with the power to pass constitutional amendments. In addition, it elected the Executive Committee, appointed the Procurator General of the USSR and formed the Supreme Court and the **Council of Ministers** *(Совет Министров)*—the highest executive and administrative body.

20. From 1985 onward, the new policies of "**glasnost**" (public voicing, *гласность*) and "perestroika" (reconstruction, *перестройка*), which were characterized by maximum openness of the governmental system and freedom of information, were introduced by *Mikhail Gorbachev*. However, that so-called liberalization shock therapy with its wide-ranging reforms, including reform of the system of government, pushed the country into a deep crisis, which it has been recovering from in the last years, reaching a relative level of stability approximately in the year 2000. Russia, that is, the Russian Soviet Federative Socialist Republic (RSFSR), being the largest republic of the USSR, became the legal successor of the Soviet Union and took up the responsibility for settling the USSR's external debts after its dissolution.[31]

V. The Judicial System

21. The organization of the judicial system is based on the principle of jurisdictional unity. Special jurisdictions are expressly forbidden by the Russian Constitution, with the only limited exception of the military courts: "The judicial system of

29. FSSS, state of 2010.
30. Kucherov, The Organs of Soviet Administration of Justice, 1970.
31. Paramonova, National characteristics, fundamental principles, and history of criminal law in Russia, 2014, p. 182.

the Russian Federation shall be instituted by the Constitution of the Russian Federation and the Federal Constitutional Law. The creation of extraordinary courts shall not be allowed" (Article 118, paragraph 3 Const.). The judicial power shall be exercised by means of constitutional, civil, administrative, and criminal proceedings (Article 1, paragraph 2 Const.).

22. The Constitution of the Russian Federation guarantees the separation of powers and judicial independence by setting out that judges are independent and are bound only by the law (Article 120 Const.). It establishes that "justice in the Russian Federation shall be administered by courts alone" (Article 118, paragraph 1 Const.). Russian judges are selected on the basis of highly competitive examinations and are appointed for their lifetime. They may only be removed, suspended, transferred, or retired on the grounds and subject to the safeguards provided for by law.[32]

23. For details on the judicial system, see *infra*, General Introduction, §2, III, trial jurisdictions and Part II, chapter I, §1, judicial organization.[33]

§2. Criminal Law, Criminal Justice, and Criminal Science

I. Definitions of Criminal Law

A. Criminal Law and Substantive Criminal Law

24. The term for **criminal law** in Russian, ***уголовное право,*** translated literally means "law regarding the head."[34] Early in its history, criminal law represented the aggregate of the rules that foresaw the most severe penalty, namely capital punishment (where persons could lose their heads).[35] While there is currently no legislative definition of criminal law, definitions can be found in the legal literature. Accordingly, criminal law ***(уголовное право),*** which is identical to **substantive criminal law** ***(материальное уголовное право)*** ,[36] is an independent branch of law that represents the embodiment of legal norms that regulate the social relations that result from the commission of the most socially dangerous acts (crimes) and that impose foreseen punishments by the state. The goal of criminal law is to protect individuals, society, and the state from the violation of interests that are

32. *See* Paramonova/Bogush, ZStW 125 (2013), pp. 703–728.
33. On the judicial system, *see* General Introduction, §1, paras. 21–23, 52–55.
34. Paramonova, National characteristics, fundamental principles, and history of criminal law in Russia, 2014, p. 238.
35. Naumov, Rossiiskoe ugolovnoe pravo, p. 1; Korobeev, Polnij kurs ugolovnogo prava, pp. 14–16.
36. Kropachev, Ugolovnoe pravo Rossii, p. 14, 69; Korobeev, Polnij kurs ugolovnogo prava, pp. 14–16; Lebedev, Kommentarij k UK RF, p. 29; Kuznezova/Tyazhkova, Kurs ugolovnogo prava, p. 67.

recognized as protected legal interests.[37] In the broadest sense, the term "criminal law" encompasses all criminal law related areas: substantive criminal law, criminal procedure, and correctional law.[38]

25. Scholars regard **crime** *(преступление)* and **punishment** *(наказание)* as fundamental subdivisions of the criminal law.[39] The main law that regulates the social relationships resulting from the commission of crimes is the Criminal Code of the Russian Federation (UKR).[40]

26. The Criminal Code is the only law that can establish criminal responsibility. None of the other laws or executive or judicial decisions can criminalize behavior independently of the UKR (principle of the complete codification of criminal offenses).[41]

B. Criminal Procedure

27. The law of **criminal procedure** *(уголовно-процессуальное право)* is the branch of law concerned with legal provisions governing the procedures by which authorities investigate, prosecute, and adjudicate crimes, and it defines the procedural rights and obligations of the participants of the criminal proceedings (suspects, defendants, witnesses, victims, experts, representatives of the prosecution and defense).[42]

28. Criminal procedure represents a self-contained branch of law. Substantive criminal law cannot be enforced without the rules of criminal procedure. The latter, likewise, is not of use without substantive criminal law. For instance, substantive criminal law determines the grounds of justification, whereas the proceedings belong to the domain of criminal procedural law (Article 75 UKR and Article 28 UPKR). Russian Code of Criminal Procedure[43] is the major law in this area.[44]

---

37. Naumov, Rossiiskoe ugolovnoe pravo, pp. 1, 16; Korobeev, Polnij kurs ugolovnogo prava, Zhuravlev/Nikulin, Ugolovnoe pravo, pp. 3–4.
38. For the correctional law, *see* infra Part III, paras. 1361–1491
39. Sergeevskij, Russkoe ugolovnoe pravo, pp. 10–13; Shargorodskij, Soviet Criminal Law, N 4, 1941, 41; Taganzev, Russkoe ugolovnoe pravo, p. 16; Ignatov/Krasikov, Kurs rossijskogo ugolovnogo prava, p. 3; Korobeev, Polnij kurs ugolovnogo prava, p. 16.
40. Criminal Code of the Russian Federation, Jun. 13, 1996, N 63-FZ (Ugolovnij Kodeks RF, UKR); Paramonova, National characteristics, fundamental principles, and history of criminal law in Russia, 2014, p. 238.
41. For the sources of criminal law, *see* below General Introduction, §5, II, B, paras. 155–167; Komissarov/Krilova/Tyazhkova, Ugolovnoe pravo RF, p. 24; Paramonova, National characteristics, fundamental principles, and history of criminal law in Russia, 2014, p. 241.
42. For crime and criminal prosecution, *see* Part II, Chapter 1, §6, paras. 858–926; Matuzov, Teorija gosudarstva i prava, p. 233; Sucharev, Kommentarij k UPK RF, pp. 16–18.
43. Russian Code of Criminal Procedure, Dec. 18, 2001, N 174-FZ (Ugolovno prozessual´nij Kodeks RF, UPKR).
44. For the sources of criminal law, *see* below General Introduction, §5, II, B. paras. 155–167.

C. Correctional Law or Enforcement of Criminal Sanctions

29. **Correctional law** ***(уголовно-исполнительное право)*** represents a self-contained branch of law. It regulates the legal status of prisoners and addresses questions pertaining to the execution and service of sentences. The Correctional Code of the Russian Federation (UIKR)[45] is the main law regulating these legal issues. Other normative acts of federal executive authorities that regulate this criminal law-related area are laid down in subordinate legislation.[46]

30. Even though some scholars regard criminal procedure and correctional law as sub-branches of a superordinate criminal law, according to the prevailing opinion, they are independent branches of law. This is because these branches of law have content, methods, and functions that are different from (substantive) criminal law.[47]

D. Criminal Offenses

31. In contemporary doctrine and legislation, there are four main indicators of criminal offense or **crime** ***(преступление)***. It should be a socially dangerous act or **omission** ***(общественно опасное деяние),*** which is prohibited by means of criminal law regulations—**illegality** ***(противоправность)*** under threat of punishment—**punishability** ***(наказуемость)***—and committed culpably—**culpability** ***(виновность)***.[48]

32. The current legal definition of the criminal offense or crime is laid down in Article 14 of the Criminal Code of the Russian Federation (UKR). This definition is regarded as a formal-substantive one. The existence of both, a formal indicator (illegality) and a substantive one (a reference to the social danger of the criminal offense), characterizes the formal-substantive concept of the crime. Thus, the criminal offense is a behavior that is illegal in its form and socially dangerous in its content.[49]

Art. 14 UKR (Definition of Crime)

(1) A socially dangerous act committed with guilt and prohibited by this Code under threat of punishment shall be deemed a criminal offense.

---

45. Correctional Code of the Russian Federation, Jan. 8, 1997, N 1-FZ (Ugolovno-isponitel´nij Kodeks RF, UIKR).
46. For the sources of criminal law, *see* below General Introduction, §5, II, B, paras. 155–167.
47. For the methodology of distinguishing between the branches of law, *see* below General Introduction, §2, II, paras. 36–42; Sucharev, Kommentarij k UPK RF, p. 16; Matuzov, Teorija gosudarstva i prava, p. 233.
48. Lebedev, Kommentarii k UK RF, p. 54; Kropachev, Ugolovnoe pravo Rossii, p. 334.
49. For the concept of the criminal offense, *see* Part I, Chapter 3, §1, paras. 317–321; Kropachev, Ugolovnoe pravo Rossii, p. 326; Paramonova, Concept and systematization of the criminal offense in Russia, 2011, p. 86.

(2) An action (or omission), although formally containing the indicia of any act provided for by the present Code but by virtue of insignificance does not represent a social danger, shall not be a criminal offense.[50]

33. The Criminal Code defines only criminal offenses. Administrative offenses that have a lower degree of social danger are defined by the Administrative Code. Substantively, criminal, administrative, and civil offenses differ as to the degree of social danger.[51] The spheres of the interests protected by these three areas of law overlap: for example, both criminal and civil law protect property. Criminal law is applied in the case of more severe infringements—crimes or criminal offenses—administrative or civil law in the case of less severe infringements.

34. The UKR distinguishes between the following categories of crimes: **crimes of small gravity** *(преступления небольшой тяжести)*, **crimes of average gravity** *(преступления средней тяжести)*, and grave crimes *(тяжкие преступления)*, and **especially grave crimes** *(особо тяжкие преступления)*. Every criminal offense falls under one of these categories.[52]

35. The terms "crime" *(преступление)* and "criminal offense" *(преступное деяние)* are equipollent.

II. Characteristics of Criminal Law

36. Criminal law, as well as administrative law, are considered parts of *public law*.[53] In contrast, civil law belongs to private law. The criterion for distinguishing between public law and private law is a matter of controversy among scholars. Distinguishing criteria can be found by combining leading theories presented in the doctrine: the **theory of the subject matter of the legal regulation** *(теория предмета правового регулирования)*, the **theory of the method of the legal regulation** *(теория метода)*, and the **theory of the protected legal interest** *(теория интереса)*.[54]

37. According to the first theory, the subject matter of the legal regulation is the decisive criterion of distinction: public law is the structural subsystem of the law that regulates legal relationships between government bodies and subordinated individuals/legal entities; private law, in contrast, regulates legal relationships between equal individuals/legal entities. The method is regarded as another distinguishing criterion: compulsory methods of legal regulation are applied primarily in public law, whereas in private law, the nonmandatory method prevails. The branches

---

50. For the concept and definition of the criminal and administrative offenses, *see* Part I, Chapter 3, §1, paras. 327–329.
51. For the concept of the criminal offense, *see* Part I, Chapter 3, §1, paras. 317–321.
52. For the classification of criminal offenses, *see* Part I, Chapter 6, §1, paras. 635–637.
53. Komissarov/Krilova/Tyazhkova, Ugolovnoe pravo RF, pp. 21–22.
54. Matuzov, Teorija gosudarstva i prava, pp. 403–406.

of public law predominantly protect the legal interests of the state and society as a whole. In contrast, in private law, individual interests have priority over collective interests.[55]

38. As a means of social control, criminal law is considered the reaction of the state to the most dangerous forms of conduct in society.[56] Criminal law as a social institution (and later on as an established, centralized legal institution) was meant to facilitate the sustainable coexistence of the community, primarily by protecting important public interests.[57] Thus, the primary, historically determined function of criminal law is its **protective function** ***(охранительная функция)***: it responds to the violation of interests that are recognized as worthy of (public law) protection.[58]

39. As a reaction to the most serious infringements of legally protected interests, criminal law fulfills both an *ultima ratio* function and a **regulative function** ***(регулятивная функция)***. The latter can be seen in the influence exerted on social behavior by criminal law norms (e.g., prohibitions against murder, theft, etc.), whose purpose is to promote law-abiding behavior.[59]

40. By means of legally binding provisions, criminal law also fulfills a **preventive function** ***(превентивная функция)***.While prevention may be considered a function of criminal law,[60] the legal literature considers it primarily a purpose of punishment (Article 43, paragraph 2 UKR).[61]

41. While incentives, as well as educational functions, are often seen as a part of the preventive function of the criminal law (i.e., prevention achieved by stimulating lawful behavior),[62] some authors consider them separate functions. The independent incentive or **stimulating function** ***(поощрительная функция)*** refers to a "positive," active prevention of crime and of the consequences of crime, despite the primarily "punitive" nature of criminal law. Examples of norms that stimulate law-abiding behavior are provisions of the General Part of the Criminal Code, such as those covering excuses (Articles 75–78 UKR) and justifications (Articles 37–42 UKR).

42. Although the repressive goal or function of criminal law as such is neither discussed explicitly in the scholarship, nor does it appear explicitly in legal provisions, criminal law cannot exist without repressive measures. These measures are

---

55. Paramonova, National characteristics, fundamental principles, and history of criminal law in Russia, 2014, p. 238.
56. Naumov, Rossiiskoe ugolovnoe pravo, p. 23.
57. Sudebniki Rusi XV–XVI. Moscow-Leningrad 1952.
58. Naumov, Rossiiskoe ugolovnoe pravo, p. 24.
59. Korobeev, Polnij kurs ugolovnogo prava, p. 25; Revin, Ugolovnoe pravo Rossii.
60. Naumov, Rossiiskoe ugolovnoe pravo, p. 25.
61. Paramonova, National characteristics, fundamental principles, and history of criminal law in Russia, 2014, pp. 221–222.
62. Naumov, Rossiiskoe ugolovnoe pravo, p. 24.

justified as necessary for the realization of criminal law's integrative, protective role. This protective role is derived from the principle of humanity (Article 21 Const., Article 7 UKR).[63]

III. Overview of the Criminal Justice System

A. *Investigating Authorities*

43. The investigating institutions and the scope of their authority are provided for by the **Code of Criminal Procedure of the Russian Federation** (*Ugolovno prozessual'nij Kodeks RF*,[64] UPKR, Articles 150, 151). There are two **forms of preliminary investigations** (*предварительное расследование,* Article 150 UPKR): **pretrial investigations** (*предварительное следствие)* and **inquiries** *(дознание).*[65] The form employed depends on the character and the gravity of the committed crime. Pretrial investigations are conducted by **investigating bodies or investigators** *(следователи),* while inquiries are conducted by **inquiry bodies or inquirers** *(дознаватели).* The investigating authorities work under the supervision of the prosecutor (Article 37, paragraph 1 UPKR).[66]

44. In contrast to inquiry bodies, which deal only with minor criminal offenses, for example, Article 112 **Criminal Code of the Russian Federation**—*Ugolovnij Kodeks RF*, hereinafter "UKR"—(intentional causing of average gravity harm to health) and Article 168 UKR (destruction or damage of property by negligence), investigating bodies deal with more serious crimes (Articles 38, 40, 41, 150, paragraph 2, 223 UPKR).

45. There are different types of investigating bodies. **Investigators of the domestic affairs bodies** *(следователи органов внутренних дел)* have jurisdiction over ordinary crimes, including aggravated theft (Article 158, paragraphs 2–4 UKR). **Investigators of the investigative committee** *(следователи следственного комитета)* deal with the same types of crimes but of a more serious nature, such as murder (Article 105 UKR), human trafficking (Article 127.1 UKR), etc. **Investigators of the bodies of the federal security service** *(следователи органов федеральной службы безопасности)* are authorized to deal with crimes related to issues of state security, such as terrorism (e.g., Article 205 UKR), treason (Article 275 UKR), smuggling (Article 188 UKR), etc. **Investigators of the bodies for the control over drug traffic and psychotropic substances** *(следователи органов по контролю за оборотом наркотических средств и психотропных веществ)* deal with drug-related crimes.

---

63. Korobeev, Polnij kurs ugolovnogo prava, p. 23; Uss, Sozialno-integrativnaya rol´ugolovnogo prava, p. 3.
64. Dec. 18, 2001, N 174-FZ.
65. Paramonova, National characteristics, fundamental principles, and history of criminal law in Russia, 2014, pp. 185–186.
66. For the criminal procedure, *see* Part II, Chapter 1, §6, paras. 858–926.

46. The following institutions are responsible for conducting inquiries, the second type of preliminary investigation (Article 151, paragraph 2 UPKR): **inquirers of the domestic affairs bodies** ***(дознаватели органов внутренних дел)***,**inquirers of the customs bodies** ***(дознаватели таможенных органов)***, **inquirers of the fire inspection bodies** ***(дознаватели органов пожарного надзора)*** as well as inquirers subordinate to various other governmental agencies. Captains of sea and river vessels and heads of diplomatic representations are also considered inquiry authorities (Article 40, paragraph 3 UPKR).

47. All investigative authorities (investigators and inquirers) are subordinate to a specific federal governmental agency according to their investigative competencies; for instance, investigative authorities under the Federal Air Transport are responsible for the investigation of the air transport offenses. However, the main burden of investigation lies on investigators and inquirers of the domestic affairs body—police ***(полиция)***. The police are subordinate to the **Ministry of the Interior** ***(Министерство Внутренних Дел—МВД)***.[67] In March 2011, the Federal Law on the Police (OtP) replaced the Law on Militia.[68] This law contains some structural changes regarding law enforcement authorities. These show a clear centralizing tendency. For instance, the structure of the regional domestic affairs bodies is determined by the President (Article 4 paragraph 4 Law on Police).[69]

B. Prosecuting Authorities

48. Prosecution on behalf of the state in criminal cases (public and private-public prosecution)[70] must be conducted by the **prosecutor** ***(прокурор)***, Articles 21, paragraph 1 and 37, paragraph 1 UPKR). Moreover, the prosecutor is entitled to supervise the procedural activity of the bodies of inquiry and the bodies responsible for preliminary investigations (cover both inquiries and pretrial investigations).[71]

49. In the course of the pretrial procedure, the main obligations of the prosecutor are as follows: to approve the decision of the inquirer and of the investigator on the termination of the proceedings in criminal cases; to approve the accusatory conclusion of the investigator and to direct the criminal case to the court; and to return a criminal case to the inquirer or the investigator with directions for conducting an additional investigation (Article 37, paragraphs 2–6 UPKR). During the preliminary court hearings (Article 236, paragraph 5 UPKR), as well as during trial court proceedings, the prosecutor may modify the charge or refuse to accuse the defendant (Article 246, paragraphs 7–8 UPKR).[72]

67. Ministry of the Interior of the Russian Federation (MVD).
68. Federal Law on Militia, Apr. 18, 1991, N 1026-1.
69. Federal Law on Police, Feb. 7, 2011, N 3-FZ; Paramonova, National characteristics, fundamental principles, and history of criminal law in Russia, 2014, pp. 185–186.
70. For the private-public prosecution, *see* Part II, Chapter 1,, paras. 832, 899, 949, 951, 952.
71. For the criminal procedure, *see* Part II, Chapter 1, §6, paras. 858–926.
72. For the criminal procedure, *see* Part II, Chapter 1, §6, paras. 858–926.

50. According to Article 5, paragraph 31 UPKR and Article 11, paragraph 1 Federal Law on the Prosecutor's Office of the Russian Federation, the prosecution system consists of the **Prosecutor General's Office of the Russian Federation** *(Генеральная прокуратура Российской Федерации)*, the **prosecutor's offices of the entities of the Russian Federation** *(прокуратуры субъектов Российской Федерации)*, the **equivalent military and other specialized prosecutor's offices** *(военные и другие специализированные прокуратуры)*, **city and district prosecutor's offices** *(прокуратуры городов и районов)*, and other specialized prosecutor's offices (including territorial and military).[73] Prosecutors are subordinate to superior prosecutors and the Prosecutor General of the Russian Federation (Article 129 Const., Article 1 paragraph 1, and Articles 21–34 Law on the Prosecutor's Office).

51. The Prosecution Service or "procuratorship" (as a state structure) is a united, federal, and centralized system of bodies that exercises supervision over the compliance with the Constitution and is also responsible for the observation of law enforcement within the territory of Russia (Article 1, paragraph 1, Articles 21–34 Law on the Prosecutor's Office).[74]

C. Trial Jurisdictions

52. Article 118, paragraph 1 Constitution establishes that "justice in the Russian Federation shall be administered by the courts alone." Criminal cases are heard in the **courts of general jurisdiction** *(суды общей юрисдикции*, Article 4 Federal Law on the Judicial System of the Russian Federation, 1996).[75]

53. The criminal judicial system consists of the following courts (from the lowest to the highest): **magistrate courts** *(мировые судьи)*, **district courts** *(районные суды)*, courts of entities of the Russian Federation—i.e., **regional courts** *(суды субъектов Российской Федерации)*, and the **Supreme Court** *(Верховный Суд)* —the highest judicial body for criminal cases. In addition, there is the **Military Panel of the Supreme Court** *(Военная Коллегия Верховного Суда)*, which is the final instance for the lower military courts: military presidial courts *(гарнизонные военные суды)* and military district courts *(военные окружные суды)* (Articles 19–22 Federal Law on the Judicial System of the Russian Federation).[76]

54. The least serious cases are heard by the magistrate courts. District courts serve as first instance courts deal with more serious cases and deal with the appeals against judgments rendered by magistrate courts. Regional courts can be both first

73. Federal Law on the Prosecutor's Office of the Russian Federation, Jan. 17, 1992, N 2202.
74. Paramonova, National characteristics, fundamental principles, and history of criminal law in Russia, 2014, pp. 188–189.
75. Federal Constitutional Law "On the Judicial System of the Russian Federation," Dec. 31, 1996, N 1-FKZ.
76. Paramonova, National characteristics, fundamental principles, and history of criminal law in Russia, 2014, p. 190.

and second instance courts. In the latter case, they have a supervisory function with regard to district courts. As first instance courts, regional courts decide cases that are more serious in nature than those heard in district courts (Article 31 UPKR). The Supreme Court is the Court of First Instance for criminal cases involving federal deputies or judges (Article 452 UPKR). At the same time, it serves as the Court of Second Instance for regional courts.

55. For details on the competencies and composition of the courts, *see infra*, Part II, Chapter 1, §1 Judicial Organization.[77]

D. Prison System and Probation Service

56. The prison system falls within the competence of the **Federal Correctional Service** (*Федеральная служба исполнения наказаний,* FSIN).[78] This is a federal executive body that exercises the functions of control and supervision in the area of enforcement of criminal punishment; it is subordinated to the Ministry of Justice.

57. For the serving of criminal punishment, there are the following types of correctional facilities: **arrest houses** (*арестные дома,* Articles 67–72 UIKR); **correctional prison camps** (*исправительные колонии,* Article 74, paragraph 1 UIKR); **prisons** (*тюрьмы,* Article 74, paragraph 7 UIKR); **specialized facilities in prison camps,** such as prisons for medical treatment during incarceration (*лечебно-профилактические учреждения,* Article 74, paragraph 8 UIKR); and **educational juvenile correctional facilities** *(воспитательные колонии)* designed for juveniles aged 14 to 18 (Article 74, paragraph 9 UIKR).

58. The correctional prison camps are subdivided into the following types: **settlement prison camps** *(колонии-поселения)* and **general** *(общий),* **strict** *(особый),* and **special regime** *(строгий режим)* prison camps, and **prison** *(тюрьма),* which represents Russia's strictest form of imprisonment. In the sphere of criminal enforcement, the type of imprisonment corresponds to a certain category of crimes (Article 58, paragraph 1 UKR). For example, according to the item c of Article 58, paragraph 1 UKR, imprisonment in strict regime correctional facilities is reserved for males sentenced for the commission of especially grave crimes, e.g., a qualified homicide, Article 105, paragraph 2 UKR. The settlement prison camps are for those who have committed crimes of negligence or intentional crimes of average gravity. Some of these so-called open prisons are located in or close to civilian settlements; most, however, are situated in very remote parts of Russia. The prison camps of special regimes are the strictest camps. They are for males recidivists convicted of particularly dangerous crimes or men who have been sentenced to life imprisonment. Another type of correctional facility is a prison

77. For details on the competencies and composition of the courts, *see* paras. 841–857.

78. Regulation "On the Federal Correctional Service" (approved by the Presidential Decree of October Oct. 13, 2004 No. 1314).

(тюрьма), which represents Russia's strictest form of imprisonment, where restrictions on visiting and communication are severe. Only some 4% to 5% of those convicted by the criminal courts are sentenced to prison.

59. One of the significant problems concerning custodial penalties remains the shortage of correctional facilities across the board. This is due to the fact that imprisonment is, for most crimes, still the most common sentence imposed by criminal courts.[79]

E. Statistical Overview

60. The criminal statistics of Russia are based on the data of the **Federal State Statistics Service** (*Федеральная Служба Государственной Статистики*, hereinafter "FSSS").

61. The total **number of registered crimes** *(зарегистрированные преступления)* for the period of 2009–2018, on average, was 2.3 million. In 2018, the total number of registered crimes was 1.9 million. In general, there was a clear decline with regard to the number of registered crimes during this period: e.g., 2.9 million in 2009, 2.6 million in 2010, 2.4 million in 2011, 2.3 million in 2012, 2.1 million in 2014, and 1.9 million in 2018.[80]

62. In 2009, more than one-third of all reported crimes—1.1 million—were thefts. Drug-related crimes were in second place (0.2 million), followed by 0.2 million burglaries. Intentional grave injuries were in fourth place.[81] In 2014, 2.1 million crimes were registered. Compared to 2012, the number of crimes, such as murder and attempted murder (12,400), intentional infliction of grievous bodily harm (34,800), rape (4,200), decreased. At the same time, the number of reported drug-related crimes as well as crimes related to the illegal use of weapons and arms trafficking (27,000) increased by 1.8%.[82] In 2018, compared to the period of 2000–2017, the number of all types of violent registered crimes decreased: murder and attempted murder (8,600), intentional infliction of grievous bodily harm (23,200), and rape (3,400). The number of registered briberies, though, increased slightly (12,000 in 2010 versus 12,500 in 2018).[83]

---

79. Ambamkin, Sokraschenie chislennosti tuyremnogo naseleniya; Paramonova, National characteristics, fundamental principles, and history of criminal law in Russia, 2014, pp. 195–196.
80. FSSS, state of 2019.
81. Ministry of the Interior of the Russian Federation (MVD), state 2009.
82. Ministry of the Interior of the Russian Federation (MVD), state 2015.
83. FSSS, state of 2019.

63. According to the statistics, custodial penalties are imposed more often than any other type of punishment. This is due to various factors, such as the undeveloped infrastructure for alternative types of penalties, the low income of the population, as well as the long history of prisons.[84] Deprivation of freedom is also often imposed for economic crimes. In the period 2004 to 2009, imprisonment was imposed in approximately 33.4% of criminal cases (32.4% in 2009); other types of penal sanctions were imposed as follows: suspended sentences of imprisonment (40.1%); fine (14.7%); compulsory work and correctional labor (5%); other penalties (7.8%).[85] However, in the period 2009 to 2018, a clear tendency toward the reduction of the imposition of imprisonment, in general, can be observed: from 290,000 prison sentences in 2009 to 190,300 in 2018.[86] In 2018, the sanctions with the total number of 658,300 convicts were imposed as follows: 190,300 (imprisonment), 182,100 (suspended sentences), compulsory work and correctional labor (114,800), fine (85,400), and other penalties (31,000).[87]

64. The **occupancy level** ***(степень занятости),*** according to the statistics of 2019 (based on official capacity), was 72.8%.[88] The situation improved in comparison to 2007, when the occupancy rate was 91.6%.[89] However, the still quite high rate leads to unbearable conditions in prisons, dissemination of dangerous diseases, and gradual inclusion of the less dangerous offenders into the "real" criminal world.[90] Compared to 2015 (ca. 674,900), the number of inmates decreased in 2018 (ca. 563,200).[91] The average **number of offenders** ***(число лиц, совершивших преступления)*** per 100,000 inhabitants is ca. 260 based on an estimated national population of 146.7 million.[92] With regard to the correctional population by sex, age, and occupation, the picture is as follows: in 2013, ca. 1,012,000 perpetrators were convicted; among them were ca. 856,000 men and 156,000 women (approx. 84.6% to 15.4%). The ratio of men to women remained relatively stable over the previous years. In 2018, about 83.7% were men, against 16.3% of women.[93]

65. With regard to age composition, of the total number of convicted persons in 2018, 1.7% were 14 to 15-year-olds, 1.6% were 16 to 17-year-olds, 11.2% were 18 to 25-year-olds, 69.5% were 26 to 60-year-olds, and 16% were aged 60 and above.[94]

---

84. Gernet, Istoriya zarskoj tuyrmi, vol. 2, pp. 459–470.
85. FSSS, state of 2019.
86. FSSS, state of 2019.
87. FSSS, state of 2019.
88. FSSS, state 2019.
89. World Prison Brief.
90. Ambamkin, Sokraschenie chislennosti tuyremnogo naseleniya.
91. FSSS, state 2019.
92. FSSS, state of 2019.
93. FSSS, state of 2019.
94. *Ibid*; Paramonova, National characteristics, fundamental principles, and history of criminal law in Russia, 2014, pp. 195–196.

§3. The Historical Background

I. Ancient Rus'

66. The history of Russian criminal law goes back to the time of the formation of **Kievan Rus',** in 882.[95] The earliest known remnants of the law were embodied in the first bilateral international treaties of *Kievan Rus'* that regulated relationships with Byzantium. They were dedicated to the regulation of (criminal) punishments, procedure, and trade and first concluded by Prince *Oleg* (later by Prince *Igor* in 944 and by Prince *Svyatoslav* in 971).[96] These treaties proclaimed punishments for specific actions, for example, compensation to be paid in silver for striking someone with a sword or for killing a Christian (Article 4 of the Treaty of 911).[97]

67. The evolution of (criminal) law in ancient Russia is closely connected with the introduction of Christianity by Grand Prince *Vladimir* in 988. One of the more important innovations introduced by the Orthodox Church was the notion of written law.[98]

68. The Russian Truth, enacted in 1016 by Prince *Yaroslav the Wise* (with subsequent amendments in 1036 and 1072), was the first written source of legal rules—the result of the codification of legal customs and princely enactments.[99] As the first written code, the Russian Truth regulated mostly criminal matters but contained some civil law-related norms as well. The criminal law part consisted of three sections: on murder, on personal insult, and on infringements of property. The Russian Truth used the term "**insult**" ***(обида)*** instead of "crime" ***(преступление)***.[100] There was no state mechanism for imposing punishments; however, the injured party had a right of vengeance against his/her offender for the "insult."[101]

69. The long-term occupation under the Mongol-Tatars (1238–1480) isolated Russia from legal developments in Western Europe. This is one of the reasons why Russian law had not advanced markedly by the end of the 15th century.[102] The **Dvina Charters** ***(Двинская уставная грамота)*** of 1397, as well as the **Pskov Judicial Charters** ***(Псковская судная грамота)*** of 1462, provided for rules similar to the norms of the Russian Truth.[103] As far as criminal law-related rules are concerned, the crucial difference was the increased control of state authorities with respect to the regulation of socially dangerous behavior. In the case of murder, for

95. Karamzin, Istoriya Gosudarstva Rossiiskogo, http://bibliotekar.ru/karamzin/index.htm [last visited Dec. 18, 2019].
96. Yushkov, Monuments of Russian Law, p. 79.
97. Karamzin, Istoriya Gosudarstva Rossiiskogo, http://bibliotekar.ru/karamzin/index.htm [last visited Dec. 18, 2019]; Smith, Reforming the Russian Legal System, p. 2.
98. Smith, *ibid.*
99. Russian Truth, http://uateka.com/ru/article/society/heritage/1221 [last visited Dec. 18, 2019].
100. Kropachev/Volzhenkin/Orechova, Ugolovnoe pravo Rossii, pp. 117–121; Komissarov/ Krilova/ Tyazhkova, Ugolovnoe pravo, p. 53.
101. Zhilzov, Pravovedenie, N 4, 1997, 1.
102. Smith, Reforming the Russian Legal System, p. 4.
103. Rossijskoe zakonodatelstvo X-XX vekov: v 9 tomach. Tom 2. Moscow 1985.

example, wergeld[104] was paid to a vicar of the **Prince** ***(княжеский наместник)*** and no longer to the family of the victim.[105]

II. Russian Centralized State

70. The epoch of the 15th and 16th centuries and the reign of *Ivan III* and *Ivan IV* marked the turning point for the centralized Russian State.

71. Under *Ivan III's* rule, historically meaningful Russian lands (Riazan, Tver, Novgorod, Pskof, Vereia, Biélozersk, Rostof, and Iaroslavl) were united around Moscow, which was transformed into the center of all Russian lands. By this time, Russia extended as far as Finland, the White Sea, the Arctic Ocean, and had already obtained a footing in Asia.

72. The final liberation of the country from the Tatar-Mongolian yoke took place in 1480. *Ivan III*, the heir of the Emperors of Byzantium and the Roman Caesars, married the Byzantine princess Sophia, the daughter of Thomas Palaeologus (a brother of the last Emperor of Byzantium). He chose the two-headed eagle for the new Russian coat of arms, which, in its archaic form, is still to be found in the Palace of Facets of the Kremlin.[106]

73. *Ivan IV* continued his grandfather *Ivan III's* political agenda. In 1552, *Ivan IV* conquered Kazan, and in 1556, he annexed the Astrakhan Khanate and destroyed the largest slave market on the river Volga. Russia's expansion into Siberia started with these campaigns and resulted in a large Muslim population joining Russia. Thereby, Russia turned into a multiethnic and multireligious state.[107]

74. The political centralization was very much connected to the idea of Moscow being the "Third Rome." With the fall of Constantinople in 1453, Russia viewed itself as the true repository of Christianity.[108] The reign of *Ivan IV (Ivan the Terrible)*, who proclaimed himself the first Czar of Russia (from the Latin "Caesar"—Emperor), was also characterized by the annexation of new lands, including Siberia, and by unprecedented terror—referred to as "oprichnina" ***(опричнина)***—in order to further strengthen the centralized state.[109]

---

104. The term Wergeld refers to a price paid by a person who has killed another to the family of the person killed, to atone for the killing and avoid reprisals, https://www.collinsdictionary.com/dictionary/english/wergeld [last visited Dec. 18, 2019].
105. *Ibid.*; Paramonova, National characteristics, fundamental principles, and history of criminal law in Russia, 2014, pp. 270–271.
106. Rambaud, Ivan III, the Uniter of the Russian Land, pp. 161–174.
107. Karamzin, Istoriya Gosudarstva Rossiiskogo, http://bibliotekar.ru/karamzin/index.htm [last visited Dec. 18, 2019].
108. *Ibid.*; Smith, Reforming the Russian Legal System, p. 5.
109. Karamzin, Istoriya Gosudarstva Rossiiskogo, http://bibliotekar.ru/karamzin/index.htm [last visited Dec. 18, 2019].

75. The main feature of the criminal law of this historical period was its repressive nature.

76. The **Law Code of Ivan III of 1497** ***(Судебник)*** was the first substantive codification of the various feudal laws. With regard to criminal matters, the interest of the state was clearly defined in the Law Code of 1497: a **dangerous act** ***(лихое дело)*** was not only perceived as damage inflicted on private persons but also as damage to state and church. For example, normal theft and theft inside a church were considered separate crimes. The right to prosecute and punish was limited to the prosecuting authorities of the state.[110]

77. The **Law Code of Ivan IV of 1550** ***(Судебник)*** reflected the historical developments of the centralization of state control, providing for an array of further crimes against the state and state power: for example, forgery, fraud, and knowingly rendering an unjust judgment. Most of these offenses were punished with the death penalty.[111]

78. The **Council Code of 1649** ***(Соборное уложение),*** enacted by *Alexej*, provided for a more sophisticated system of criminal liability and crime classification in comparison to previous legislation.[112] It distinguished, for example, between intentional and negligent crimes[113] and between forms of criminal conduct prior to achievement of the criminal goal: mere intent was not considered an attempt to commit a crime,[114] etc. Crimes against the church and religion were regarded as the most dangerous and serious crimes, followed by crimes against state power. "Crime" was regarded as disobedience to the czar's (God's representative on earth) will and was no longer considered a private matter.[115]

III. Russian Empire (1721–1917)

79. The epoch of *Peter I* (1682–1725) was characterized by major changes in the state administration, the economy, and the military, as well as by the reception of Western schools of legal thought. These developments favored Russia's transformation from a traditional and isolated state into a dynamic, partially westernized,

110. Kropachev/Volzhenkin/Orechova, Ugolovnoe pravo Rossii, pp.124–125.
111. Kropachev/Volzhenkin/Orechova, Ugolovnoe pravo Rossii, p. 127; Komissarov/Krilova/Tyazhkova, Ugolovnoe pravo, p. 53; Paramonova, Death Penalty in Russia, forthcoming.
112. Taganzev, Russkoe ugolovnoe pravo, p. 141.
113. On the subjective aspects of the offense, *see* Part I, Chapter 3, §4, paras. 383–428.
114. On attempt, *see* Part I, Chapter 5, paras. 544–589.
115. Rossijskoe zakonodatelstvo X–XX vekov: v 9 tomach. Tom 4. Moscow 1986; Paramonova, National characteristics, fundamental principles, and history of criminal law in Russia, 2014, pp. 271–272.

and secularized Russian Empire. *Peter I's* wrenching westward reforms on education, government, army, navy, and industry directed at strengthening the power of the state inevitably influenced the development of (criminal law) legislation.[116]

80. Approximately 372 criminal law-related acts and decrees were enacted during the reign of *Peter I.* The most important of these were the **Military Statute** ***(Воинский Устав)*** of 1716, and the **Naval Statute** ***(Морской Устав)*** of 1720. These legal rules also applied to civilians.[117] Crime was understood not only as disobedience to the czar's will but also as "anything that could cause harm"[118] to church and state. The Military Statute allowed the expansion of criminal law by analogy, i.e., extensive interpretation of the law, which allows ruling a case that is not explicitly considered by a legal provision.[119] Juvenility was regarded as a mitigating circumstance, although the Naval Statute did not specify the exact age of a juvenile (Article 131 Naval Statute).

81. The conception that "crime" is behavior forbidden by law was comprehensively anchored for the first time in the Proclamation of 1763 of *Catherine II.* This Proclamation was based on the ideas of French philosophers, such as *Montesquieu* and *Rousseau.*[120] During the reign of *Catherine II* (1762–1796), natural law ideas gained ground, and the writings of *Montesquieu*, *Beccaria*, *Feuerbach*, etc., were translated into Russian.[121]

82. According to the famous criminal law scholar, *Gernet*, the period from the end of the 18th century until the revolution (1917) was characterized by a shift in the emphasis of criminal policy from "intimidation" to "prevention of new crimes" and "reformation of offenders."[122] Further codifications of legal rules in the 19th century were directly influenced by the liberalization processes that had been taking place in Europe and, primarily by the ideas of the French Revolution, which entered Russia largely as a result of its victory over *Napoleon's* army.[123]

83. At the beginning of the 19th century, legal concepts and institutions that were accepted by universities and lawyers were those derived from Roman law. *Alexander I* (1801–1825), a progressive and reform-minded czar who admired the

116. Komissarov/Krilova/Tyazhkova, Ugolovnoe pravo, p. 53; *see also* Early Imperial Russia, http://countrystudies.us/russia/4.htm [last visited Dec. 18, 2019].
117. Rossijskoe zakonodatelstvo X–XX vekov: v 9 tomach. Tom 4. Moscow 1986.
118. *Ibid.*; Kropachev/Volzhenkin/Orechova, Ugolovnoe pravo Rossii, pp. 128–130.
119. Kropachev/Volzhenkin/Orechova, ibid., p. 129.
120. Rossijskoe zakonodatelstvo X-XX vekov: "Order of Ekaterina II," 1767; Latkin, Uchebnik istorii russkogo prava, p. 415.
121. Feldstein, Glavnie techeniya v istorii nauki ugolovnogo prava, p. 568.
122. Iljin et al., Osnovi zakonovedeniya, pp. 344–345; Komissarov/Krilova/Tyazhkova, Ugolovnoe pravo, pp. 48–49.
123. Smith, Reforming the Russian Legal System, p. 10.

logical consistency of the German and French codes, expanded university law faculties and invited foreign scholars to teach.[124] Hence, German and French (criminal) law had a significant influence on the Russian legal system. Many Russian lawyers were educated abroad in Germany and France, and in Russia under the influence of those legal systems.[125]

84. The **Digest of the Laws of the Russian Empire of 1835** ***(Свод Законов Российской Империи)***—one of the most significant codifications of the Russian Empire—was finished and entered into force in 1835 under the reign of *Nikolai I* (1825–1855). *Nikolai I*—in contrast to *Alexander I* and to *Nikolai I's* successor, *Alexander II*—made little effort to support democratic legal reforms and was known for the suppression of the famous Decembrist uprising (in which members of the military agitated for human rights and democracy) in 1825.[126] The Digest consisted of fifteen volumes and distinguished between state, civil, administrative, criminal, and procedural law. It organized the existing laws into a workable form: most obsolete legal provisions were abolished, and many legal acts originating from 1649 were systematized. The part regulating the criminal law distinguished between a General and a Special Part, and "crime" was defined as "any act that is forbidden by law under the fear of punishment."[127]

85. In 1845, the **Code on Criminal and Correctional Punishments** ***(Уложение о наказаниях)***[128] was introduced. It updated legal provisions of the codified laws of 1835 and remained in force with certain changes (introduced in 1857, 1866, and 1885) until the revolution of 1917. The Code distinguished between "misdemeanors" and "felonies," depending on the nature of the infringement. Crimes against state power, church, and society were regarded as the gravest offenses (felonies). Infringements of the rules that protected individual interests, in contrast, were regarded as misdemeanors (Article 1 Code).[129] Children under the age of 10 were not criminally liable. Insane individuals and persons who committed a crime in a state of delirium or unconsciousness were not subject to criminal responsibility (Article 96 Code). Interestingly, puberty and pregnancy were deemed (under certain circumstances) to be sufficient grounds for excluding criminal responsibility.[130]

124. *Ibid.*, pp. 10–11.
125. Kuznezova/Tyazhkova, Kurs ugolovnogo prava, p. 166; Shershenevich, Uchebnik russkogo grazhdanskogo prava, p. 546.
126. Svod Zakonov Rossijskoj Imperii 1835, http://civil.consultant.ru/reprint/books/181/3.html [last visited Dec. 18, 2019]; Solodkin, Ocherki po istorii russkogo ugolovnogo prava.
127. Rossijskoe zakonodatelstvo X–XX vekov: v 9 tomach. Tom 6. Moscow 1988; Paramonova, National characteristics, fundamental principles, and history of criminal law in Russia, 2014, pp. 272–275.
128. *Ibid.*
129. Proekt novogo Ulozheniya o nakazaniyach. St. Petersburg 1844, p. 5.
130. Taganzev, Russkoe ugolovnoe pravo, pp. 487–488; Dostoevskij, Dnevnik pisatelya, pp. 201–209, 215–225.

86. The period of the 1860s, which is considered to be the time of the formation of criminal law scholarship, is often called "the Golden Age of Russian law."[131] This period is primarily associated with outstanding scholars, such as *Tagantsev Nikolaj*,[132] *Kistyakovskij Alexander*,[133] *Fojnitskij Ivan*, *Spasovich Vladimir*, and *Neklyudov Nikolaj*.[134] Developments during this period were influenced by the progressive social, political, and legal reforms of *Alexander II* (1855–1881), famous for the emancipation of the serfs in 1861. In 1864, he initiated judicial reforms that contributed to the development of the rule of law. Independent courts were, for example, established, and a jury system and professional bar were also introduced.

87. The conflict between Western European influences on Russian law and indigenous Slavic mores and traditions manifested itself in two opposing schools of thought. On the one hand, there were the **Westernizers** ***(западники),*** who advocated a Western model of development for Russia, and on the other hand, the **Slavophiles** ***(славянофилы),*** who adhered to Russia's unique social, political, and legal evolution.[135]

88. The last significant codification of criminal law norms during the period of the czars was the **Criminal Code of 1903** ***(Уголовное уложение).*** It was mostly influenced by classical criminal law school.[136] The influence of the sociological school was also apparent, but less. It appeared, for instance, in a provision that foresaw the possibility of conditional early relief from punishment.[137] The Criminal Code of 1903 was expected to enter into force gradually. By 1917, however, only 158 of the Code's 687 articles had entered into force. The resulting gaps in coverage were filled by the Code on Criminal and Correctional Punishments of 1845 (which remained in force until 1917).

89. Hopes awakened by the incorporation of the concept of the rule of law and by human rights-based developments under *Nikolai II*—the gradual integration of which could be seen in the establishment of the State Duma (first Russian Parliament)[138] and the enactment of the Proclamation on basic human rights, both in 1905[139]—vanished. On the crisis at the beginning of the 20th century, *Nikolai II*

---

131. Kropachev/Volzhenkin/Orechova, Ugolovnoe pravo Rossii, pp. 171–172.
132. Taganzev, Russkoe ugolovnoe pravo.
133. Kistyakovskij, Issledovanie o smertnoj kazni, 1867.
134. Neklyudov, Ugolovno-statisticheskie etyudi, 1865; Nabokov, Pravo, N 44, 1915, 14; Komissarov/Krilova/Tyazhkova, Ugolovnoe pravo, pp. 60–61.
135. Solodkin, Ocherki po istorii russkogo ugolovnogo prava; Smith, Reforming the Russian Legal System, p. 14.
136. Classical school of criminology/ criminal law, https://www.open.edu/openlearn/society-politics-law [last visited Dec. 18, 2019].
137. Kropachev/Volzhenkin/Orechova, Ugolovnoe pravo Rossii, pp. 135, 142; Paramonova, National characteristics, fundamental principles, and history of criminal law in Russia, 2014, pp. 272–275.
138. Law "On the Establishment of the State Duma," Aug. 6, 1905; Regulation "On Elections to the State Duma," Aug. 6, 1905.
139. Proclamation "On the Improvement of Public Order," Oct. 17, 1905.

wrote in his diary that "granting civil rights—freedom of speech, press, assembly, and association, and personal integrity […] is risky," but still "the only right thing at the moment."[140]

IV. Soviet Period (1917–1991)

90. The criminal law of the Soviet period is characterized by the prevalence of the power of the state and the ideology of the communist party over the rule of law.

91. After the Bolsheviks seized power in the **October Revolution of 1917**, the czar's state apparatus and social order were overthrown, and a dictatorship of the proletariat was proclaimed. All previous legislation (including codified criminal law provisions) was abolished because it was considered an embodiment of the hostile imperial regime.

92. According to the new Bolshevik ideology, which was based on Marxist concepts, law and the state would wither away with the passage of time.

93. Crime was seen as a manifestation of class antagonism. Hence, if under communism the suppression of one class by another disappeared, there would be no further need for (criminal) law. Nonetheless, the necessity of legal rules soon became apparent.

94. The first systemized statute of post-revolutionary Russian criminal law, the Fundamentals of the **Criminal Law of the Russian Soviet Federal Socialist Republic of 1919**,[141] reflected the main feature of the criminal law of post-revolutionary Russia: its class-based nature.[142]

95. The provisions of the first **Criminal Code of the Russian Soviet Federal Socialist Republic of 1922** were also designed to protect the interests of the working class (workers and peasants) from "antisocial elements" (Article 5 Criminal Code RSFSR).[143] The definition of crime did not contain the feature of illegality. Furthermore, the Code permitted the broad application of analogy in criminal law (Articles 7, 10 Criminal Code RSFSR); criminally liable were not only those individuals who had committed crime but also those who were deemed to be dangerous

---

140. http://historic.ru/books/item/f00/s00/z0000097/st001.shtml [last visited Dec. 18, 2019]; Paramonova, National characteristics, fundamental principles, and history of criminal law in Russia, 2014, p. 276.
141. Fundamentals of the Criminal Law of the Russian Soviet Federative Socialist Republic, Dec. 12, 1919, N 66, Art. 590 (Rukovodyaschie nachala po ugolovnomu pravu RSFSR).
142. Kropachev/Volzhenkin/Orechova, Ugolovnoe pravo Rossii, p. 148.
143. Criminal Code of the Russian Soviet Federal Socialist Republic, May 26, 1922, N 15, Art. 153 (Ugolovnij Kodeks RSFSR).

because of their connection to the criminal environment, for example, relatives, or persons with an "anticommunist" past.[144]

96. The next **Criminal Code of the Russian Soviet Federal Socialist Republic was enacted in 1926**[145] and was based on the principles of the previous Criminal Code. This legislation, as well as the criminal policies of the 1920s and 1930s, foreshadowed *Stalin's* terror in the 1930s.

97. 1937–1938 are known as the years of "**the big terror**." While approximately 5 million persons were convicted of so-called counterrevolutionary crimes between 1918 and 1958, of whom about 838,000 were executed, the vast majority of these executions—approximately 681,692—took place during the terror of 1937–1938.[146] These executions were authorized by the executive. For instance, the notorious *Stalin* Decree on the Protection of Social (Socialistic) Property of 1932,[147] and the so-called **Law of the Three Spikelets** ***(Закон о трёх колосках)*** that was in force until 1947[148] provided for the death penalty (or under mitigating circumstances at least ten years of deprivation of freedom) for the theft of any kind of public property (state, collective, cooperative). Since private property did not exist in a socialist society, all property was public and was proclaimed to be "sacred and inviolable."[149] Stalin era was characterized by forced labor camps. These camps were first under the control of the People's Commissariat of Justice and later under the control of the **General Directorate of Corrective Labor Camps and Labor Camps** (***Главное Управление исправительно-трудовых лагерей и трудовых колоний,*** **GULAG**), which was established on July 10, 1934.[150] According to some data, up to 15 million prisoners—including representatives of the Russian aristocracy and the state apparatus of pre-revolutionary Russia, dispossessed peasants, intellectuals, political and war prisoners—were held in these camps (e.g., in the Ural, Siberia, and the Russian Far East) during the Soviet period.[151] The statement made by *Stalin's* prosecutor general *Vyshinskii* that "the formal law is subordinate to the law of the Revolution"[152] precisely describes the spirit of criminal policy in this period of state-sanctioned arbitrariness and terror—a time period that lasted from the Bolshevik October Revolution of 1917 until the 1960s (Khrushchev's era).

---

144. Kuznezova/Tyazhkova, Kurs ugolovnogo prava, p. 37; Kropachev/Volzhenkin/Orechova, Ugolovnoe pravo Rossii, p. 153.
145. Criminal Code of the Russian Soviet Federal Socialist Republic, Nov. 22, 1926, N 80, Art. 600 (Ugolovnij Kodeks RSFSR).
146. Luneev, Prestupnost'XX veka, p. 180.
147. Decree "On Protection of Social (Socialistic) Property," Aug. 7, 1932, N 62, Art. 360.
148. Decree "On the Criminal Responsibility for the Crimes against State and Social Property," Jun. 4, 1947.
149. Decree "On Protection of Social (Socialistic) Property," Aug. 7, 1932.
150. Yakovlev/Burtsov, Concentration Camps in the USSR, http://javot.net/arhiv/8.htm [last visited Dec. 18, 2019].
151. *Ibid.*
152. Vyshinskii, Stalin's Prosecutor general: Reforming the Russian Legal System 1935 (Bolshevik experience); Smith, Reforming the Russian Legal System, p. 27.

98. The death of *Stalin* in 1953 was followed by the so-called **Khrushchev Thaw** ***(Хрущевская оттепель).*** This was a period of more moderate politics in interior and foreign affairs that saw the dethroning of *Stalin's* cult of personality, a decrease in (political) repression, the release of German and Japanese war prisoners, and the release of thousands of political prisoners from forced labor camps.[153]

99. The third and last **Soviet Criminal Code**, which was enacted in **1960**,[154] reflected the tendencies of the milder criminal policy of that time. The establishment of the so-called illegality requirement brought relative stability and predictability. Crime was defined as a socially dangerous act prohibited by the Criminal Code (Article 7 Criminal Code 1960), the nonjudicial imposition of criminal punishment was prohibited, and prosecution based on analogy as well as on the "social instability and dangerousness" of an individual ceased.[155]

100. The period from the 1960s to the late 1980s retained the spirit of a totalitarian regime based on Marxist ideology and on executive control of social, economic, and political spheres in the criminal law. The changes introduced to the Criminal Code 1960 in the 1980s—the time of "perestroika" ***(перестройка)***—did not change the fact that the priority of the Soviet legal system, including criminal law, was state interests rather than the rights and freedoms of the individual.[156] The Code of 1960 remained in force until the introduction of the modern Criminal Code of the Russian Federation of 1996.[157]

§4. The Criminal Code of 1996 and the Code of Criminal Procedure of 2001: Recent Developments in Criminal Law and Criminal Procedure

101. The **Criminal Code of the Russian Federation** that is still in force today was enacted in **1996** and entered into force in 1997. It became a model for most of the post-Soviet republics.

102. The new **Code of Criminal Procedure of 2001**, which is still in force today with many amendments, refers to a "**neo-inquisitorial**" (mixed or hybrid) model of criminal procedure[158] (*see infra*—Part II, Chapter 1, §2: basic concepts of criminal procedure, paragraphs 809–813).

153. Naumov, Rossijskoe ugolovnoe pravo, pp. 137–141; *see also* http://dic.academic.ru/dic.nsf/ruwiki/341690 [last visited Dec. 18, 2019].
154. Criminal Code of the Russian Soviet Federative Socialist Republic Oct. 27, 1960 (Ugolovnij Kodeks RSFSR).
155. Kropachev/Volzhenkin/Orechova, Ugolovnoe pravo Rossii, p. 158.
156. *Ibid.*, p. 162.
157. Paramonova, National characteristics, fundamental principles, and history of criminal law in Russia, 2014, pp. 276–278.
158. Bozhjev, Ugolovnij process, p. 16; Paramonova/Bogush, ZStW 125 (2013), 703–728.

103. Today, the legal system is still struggling with its origins and with the Soviet legacy. It is, therefore, hardly surprising that the criminal law of modern Russia has changed quite extensively in recent decades.[159] Between its enactment and the end of 2019, the Criminal Code 1996 had undergone more than 3,000 amendments.[160] Some of the changes, as well as the tendencies associated with them, are controversial, as will be explained below.[161]

104. The reform of 2001—guided by the idea of humanization of criminal law—provided for an expansion of the use of deprivation of freedom served in open-type colonies and softened the rules for parole as well as the requirements for the replacement of non-served parts of sentences with a milder punishment.[162]

105. One of the major reforms of the criminal law in 2003[163] was directed toward the mitigation of punishment in general, for instance, in terms of repeated offenses.[164] In addition, among other offenses, the negligent infliction of bodily harm, some cases of hooliganism, and the illegal purchase and carrying of gas and cold weapons (so-called white arms) were decriminalized. The amended Criminal Code differentiated criminal punishment with regard to juvenile offenders into two groups: 14 to 15-year-olds and 16 to 17-year-olds. It substantially reduced their criminal responsibility and introduced special closed-type educational institutions for juveniles (Article 87, paragraph 2 UKR). Juveniles were defined as persons who, at the time of the commission of a crime, were at least 14 years of age but not yet 18 years of age (Article 87, paragraph 1 UKR).[165]

106. However, since 2003, there has been a tendency toward increasing criminal sanctions with regard to crimes, such as terrorism, corruption, organized crime, and crimes against life, health, and the sexual integrity of children.[166] New crimes against the sexual integrity of minors with increased criminal penalties were also introduced.[167] The amendments introduced life imprisonment as a separate penalty (previously it was only imposed as an alternative to the death penalty) that can be imposed not only for crimes against life but also for crimes against public security, public health, and morals.[168]

107. Next, the Federal Law 2011 on Changes to the Criminal Code and Other Legal Provisions was enacted. It symbolized one of the most far-reaching reforms

---

159. Paramonova, Revista Penal 2012, 264–268.
160. Supreme Court of the Russian Federation, http://www.supcourt.ru/ [last visited Dec. 18, 2019].
161. Paramonova, National characteristics, fundamental principles, and history of criminal law in Russia, 2014, p. 280.
162. Federal Law on Changes to the Criminal Code, N 25-FZ, Mar. 9, 2001.
163. Federal Law on Changes to the Criminal Code, N 162-FZ, Dec. 8, 2003.
164. On recidivism, *see* Part I, Chapter 7, §6, paras. 754, 771–774.
165. For a discussion of juveniles, *see* Part I, Chapter 7, §6, paras. 765–767.
166. *See* Federal Law on Changes to the Criminal Code, N 73-FZ, Jul. 21, 2004.
167. Federal Law on Changes to the Criminal Code, N 162-FZ, Dec. 8, 2003.
168. Bogush, Criminal Law Reform in Russia, pp. 49–60.

that started in 2009.[169] Its main goals were the humanization of criminal law, the "reduction of the prison population" of prisons, the recovery of the business environment by reducing custodial penalties for economic crimes, reducing pressure on law enforcement authorities, and creating a more favorable investment climate.

108. The amendments of the General Part that have taken place since 2009 are remarkable in that they provide broader discretion to judges in sentencing matters. First, the lower threshold for penalties for offenses of small gravity decreased (e.g., for kidnapping, Article 126 UKR; the lower limit punishment was changed from four years to two months). Second, courts were given the authority to change the way a crime is categorized: they may reduce a crime's category by one level (Articles 61, 63, 15, paragraph 6 UPKR and Article 299, paragraph 1 N 6.1. UPKR), for example, from the category "especially grave crimes" to the category "crimes of average gravity." These reforms have, however, been met with mixed responses. On the one hand, as reform supporters argue, they permit judges to individualize sentences to a larger extent, thus making criminal law more flexible and humane.[170] On the other hand, they raise concerns about the expanded discretion of judges and especially the lack of judicial independence from the executive.[171]

109. With regard to the Special Part, the provisions regulating economic crimes (Chapter 22 UKR) have undergone the most significant changes.[172] Some economic crimes were abolished as, for example, pseudo-entrepreneurship (Article 173 UKR).[173] However, a number of entirely new offenses were introduced in this area, for example, illegal organization associated with the conduct of gambling activities (Article 171.2 UKR). Furthermore, from January 1, 2010,[174] the application of detention as a pretrial restriction is no longer an option with regard to most economic offenses (Article 108, paragraph 1.1 UPKR).[175]

110. In general, the period 2009–2014 is characterized by contradictory tendencies and inconsistency. For instance, parallel to the trend of the amendments that soften the impact of criminal policy, there was also a tendency toward more criminalization and more severe criminal penalties.

111. The trend toward criminalization can be observed in other spheres. For example, computer crimes (Articles 272–274 UKR) have also undergone changes,

169. Federal Law on Changes to the Criminal Code and Other Legal Provisions, N 420-FZ, Dec. 7, 2011; Conception of the Modernization of the Criminal Law Legislation in Economic Sphere. Institute of Modern Development (INSOR) authorized by President Medvedev D.A., Jan. 14, 2011, http://www.insor-russia.ru [last visited Dec. 18, 2019]; Panov, Expert, N 28, 2011, http://expert.ru/expert/2011/28/tihaya-reforma/ [last visited Dec. 18, 2019]; Paramonova, Revista Penal 2012, 264–268.
170. Panov, ibid.
171. Paramonova, Revista Penal 2012, 264–268.
172. *Ibid.*, 251–254.
173. Federal Law on Changes to Various Legal Provisions, N 60-FZ, Apr. 7, 2010.
174. Federal Law on Changes to Tax Law and Other Legal Provisions, N 383-FZ, Dec. 29, 2009.
175. Paramonova, Revista Penal 2011, 255–260; Federal Law on Changes to Various Legal Provisions, N 60-FZ, Apr. 7, 2010.

as new crimes with more severe punishments were introduced.[176] Moreover, the laws of 2009,[177] 2011,[178] and 2012[179] introduced new crimes of violence against minors as, for example, the use of minors for the production of pornographic materials or objects (Article 242.2 UKR).[180] The voluntary chemical castration of pedophiles was also introduced.[181]

112. As indicated, the tendency toward liberalization (i.e., less criminalization, less severe penalties) is an opposite trend in this period of time. For instance, the possibility of the suspension of enforcement of a sentence for up to five years was introduced with regard to drug-dependent offenders (Article 228, paragraph 1, Article 231, paragraph 1, Articles 233, and Article 82.1 UKR).[182] Besides, some criminal acts were decriminalized and became administrative offenses.[183] For instance, former criminal offenses, such as slander (Article 129 UKR) and insult (Article 130 UKR), were moved to the Administrative Code[184] (Articles 5.60 and 5.61 KoAPR, respectively).[185] The violation of equality of human rights and freedoms (Article 136, paragraph 1 UKR) became punishable under Article 5.62 KoAPR (discrimination).[186] One of the main legal consequences of this shift toward administrative offenses is that legal persons—who cannot be held criminally responsible under Russian law—do bear (administrative) responsibility.[187] Nonetheless, taking into account the problem of the distinction between criminal law and administrative law with a quasi-criminal function, there is a likelihood that these changes will lead to an expansion of the number of de facto criminally liable persons—including legal persons. It has partially to do with the influence of the ECtHR and its broad interpretation of the term "criminal."

113. Many other amendments from this period are contradictory. The introduction of relief from criminal responsibility for most crimes in the economic sphere (Article 76.1 UKR and Article 28.1 UPKR) reveals, for example, the tendency

176. Federal Law on Changes to the Criminal Code and Other Legal Provisions, N 420-FZ, Dec. 7, 2011, *see also* Paramonova, Internationales Strafrecht im Cyberspace, pp. 77–123.
177. Federal Law on Changes to the Criminal Code, N 377-FZ, Dec. 27, 2009.
178. Federal Law on Changes to the Criminal Code and Other Legal Provisions, N 420-FZ, Dec. 7, 2011.
179. Federal Law on Changes to the Criminal Code and Other Legislative Acts that Aggravate the Penalties for the Sexual Offenses Committed against Minors, N 14-FZ, Feb. 29, 2012.
180. Federal Law on Changes to Various Legal Provisions, N 14-FZ, Mar. 1, 2012.
181. On sex offenders, *see* Part I, Chapter 7, §6, para. 770.
182. Federal Law on Changes to the Criminal Code and Other Legal Provisions, N 420-FZ, Dec. 7, 2011.
183. Paramonova, Revista Penal 2012, 264–268.
184. Code of Administrative Offenses of the Russian Federation, Dec. 30, 2001, N 195–FZ (Kodeks RF ob administrativnih pravonarusheniyah, KoAPR).
185. Federal Law on Changes to the Criminal Code and Other Legal Provisions, N 420-FZ, Dec. 7, 2011; Federal Law on Changes to the Criminal Code, N 60-FZ, Apr. 7, 2010.
186. Federal Law on Changes to the Criminal Code and Other Legal Provisions, N 420-FZ, Dec. 7, 2011; Federal Law on Changes to the Criminal Code, N 60-FZ, Apr. 7, 2010; on the distinction between criminal and administrative offenses, *see* paras. 218, 327–330.
187. For criminal liability of legal persons, *see* paras. 112, 379.

toward favoring the fiscal interests of the state.[188] A person who has committed an economic crime for the first time is to be relieved of criminal responsibility if he/she pays compensation calculated at five times the amount of damage caused by the offense to the federal budget. However, this rule raises a contradiction: On the one hand, such a norm humanizes the criminal law and simplifies the work of judges. On the other hand, with relief from criminal responsibility, any new investigation of the relieved person for the same offense would always be the "first," thus each time allowing the person to "buy" his/her way out of criminal responsibility.[189]

114. An important, recent development in the context of criminal procedure was the introduction of a new institution, the purpose of which was to enhance the adversarial nature of Russian criminal procedure.[190] This institution, created in 2009, is a special procedure of pretrial cooperation between prosecution and defense (Chapter 40.1. UPKR)—an *analog* of plea bargaining.[191]

115. Another development that resonated broadly with the public was the Federal Law that reduced the competence of the jury, for instance, in the cases involving terrorism (Article 205 UKR).[192] This was regarded as a negative development since jury trials are considered more independent than trials with professional judges: jurors hand down fewer guilty verdicts than professional judges.[193]

§5. Sources of Criminal Law

I. International Sources

(1) The Problem of Supremacy

116. The Criminal Code is "based on the Constitution of the Russian Federation and the generally recognized principles and norms of international law" (Article 1, paragraph 2 UKR). The question of whether the Constitution has supremacy over national laws or the norms of international treaties have supremacy over national laws, including the Constitution, has a direct impact on the structure of the hierarchy of the sources of law. However, the problem of supremacy has not yet been

188. Federal Law on Changes to the Criminal Code and Other Legal Provisions, Dec. 7, 2011, N 420-FZ.

189. Paramonova, National characteristics, fundamental principles, and history of criminal law in Russia, 2014, pp. 280–284, 288–289.

190. Paramonova, Revista Penal 2012, 264–268.

191. Federal Law on Changes to Code of Criminal Procedure, Jun. 29, 2009, N 141-FZ. For plea bargaining, *see* paras. 114, 810, 961, 1273–1278. For special court procedures, *see* paras. 1270–1271.

192. Federal Law on Changes to Legal Provisions on Fight Against Terrorism, Dec. 30, 2008, N 321-FZ; Decision of the Constitutional Court of the Russian Federation, N 8-II, Apr. 19, 2010, http://www.ksrf.ru/ [last visited Dec. 18, 2019].

193. Federal Law, Dec. 30, 2008, N 321-FZ; Golovko, Konstituzionnij sud vs sud prisyazhnich; for more details on jury trials, *see* paras. 1280–1302; Golubkova, Mariya/Kozlova, Natalya. Bud'te sudimi, Rossijskaya Gazeta 25.02.2016: http://rg.ru/2016/02/25/ks-rf-rasshiril-polnomochiia-prisiazhnyh-i-razreshil-im-sudit-zhenshchin.html.

solved in Russia and thus remains a controversial issue among scholars and in legal practice since the adoption of the Constitution in 1993. Legal scholars sometimes refer to this situation as the "war of supremacies."[194]

117. The rules of the Constitution, as such, create ambiguity in this context: On the one hand, the supremacy of the Constitution is proclaimed (Article 4, paragraph 2 Const.); on the other hand, national laws are required to conform to the norms and general principles of international law, which are a "component part" of the Russian legal system (Article 15, paragraph 4 Const.).

Art. 4 Const.

(1) […].
(2) The Constitution of the Russian Federation and Federal Laws have the supremacy on the whole territory of the Russian Federation.
(3) […].

Art. 15 Const.

(1) The Constitution of the Russian Federation has the supreme legal force, direct application and is valid on the whole territory of the Russian Federation. Laws and other legal provisions adopted in the Russian Federation shall not contradict the Constitution of the Russian Federation.
(2)-(3) […].
(4) The universally recognized principles and norms of international law as well as international agreements of the Russian Federation are a component part of its legal system. If an international agreement of the Russian Federation establishes other rules than those provided for by law, the rules of the international agreement shall be applied.

(2) "Internationalists" versus "Constitutionalists"

118. According to the "**internationalists**" (in contrast to the "**constitutionalists**"), the Constitution, being national law in the sense of Article 15, paragraph 4 Const., is subordinate to international law; hence, international law must be at the top of the hierarchy of the sources of law.[195]

119. Although "norms of international law" as well as "generally recognized principles" are each proclaimed a "**component part**" of the legal system (Article

194. Ivanenko, Pravovedenie, N 3, 2010, 140; for a discussion of international ties, *see* General Introduction, §5, paras. 116–144; Paramonova, Der rechtliche Status der Europäischen Konvention zum Schutze der Menschenrechte und EGMR, KritV, N 3, 2013, pp. 188–211.

195. *Ibid.*, pp. 135–161; Gavrilov, Mezhdunarodnaya i nazional´naya pravovaya sistema, p. 11; Bachin, Pravovedenie, N 6, 2007, 126; Chernichenko, Pravovedenie, N 1, 2009, 18.

15, paragraph 4 Const.), they nonetheless cannot directly provide for criminal liability. This is because the Russian Federation has adopted the dualist approach to international treaties: international norms and principles must be incorporated into domestic law before they can take effect.[196] Norms of international treaties that in any way affect criminal liability must be implemented through the Criminal Code in order to take effect in national law, i.e., introduce or amend national regulations (Articles 1, 3 UKR).[197] In general, the direct application of international regulations that do not provide for concrete sanctions would contradict the rule *nullum crimen sine lege certa.*[198]

120. The dualist approach contributes to partial clarity in the supremacy question to the extent that only those international norms that have been implemented into the Russian legal system (enacted by the Parliament in the form of a Federal Law) can prevail over national law.[199]

121. In the legal scholarship, however, followers of the monist concept argue for the direct application of the rules of international agreements. In their opinion, even in the absence of implementation, such rules should take precedence over national laws.[200]

122. In that respect, it is, however, important to mention the role of "the universally recognized principles and norms of international law" (Article 15 Const.) in shaping the Russian legal system as far as human rights standards are concerned, as will be explained further below.

123. In general, provisions of the international treaties can be applied in the domestic legal system if they were ratified by the Russian Federation and incorporated accordingly into the domestic legal system. An exception is the European Convention on Human Rights (ECHR) and the protocols thereto that were ratified by Russia.

124. The ECHR and the protocols (Nos. 1, 2, 4, 7, 9, 10, 11) can exceptionally be directly enforced on Russian territory. The reason for it is that Russia accepted the jurisdiction of the **European Court of Human Rights** (ECtHR).[201] The Supreme Court stated that "the application of the ECHR by domestic courts must occur with due consideration of the practice of the European Court of Human Rights

196. Zimnenko, Rossijskaya Justiziya, pp. 10–13.
197. For the principle of legality, *see* Part I, Chapter 1, paras. 197–226.
198. For the principle of legality, *see* Part I, Chapter 1, paras. 197–226; Paramonova, Revista Penal, 2010, 220–222; Resolution of the Supreme Court of the Russian Federation, Oct. 10, 2003 N 5.
199. For the procedure, *see* Federal Law on International Treaties, Jul. 15, 1995, N 101-FZ; Resolution of the Supreme Court of the Russian Federation, Oct. 10, 2003, N 5.
200. Chernichenko, Pravovedenie, N 1, 2009, 18; Tichomirov/Talapina, Vvedenie v rossijskoe pravo, p. 50.
201. Art. 1 Federal Law on Ratification of the ECHR, Mar. 30, 1998, N 54-FZ; http://www.echr.ru/convention/protocols.htm [last visited Dec. 18, 2019]; Ivanenko, Pravovedenie, N 3, 2010, 152–153; Baglaj, Konstituzionnoe pravo RF, p. 178.

in order to avoid any infringement of the ECHR."[202] With regard to the decisions of the ECtHR, on April 19, 2016, the Constitutional Court of the Russian Federation ruled for the first time that a decision of ECtHR cannot be implemented in Russia because measures aimed at its implementation would contradict the Russian Constitution.[203] This decision followed an earlier ruling of the Constitutional Court rendered in July 2015, where the Court held that, in exceptional cases, Russia could deviate from its obligation to enforce an ECtHR judgment if this was the only possible way to avoid a violation of the fundamental principles and norms of the Russian Constitution. The Constitutional Court noted that a special legal mechanism needed to be established under which the Constitutional Court would decide whether or not the enforcement of ECtHR judgments was contradictory to the Constitution.[204] Unlike the situation in EU countries, there is no supranational criminal law that can be directly applied to Russian territory. Approximately equivalent to the rules that have some features of supranational law are the regulations of the **Commonwealth of Independent States** (*Содружество Независимых Государств*, CIS). This regional organization on the territory of the former Soviet Union consists of eleven members, including Russia; it is, however, a loose association of states and cannot be compared to a supranational union such as the EU.[205]

125. Despite the above discussion on the supremacy of international treaties, a significant part of Russian criminal legislation has been shaped by the rules and standards of international treaties, which are considered to be a "component part of the Russian legal system" (Article 15, paragraph 4 Const.). The fact that the Russian Federation is a party to a large number of international agreements devoted to the establishment of international human rights institutions and to the joint combating of various forms of crime makes the international "impact factor" on the national level considerable.[206]

126. It is important to know that, as the legal successor of the Soviet Union, Russia took on the international obligations of the USSR, including all debts of the post-Soviet republics.[207]

---

202. Resolution of the Supreme Court of the Russian Federation, Oct. 10, 2003 N 5; for international sources of criminal law, *see* General Introduction, §5, paras. 116–144.
203. Press Release, RF Constitutional Court, Constitutional Court Announced Its Judgment in Case on the Possibility of Implementing the ECHR Ruling of July 4, 2013, in Anchugov and Gladkov v. Russia (Apr. 19, 2016), RF Constitutional Court website (in Russian).
204. Resolution of the Constitutional Court of the Russian Federation No. 21-P of July 14, 2015, on the Matter of Verifying the Constitutionality of Provisions of Article 1 of the Federal Law on Ratification of the Convention on Human Rights and Fundamental Freedoms, ROSSIISKAIA GAZETA (RG) (official publication) (June 27, 2015) (in Russian).
205. Paramonova, National characteristics, fundamental principles, and history of criminal law in Russia, 2014, pp. 257–259.
206. Paramonova, Revista Penal 2010, 220.
207. Paramonova, National characteristics, fundamental principles, and history of criminal law in Russia, 2014, pp. 204–209.

127. Article 46, paragraph 3 Const. provides that:

> Everyone shall have the right to appeal, according to international treaties of the Russian Federation, to international bodies for the protection of human rights and freedoms, if all the existing domestic state means of legal protection have been exhausted.

(3) Human Rights-related International Treaties

128. The efficiency of this mechanism is determined by the Russian Federation's international obligations to human rights.

129. Russia is a party to the following important **UN human rights agreements**: International Bill of Human Rights consisting of the Universal Declaration of Human Rights of 1948, the International Covenant on Civil and Political Rights of 1966 (ICCPR), and the International Covenant on Economic, Social and Cultural Rights of 1966 (ICESCR).

130. Both of the covenants were ratified in 1973.[208] The importance of the documents is hard to overestimate. Their provisions served as a basis for the key part of the new post-Soviet Constitution of the Russian Federation of 1993 and, more precisely, for its Chapter 2 entitled "Human and Civil Rights and Freedoms."

131. The Russian Federation is also a party to the core treaty of the **Council of Europe** (CoE) in the area of human rights, that is, to the ECHR and the protocols thereto.[209] The ECHR was ratified and entered into force in 1998.[210] The following protocols to the ECHR were ratified by Russia in 1998: Protocol No. 1, Protocol No. 2 (conferring upon the ECtHR competence to give advisory opinions), Protocol No. 3, Protocol No. 4 (securing certain rights and freedoms other than those already included in the Convention and in the first Protocol thereto), Protocols Nos. 5, 7, 8, 9, 10 and Protocol No. 11 (restructuring the control machinery established thereby).[211] Russia signed Protocol No. 12 in 2000 and ratified Protocol No. 14 in 2010. The ECHR also provided for the establishment of the ECtHR.

132. The important international monitoring bodies that have a restraining effect on the infringement of basic human rights on the national level are the UN Committee Against Torture (CAT) and the European Committee for the Prevention of Torture and Inhuman and Degrading Treatment or Punishment (CPT). The CAT and the CPT monitor the implementation of the Convention against Torture and Other

208. UN Treaties, http://treaties.un.org/ [last visited Dec. 18, 2019].
209. Ivanenko, Pravovedenie, N 3, 2010, 152–153; Baglaj, Konstituzionnoe pravo RF, p. 178; Paramonova, Der rechtliche Status der Europäischen Konvention zum Schutze der Menschenrechte und EGMR, KritV, N 3, 2013, pp. 188–211.
210. Treaties of Council of Europe, http://conventions.coe.int/treaty/ [last visited Dec. 18, 2019].
211. *Ibid.*

Cruel, Inhuman or Degrading Treatment or Punishment of 1984 (ratified 1987) and of the European Convention for the Prevention of Torture and Inhuman and Degrading Treatment or Punishment of 1987 (ratified 1998). Russia is thus a party to both these conventions.[212] Corresponding provisions are reflected in the Constitution (Article 21). However, corresponding criminal law norms that led to the offense of torture embracing "mental suffering" in compliance with the Convention were not introduced until 2003 (see Article 117 UKR).[213]

133. The UN Convention on the Rights of the Child of 1990, which was already ratified by the USSR in 1990, served as the basis for corresponding national legislation.[214] As a consequence, the rights of children were introduced into the Russian Family Code (part IV).[215] However, the CoE Convention on Action against Trafficking in Human Beings of 2005, as well as the Convention on the Protection of Children against Sexual Exploitation and Sexual Abuse of 2007, have neither been ratified nor signed by the Russian Federation. The non-signing, especially of the latter, has caused discontent among human rights activists.[216]

134. Among the main treaties ratified by the USSR (inherited by Russia as its legal successor) that are directed toward the fighting of crimes against the peace and security of mankind are the following: the Convention on the Prevention and Punishment of the Crime of Genocide of 1948 (ratified by the USSR in 1954), the Geneva Conventions I to IV of 1949 with their additional Protocols, the Hague Convention for the Protection of Cultural Property in the Event of Armed Conflict of 1954 (ratified in 1957), the Convention on the Non-Applicability of Statutory Limitations to War Crimes and Crimes Against Humanity of 1968 (ratified in 1969), the Convention on the Suppression and Punishment of the Crime of Apartheid of 1973 (ratified in 1975), the Convention on Certain Conventional Weapons of 1980 (ratified in 1982), and the Convention on the Physical Protection of Nuclear Material of 1980 (ratified in 1983). The Rome Statute was signed by Russia in 2000; nevertheless, it has not yet been ratified.[217] The main regulations of international humanitarian law were also adopted on the national level. Chapter 34 of the UKR is devoted to "crimes against the peace and security of mankind," which partly embrace the crimes of the Geneva Conventions. The chapter of the UKR does not include all the crimes of the Geneva Conventions.

212. UN Treaties, http://treaties.un.org/ [last visited Dec. 18, 2019]; Council of Europe, http://conventions.coe.int/Treaty/Commun/ListeTraites.asp?CM=8&CL=ENG [last visited Dec. 18, 2019].
213. Federal Law, Dec. 8, 2003, N 162-FZ.
214. UN Treaties, http://treaties.un.org [last visited Dec. 18, 2019].
215. Family Code of the Russian Federation, Mar. 1, 1996, N 223-FZ.
216. The Regional Report of the Ombudsman, http://ombudsmannao.ru [last visited Dec. 18, 2019]; Paramonova, National characteristics, fundamental principles, and history of criminal law in Russia, 2014, pp. 205–206.
217. Ministry of Foreign Affairs of the Russian Federation, http://www.ln.mid.ru/bl.nsf [last visited Dec. 18, 2019].

(4) International Treaties on Terrorism

135. The process of establishing anti-terrorist legislation in the Russian Federation was directly influenced by terrorism-related international agreements. Core treaties on both the international and the regional level became binding on the Russian Federation. Among them are the following: the Tokyo Convention on Offenses and Certain Other Acts Committed on Board Aircraft of 1963 (ratified in 1988),[218] the Hague Convention for the Suppression of Unlawful Seizure of Aircraft of 1970 (ratified in 1971) and the Montreal Convention for the Suppression of Unlawful Acts against the Safety of Civil Aviation of 1971 (ratified in 1973).[219] In 1973, Article 213 (2), which established criminal responsibility for hijacking, was already included in the Criminal Code of the RSFSR.[220] In the current UKR, the hijacking of an aircraft, a ship, or a train is criminalized by Article 211.

136. Additional international treaties that had a significant impact on the shaping of Russia's anti-terrorist legislation are the International Convention Against the Taking of Hostages of 1979 (ratified in 1987), the International Convention for the Suppression of Terrorist Bombings of 1997 (ratified in 2001), the International Convention for the Suppression of the Financing of Terrorism of 1999 (ratified in 2002), and the International Convention for the Suppression of Acts of Nuclear Terrorism of 2005 (ratified in 2007).[221]

137. Among the regional conventions on terrorism that influenced the national terrorism-related legislation are the European Convention on the Suppression of Terrorism of 1977 (ratified in 2001) as well as its amending Protocol (ratified in 2006),[222] and the Council of Europe Convention on the Prevention of Terrorism of 2005 (ratified in 2006).[223] The CoE Convention on Laundering, Search, Seizure and Confiscation of the Proceeds from Crime and on the Financing of Terrorism of 2005 was signed by Russia in 2009, ratified in 2017 and entered into force in 2018. Furthermore, the Member States of the CIS adopted the Minsk Treaty on Cooperation in Combating Terrorism of 1999.

138. Several domestic laws based on provisions of the aforementioned conventions were passed for the purpose of countering terrorism, for example, the Federal Law on Counteraction of Legalization (Laundering) of Criminally Obtained

---

218. http://www.icao.int/secretariat/legal/List%20of%20Parties/Tokyo_EN.pdf [last visited Dec. 18, 2019].
219. http://treaties.un.org/doc/db/Terrorism/Conv2-english.pdf [last visited Dec. 18, 2019].
220. Komissarov, Responsibility for Terrorism According to the Criminal Code of the Russian Federation (forthcoming).
221. http://treaties.un.org/Pages/DB.aspx?path=DB/studies/page2_en.xml&menu=MTDSG [last visited Dec. 18, 2019].
222. http://conventions.coe.int/treaty/Commun/ListeTraites.asp?CM=8&CL=ENG [last visited Dec. 18, 2019].
223. http://conventions.coe.int/Treaty/EN/Treaties/HTML/196.htm [last visited Dec. 18, 2019].

Incomes and of Financing Terrorism (2001) and the new Federal Law on Counteraction of Terrorism of 2006.[224] Furthermore, new crimes were introduced in the UKR.

(5) Treaties on Organized Crime, Drug Trafficking and Cybercrime

139. The key international conventions on organized crime and drug trafficking have also been ratified: the UN Convention against Transnational Organized Crime of 2000 and its supplementing Protocols, that is, the Protocol to Prevent, Suppress and Punish Trafficking in Persons, Especially Women and Children and the Protocol against the Smuggling of Migrants by Land, Sea and Air of 2000 (ratified in 2004). In 1990, Russia also ratified the UN Convention against Illicit Traffic in Narcotic Drugs of 1988. As a consequence, many new offenses were created and introduced into the UKR, for example, laundering of proceeds of crimes and the crimes of the organization of a criminal group, and participation in an organized criminal group.[225] Russia has not signed the Third Protocol against the Illicit Manufacturing of and Trafficking in Firearms, their Parts and Components and Ammunition of 2001.

140. Russia has signed but not ratified the CoE Convention on Cybercrime of 2001, which contains a list of core cybercrimes.[226] The signature given in November 2005 was even recalled in 2008. The main reason for non-ratification and for recalling the signature was Russia's concern that its sovereignty and national security could be infringed through Article 32 of the Convention (transborder access to stored computer data with consent or where publicly available).[227] The failure to ratify the Cybercrime Convention is one of the reasons why Russia's national legislation in regard to cybercrime is still based on outdated substantive and procedural norms.[228]

141. Moreover, Russia is not a member of the Organization for Economic Co-operation and Development (OECD) and has not signed the Convention on Combating Bribery of Foreign Public Officials in International Business Transactions of 1997. It did, however, sign (in 2003) and ratify (in 2006) the UN Convention against Corruption of 2003. In order to comply with the Convention's demand for the establishment of national anti-corruption bodies, Russia set up the Council for the Fight against Corruption, whose main task is to determine the priorities of anti-corruption policies. In general, in spite of the introduction of preventive anti-corruption measures on the national level, corruption remains a severe problem on

224. Federal Law on Counteraction of Terrorism, Mar. 6, 2006, N 35-FZ, http://www.garant.ru/doc/law/antiterror/ [last visited Dec. 18, 2019].
225. On parties to crime, *see* Part I, Chapter 5, §2, paras. 590–634.
226. Paramonova, Internationales Strafrecht im Cyberspace, pp. 41–75.
227. Walden, Security in Cyberspace; Schjolberg, Cyberspace Treaty.
228. Paramonova, ZSP, N 4, 2009, 77–79; Paramonova, Internationales Strafrecht im Cyberspace, pp. 77–123.

different levels and in many social spheres. According to recent polls, the most problematic area is corruption within the law enforcement authorities.[229]

(6) Treaties on Mutual Legal Assistance and Judicial Cooperation in Criminal Matters

142. With regard to mutual legal assistance and judicial cooperation in criminal matters, Russia has signed over 60 bilateral agreements with various countries. Among the multilateral agreements, the most important ones are the CoE Convention on Mutual Assistance in Criminal Matters of 1959 (ratified in 1999), the CoE Convention on Extradition of 1957 (ratified in 1999) and its first two additional Protocols (ratified in 1977 and 1999), the CoE Convention on the Transfer of Sentenced Persons of 1983 (ratified in 2007),[230] and the Minsk Convention on Legal Assistance for the CIS States of 1993 (entered into force in 1994).[231]

143. In terms of multilateral agreements, it is important to distinguish between two "regional regulative systems," the CoE and the CIS, which sometimes have overlapping regulations.[232] Nonetheless, they coexist due to their consistent implementation into national law, although the extent of implementation varies. For instance, Russia has two main international regulative subsystems on extradition. The first is based on the CoE Convention on Extradition of 1957, the second on the Minsk Convention on Legal Assistance of 1993 within the CIS States. One of the central principles of the Minsk Convention, which is also reflected in Russia's domestic criminal norms, is the principle of no surrender of nationals (Article 57, paragraph 1 Minsk Convention and Article 61, paragraph 1 Const.).[233] In contrast, the CoE Convention does not recognize nationality as a sufficient ground to refuse extradition. Nevertheless, the Minsk Convention does not contradict the rules of the CoE Convention that are binding upon the Russian Federation because, first, the CoE Convention allows a uniform law between two or more contracting parties (Article 28, paragraph 3), here between the CIS States, and second, Russia made a declaration in the instrument of ratification of the CoE Convention on Extradition according to which a citizen of the Russian Federation may not be extradited to another state.[234]

(7) Other Treaties

144. Additional UN international treaties that were ratified and are binding upon Russia are the Convention on the Law of the Sea of 1982 (ratified in 1997), the

229. Panfilova, The Barometer of the World Corruption 2007, http://www.transparency.org.ru/doc/2RUS [last visited Dec. 18, 2019].
230. http://conventions.coe.int/Treaty/Commun/ListeTraites.asp?CM=8&CL=ENG [last visited Dec. 18, 2019].
231. Ministry of Justice of the Russian Federation, http://government.ru/en/docs/ [last visited Dec. 18, 2019].
232. Paramonova, Revista Penal 2010, 220–223.
233. *Ibid.*
234. *Ibid.*

Convention on the High Seas of 1958 (ratified in 1960), the Convention on the Territorial Sea and the Contiguous Zone (ratified in 1960), and the Vienna Convention for the Protection of the Ozone Layer (ratified in 1986).[235]

II. National Sources

A. *The Constitution*

145. The Constitution is the supreme Russian law. It establishes fundamental human rights and guarantees, principles that impose limits on the criminal law, and fundamental principles of criminal procedure.[236]

146. The present **Constitution of the Russian Federation of 1993** (*Konstitucija Rossijskoj Federacii*, Const.)[237] is the fifth such document to be enacted since the October Revolution of 1917, after the constitutions of the Russian Soviet Federative Socialist Republic (RSFSR) of 1918, 1925, 1937, and 1978. The 1993 Constitution of the Russian Federation replaced the last constitution of the RSFSR of 1978.[238] The creeping process of democratization connected with the new policies of "glasnost" and "perestroika" of the 1980s, as well as the dissolution of the Soviet Union in late 1991, had made the enactment of a new constitution urgent.[239]

147. The Constitution has **supreme legal force** *(высшая юридическая сила)* on Russian territory (Article 4, paragraph 2 Const.). However, not all academics and legal practitioners agree on this feature,[240] primarily because its rules create conflicts and ambiguity in terms of whether the Constitution or the norms of international treaties have the supremacy (Article 15, paragraphs 1 and 4 Const.).[241]

148. The "supreme value of human rights" is proclaimed at the beginning of the Constitution (Article 2 Const., Chapter I). Chapter II of the Constitution (Articles 17–64), entitled "Rights and Freedoms of Man and Citizen," is completely devoted to human and civil rights and freedoms. These rights and freedoms are "inalienable

235. UN Treaties, http://treaties.un.org/ [last visited Dec. 18, 2019]; Paramonova, National characteristics, fundamental principles, and history of criminal law in Russia, 2014, pp. 206–209.
236. On the principles of criminal law, *see* Part I, Chapter 1, paras. 194–196, and on the principles of the criminal procedure, *see* Part II, Chapter 1, §3, paras. 814–827.
237. Constitution of the Russian Federation, Dec. 12, 1993.
238. Constitutions of the Russian Soviet Federative Socialist Republic (RSFSR) of Jul. 10, 1918; May 11, 1925; Jan. 21, 1937; Apr. 12, 1978.
239. Solomon, Reforming Justice in Russia, pp. 282–347; Smith, Reforming the Russian Legal System, pp. 79–103.
240. For a discussion of the supremacy of the Constitution and for national sources of criminal law, *see* General Introduction, §5, I, paras. 145–181; Chernichenko, Pravovedenie, N 1, 2009, 18.
241. On the sources of law and their hierarchy, *see* General Introduction, §5, I, paras. 116–181; for criminal liability of legal persons, *see* paras. 112, 379.Ivanenko, Mezhdunarodnie dogovori i konstituziya, pp. 135–161; Gavrilov, Mezhdunarodnaya i nazional'naya pravovaya sistema, p. 11; Bachin, Pravovedenie, N 6, 2007, 126; Paramonova, National characteristics, fundamental principles, and history of criminal law in Russia, 2014, pp. 212–213.

and shall be enjoyed by everyone from birth" (Article 17 Const.), and everyone is free to protect his or her rights and freedom by all means not prohibited by law (Article 45, paragraph 2 Const.). Thus, the supremacy of the institution of human and civil rights and freedoms is emphasized by the very structure of the Constitution of 1993. In contrast, the Constitution of the Russian Soviet Federative Socialist Republic of 1978 placed articles that dealt with civil rights only in Chapter VI (in the section "State and Individual").[242]

149. In the legal scholarship, the institution of human and civil rights and freedoms is regarded as the core element of the legal system as a whole and of the constitutional law, in particular. The main principle upon which it is based is that individual liberty may only be encroached upon pursuant to Federal Law (Article 55 Const.).[243]

150. There is a group of rights and freedoms that cannot be abolished or suspended by any laws, the so-called fundamental rights and freedoms (Article 55, paragraph 3 Const.). Prohibition of torture is the only absolute fundamental right that is not subject to limitation by any law. According to Article 56, paragraph 3 Const., these fundamental rights and freedoms are provided for in Articles 20, 21, 23, paragraph 1, 24, 28, 34, paragraph 1, 40, paragraph 1, as well as in Articles 46–54 Const.:

– right to life (Article 20 Const., Article 2 ECHR);
– protection of human dignity (Article 21, paragraph 1 Const.);
– prohibition of torture, violence, and other severe or humiliating treatment or punishment; prohibition of medical, scientific, and other experiments without the free consent of a person (Article 21, paragraph 2 Const., Article 3 ECHR);
– right to the inviolability of private life, personal and family secrets, and the protection of honor and good name (Article 23, paragraph 1 Const., Article 8 ECHR);
– prohibition of the dissemination of information about the private life of a person (Article 24 Const.);
– freedom of conscience and religion (Article 28 Const., Article 9 ECHR);
– right to the free use of a person's abilities and property for entrepreneurial and other economic activities (Article 34, paragraph 1 Const.);
– right to a home and social dwelling (i.e., a low-income housing offered by the State)(Article 40, paragraph 1 Const.).

151. The fundamental rights and freedoms provided for by Articles are particularly relevant to criminal law and criminal procedure. They contain due process guarantees and rights ***(процессуальные гарантии и права)*** and cannot be abolished or suspended:

242. Paramonova, National characteristics, fundamental principles, and history of criminal law in Russia, 2014, pp. 214–215.
243. Baglaj, Konstituzionnoe pravo RF, p. 176.

- guarantee of judicial protection of individual rights and freedoms (Article 46, paragraph 1 Const.);
- right to appeal to higher domestic courts, to interstate bodies for the protection of human rights and freedoms, if all available internal means of legal protection have been exhausted (Article 50, paragraph 3, Article 46, paragraph 2 Const.);
- right of the individual to the consideration of his or her case in the court and by the judge—"natural" judge—in whose jurisdiction the given case belongs according to the law (Article 47, paragraph 1 Const.);
- right of the individual to the examination of his or her case by a jury (Article 47, paragraph 2 Const.);
- right to qualified legal assistance, also free of charge, from the moment of detention, custody, or facing charges (Article 48 Const.);
- presumption of innocence (Article 49 Const.);
- nobody may be convicted twice for one and the same crime *(ne bis in idem)* (Article 50, paragraph 1 Const.);
- prohibition of the use of evidence received in violation of Federal Law in administering justice; right to appeal to a superior court as well as pardon or mitigation of punishment (Article 50, paragraph 2 Const.);[244]
- no obligation to testify against oneself, one's spouse, or close relatives (Article 51, paragraph 1 Const.);
- protection of rights of victims of crimes and of abuses of office (Article 52 Const.);
- right to state compensation for damages caused by unlawful action (omission) of bodies of state authority and their officials (Article 53 Const.);
- prohibition of retrospective force of laws introducing or aggravating responsibility (Article 54, paragraph 1 Const., Article 7 ECHR);[245]
- principle of legality (Article 54, paragraph 2 Const., Article 3 UKR, Article 7 ECHR).[246]

152. Other human and civil rights and freedoms may be limited by the Federal Law but only to the extent necessary for the protection of the fundamental principles of the constitutional system, morality, health, the rights and lawful interests of other people, and for ensuring the defense of the country and security of the state (Article 55, paragraph 3 Const.).

153. These rights include the following:

- equality before the law and court (Article 19, paragraph 1 Const.);
- equality of human and civil rights and freedoms regardless of sex, race, nationality, language, origin, property and official status, place of residence, religion, convictions, membership in public associations, or of other circumstances (Article 19, paragraph 2 Const., Article 14 ECHR);

244. For the principle of legality, *see* Part I, Chapter 1, paras. 197–226.
245. For the principle of legality, *see* Part I, Chapter 1, paras. 197–226.
246. For the principle of legality, *see* Part I, Chapter 1, paras. 197–226.

- right to freedom and personal inviolability (Article 22, paragraph 1 Const., Article 5 ECHR);
- prohibition of unlawful arrest, detention, and keeping in custody (Article 22, paragraph 2 Const., Article 5 ECHR);
- right to privacy of correspondence, of telephone conversations, postal, telegraph, and other messages (Article 23, paragraph 2 Const., Article 8 ECHR);
- right to the inviolability of the home (Article 25 Const., Article 8 ECHR);
- right of an individual to determine and declare his or her nationality and the right of an individual to use his or her native language (Article 26, paragraph 1 Const.);
- freedom of thought and expression (Article 29, paragraph 1 Const., Article 10 ECHR);
- freedom of mass media, prohibition of censorship (Article 29, paragraph 5 Const.);
- right to assembly and association (Articles 30, 31 Const., Article 11 ECHR);
- right of citizens of the Russian Federation to participate in managing state affairs both directly and through their representatives, to elect and be elected to state bodies (Article 32, paragraphs 1–2 Const.);
- right to participate in the administration of justice (Article 32, paragraph 5 Const.);
- right of citizens of the Russian Federation to appeal to state bodies (Article 33 Const.);
- right to own property (Articles 35, 36 Const.);
- guarantee of social security (Article 39 Const.);
- right to education (Article 43, paragraph 1 Const.);
- freedom of teaching, literary, artistic, scientific, technical, and other types of creative activity (Article 44, paragraph 1 Const.).

154. According to the principle "what is not forbidden is allowed," the list of human and civil rights and freedoms is not exhaustive and is extended by further domestic laws and international treaties. International treaties can provide rights and guarantees in addition to those established by the Constitution. They could be applied directly in the domestic legal system if they were ratified by the Russian Federation and incorporated accordingly into the domestic legal system. An exception is the ECHR and its protocols that were ratified by Russia.[247]

B. Statutory Legislation

155. Besides the Constitution, there are three levels of criminal law-related national legislation in Russia.[248]

---

247. For international sources of criminal law, *see* General Introduction, §5, paras. 116–144.
248. Paramonova, National characteristics, fundamental principles, and history of criminal law in Russia, 2014, pp. 254–257.

156. The first level—criminal law in a narrow sense—consists solely of the Criminal Code.

157. The Criminal Code is applicable—without exception—to the entire territory of the Russian Federation (Article 4, paragraph 2 Const., Article 1 UKR).

158. It was enacted by the Russian Parliament—**Federal Council *(Федеральное Собрание)***—on June 13, 1996, and entered into force on January 1, 1997. It replaced the Criminal Code of the Russian Soviet Federative Socialist Republic of 1960.[249]

159. The Criminal Code is the only law that can establish criminal responsibility in Russia, and new legal provisions establishing criminal responsibility must be enacted as part of the Criminal Code (Article 1, paragraph 1, principle of the complete codification of the criminal offenses).[250] Juvenile criminal law is also regulated by the Criminal Code (Chapter 14). As provided by Article 3 UKR, none of the other laws and no executive or judicial decisions can criminalize behavior independently of the Criminal Code.

160. Criminal liability, punishability, and other criminal legal consequences shall be determined by the Criminal Code alone.[251]

161. The idea behind the complete codification of criminal offenses in the Criminal Code is the guarantee of the principle of legality.[252] Its elements *nullum crimen sine lege scripta* and *nullum crimen sine lege certa* are embodied in concrete legal regulations that require that legal provisions be officially published (Article 15 paragraph 3 Const.). This requirement applies to the legal norms of all branches of law, including criminal law. It means that in order to be a source of criminal law, legal norms and any amendments to them must always be announced in official publications so that individuals can become aware of their rights and obligations. The following are the official publications: *Sobranie zakonodatelstva RF*, *Rossijskaja Gazeta*, *Parlamentskaja Gazeta*, as well as the official websites of the various state authorities.[253] Unpublished laws are inapplicable and invalid, as provided by Article 15 Constitution:[254]

---

249. Criminal Code of the Russian Soviet Federative Socialist Republic, Oct. 27, 1960 (Ugolovnij Kodeks RSFSR).
250. For national sources of criminal law, *see* General Introduction, §5, II, paras. 145–181, and for the principle of legality, *see* Part I, Chapter 1, paras. 197–226; Komissarov/Krilova/Tyazhkova, Ugolovnoe pravo RF, p. 24.
251. On the principles of criminal law, *see* Part I, Chapter 1, paras. 194–196, and on the principles of the criminal procedure, *see* Part II, Chapter 1, §3, paras. 814–827.
252. For the principle of legality, *see* Part I, Chapter 1, paras. 197–226.
253. Matuzov, Teorija gosudarstva i prava, pp. 371, 418; e.g., Federation Council, http://www.council.gov.ru/fedzak/index.html [last visited Dec. 18, 2019].
254. Plenum of the Highest Court of the Russian Federation, Oct. 31, 1995, N 8.

(1)-(2) […].

(3) Laws shall be officially published. Unpublished laws shall not be applied. Any normative legal provisions concerning human rights, freedoms and duties of man and citizen cannot be applied if they are not officially published for general knowledge.

(4) […].

162. The second level contains numerous pieces of special legislation that are directly related to criminal law. Federal Codes traditionally retain their preeminence as main sources of law in a given area. Thus, other Federal Laws must comply with the norms of the relevant Code. For example, the norms of the Federal Law on the Prosecutor's Office of the Russian Federation[255] must comply with the legal provisions of the Criminal Code, the Code of Criminal Procedure, and the Correctional Code.[256]

163. The following are examples of important crime-related Federal Laws: Federal Law on Interior Troops of the Russian Federation,[257] Federal Law on Police,[258] Federal Law on Detention of Suspects and Accused Persons,[259] Federal Law on Counteraction Against Terrorism,[260] Federal Law on Narcotic Drugs and Psychotropic Substances,[261] Federal Law on Weapons,[262] and Federal Law on State Fingerprinting Procedure.[263] These legal acts cannot establish criminal responsibility.

164. Federal Constitutional Laws, executive acts, and decrees and directives are also part of level two. Federal Constitutional Laws have supremacy over all other Federal Laws, including codes. The list of Federal Constitutional Laws is prescribed by the Constitution and includes, for instance, the Federal Constitutional Law "On the Judicial System of the Russian Federation."[264] Federal Constitutional Laws cannot create criminal offenses.

165. A large number of executive acts issued by the federal government, ministries, federal agencies, committees, etc., are part of the criminal law-related sphere. They are subordinate to all laws. Examples include the "Regulations on the

---

255. Federal Law on the Prosecutor's Office of the Russian Federation, Jan. 17, 1992, N 2202.
256. Sucharev, Commentaries to the Code of Criminal Procedure RF, p. 16; Matuzov, Teorija gosudarstva i prava, p. 233.
257. Federal Law on Interior Troops of the Russian Federation, Feb. 6, 1997, N 27-FZ.
258. Federal Law on Police, Feb. 7, 2011, N 3-FZ.
259. Federal Law on Detention of Suspects and Accused Persons, Jul. 15, 1995, N 103-FZ.
260. Federal Law on Counteraction Against Terrorism, Jul. 25, 1998, N 130-FZ.
261. Federal Law on Narcotic Drugs and Psychotropic Substances, Jan. 8, 1998, N 3-FZ.
262. Federal Law on Weapons, Dec. 13, 1996, N 150-FZ.
263. Federal Law on State Fingerprinting Procedure, Jul. 25, 1998, N 128-FZ.
264. Federal Constitutional Law on the Judicial System of the Russian Federation, Dec. 31, 1996, N 1-FKZ.

Ministry of Internal Affairs of the Russian Federation"[265] and the "Regulations on the Federal Security Service of the Russian Federation and Its Structure."[266]

166. Decrees and directives of the Russian President make up a separate category of legal acts (Article 90 Const.). If there is no valid Federal Law regulating a certain question, the President can issue a decree regarding this question. Such decrees may not be issued, however, when the Constitution directly requires the adoption of a Federal Law in this area. This presidential competence does not include the power to criminalize conduct.

167. The third level consists of legislation pertaining to the criminal law in its broadest sense: potentially, any legal provision that is to any extent relevant to the criminal law can be included in this level. Such legal norms usually define terms and definitions relevant to a particular criminal offense. These legal provisions can never be relied on as a ground for establishing criminal responsibility. For instance, the legal provisions of the Civil Code[267] must be taken into consideration when defining "property" in cases of economic crime. Also, all four tax crime articles (Articles 198–199.2 UKR) employ the terms "tax" and "fee." These terms are applied in accordance with their definitions in the Tax Code of the Russian Federation (*Nalogovij Kodeks RF*, NKR[268]) in the context of the criminal law. This is of particular relevance for the list of obligatory taxes and fees: Article 3, paragraph 5 and Articles 12–15 NKR contain an exhaustive list of federal, regional, and local types of taxes and fees of the Russian Federation. Hence, the failure to pay any charges that are not on this list of taxes and fees cannot be treated as a "tax crime."[269]

C. Statutory Delegated Legislation

168. In the field of criminal law, in compliance with the principle of legality, there is no possibility of delegated or secondary legislation.

---

265. "Regulations on the Ministry of Internal Affairs of the Russian Federation, Mar. 1, 2011, N 248.
266. "Regulations on the Federal Security Service of the Russian Federation and Its Structure, Aug. 11, 2003, N 806.
267. Civil Code of the Russian Federation, Nov. 28, 2001.
268. Tax Code of the Russian Federation. Part I, Jul. 31, 1998, N 146-FZ; Part II, Aug. 5, 2000, N 117-FZ.
269. Paramonova, Revista Penal 2011, 255–260; Plenum of the Highest Court of the Russian Federation, Dec. 28, 2006 (pa. 1,2); Paramonova, National characteristics, fundamental principles, and history of criminal law in Russia, 2014, pp. 254–257.

D. Case Law

169. In compliance with the principle of legality, judicial decisions of any level, including decisions of the Supreme Court, are not considered as a source of criminal law (Articles 1, 3 UKR) but as a means to interpret criminal law norms.[270]

170. According to the Constitution, judges are independent and only bound by the Constitution and the Federal Laws (Article 120 Const.). Decisions of the upper courts are not binding on the inferior courts in deciding subsequent cases. Decisions of the Supreme Court also do not create a precedent that can be a source of law for equivalent cases.[271] According to Article 126 Const.:

> The Supreme Court of the Russian Federation […] shall exercise judicial supervision […] according to procedural forms provided for by Federal Law and shall provide interpretations on the issues of judicial practice.

171. Theoretically, any judicial decision of any level can be overridden by judges. Nonetheless, the decisions of the upper courts, although not binding, are usually taken into consideration by inferior courts.

172. Resolutions of the Supreme Court's Plenary Assembly ***(постановления Пленума Верховного Суда РФ)*** and reviews of the judicial practice of the Supreme Court ***(обзоры судебной практики Верховного Суда РФ)*** play a central role in the shaping of a unified judicial practice.

173. Resolutions of the Supreme Court's Plenum address specific problems in a particular area and are designed to harmonize legal practice regarding these questions.[272] Reviews of the judicial practice of the Supreme Court consist of a general analysis of judicial practice over a certain time period.[273] In addition to general information (such as case statistics), the reviews include analysis of judicial mistakes, criminal liability, imposition of punishment, and procedural questions. Domestic courts normally follow resolutions and reviews of the Supreme Court. In practice, they are considered to be more than recommendations and are regarded by the courts and lawyers as quasi-legislative acts.[274] This way, the highest judicial body, by providing guidelines for uniform judicial practice, sets out the limits of

270. For the principle of legality, *see* Part I, Chapter 1, paras. 197–226.
271. Supreme Court of the Russian Federation, http://www.supcourt.ru [last visited Dec. 18, 2019].
272. E.g., Resolution of the Supreme Court RF on Judicial Practice of Application of Compulsory Measures of Medical Nature, Apr. 7, 2011 or Resolution on Money Laundering, Nov. 18, 2004, http://www.supcourt.ru [last visited Dec. 18, 2019].
273. E.g., Review of the Legislation and Judicial Practice of the fourth quarter of 2009 or Review on the Judicial Practice in Judicial Supervision of the Panel for Criminal Cases of the Supreme Court of the first quarter of 2009, http://www.supcourt.ru [last visited Dec. 18, 2019].
274. Burov, The Status of the Resolutions of the Supreme Court's Plenary Assembly; Paramonova, National characteristics, fundamental principles, and history of criminal law in Russia, 2014, pp. 253–254.

interpretation and fulfills its function of judicial supervision. However, the judiciary can never create new rules that establish criminal responsibility.[275]

174. For instance, with regard to the international obligations of Russia, the Supreme Court stated that "the application of the ECHR by domestic courts must occur with due consideration of the practice of the European Court of Human Rights in order to avoid any infringement of the ECHR."[276] Since the ECHR and the protocols (Nos. 1, 2, 4, 7, 9, 10, 11) were ratified, their rules can be directly enforced on the Russian territory.[277] It is important to mention that with regard to the case law of the ECtHR, the Constitutional Court of the Russian Federation ruled in 2015 that decisions of the ECtHR shall be executed based on the supremacy of the Constitution. In case of collision between the interpretation of the Convention given by the ECtHR in a particular case and the norms of the Constitution, the supremacy of the constitutional provisions can be recognized, however, only by the Constitutional Court. Considering that the Constitution is based on the provisions of the ECHR, collisions between them are barely likely to appear.[278]

175. The publication of judicial decisions is not obligatory.[279] Nonetheless, court decisions are published in written or electronic form in the law reports of the various courts. There are, for example, the Bulletin of the Highest Court of the Russian Federation[280] and the Bulletin of the Krasnoyarsk Regional Court.[281] The consolidated database of judicial decisions of all Russian courts is the State Automated System of the Russian Federation "Justice"—**GAS** ***(Государственная Автоматизированная Система РФ "Правосудие," ГАС)***.[282]

176. The **Constitutional Court of the Russian Federation** ***(Конституционный Суд Российской Федерации),*** which has a monopoly over the interpretation of the Constitution (also in conjunction with the norms of international treaties, Article 125 Const.), plays a significant role in the establishment of the constitutional framework by shaping its homogenous application throughout the domestic legal system. The importance of this court cannot be overestimated, especially given the fact that

275. For the principle of legality, *see* Part I, Chapter 1, paras. 197–226.
276. Resolution of the Supreme Court of the Russian Federation, Oct. 10, 2003 N 5; for international sources of criminal law, *see* General Introduction, §5, paras. 116–144.
277. Art. 1 Federal Law on Ratification of the ECHR, Mar. 30, 1998, N 54-FZ; http://www.echr.ru/convention/protocols.htm [last visited Dec. 18, 2019].
278. Decision of the Constitutional Court of the Russian Federation, Jul. 14, 2015, N 21-II .For international sources of criminal law, *see* General Introduction, §5, paras. 116–144.
279. For the principle of legality, *see* Part I, Chapter 1, paras. 197–226.
280. Supreme Court of the Russian Federation, http://www.supcourt.ru/ [last visited Dec. 18, 2019].
281. Krasnoyarsk Regional Court, http://kraevoy.krk.sudrf.ru [last visited Dec. 18, 2019].
282. State Automated System of the Russian Federation "Justice," GAS, http://www.sudrf.ru/ [last visited Dec. 18, 2019]; Paramonova, National characteristics, fundamental principles, and history of criminal law in Russia, 2014, pp. 260–262.

its decisions are basically of a normative nature since they apply to an undetermined number of individuals and normally for an undetermined range of time. A 2009 decision represented, for instance, a turning point with regard to the abolition of capital punishment.[283]

E. Others

177. According to the principle of legality, written law is the sole source of criminal law (Articles 1, 3 UKR, Article 15 Const.).[284] Consequently, national as well as international legal customs must be written down before they can attain the status of criminal law.[285]

178. National customs being part of unwritten law cannot contain criminal offenses or definitions determining Russian criminal law. This is different from civil law, such as maritime law, where customary law is considered an official source of law (Article 6 Civil Code RF). Thus, customary law is neither a source of substantive criminal law nor of the law of criminal procedure.

179. The same applies to international customs and general principles: although the "generally recognized principles" are seen as a "component part" of the Russian legal system (Article 15, paragraph 4 Const.), they cannot be legal sources for criminal liability, punishability, and other criminal legal consequences on Russian territory unless they are implemented into domestic law.[286] They serve only as the "basis" or guideline for domestic legal provisions.[287]

180. There are, however, different views on this issue among academics; according to some, international customs and "generally recognized principles" of international law are official sources of criminal law.[288]

181. Legal literature is not regarded as a source of criminal law. As a complementary means of interpreting and understanding legal provisions, it plays a consultative role in judicial practice. The influence and importance of a particular academic opinion depend less on the authority of its author but more on the author's affiliation with a certain (academic or state) organization. Thus, in practice, courts normally take into consideration the opinions expressed in the various commentaries, academic journals, and textbooks published by institutions, such as the Supreme

283. On death penalty in Russia, *see* Part I. Chapter 7, paras. 723–724, 1283–1285, ; Paramonova, in: Arroyo/Biglino/Schabas (eds.), Towards Universal Abolition of the Death Penalty, pp. 168–175; Paramonova, National characteristics, fundamental principles, and history of criminal law in Russia, 2014, p. 214.
284. For the principle of legality, *see* Part I, Chapter 1, paras. 197–226.
285. Naumov, Rossiiskoe ugolovnoe pravo, pp. 200–214; Zhuravlev, Ugolovnoe pravo, pp. 19–25; Encyclopedia of a lawyer, http://dic.academic.ru/dic [last visited Dec. 18, 2019].
286. Plenum of the Highest Court of the Russian Federation, Oct. 31, 1995, N 8.
287. For the principle of legality, *see* Part I, Chapter 1, paras. 197–226.
288. Konyachin, Mezhdunarodnij dogovor, p. 154.

Court of the Russian Federation and the Institute of Legislation and Comparative Law of the Government of the Russian Federation.[289]

§6. Classifications and Techniques of Criminal Law

182. Russian law belongs to the **continental** ***(континентальная)*** or **Romano-Germanic legal system** ***(романо-германская правовая система).*** Throughout history, the systematization and codification of legislative acts has been a decisive feature in the development of Russian criminal (procedural) law.

183. The first written source of legal (criminal) rules of the *Kievan Rus´* is **Russkaya Pravda** ***(Русская Правда).***[290]

184. The first codifications of law in centralized Russia (**Law Code of Ivan III**, ***Судебник Ивана** III*, 1497, and **Law Code of Ivan IV**, ***Судебник Ивана** IV*, 1550) provided for the inquisitorial criminal procedure instead of a private accusatorial procedure. The most serious crimes, especially political ones, were prosecuted by the state, independent of a private initiative.

185. Further codifications of legal rules in the 19th century were directly influenced by the liberalization processes that had been taking place in Europe, primarily by the French Revolution. The **Complete Collection of Codified Laws of the Russian Empire** ***(Свод Законов Российской Империи)*** was mostly finished by 1835.[291] By the end of the 19th century, a solid, codified legal base had been formed that was comparable to French and German codifications. These legal systems had a significant influence on the Russian legal system.[292]

186. The (criminal) legal system after 1917 must be considered separately. In foreign as well as in the Russian legal literature, Russian law in general and the criminal law, in particular, is often seen as belonging to the so-called **socialist legal system** ***(социалистическая правовая система),*** which, however, is derived from continental law.[293] As a phenomenon, socialist law traces its roots to 1917 (the October Revolution) and 1922 (the year the Soviet Union was established). The key idea behind socialist law and its historical mission was to engineer the creation of

289. E.g., Lebedev, Kommentarii k UK RF; The Institute of Legislation and Comparative Law of the Government of the Russian Federation (IZISP), http://www.izak.ru [last visited Dec. 18, 2019]; Paramonova, National characteristics, fundamental principles, and history of criminal law in Russia, 2014, pp. 259–260, 262.

290. Russkaya Pravda, www.consultant.ru [last visited Dec. 18, 2019].

291. Svod Zakonov Rossijskoj Imperii 1835, http://civil.consultant.ru/reprint/books/181/3.html [last visited Dec. 18, 2019].

292. Kuznecova, Kurs ugolovnogo prava, p. 166; Shershenevich, Uchebnik russkogo grazhdanskogo prava, p. 546.

293. David/Brierly, Major Legal Systems, pp. 150–256; Glendon et al., Comparative Legal Traditions, pp. 395–405; Tichomirov, Kurs sravnitelnogo pravovedeniya, pp. 124–129.

a "stateless" and "lawless" society since "state" and "law" were considered repressive tools of state power.[294] That was the reason for the absence of a clear distinction between private and public law. According to this logic, no actual separation of powers and no system of checks and balances were needed. And instead of the supremacy of law, the decisions of the executive power were regarded as supreme.

187. However, in spite of the many profound substantive differences between the socialist system and the continental legal system, Russian law in the Soviet period retained many, for the most part, "technical" characteristics of continental law. These included the distinction between branches of law, the codification of legal norms, the supremacy of written sources of law, and the formal recognition of the separation of powers.

188. Another view found in the legal scholarship places the Russian legal system within the **Slavic legal family or system** *(славянская правовая семья)* together with the Czech Republic, Poland, Ukraine, and several other countries. This view is based on the substantial similarities of these legal systems. The countries belonging to this legal family share—to some extent—a common legal mentality (e.g., no tradition of the strong protection of private property), common historical sources of law, and a tradition of common legal terms and institutions independent of the Soviet period.[295]

189. The main features of the continental legal system, which characterize contemporary Russian law, are the following: the distinction between private and public law; the differentiation between constitutional, civil, administrative, criminal, civil procedural, and criminal procedural branches of law; the vertical and horizontal separation of powers on the constitutional level (Articles 71–73 Constitution); the stable hierarchy of the sources of law with the Constitution at the top of the hierarchy;[296] the systematization and codification of legislative acts; and the supremacy of law.[297]

190. Legislative statutes—federal and regional laws—are the primary sources of law in general and in terms of criminal law in particular. Case law, customary law, as well as legal scholarship are not, de jure, considered official sources of law (Article 120 Const.).[298] However, de facto, inferior courts are following the upper

294. Glendon et al., Comparative Legal Traditions, p. 396; Tichomirov, Kurs sravnitelnogo pravovedeniya, p. 128.
295. Danilevskij, Rossiya i Evropa, pp. 469–509; Paramonova, National characteristics, fundamental principles, and history of criminal law in Russia, 2014, pp. 200–202.
296. For a discussion of the supremacy of the Constitution, *see* General Introduction, §5, II, paras. 145–181.
297. Tichomirov, Kurs sravnitelnogo pravovedeniya, p. 124; Glendon et al., Comparative Legal Traditions, pp. 114–120; Paramonova, National characteristics, fundamental principles, and history of criminal law in Russia, 2014, pp. 200–202.
298. For the sources of criminal law, *see* General Introduction, §5, II, B, paras. 155–167.

courts in their decisions, for instance, the **Supreme Court of the Russian Federation's** *(Верховный Суд Российской Федерации)* decisions in cases involving criminal law.

191. In accordance with the principle of legality, written law must be officially published.[299] It is the sole source of criminal law in the Russian Federation. Due to the fact that substantive criminal law, the law of criminal procedure, as well as the law of criminal corrections fall within the jurisdiction of the Federation (Article 71 item "n" Const.),[300] criminal law norms are determined exclusively by Federal Laws or Federal Constitutional Laws. Neither the constituent **entities of the Federation** *(субъекты Российской Федерации)* [301] nor any other authority has competence over these matters.

192. As explained above, the following Federal Laws are the main sources of criminal law in its broadest sense: Criminal Code of the Russian Federation, the Criminal Procedure Code of the Russian Federation, and the Correctional Code of the Russian Federation.[302] Nevertheless, legal scholarship equates "criminal law" with substantive criminal law. Thus, the Criminal Code is considered the main source of criminal law.[303]

193. Finally, it is noteworthy that different methods of legal interpretation are applied: grammatical (or linguistic), functional, historical, systematic as well as logical and teleological interpretation methods.

---

299. For the principle of legality, *see* Part I, Chapter 1, paras. 197–226.
300. Constitution of the Russian Federation, Dec. 12, 1993 (Konstituciya Rossijskoj Federacii, Const.).
301. For political and administrative structure, *see* General Introduction, §1, IV, paras. 11–20.
302. For national sources of criminal law, *see* General Introduction, §5, II, paras. 145–181.
303. Paramonova, National characteristics, fundamental principles, and history of criminal law in Russia, 2014, pp. 253–254.

Part I. Substantive Criminal Law

Chapter 1. General Principles

§1. System of General Principles

194. As criminal law is considered *ultima ratio*, that is, the final and most severe means of protecting recognized legal values, it is extremely important to have a coherent system of rules that place limitations on its form and content. This system of rules is based on the **principles of criminal law** *(принципы уголовного права),* and the framework for these principles is formulated in the legal literature and in the Constitution of the Russian Federation.

195. The question of how many discrete criminal law principles there are is a source of controversy.[304] Also, the fact that some of these principles are expressed in concrete legal norms (e.g., the principle of justice, Article 6 UKR) is regarded critically: some authors argue that these principles—as fundamental values that impose limits on the criminal law—can only be adequately (i.e., with sufficient detail) formulated in the legal literature and can only be appropriately developed in criminal policy. Others argue that it is possible through the case law. This approach would facilitate the avoidance of the brief, formalized wording, typical for legal provisions, and that could lead to unjustified limitations on the application of the various principles.[305] The main principles of criminal law are included in the Criminal Code (Articles 3–7 UKR).

- *Principle of Legality:* The **principle of legality** *(принцип законности)* is binding upon all state authorities: legislative, executive, and judicial. According to this principle, criminal liability, punishment, and other criminal legal consequences must be determined by the Criminal Code alone, based on the Constitution and international norms. No one may be held criminally responsible for an action (or omission) that was not regarded as a crime when it was committed (Article 4, paragraph 2, Articles 15 and 54 Const., Article 3 UKR).[306]
- *Principle of Equality:* The **principle of equality of individuals before the law** *(принцип равенства граждан перед законом)* means that persons accused

304. Korobeev, Polnij kurs ugolovnogo prava, p. 86; Filimonov, Principi ugolovnogo prava, p. 1; Malzev, Principi ugovnogo prava i ich realisaziya, pp. 1–20.
305. Korobeev, ibid., pp. 87–88.
306. For the principle of legality, *see* Part I, Chapter 1, paras. 197–226.

of having committed crimes are equal before the law and that criminal responsibility must be determined regardless of the accused's sex, race, nationality, language, origin, property and official status, place of residence, attitude to religion, convictions, membership in public associations, and other circumstances (Article 19 Const., Article 4 UKR). In the legal literature, the principle of equality is often regarded as part of the principle of justice.[307]

The principle also finds expression in Article 300 UKR, which criminalizes the illegal release from criminal responsibility by a prosecutor, investigator, or inquirer[308] of a person suspected or accused of committing a crime.

– *Principle of Culpability:* According to the **principle of culpability** ***(принцип вины),*** objective imputability, that is, the attribution of criminal responsibility for the causing of harm without proof of culpability, is not permitted. A person can be held criminally responsible only for those socially dangerous actions (or omissions) and consequences in respect of which his or her culpability has been established (Article 5 UKR).[309] In contrast, for instance, according to Soviet law, relatives of "traitors of the motherland" could be held criminally responsible solely by virtue of their family relationships.[310]
– *Principle of Humanity:* According to the **principle of humanity**, the purpose of criminal legislation is to ensure the safety of the person. Punishment and other measures of a criminal-law character that are imposed upon a person who has committed a crime may not pursue the aim of causing physical suffering or demeaning human dignity (Article 21 Const., Article 7 UKR). This principle can be seen in the de facto abolition of the death penalty in Russia since 1996.[311] It can also be seen in the possibility of early conditional relief from serving punishment (Article 79 UKR) and in the institutions of amnesty and pardon (Articles 84, 85 UKR).[312]
– *Principle of Justice:* The **principle of justice** ***(принцип справедливости)*** holds that punishment and other measures of a criminal-law character that can be imposed on a person who has committed a crime must be just, that is, must correspond to the character and degree of the social danger of the crime, the circumstances of its commission, and the personality of the accused.

The double jeopardy prohibition (Article 50, paragraph 1 Const.) is explicitly regarded as an element of the principle of justice (Article 6, paragraph 2 UKR).

---

307. Ignatov/Krasikov, Kurs rossijskogo ugolovnogo prava, pp. 14–16; Korobeev, Polnij kurs ugolovnogo prava, pp. 95–99. *See* discussion of the principle of justice paras. 194–196, 206, 244, 656.
308. In accordance with Arts. 38, 40, 41, 150, 223 Code of Criminal Procedure, "inquirers" deal with minor criminal offenses, e.g., Art. 112 UKR, intentional causing of average gravity harm to health.
309. On the subjective aspects of the offense, *see* Part I, Chapter 3, §4, paras. 383–428.
310. Statute "Treason against the Motherland," Jun. 8, 1934, available at http://www.allpravo.ru/library [last visited Dec. 18, 2019].
311. Paramonova, in: Arroyo/Biglino/Schabas (eds.), Towards Universal Abolition of the Death Penalty, p. 175; Decision of the Constitutional Court of Russia, Nov. 19, 2009, http://www.ksrf.ru/ru/Decision/Pages/default.aspx [last visited Dec. 18, 2019]. For capital punishment, *see* Part I. Chapter 7, paras. 723–724, 1283–1285.
312. Paramonova, Grounds for excluding criminal liability in Russia, 2016, pp. 344–349.

As mentioned above, according to the legal literature, the principle of justice also includes the principle of equality of individuals before the law, on the one hand, and the principle of differentiation or individualization of responsibility, on the other.

- *Principle of Differentiation or Individualization of Responsibility*: The **principle of individualization of responsibility** (принцип дифференциации и индивидуализации ответственности) can be seen in the difference between criminal law consequences for healthy persons and those for insane persons, for adults and for minors, and in some cases for men and for women.[313] For example, pregnancy or parenthood with young children are circumstances that may lead to mitigation of punishment (Article 61, paragraph 1 items c, d UKR). In contrast, committing a crime by taking advantage of the vulnerability of the victim or with special cruelty are examples of circumstances that lead to an aggravation of punishment (Article 63 UKR).

  The principle of individualization of responsibility comprises the principle of personal responsibility and the principle of proportionality.
- *Principles of Personal Responsibility and Proportionality:* The **principle of personal responsibility** (no punishment without personal blameworthiness) and the principle of proportionality (punishment must be proportional to the individual culpability of the offender) are both parts of the principle of justice. They are, for example, reflected in Article 34, paragraph 1 UKR, which states:

> The responsibility of parties to crime shall be determined by the character and degree of the actual participation of each of them in the commission of the crime.

- *Principles of Criminal Policy:* The legal literature distinguishes between principles of criminal law, on the one hand, and **principles of criminal policy** *(принципы уголовно-правовой политики),* on the other. While principles of criminal law serve as a basis for criminal policy, principles of criminal policy, in turn, reflect the implementation, in practice, of principles of criminal law.

196. Principles of criminal policy include the following: minimization of forms of repression, inevitability of criminal responsibility, appropriateness, and justice.[314]

313. For more details, *see* Part I, Chapter 7, §6, paras. 762–774.
314. Korobeev, Polnij kurs ugolovnogo prava, pp. 88–99.

§2. The Principle of Legality

I. Statement and Content

A. Historical Background of the Concept of the Principle of Legality

197. The **concept of the principle of legality** *(принцип законности)* has changed according to historical epochs and developments.

198. During the period of the czars, as all legal sources emanated from the czar and were considered to be the only sources of valid law, any violation of the czar's will was illegal. In 1550, the **Law Code of Ivan IV** *(Судебник Ивана IV),* which was the first codification of law in centralized Russia, was adopted. In the 18th century, during the ruling of *Peter the Great* and *Ekaterina II*, a further and more detailed codification of the law was carried out.

199. By the end of the 18th century, it became necessary to consolidate all current laws in one Code, and in doing so, to retain those laws that were "the most useful for the welfare of the people and correspond to the spirit of the nation and the natural conditions of the state."[315] This reform, known as the **Complete Collection of Codificated Laws of the Russian Empire** *(Свод Законов Российской Империи),* was finished by 1835 and created a distinction between state, civil, administrative, criminal, and procedural branches of law.[316]

200. Administrative, educational, and judicial reforms that were implemented by the liberal Czar Alexander II in the mid-19th century appeared to create a turning point with regard to the concept of the principle of legality in Russian law. These reforms established some government positions that were elected (before all of them were appointed by the czar) and a unified system of the national courts based on the principle of equality of all social groups before the law. The new codified legal provisions, including criminal law, were considered to be a "juridical barrier" against the arbitrariness of state power.[317] Notwithstanding this, the czar retained unlimited power.

201. In the Soviet period, the principle of legality was given a very broad interpretation. Noncompliance with ideology was considered to be illegal regardless of official written law. The application of analogy in the field of criminal law was, for instance, permitted until the adoption of the new Criminal Statute in 1958.[318] Analogy was provided for by the Criminal Codes of RSFSR of 1922 and 1926 as follows:

---

315. Karamzin, Istoriya Gosudarstva Rossiiskogo: http://bibliotekar.ru/istoria-prava-rossii/index.htm.
316. Paramonova, Principle of legality in Russia. In: Sieber, U. / Forster, S. / Jarvers, K. (ed(s).): National Criminal Law in a Comparative Legal Context. Volume 2.1: General limitations on the application of criminal law. Berlin, Duncker & Humblot, 2011, p. 103.
317. Kropachev, Ugolovnoe pravo Rossii, p. 69; Kruglikov, Kommentarii k Ugolovnomu Kodeksu RF, p. 10.
318. Art. 7 Osnovi Ugolovnogo Zakonodatel´stva Dec. 25, 1958.

> [i]f any socially dangerous acts are not explicitly provided for by the present Code, the grounds and limits of criminal responsibility for the act shall be determined in conformity with those articles of the Code which are, according to the type of a crime, most similar to the act.[319]

202. In the legal doctrine, "the historical inevitability" of the application of analogy was justified by the impossibility to completely foresee in the written law the diversity of forms of criminal activity. This rationale permitted judges to fill gaps in the criminal law by following their "socialistic legal consciousness" in order to find an appropriate solution.[320] In such a way, practically every socially dangerous act could be qualified as criminally illegal.[321]

B. The Current Concept of the Principle of Legality

203. The current concept of the principle of legality is based, first of all, on constitutional rules since the Constitution[322] has supremacy in the hierarchy of laws (paragraph 2 Article 4 Constitution, paragraph 2 Article 1 UKR).[323] In the Criminal Code of the Russian Federation and the Code of Criminal Procedure of the Russian Federation, aspects of the principle of legality are enshrined in a more detailed fashion.

204. The principle of legality is laid down, first, in, Article 15, paragraph 2 Constitution, which states that "the bodies of State authority, the bodies of local self-government, officials, private citizens and their associations shall be obliged to observe the Constitution and laws of the Russian Federation."

205. Another essential constitutional norm requires that "no one may bear responsibility for the action (or omission) which was not regarded as a crime when it was committed" (Article 54, paragraph 2). In regard to the criminal law, this constitutional norm is transformed into the principle *nullum crimen sine lege scripta.*

206. In legal doctrine, the principle of legality is regarded as a formal **organizational principle (организационный принцип),** which is distinct from the group of substantial principles, such as the principle of justice.[324] The principle of legality determines the unified form of the law, which governs rules of social behavior. The exercise of the state's power must be predictable for the citizens; this is achieved through definite, prior-known, publicly established legal regulations and by the non-application of unknown and uncertain rules (e.g., prohibition of analogy in criminal law, Article 3 UKR).

319. Art. 10 Ugolovnij Kodeks RSFSR June 1, 1922; Art. 16 Ugolovnij Kodeks RSFSR Nov. 22, 1926.
320. Kurskii, Ugolovnij Kodeks 1922, pp. 86–87.
321. Trajnin, Textbook on the Criminal Law, p. 101.
322. Constitution of the Russian Federation, Dec. 12, 1993.
323. For the sources of criminal law, *see* General Introduction, §5, II, paras. 116–181.
324. Kropachev, Ugolovnoe pravo Rossii, p. 67.

207. However, the principle of legality cannot be regarded as only an organizational principle. In order to avoid pure formal punishment (objective imputability-principle of legality in its very narrow approach), it is important to note that in Russian criminal law, the principle of legality can be applied only together with the principle of culpability or *mens rea* (Article 5 UKR) as well as the principle of individual responsibility (pa. 1 Article 34 UKR).[325]

C. Legal Regulation and Scope of the Principle of Legality

Legal Provisions

208. The principle of legality as one of the main principles of criminal law is rooted in several provisions of constitutional law.[326]

Art. 4 para. 2 Constitution of the Russian Federation[327]

(2) The Constitution of the Russian Federation and federal laws shall have supremacy in the whole territory of the Russian Federation.

Art. 15 Constitution of the Russian Federation

(1) The Constitution of the Russian Federation shall have supreme juridical force, direct application and shall be valid in the whole territory of the Russian Federation. Laws and other legal provisions adopted in the Russian Federation shall not contradict the Constitution of the Russian Federation.
(2) The bodies of State authority, the bodies of local self-government, officials, private citizens and their associations shall be obliged to observe the Constitution of the Russian Federation and laws.
(3) Laws shall be officially published. Unpublished laws shall not be applied. Any normative legal provisions concerning human rights, freedoms and duties of man and citizen cannot be applied if they are not officially published for general knowledge.
(4) The universally-recognized norms of international law and international treaties and agreements of the Russian Federation shall be a component part of its legal system. If an international treaty or agreement of the Russian Federation fixes other rules than those provided for by law, the rules of the international agreement shall be applied.

325. On the principles of criminal law, *see* Part I, Chapter 1, paras. 194–196, and on the principles of the criminal procedure, *see* Part II, Chapter 1, §3, paras. 814–827; Paramonova, Principle of legality in Russia, 2011, pp. 103–105.
326. Lebedev, Kommentarii k UK RF, p. 29; Naumov, Rossiiskoe ugolovnoe pravo, p. 51.
327. All translations of the provisions of the Constitution in this chapter are taken from: http://www.constitution.ru/en/10003000-01.htm, last visited: May 26, 2016.

Art. 54 Constitution of the Russian Federation

(1) A law introducing or aggravating responsibility shall not have retroactive effect.
(2) No one may bear responsibility for an action (or omission) which was not regarded as crime when it was committed. If after violating a law responsibility for that violation is eliminated or mitigated, the new law shall be applied.

209. The main aspects of the principle of legality are thus explicitly provided for by the Constitution of the Russian Federation but also by the UKR, and by the UPKR;[328] the constitutional rules referring to the principle of legality in the criminal law are specified in the following provisions of the UKR and the UPKR:

Art. 1 UKR (The Criminal Law of the Russian Federation)

(1) The criminal law of the Russian Federation consists of the present Code. New laws providing for criminal responsibility are subject to inclusion in the present Code.
(2) The present Code is based on the Constitution of the Russian Federation and the generally recognized principles and norms of international law.

Art. 3 UKR (The Principle of Legality)

(1) Criminal liability, punishability and other criminal legal consequences shall be determined by the present Code alone.
(2) The application of a criminal law by analogy shall not be allowed.

Art. 10 UKR (The Retroactive Force of a Criminal Law)

(1) A criminal law which eliminates the criminality of an action (or omission), mitigates punishment, or in any other way improves the position of a person who has committed a crime shall have a retroactive force, that is, extend to the persons who have committed the respective actions (or omissions), before the entry of such law into force, including to persons who are serving or have served a sentence. A criminal law that establishes the criminality of an action (or omission) and increases punishment or in any other way worsens the position of a person shall have no retroactive force.
(2) If a new criminal law mitigates the punishment which is then being served by a person, for an action (or omission), then this punishment shall be subject to reduction within the limits provided for by the new criminal law.

328. Paramonova, Principle of legality in Russia, 2011, p. 105.

Art. 14 UKR (The Concept of Crime)

(1) A socially dangerous act committed with guilt and prohibited by this Code under threat of punishment shall be deemed to be a criminal offense.

Art. 7 UPKR (Legality in the Criminal Procedure)[329]

(1) The court, the prosecutor, the investigator, the body of inquiry and the inquirer shall have no right to apply a federal law contradicting the present Code.
(2) The court having established the non-correspondence of a federal law or of another legal normative act to the present Code in the course of the criminal case shall take the decision in conformity with the present Code.
(3) Violation of the norms of the present Code by the court, by the prosecutor, by the body of inquiry or by the inquirer in the course of the criminal court proceedings shall have the effect that the proof of evidence so obtained shall be inadmissible.
(4) The rulings of the court, the resolutions of the judge, of the prosecutor, the investigator and the inquirer shall be lawful, substantiated and reasoned.

Art. 297 UPKR (Legality, Substantiation and Justice of the Sentence)

(1) The court sentence shall be legal, substantiated and just.
(2) The sentence shall be recognized as legal, substantiated and just, if it is passed in conformity with the demands of the present Code and relies on the correct application of the criminal law.

Scope of the Principle of Legality

210. It should be mentioned that due to the fact that substantive criminal law, criminal procedure as well as the correctional law are regulated at the federal level (Article 71 (o) Constitution), the relevant legal norms are determined exclusively by federal statutes and codes (the UKR, the UPKR and the UIKR).

211. The principle of legality, enshrined in the Constitution, is furthermore binding upon all state authorities: legislative, executive, and judicial ones.[330] The maxim: “the bodies of the State, the bodies of local self-government, officials, private citizens and their associations shall be obliged to observe the Constitution of the Russian Federation and laws“ extends to all branches of the law and is regulated by appropriate legal provisions (Article 15, paragraph 2 Const.). The principle of

329. All translations (with revision of the author) of provisions of the UPKR in this chapter are taken from: http://www.legislationline.org/documents/section/criminal-codes, last visited: May 26, 2016.
330. Paramonova, Principle of legality in Russia, 2011, p. 107.

legality is, for instance, also provided for by the **Administrative Code of the Russian Federation** (*Kodeks ob administrativnih pravonarusheniyah Rossijskoj Federacii*, hereinafter ACR).[331]

212. Each of the constitutional provisions mentioned above deals with the following elements of the principle of legality: *nullum crimen sine lege scripta* (Articles 1, 15, paragraph 3 Constitution, Articles 14, paragraph 1, 3 UKR, Article 297 UPKR), *nullum crimen sine lege certa* (Article 15, paragraph 3 Const., Article 3 UKR, Article 7 paragraph 3 UPKR), *nullum crimen sine lege stricta* (Article 15, paragraph 3 Const., Articles 1, 3 UKR, Article 297 UPKR), *nullum crimen sine lege praevia* (Article 54 Constitution, Article 10 UKR).

213. The principle *nullum crimen sine lege scripta* states that criminal responsibility can be assigned only for the commission of a socially dangerous act that is explicitly forbidden by written criminal law enacted by the legislature.[332]

214. The formal requirement *nullum crimen sine lege scripta* is furthermore embodied in concrete legal rules. According to Article 15, paragraph 3 Constitution, legal provisions shall thus be officially published. This applies to federal and regional laws enacted by the legislature ***(законы)*** as well as to regulations enacted by the executive ***(нормативные правовые акты)*** if they "concern human and civil rights, freedoms and obligations." The laws must always be published in official publications[333] so that citizens can become aware of their rights and obligations. Unpublished laws and regulations that should have been published are inapplicable and invalid.

215. In compliance with the norms provided for by the UKR (Articles 1, paragraph 1, 3, paragraph 1, 14, paragraph 1), all criminal offenses, the elements of criminal liability, the type of punishment, the sentencing range, and other legal criminal consequences shall be determined only by the UKR, not by any other federal or regional laws or normative legal provisions (e.g., administrative provisions).

216. However, some provisions of criminal law may require additional information in order to determine whether or how they apply to a particular conduct. For example, technical terms are defined in other federal laws like in the Federal Weapons Law.[334]

217. As a result, criminal responsibility occurs only on the basis of regulations codified in the UKR that are published in an appropriate way. Case law, customary

331. Code of Administrative Offenses of the Russian Federation, Dec. 30, 2001, N 195—FZ (Kodeks RF ob administrativnih pravonarusheniyah).
332. Kropachev, Ugolovnoe pravo Rossii, p. 71.
333. Official publications: "Sobranie zakonodatelstva RF," "Rossijskaja Gazeta," "Parlamentskaja Gazeta": Matuzov, Teorija gosudarstva i prava, pp. 371, 418.
334. Federal Law on weapons, Dec. 13, 1996, N 150-FZ.

law as well as doctrinal interpretation serve as orientation points, but without any exceptions, are not considered to be official sources of criminal law.[335]

218. The less serious offenses—**administrative offenses** *(административные правонарушения)*—are not subject to the regulation of the criminal law, but to administrative law. However, the principle of legality applies in the field of administrative law as well. Article 1.6 ACR requires that the grounds for administrative responsibility, as well as the procedural rules, be based on the legal provisions of the ACR. Article 2.1 ACR states that administrative offenses can be provided for only in federal and regional administrative offenses codes.[336] Unlike criminal law, however, administrative law lies within the joint jurisdiction of the Russian Federation and the Regions (Article 72 (k) Constitution). Administrative offenses are less dangerous in comparison to criminal offenses, and the range of punishment, which is determined by federal and regional codes on administrative offenses, is smaller than for criminal offenses provided for only by the UKR (federal law).

219. As to the law of criminal procedure and with respect to sentencing and the execution of sentences, decisions of the state authorities, including rulings of the court, as well as the decisions of the judge, prosecutor, and investigator must be "lawful, substantiated and motivated" (Article 7, paragraph 4 UPKR, Article 8 UIKR). Thus, the violation of the principle of legality "by the court, the prosecutor, the inquiring body or the inquirer in the course of criminal court proceedings" has the effect that the evidence so obtained is inadmissible (Article 7, paragraph 3 UPKR).[337]

220. The requirement of reasonable clarity in criminal law is part of the principle of legality and refers to two components: clarity with regard to the prohibited conduct and foreseeability of the expected punishment.

221. The requirement of reasonable clarity refers to all criminal law provisions contained in the UKR (e.g., rules of defenses and excuses, regulations of criminal liability, etc. [General Part] or elements of concrete crimes [Special Part]). Hence, the consequences of the forbidden behavior and the established sentencing range must be provided for by criminal provisions with maximum clarity. This is required in order to ensure the citizens' awareness of their legal obligations and liabilities with regard to all serious infringements.[338]

---

335. Kropachev, Ugolovnoe pravo Rossii, p. 69; Lebedev, Kommentarii k UK RF, p. 29; Kuznezova, Uchenie o prestuplenii, p. 67; for the sources of criminal law, *see* General Introduction, §5, II, B, paras. 155–167.
336. Code of Administrative Offenses of the Russian Federation, Dec. 30, 2001, N 195-FZ (Kodeks RF ob administrativnih pravonarusheniyah).
337. Paramonova, Principle of legality in Russia, 2011, p. 108.
338. Kropachev, Ugolovnoe pravo Rossii, p. 71; Paramonova, Principle of legality in Russia, 2011, pp. 105–111.

222. The requirement of clarity concerning criminally prohibited conduct is based on the idea that clear and precise determination of all characteristics of a criminal act are necessary in order to avoid judicial arbitrariness.[339]

223. Criminal law norms contain thus an explicit designation of the conduct which is prohibited. In this regard, Article 8 UKR states that "the ground for criminal responsibility is the commission of an act containing all indicia of the 'elements of crime'" provided for by the UKR (in the General and the Special Part of the UKR).[340]

224. In compliance with Article 14, paragraph 1 UKR, "a socially dangerous act committed with guilt and prohibited by the UKR under threat of punishment shall be deemed to be a criminal offense." Additional crimes (e.g., behaviors that might go against good morals and customs) or elements of the crime may not be created by the courts; they only must interpret the written rules of the legislature.[341]

225. The rule of clarity with regard to the prescribed criminal penalties and sentencing ranges means that the list of penalties should be exhaustive and that the sentencing range concerning a specific crime must have a maximum limit.[342] According to, Article 43, paragraph 1 UKR, criminal punishment is regarded as "a measure of state compulsion assigned by a court's judgment," which "consists of the depreciation or restriction of the rights and freedoms of the person, as provided for by the Criminal Code." The list of the possible types of criminal penalties (twelve) is provided for by Article 44 UKR. Each type of penalty contains a maximum sentencing range (Articles 45–59 UKR). The maximum limit is also specified with respect to cumulative crimes and sentences (Articles 69, 70 UKR).

226. At last, with regard to offenses committed during the war, it should be mentioned that the Geneva Conventions and their Additional Protocols, to which Russia is a signatory, constitute international treaties that prevail over domestic criminal law.[343] According to the internationalists, the legal provisions of the Geneva Convention and their Protocols shall be applied directly to the territory of Russia based on the principle of legality. The legal basis for the supremacy of ratified international treaties rules is Article 15, paragraph 4 Constitution, which states that:

> if an international treaty or agreement of the Russian Federation fixes rules other than those provided for by law, the rules of the international agreement shall be applied.[344]

---

339. Kropachev, Ugolovnoe pravo Rossii, p. 71.
340. For elements of crime, *see* Part I, Chapter 3, §1 paras. 331–341.
341. For the sources of criminal law, *see* General Introduction, §5, II, paras. 116–181.
342. Kropachev, Ugolovnoe pravo Rossii, p. 72.
343. For international sources of criminal law and for the discussion on the supremacy of the Constitution, *see* General Introduction, §5, paras. 116–144; Geneva Conventions of Aug. 12, 1948. Ratification of Russia: May 10, 1954.
344. *See* Art. 15 Federal Law on International Treaties of the Russian Federation Jul. 15, 1995, N 101-FZ.

II. Legality and Interpretation

227. Setting limits to criminal law is necessary in order to avoid arbitrariness of state power with regard to serious violations of human rights.[345]

228. The complete prohibition of analogy in contemporary Russian criminal law is invoked to fulfill this goal. It is closely connected with the requirement of reasonable clarity of criminal provisions and also serves to make citizens aware of their legal obligations.[346]

229. During the Soviet period, when judges applied analogy and were allowed to fill gaps in the criminal law by creating new insignificant offenses according to their "socialistic legal consciousness," this often led to arbitrariness. In this way, Article 10 of the Criminal Code of 1922 provided that "if socially dangerous action (or omission) was not provided for by the present Code, the ground and the limits of criminal responsibility shall be determined in accordance with the most similar criminal offenses enshrined in the Code."[347] This remained the law until 1958 when Article 7 Criminal Statute declared "illegality" (prohibition by means of criminal law regulations) as an inherent feature of a criminal offense which led to relatively clear limits on criminally punishable conduct.

230. Analogy as a method of filling gaps is not accepted by the present criminal law, unlike private law. Article 3, paragraph 2 UKR directly prohibits the application of the criminal law by analogy in all cases, regardless of whether it favors the criminal defendant or not. It refers to all criminal law norms, namely regulations regarding defenses, excuses, criminal liability, etc. (norms of the General Part) and regulations concerning individual elements of concrete crimes, for example, terrorism (Special Part regulations).

231. Article 14 UKR requires furthermore "illegality" as a foundation for a criminal offense.[348] Therefore, a behavior that is not precisely prohibited by criminal provisions cannot be subject to criminal responsibility. When a gap in the criminal law is discovered, judges can only refer to the representatives of the legislature, so they can initiate the adoption of a new rule (Article 104, paragraph 1 Const.). Only the legislature has the legal power to fill gaps in the criminal law by passing new legal provisions. Courts are merely allowed to interpret the written criminal law rules.[349]

345. Kropachev, Ugolovnoe pravo Rossii, pp. 75–76.
346. Paramonova, Principle of legality in Russia, 2011, p. 111.
347. Art. 10 Ugolovnij Kodeks RSFSR Jun. 1, 1922.
348. For elements of crime, *see* Part I, Chapter 3, §1 paras. 331–341.
349. For the sources of criminal law, *see* General Introduction, §5, II, paras. 116–181.

232. Depending on the tasks of interpretation, different methods of legal interpretation need to be distinguished: grammatical (or linguistic), functional, historical, systematical as well as logical and teleological. In practice, different methods of legal interpretation are applied cumulatively without specifying a concrete method.

233. Legal interpretation by individuals may furthermore be classified into three categories: ordinary (by laymen), professional (by professional lawyers), and doctrinal.

234. Another differentiation of legal interpretation is based on the juridical force of the results of interpretation. Here, a distinction is made between an official interpretation (given by state authorities in practice normally binding) and a nonofficial interpretation (given by organizations without state power, has a recommendatory nature).[350]

235. None of these methods or rules of interpretation are binding upon a judge, except the "official interpretation" to some extent. Official interpretations can namely be overridden by judges on the basis of Article 120 Constitution, which states that "judges are independent and are bound only by the Constitution and the federal laws."

236. As mentioned above (General Introduction, §5 Sources of Criminal Law), case law, customary law as well as doctrinal interpretation are not considered to be official sources of law,[351] but a means to interpret criminal law norms. Even the reviews of the judicial practice of the Supreme Court of the Russian Federation[352] are not regarded as official sources of the (criminal) law. Decisions of the upper courts (including the Supreme Court of the Russian Federation) are also not binding upon the inferior courts in considering any other (also similar) cases. However, the reviews and the decisions of the upper courts are of great significance in judicial practice and are usually followed by inferior courts. One can say that this way, the reviews and the decisions of the upper courts impose limits on the interpretation of laws: the decisions of the upper courts provide guidelines to the inferior courts for unified judicial practice, especially in the interpretation of estimative categories (e.g., social danger). They may never be used as a ground for establishing criminal responsibility.[353]

350. Matuzov, Teorija gosudarstva i prava, pp. 418–420.
351. For the sources of criminal law, *see* General Introduction, §5, II, paras. 116–181.
352. Supreme Court of the Russian Federation: http://www.supcourt.ru, last visited: May 26, 2016.
353. For the sources of criminal law, *see* General Introduction, §5, II, paras. 116–181; Paramonova, Principle of legality in Russia, 2011, pp. 111–112.

§3. THE PRINCIPLE OF INDIVIDUAL RESPONSIBILITY

237. The central principle of criminal liability is the principle of **individual or personal criminal responsibility or guilt** *(принцип индивидуальной уголовной ответственности).*[354]

238. It is fully applicable to persons in leadership positions in companies, associations, and other collective legal entities as well as to their subordinates. The Criminal Code does not make any exceptions to this principle. Hence, according to the principle of individual responsibility and the principle of legality (criminal conduct must be defined in the Criminal Code, including individuals in leadership positions),[355] individuals holding leadership positions, such as chief executive officers, directors, and others, cannot incur criminal liability for offenses committed by their subordinates.[356]

239. Due to the principle of **individual criminal responsibility, vicarious liability** *(субститутивная ответственность)*—that is, the transfer of responsibility for action from one person to another due to the special relationship between them, for example, a parent may be held vicariously liable for the tort of a child in civil law[357]—is prohibited in criminal law in general and, more specifically, in the context of collective legal entities.

240. The criminal liability of persons in leadership positions, as well as the criminal liability of "normal" employees of companies, associations, and other collective legal entities, is based on accomplice liability.[358] This means that criminal responsibility depends on the character and the degree of the actual participation of the offender in the commission of a crime[359] and his or her complicity with other criminal actors (Article 34, paragraph 1 UKR).[360]

241. The rationale can be found in the principle of individual criminal responsibility, which, in turn, is based on the principle of (personal) culpability (Article 5 UKR),[361] which excludes any form of collective criminal responsibility. Thus, individuals, including persons in leadership positions in organizations, are criminally accountable only for their own conduct and not for the conduct of others.

---

354. Hellmann et al., Opredelenie subjekta, p. 47.
355. For the principle of legality, *see* Part I, Chapter 1, paras. 197–226.
356. Paramonova, Criminal liability for crimes in legal entities in Russia. In: Sieber, U. / Jarvers, K. /Silverman, E. (ed(s).): Criminal liability for crimes in legal entities. Berlin, Duncker & Humblot, 2015, pp.340–341.
357. *See* Nikoforov, Juridicheskoe lizo kak subjekt prestupleniya; Naumov, Rossiiskoe ugolovnoe pravo, pp. 361–363; Adel'chanyan, Ugolovnoe pravo Rossii, pp. 80–81.
358. *See* Resolution of the Supreme Court RF on taxes, Dec. 31, 2006 (pa. 7); on the sentencing of attempted crimes, *see* Part I, Chapter 5, paras. 544–589.
359. For parties to crime, *see* Part I, Chapter 5, §2, paras. 590–634.
360. For parties to crime, *see* Part I, Chapter 5, §2, paras. 590–634.
361. For principle of culpability and other principles of criminal law, *see* Part I, Chapter 1, paras. 194–196, 388, 425.

242. Strict liability or **objective imputability** *(объективное вменение)*,[362] that is, criminal responsibility for the causing of harm despite the absence of personal culpability, is thus not permitted.

243. It should be reminded that during the Soviet era, many violations of individual rights took place as a result of the then-prevailing principle of collective (criminal) responsibility based on the concept of strict liability; criminal responsibility for an offense was transferred from one person to another due to the special relationship between them, for example, due to a familial relationship or due to belonging to the same union/entity.[363] The current legal situation—which is based on the opposite principle, the principle of individual criminal responsibility—is, in part, a reaction to this negative historical experience.[364]

§4. The Principle of Proportionality

244. The principle of proportionality is not explicitly stated in the criminal law provisions. In the criminal law theory, this principle is regarded as an element of the **principle of justice (принцип справедливости)** that holds that punishment and other measures of a criminal-law character that can be imposed on a person who has committed a crime must be just, that is, must correspond to the character and degree of the social danger of the crime, the circumstances of its commission, and the personality of the accused.[365]

245. Objectively, the principle of proportionality holds that punishment and other measures of a criminal-law character provided for by legal provisions shall be proportionate to the character and the degree of the social danger of the particular type of criminalized behavior. This way, it is part of the principle of equality of individuals before the law.

246. Subjectively, the principle of proportionality is seen in the difference or similarity of criminal penalties with regard to individual situations in concrete criminal cases. In other words, it can be regarded as a **principle of differentiation or individualization of responsibility** *(принцип дифференциации и индивидуализации ответственности)*.

247. On the one hand, for committing the same or a similar crime under the same/similar circumstances, criminal penalties shall be comparable. On the other hand, the principle of individualization of responsibility requires to make a difference between criminal law consequences, including criminal penalties, for various

362. On the principles of criminal law, *see* Part I, Chapter 1, paras. 194–196.
363. For the principles of criminal law, *see* Part I, Chapter 1, paras. 194–196.
364. Paramonova, Criminal liability for crimes in legal entities in Russia. In: Sieber, U. / Jarvers, K. /Silverman, E. (ed(s).): Criminal liability for crimes in legal entities. Berlin, Duncker & Humblot, 2015, pp.341–348.
365. Paramonova, National characteristics, fundamental principles, and history of criminal law in Russia, 2014, p. 225.

individuals, e.g., for healthy persons and for insane persons, for adults and for minors, and in some cases for men and for women.[366]

366. *See* Part I, Chapter 7, §6, paras. 762–774; Paramonova, National characteristics, fundamental principles, and history of criminal law in Russia, 2014, p. 225.

Chapter 2. Scope of Application of Criminal Statutes

§1. Principles Concerning the Applicability of Criminal Statutes with Respect to Time

I. Principle of Nonretroactivity/Prohibition of Retroactive Criminal Law

248. According to Article 54, paragraph 2 Const., "no one may bear responsibility for an action (or omission) which was not considered a crime when it was committed," regardless of the legal provisions which were in force before and after committing an offense. The courts, as well as the legislature, are obliged to follow this nonretroactivity principle.

249. The general rule for determining the time of committing an offense is legally defined in Article 9 UKR, which states:

(1) Criminal liability and punishability of an action (or omission) shall be determined by the criminal law that was in force during the commission of the action (or omission).
(2) The time a socially dangerous action (or omission) is committed shall be deemed to be the time of committing a crime, regardless of the time of occurring of the harmful consequences.

250. The following example illustrates the mechanism of Article 9, paragraph 2. UKR: a teenager aged 13 years 11 months and 25 days has caused grave harm to health (Article 111 UKR), and the victim died ten days later. In accordance with Article 20, paragraph 2. UKR, minors who have attained the age of 14, bear criminal responsibility for certain criminal offenses, including grave harm to health. In this case, if the time of the commission of the offense was determined by the "occurring of the harmful consequences," the teenager would be criminally liable. However, on the basis of Article 9 UKR, he cannot be subject to criminal responsibility because, at the "time of committing" the crime, he was a criminally "non-liable" person.[367]

251. Until the adoption of the UKR, the rule for determining the time of offense was subject to controversy. Now, Article 9 UKR provides that the time of committing a crime is the time of the actual committing (or omitting), regardless of the occurring of certain results.

252. Therefore, the new rule of Article 9 UKR is universal with regard to the classification of criminal offenses: it encompasses regulations for both material (substantial) and formal crimes.

---

367. Paramonova, Principle of legality in Russia, 2011, p. 113.

253. Material crimes (result crimes) require that a certain result is provided for by the particular legal provision and criminal conduct leads to that harmful result in order to entail criminal responsibility. Formal crimes (conduct crimes)—in contrast—do not connect criminal responsibility with any concrete harmful results.[368] This understanding of Article 9 UKR has the broader consequence that it fulfills the requirement of reasonable clarity.

254. In judicial practice, as well as in doctrine, there is a general rule concerning offenses that by definition consist of a **series of acts** *(продолжаемые преступления)*, for instance, Article 117 UKR (torture), or cases of **continuing offenses** *(длящиеся преступления)*, for example, nonpayment of maintenance (Article 157 UKR). In these cases, the time of the commission of the last action (or omission) of the offense is deemed to be the time of the commission of the offense.[369]

II. Exceptions to the Principle Nonretroactivity: Retroactivity of the Milder Statute

255. Under certain circumstances, retroactive application of criminal law is allowed. However, this possibility of **retroactive application** *(обратная сила уголовного закона)* is an exception to the general rule that only the criminal law that was in force at the time of the commission of an offense is applicable (Article 9 UKR).

256. Retroactive applicability of criminal law provisions that eliminate or mitigate criminal responsibility is possible. This principle, as well as the prohibition on the application of criminal law which worsens the position of a person who has committed a crime, has been raised to the rank of a constitutional principle. According to Article 54 Constitution, "if, after violating a law, responsibility for that violation is eliminated or mitigated, the new law shall be applied" and "a law introducing or aggravating responsibility shall not have retrospective effect."

257. It should be noted that the aforementioned provision of the Constitution also applies to administrative responsibility; administrative law is a separate branch of law in the Russian legal system, with separate grounds of administrative responsibility.

258. The regulations of the UKR, based on constitutional norms, determine retroactive application of the criminal law in greater detail (Article 10 UKR).

259. Thus, criminal law, which "eliminates the criminality," that is, which decriminalizes a certain action (or omission), can be applied retroactively. Criminal

368. On the objective aspects of the offense, *see* Part I, Chapter 3, §2, paras. 342–371.
369. Lebedev, Kommentarii k UK RF, p. 40; Kruglikov, Kommentarii k Ugolovnomu Kodeksu RF, p. 10; Billuten´Verhovnogo Suda RF, 1997, N 8, p. 12.

law which "mitigates punishment" has the same effect: subsequent legal provisions which set lower limits of punishment or which provide for an alternative sanction and thus allow a milder punishment may similarly be applied retroactively. The main criterion of application is the enhancement of the position of a person who has committed the crime as compared to his position under the previous law.

260. The principle of retroactive application of a norm when "improving the position of the accused" applies to all criminal law norms, that is, to both substantive criminal law regulations (provisions in the General and Special Parts of the UKR, e.g., criminal liability, defenses, excuses, or provisions on concrete criminal offenses) as well as procedural rules.

261. Three criteria need to be taken into account in order to determine if a legal provision can be interpreted as "improving the position of a person who has committed a crime." First, all circumstances that are favorable to the offender should be taken into consideration. For instance, some regulations of the General Part, such as the calculation of the terms of punishment or grounds for excluding criminal liability, can be changed retrospectively. This way, a new ground for excluding criminal liability shall be applied as well to the offenders who have committed crimes earlier. All these new circumstances should be applied, even if they improve the position of the criminal defendant in an insignificant way. Second, the rule of retrospective application of the criminal law extends to all persons who have committed a crime regardless of the time of commission. Hence, persons who are serving a sentence and those who have served a sentence and have a criminal record (Article 86 UKR) are included as well. The legal consequence is a new trial under consideration of the new legal provisions. Third, all state authorities, including courts, must apply the new rules from the day of their official publication. Furthermore, a criminal investigation should be dismissed at any stage if the offense being subject to criminal investigation is decriminalized.[370]

262. On the other hand, criminal law that criminalizes an action (or omission) increases punishment or in any other way worsens the position of a person shall have no retroactive force. There are no exceptions to this prohibition of retroactive laws for specific crimes; it includes, for example, new laws that criminalize offenses against humanity.[371]

---

370. For the principle of legality, *see* Part I, Chapter 1, paras. 197–226.

371. On justification, excuse, and other grounds of impunity, *see* Part I, Chapter 4, paras. 429–528; Paramonova, Principle of legality in Russia, 2011, pp. 114–116.

§2. Principles Concerning the Applicability of Criminal Statutes with Respect to Space

I. Major Principles and Location within Legal System

263. The following principles governing the exercise of criminal jurisdiction are recognized under Russian law: the principle of territoriality, the nationality principle, the protective principle, and the universality principle. Several authors specify the patronizing principle as an additional principle.[372]

264. Both in judicial practice and in the doctrine, the application of the domestic criminal law is primarily based on the principle of territorial sovereignty, but rules of extraterritorial jurisdiction are also included in the Codes mentioned above. In the doctrine, respective rules have been turned into principles of extraterritorial criminal jurisdiction.[373]

265. The rules of applicability of domestic criminal law with a foreign nexus are contained in Article 67 of the Constitution (general provisions regarding the jurisdiction of the Russian Federation), in Articles 9–13 of the Criminal Code (UKR), in Articles 2–3 of the Code of Criminal Procedure (UPKR), and in Article 6 of the Correctional Code of the Russian Federation (UIKR).

266. Although regulations concerning the applicability of domestic criminal law are provided for by the provisions of various branches of criminal law, the jurisdictional principles are regarded as being part of the substantive law, and the main aspects are treated in the substantive criminal law, not in the criminal procedure law.[374]

II. The Territorial Principle

267. The **principle of territoriality** *(территориальный принцип)* is regarded as a major principle of criminal jurisdiction.[375] It is based on the idea of the sovereignty of a state that has legal authority over the people within its borders.[376]

---

372. Kruglikov, Kommentarii k Ugolovnomu Kodeksu RF, pp. 28–31; Naumov, Rossiiskoe ugolovnoe pravo, p. 231; Paramonova, Extraterritorial jurisdiction in Russia. In: Sieber, U. / Forster, S. / Jarvers, K. (ed(s).): National Criminal Law in a Comparative Legal Context. Volume 2.1: General limitations on the application of criminal law. Berlin, Duncker & Humblot, 2011, p. 299.

373. Paramonova, Extraterritorial jurisdiction in Russia. In: Sieber, U. / Forster, S. / Jarvers, K. (ed(s).): National Criminal Law in a Comparative Legal Context. Volume 2.1: General limitations on the application of criminal law. Berlin, Duncker & Humblot, 2011, p. 298.

374. Kruglikov, Kommentarii k Ugolovnomu Kodeksu RF, pp. 28–31; Lebedev, Kommentarii k UK RF, p. 19 ff.; Naumov, Rossiiskoe ugolovnoe pravo, pp. 223–231.

375. For the territorial principle in cyberspace, *see* Paramonova, Internationales Strafrecht im Cyberspace: Strafrechtliche Analyse der Rechtslage in Deutschland, Russland und den USA (Criminal Jurisdiction in Cyberspace: Legal Situation in Germany, Russia and the USA). Wiesbaden / Berlin, Springer-Verlag, 2013, pp. 128–158.

376. Naumov, Rossiiskoe ugolovnoe pravo, pp. 231–235; Ignatov/Krasikov, Course of the Russian Criminal Law, p. 49.

268. Article 11 UKR serves as a legal basis for the principle of territoriality. It lays down the locus of the commission of the offense as the link for the application of the law. Any person who has committed a crime on the territory of the Russian Federation, irrespective of his/her nationality, falls under its territorial jurisdiction. Russian criminal law, in both its substantive and procedural aspects, is applied.[377]

Art. 11 UKR (Operation of Criminal Law in Respect of Persons Who Have Committed Crimes on the Territory of the Russian Federation)

(1) Any person who has committed a crime on the territory of the Russian Federation shall be subject to criminal responsibility according to the present Code.
(2) Crimes committed within the limits of the territorial waters or airspace of the Russian Federation shall be deemed to be committed on the territory of the Russian Federation. The operation of this Code shall also be extended to offenses committed on the continental shelf and in the exclusive economic zone of the Russian Federation.
(3) A person who has committed a crime on a vessel registered in a port of the Russian Federation and which is situated on the open water or in airspace outside the confines of the Russian Federation shall be brought to criminal responsibility under this Code, unless provided otherwise by an international agreement of the Russian Federation. A person who has committed a crime on board of a warship or in a military aircraft of the Russian Federation, regardless of the place of their location, shall also bear criminal responsibility under this Code.
(4) The question concerning criminal responsibility of diplomatic representatives of foreign States and other individuals who enjoy immunity, if these persons have committed crimes on the territory of the Russian Federation, shall be settled in conformity with the standards of international law.

Art. 2 UPKR (Operation of the Criminal Procedural Law in Space)

(1) Proceedings in a criminal case in the territory of the Russian Federation, regardless of the place of committing a crime, shall be conducted in conformity with this Code, unless provided otherwise by an international treaty of the Russian Federation.
(2) The norms of the present Code shall also be applied in the procedure of a criminal case for a crime committed on a vessel carrying the flag of the Russian Federation in the air, at sea or on a river, and which is situated outside the territory of the Russian Federation, if the respective vessel is registered in a port of the Russian Federation.

---

377. Paramonova, Extraterritorial jurisdiction in Russia. In: Sieber, U. / Forster, S. / Jarvers, K. (ed(s).): National Criminal Law in a Comparative Legal Context. Volume 2.1: General limitations on the application of criminal law. Berlin, Duncker & Humblot, 2011, pp. 303–304.

269. As mentioned above, Article 11 UKR states that "any person who has committed a crime on the territory of the Russian Federation" is criminally liable under Russian law.

270. According to the prevailing opinion in the doctrine[378] and the position of the Highest Court of the Russian Federation,[379] this regulation, read in conjunction with other legal provisions, is interpreted as being in favor of the **location of the act** *(место совершения преступления)*, not the location of the harmful consequences. This differs from other countries (e.g., Germany or Italy), which follow the "ubiquity theory," which includes both location of the act and the consequences.[380] In Russian criminal law, territorial jurisdiction extends first to cases where a criminal act has been started and completed on Russian territory, including instances of the occurrence of harmful results on the territory; and second to cases where a criminal act was committed on the Russian territory, but the criminal effect occurred outside its borders. Hence, in order to confirm criminal jurisdiction on the basis of the principle of territoriality, it is enough that a criminal act has been started within the territory of the Russian Federation; the **location of the effect** *(место наступления преступного результата)* is irrelevant in regard to territorial jurisdiction.[381] In other words, in regard to formal ("non-result crimes") as well as to material offenses ("harmful result crimes"),[382] a criminal action (or omission) must be committed within Russian territory (at least at the attempt stage) in order to invoke the principle of territoriality, while the results of criminal activity do not necessarily have to occur within Russian territory.

271. As far as the occurrence of the criminal results of a crime committed abroad on Russian territory is concerned, they would fall, in principle, under the category of cases legitimated by the protective principle[383] and not by the territorial principle.

272. Thus, according to the concept of the locus of the act, an attempt (Article 30 UKR)[384] conducted inland (i.e., within Russian territory) would, for instance, be a sufficient ground for the application of domestic criminal law on the basis of the principle of territoriality, while the occurrence of the criminal effects on Russian territory would not suffice.

378. Naumov, Rossiiskoe ugolovnoe pravo, p. 235; Kuznezova, Uchenie o prestuplenii, p. 102.
379. Verhovnij Sud RF (Highest Court of the Russian Federation), Appeal decision, Feb. 5, 2009, N 25-009-4: http://www.supcourt.ru, last visited: May 26, 2016.
380. For the territorial principle in cyberspace, *see* Paramonova, Internationales Strafrecht im Cyberspace: Strafrechtliche Analyse der Rechtslage in Deutschland, Russland und den USA (Criminal Jurisdiction in Cyberspace: Legal Situation in Germany, Russia and the USA). Wiesbaden / Berlin, Springer-Verlag, 2013, pp. 128–158.
381. Paramonova, Extraterritorial jurisdiction in Russia. In: Sieber, U. / Forster, S. / Jarvers, K. (ed(s).): National Criminal Law in a Comparative Legal Context. Volume 2.1: General limitations on the application of criminal law. Berlin, Duncker & Humblot, 2011, pp. 304–305.
382. On formal (conduct) and result offenses, *see* Part I, Chapter 3, §2, paras. 252, 253, 363–368.
383. For the extraterritorial jurisdiction, *see* paras. 282–303.
384. On attempt, *see* Part I, Chapter 5, paras. 544–589.

273. In general, the concept of the locus of the act is applicable to all kinds of offenses. However, in regard to some offenses, the definition of the location itself can be problematic. For instance, in the area of cybercrime, the question arises what actually is considered "the location of an act." Concerning transit offenses that are very common in cyberspace, in which any of those factors could be regarded as the location of the act: the location of the computer, the offender or the server.[385]

274. The concept of the locus of the act is also followed with regard to cases where several persons contribute to the commission of the crime in different countries. It is a sufficient basis for Russia's territorial jurisdiction over all the parties if one of the parties to the crime, that is, the organizer, instigator, accessory, or perpetrator (Article 33 UKR types of parties to crime)[386] is found in the territory of the Russian Federation. However, it is necessary to establish the connection between the parties to a crime; in particular, causality[387] must be established between the actions of the parties (objective element) and their joint intent (subjective element).[388]

275. The norms which define the territory of the Russian Federation are laid down in several documents, namely the Constitution (Article 67), the UKR (Article 11), as well as in the Federal Law on the State Border of the Russian Federation,[389] the Federal Law on Exclusive Economic Zone of the Russian Federation,[390] and the Federal Law on the Continental Shelf of the Russian Federation.[391]

Art. 67 Constitution of the Russian Federation

(1) The territory of the Russian Federation shall include the territories of its constituencies (subjects of the federation), inland waters and territorial sea, and the airspace over them.
(2) The Russian Federation shall possess sovereign rights and exercise jurisdiction on the continental shelf and in the exclusive economic zone of the Russian Federation according to the rules fixed by the Federal Law and the norms of international law.
(3) The borders between the subjects of the Russian Federation may be changed upon their mutual consent.

---

385. Paramonova, *Challenges for Criminal Law and International Criminal Law in Cyberspace*. In: Justice Report. Canadian Criminal Justice Association, 2014, Issue/Volume 29, N 4, pp. 26–29; Paramonova, Ugolovnaja Jurisdikzija v Internet-prostranstve, pp. 77–79.
386. For parties to crime, *see* Part I, Chapter 5, §2, paras. 590–634.
387. On the objective aspects of the offense, *see* Part I, Chapter 3, §2, paras. 342–371.
388. Paramonova, Extraterritorial jurisdiction in Russia. In: Sieber, U. / Forster, S. / Jarvers, K. (ed(s).): National Criminal Law in a Comparative Legal Context. Volume 2.1: General limitations on the application of criminal law. Berlin, Duncker & Humblot, 2011, p. 305.
389. Federal Law on the State Border of the Russian Federation, Apr. 4, 1993, N 4730-1.
390. Federal Law on the Exclusive Economic Zone of the Russian Federation, Dec. 17, 1998, N 191-FZ.
391. Federal Law on the Continental Shelf of the Russian Federation, Nov. 30, 1995, N 187-FZ.

276. The territorial jurisdiction of Russia extends to its land, inland waters (rivers, lakes, canals, floodplains, reservoirs, wetlands, etc.), territorial sea, subsoil below the territory, the airspace above the territory, as well as the continental shelf and the exclusive economic zone of the Russian Federation (Article 11 UKR, Article 1 Federal Law on the State Border of the Russian Federation).[392]

277. The Russian territorial sea extends up to 12 nautical miles (22 km) from its baseline (maximum range of low tide on the continent or islands); the exact geographical coordinates are determined by the Government of the Russian Federation.[393]

278. The continental shelf—a part of the seabed beyond the territorial waters—and the exclusive economic zone extend to a distance of 200 nautical miles into the sea from the shore baseline, including the baselines of the islands.

279. Territorial claim based on the continental shelf or exclusive economic zone is interpreted in accordance with the United Nations Convention on the Law of the Sea of 1982.[394] The territorial jurisdiction on the continental shelf and the exclusive economic zone of the Russian Federation can be exercised only within the purpose of the respective "territorial" claim area: continental shelf or exclusive economic zone. Hence, the extension of criminal jurisdiction on the basis of territory over the continental shelf is legitimated for crimes connected with the exploration and use of the underground sources of the continental shelf, illegal facilities in this area, as well as environmental criminal cases. The territorial jurisdiction over the exclusive economic zone is extended, for instance, to crimes concerning research, exploration, and exploitation of the natural sources in this zone (e.g., poaching). Therefore, Article 11, paragraph 2 UKR, which proclaims territorial jurisdiction over the continental shelf and the exclusive economic zone, has to be interpreted in line with the provisions of international law and other relevant domestic laws.

280. According to the Treaty on Principles Governing the Activities of States in the Exploration and Use of Outer Space, Including the Moon and Other Celestial Bodies of 1967,[395] the territorial jurisdiction of the Russian Federation extends to its space facilities in outer space.[396]

281. In compliance with Russian law (paragraph 3 art 11 UKR), the criminal jurisdiction based on the territorial principle is also extended to offenses committed

392. For the geography of Russia in general, *see* General Introduction, §1, I, paras. 1–3; Paramonova, Extraterritorial jurisdiction in Russia. In: Sieber, U. / Forster, S. / Jarvers, K. (ed(s).): National Criminal Law in a Comparative Legal Context. Volume 2.1: General limitations on the application of criminal law. Berlin, Duncker & Humblot, 2011, p. 306.

393. Naumov, Rossiiskoe ugolovnoe pravo, p. 232.

394. United Nations Convention on the Law of the Sea of 1982.

395. Treaty on Principles Governing the Activities of States in the Exploration and Use of Outer Space, Including the Moon and Other Celestial Bodies of 1967.

396. Kruglikov, Kommentarii k Ugolovnomu Kodeksu RF, p. 30; Naumov, Rossiiskoe ugolovnoe pravo, p. 235.

on all vessels, aircraft, and ships registered in Russia, including warships and military aircraft (flag principle). In the doctrine, the **flag principle** (*принцип флага*) is considered to be a part of the principle of territoriality.[397]

III. Extraterritorial Criminal Jurisdiction

A. Principles

1. Protective Principle

282.

> Art. 12 UKR (The Operation of Criminal Law in Respect of Persons Who Have Committed Offenses Outside the Boundaries of the Russian Federation)
>
> (3) Foreign citizens and stateless persons who do not reside permanently in the Russian Federation and who have committed a crime outside the boundaries of the Russian Federation shall be subject to criminal responsibility under this Code in cases, if the crime is directed against the interests of the Russian Federation, or the interests of a Russian citizen or of a stateless person who permanently resides in the Russian Federation, and in cases provided for by an international agreement of the Russian Federation, and if they have not been convicted in a foreign State and are brought to criminal responsibility on the territory of the Russian Federation.

283. The Russian Criminal Code recognizes the exercise of criminal jurisdiction based on the **protective principle** *(реальный принцип)*. The aim of this principle is, by means of national regulations, to protect domestic interests that can be injured by foreign nationals outside the territory of the Russian Federation.[398] It has a rather broad range of applications and is directed toward the protection of domestic legal interests that include not only state interests but also individual legal interests (Article 12, paragraph 3 UKR). Basically, all legal interests of the state or an individual that are protected by domestic law are included in the protection scope of the principle unless an explicit legal requirement of the UKR is not fulfilled.

284. For instance, under the general requirements of the principle, treason falls within the category of protected interests. However, treason can be committed only by a Russian citizen (Article 275 UKR). In this case, even if the criminalization of

397. Lebedev, Kommentarii k UK RF, p. 22; Kruglikov, Kommentarii k Ugolovnomu Kodeksu RF, p. 31'; Paramonova, Extraterritorial jurisdiction in Russia. In: Sieber, U. / Forster, S. / Jarvers, K. (ed(s).): National Criminal Law in a Comparative Legal Context. Volume 2.1: General limitations on the application of criminal law. Berlin, Duncker & Humblot, 2011, pp. 306–307.

398. Paramonova, Extraterritorial jurisdiction in Russia. In: Sieber, U. / Forster, S. / Jarvers, K. (ed(s).): National Criminal Law in a Comparative Legal Context. Volume 2.1: General limitations on the application of criminal law. Berlin, Duncker & Humblot, 2011, p. 308.

treason is meant to protect state interests, criminal jurisdiction cannot be legitimated on the basis of the protective principle, but only on the basis of the active personality principle. In contrast, espionage (Article 276 UKR) can be committed only by foreign nationals or stateless persons. Therefore, it falls under the regulation of the protective principle.

285. It is of interest to note that before the changes of the UKR in 2006, the formulation of, Article 12, paragraph 3 UKR was ambiguous. Only "state interests" were protected under this norm. Nonetheless, in the judicial practice and the doctrine, the regulations of, Article 12, paragraph 3 UKR were interpreted in a broad manner so that individual interests were automatically included in the scope of protection of state interests.[399]

286. Offenses that are covered by the protective principle in regard to state interests are primarily crimes provided for by the Special Part of the UKR that concern the protection of state power, public security, public order, etc. To this extent, Article 10 UKR "Crimes against State Power" contains four chapters devoted to respective "protection areas": crimes against the foundations of the constitutional system, crimes against state power and state interests, crimes against justice, and crimes against the administrative order. However, the formulation of Article 12, paragraph 3 UKR "against the interests of the Russian Federation," is interpreted according to the prevailing doctrine in a broad manner and is not confined by the "crimes against state power" in terms of section 10 UKR.[400] Therefore, in the list of the offenses of the Special Part UKR, practically any further crime can be included because many criminalized acts are connected, in differing degrees, with state interests, for example, offenses against public health (Chapter 25 UKR) or crimes against military service (Chapter 33 UKR), etc. An exception would be crimes that rather fall under the category of offenses against individual interests.

287. In accordance with the rules of, Article 12, paragraph 3 UKR, the applicability of the passive personality principle is legitimated "if the interests of a Russian citizen or of a stateless person who permanently resides in the Russian Federation" are infringed by foreign nationals or stateless persons who do not have permanent residence in Russia. Normally, people who have resided in the territory of Russia for more than three years can become permanent residents. The individual interests are meant to include all the interests protected under Russian criminal law besides "state interests."[401]

288. Double criminality is not regarded as an impediment to the application of the passive personality principle according to Russian criminal law (Article 12, paragraph 3 UKR). However, foreign criminal judgments have to be taken into

399. Lebedev, Kommentarii k UK RF, p. 23; Kruglikov, Kommentarii k Ugolovnomu Kodeksu RF, p. 31; Paramonova, Criminal Jurisdiction in Cyberspace, p. 80.
400. Naumov, Rossiiskoe ugolovnoe pravo, p. 238.
401. Naumov, Rossiiskoe ugolovnoe pravo, p. 238; Kruglikov, Kommentarii k Ugolovnomu Kodeksu RF, p. 31.

account. In compliance with the *ne bis in idem* principle (Article 50, paragraph1 Constitution, Article 6, paragraph 2 UKR) and the rules of, Article 12, paragraph 3 UKR, Russian criminal law is not applicable if foreign citizens or stateless persons have already been convicted in a foreign state.[402]

2. Nationality Principle

289. The active **personality principle** *(принцип гражданства)* allows an extension of criminal jurisdiction over citizens and stateless persons who permanently reside in the Russian Federation if they commit a crime outside the boundaries of the Russian Federation. The legal basis for the active personality principle is Article 12, paragraph 1 UKR. Its provisions were substantially changed in 2006.

> Art. 12 UKR (The Operation of Criminal Law in Respect of Persons Who Have Committed Offenses Outside the Boundaries of the Russian Federation)
>
> (1) Citizens of the Russian Federation and stateless persons who permanently reside in the Russian Federation and who have committed a crime outside the boundaries of the Russian Federation, if the crime is directed against interests protected under this Code, shall be subject to criminal responsibility according to the present Code, if these persons were not convicted in a foreign State.

290. The requirement of double criminality was laid down until 2006 in the UKR with regard to some principles. For instance, in the original version of Article 12, paragraph 1 UKR, the applicability of the active personality (or nationality) principle was justified under the condition of an act being recognized as a crime in the state on whose territory it was committed. Moreover, the punishment could not exceed the upper limit of the sanction provided for by the laws of the foreign state on whose territory a crime was committed. In the revised version of the UKR, none of the principles justifying the applicability of national criminal law, including the active personality principle, now require double criminality.

291. Double criminality is not a requirement for the legitimate application of the principle, so an act does not necessarily need to be criminalized under the law of any other country to be prosecuted according to Russian criminal law. However, the restriction of double jeopardy has to be taken into consideration because Article 12, paragraph 1 UKR states that a person shall be subject to criminal responsibility according to the present Code if he/she was not convicted in a foreign state for the same crime (Article 50, paragraph1 Constitution, Article 6, paragraph 2, UKR).

---

402. Paramonova, Extraterritorial jurisdiction in Russia. In: Sieber, U. / Forster, S. / Jarvers, K. (ed(s).): National Criminal Law in a Comparative Legal Context. Volume 2.1: General limitations on the application of criminal law. Berlin, Duncker & Humblot, 2011, pp. 308–309.

292. The idea behind the active personality principle is that a state justifies the applicability of its power over its own citizens regardless of where criminal conduct took place.[403] In this way, the state ensures jurisdiction over its own nationals in cases where an act criminalized under Russian law took place on a foreign territory.

293. On the basis of the regulations of Article 12, paragraph 1 UKR, the active personality principle extends jurisdiction not only to Russian citizens but also to stateless persons who permanently reside (normally for not less than three years) in the Russian Federation. These two groups of individuals are treated equally from the perspective of the active personality principle. With regard to any foreign nationals, other principles are applied as for example, the protective principle.[404]

294. Moreover, according to, Article 13, paragraph 1 UKR, citizens of the Russian Federation who committed a crime on the territory of a foreign state cannot be extradited.

3. Universality Principle

295. According to one of the opinions represented in the literature, the **principle of universality** *(универсальный принцип)* has absolute priority to the other jurisdictional principles.[405] This is due to the fact that it is invoked to protect the well-being of the entire international community by prosecuting crimes that are regarded as dangerous if not by all, at least by most states that agreed to it in respective international treaties. The Russian Federation being part of the international community acts in compliance with its international obligations. In accordance with paragraph 4, Article 15 Constitution, "universally recognized principles and norms of international law" are considered to be "an integral part of the Russian legal system."[406]

296. The legal basis for the principle is Article 12, paragraph 3 UKR (alternative 3). In compliance with this norm, foreign nationals and stateless persons who do not permanently reside in the Russian Federation shall be subject to criminal responsibility in cases provided for by international agreements of the Russian Federation.

403. Korobeev, Polnij kurs ugolovnogo prava, pp. 766–771.

404. Paramonova, Extraterritorial jurisdiction in Russia. In: Sieber, U. / Forster, S. / Jarvers, K. (ed(s).): National Criminal Law in a Comparative Legal Context. Volume 2.1: General limitations on the application of criminal law. Berlin, Duncker & Humblot, 2011, pp. 310–311.

405. Korobeev, Polnij kurs ugolovnogo prava, p. 772; Kruglikov, Kommentarii k Ugolovnomu Kodeksu RF, pp. 30–31.

406. Paramonova, Extraterritorial jurisdiction in Russia. In: Sieber, U. / Forster, S. / Jarvers, K. (ed(s).): National Criminal Law in a Comparative Legal Context. Volume 2.1: General limitations on the application of criminal law. Berlin, Duncker & Humblot, 2011, pp. 311–313.

297. The universality principle, as laid down in, Article 12, paragraph 3 UKR, is applied in a limited manner. First, it extends only to foreign nationals and stateless persons who do not permanently reside in the Russian Federation. However, on the basis of the active personality principle, Russian nationals and stateless persons with a permanent residence in the Russian Federation are subject to the regulations of international treaties in the same way as foreign nationals if the crime is directed against interests protected under national criminal law (Article 12, paragraph 1 UKR). This is due to the rules of the Constitution, which state that the supremacy of the regulations of international treaties (Article 15, paragraph 4) applies equally to both nationals and foreigners. Moreover, all offenses are to be implemented into domestic law in order to become criminal offenses even if they are initially provided for by international agreements. Hence, both groups (nationals and foreigners) ultimately can be subject to criminal responsibility only on the basis of national criminal law, which includes the offenses contained in international agreements that can be taken into account.[407] Major crimes that are of concern to the international community have thereby been implemented into domestic law, for example, genocide (Article 357 UKR), war crimes (Chapter 34 UKR), and terrorism-related crimes (e.g., Article 205.1 UKR). Domestic criminal law has thus, a broad scope of protection.

298. Second, a double jeopardy restriction is applicable in regard to the universality principle as well as in the case of the active personality principle (Article 50 Constitution, Article 12, paragraph 1 and 3 UKR).

299. However, the main difference regarding both groups lies in the regulations relating to extradition proceedings. Russian citizens, in comparison to foreign citizens and stateless persons, cannot be extradited to another state (Article 61, paragraph 1 Constitution, Article 13 UKR). On the contrary, foreign nationals and stateless persons may be extradited to a foreign state in order to bring them to criminal responsibility or for the purpose of serving punishment in accordance with an international agreement of the Russian Federation (Article 13, paragraph 2 UKR). Nonetheless, in compliance with Article 63 Constitution, it is forbidden to extradite a person (Russian or foreign national) to other states for an act, which is not criminally punishable under Russian law.

Art. 61 para. 1 Constitution of the Russian Federation

(1) A citizen of the Russian Federation may not be deported from Russia or extradited to another State.

Art. 63 para. 2 Constitution of the Russian Federation

(1) …

407. Paramonova, Ugolovnaja Jurisdikzija v Internet-prostranstve, p. 83.

(2) In the Russian Federation it shall not be allowed to extradite to other States persons who are persecuted for their political convictions or for actions (or omissions) not recognized as a crime in the Russian Federation.

Art. 13 UKR (The Extradition of Persons Who Have Committed Crimes)

(1) Citizens of the Russian Federation who have committed a crime on the territory of a foreign State shall not be subject to extradition to that State.
(2) Foreign nationals and stateless persons who have committed a crime outside the boundaries of the Russian Federation and who are situated on the territory of the Russian Federation may be extradited to a foreign State for the purpose of bringing them to criminal responsibility or in order to serve punishment in accordance with international agreements of the Russian Federation.

300. The prohibition to surrender its own nationals is not only laid down in the Constitution (Article 61, paragraph 1) but also in the declaration made by the Russian Federation when signing the European Convention on Extradition.[408] The principle of non-surrender of one's own nationals is also applied within the **Commonwealth of Independent States** (*Содружество Независимых Государств*, CIS) and is based on the provisions of the Minsk Convention on Legal Aid for CIS States of 1994 (Article 57, paragraph 1).[409]

4. Patronizing Principle

301. In addition to the major principles governing the exercise of criminal jurisdiction, several authors specify a separate principle, the **patronizing principle** *(покровительственный принцип)*.[410] By means of this principle, Russian citizens are exempt from the criminal jurisdiction of foreign states. For instance, military servicemen of military units of the Russian Federation located outside its territory shall bear criminal responsibility for their crimes committed on the territories of foreign states according to Russian criminal law (Article 12, paragraph 2 UKR), and not according to the law of the state where the military unit is based. This case is covered by the patronizing principle as *lex specialis* instead of the active nationality principle, which is regarded as *lex generalis* for this matter.[411]

408. Art. 6, para. 1 item a European Convention on Extradition; Art. 1, para. 5 Federal Law on Ratification of the European Convention on Extradition and its Protocols, Oct. 25, 1999, N 190-FZ.
409. Paramonova, Universality Principle and Extradition in Russia, pp. 220–222.
410. Kruglikov, Kommentarii k Ugolovnomu Kodeksu RF, p. 31; Naumov, Rossiiskoe ugolovnoe pravo, p. 31.
411. Ragog, Ugolovnoe Pravo Rossii. Chasti Obschaya i Osobennaya, p. 27; Paramonova, Extraterritorial jurisdiction in Russia. In: Sieber, U. / Forster, S. / Jarvers, K. (ed(s).): National Criminal Law in a Comparative Legal Context. Volume 2.1: General limitations on the application of criminal law. Berlin, Duncker & Humblot, 2011, p. 314.

302. The legal basis for the patronizing principle is provided in, Article 61, paragraph 1 Constitution.

> Art. 61 Constitution of the Russian Federation
>
> (2) The Russian Federation shall guarantee its citizens protection and patronage abroad.

303. Apart from the principles described above, which are all provided for in the UKR, there are no other jurisdictional principles that can legitimate the applicability of national criminal law. However, as these traditional jurisdictional principles are applicable to all types of crimes without any exceptions, they may have to be interpreted differently in respect of offenses with special features, for example, cybercrimes.[412] Determination of the criminal jurisdiction could be difficult with regard to many cybercrime offenses, for instance, spreading a computer virus. Harmful consequences can occur in computers all over the world. This way, many countries could legitimately claim their jurisdiction based on the territoriality or protective principle.[413]

B. Taking Foreign Criminal Judgments into Account

304. As a general rule, foreign criminal judgments are taken into account within domestic criminal law. Respective norms can be found in the Constitution as well as in UPKR.

305. Article 50 of the Constitution states that "no one may be convicted twice for one and the same crime" and therewith lays down the *ne bis in idem* principle, also known as the "prohibition of double jeopardy." Moreover, the prohibition of double jeopardy is explicitly provided for in, Article 6, paragraph 2 UKR. Therefore, any possibility of a subsequent prosecution for the same crime in Russia is excluded after serving a sentence in any other state.[414]

306. The procedure involving an execution of a sentence passed by a foreign court is laid down in Article 472 UPKR. In compliance with this article, Russian courts shall, in principle, recognize a sentence of a foreign state and issue a decision on its execution unless there are impediments listed in, Article 472, paragraph 1 UPKR, for instance, the expiry of the limitation period according to Russian law or grounds provided for by the international treaties ratified by Russia.

307. Any decision of a foreign court shall be executed if a crime, for which the citizen of the Russian Federation was convicted, is criminally punishable under

---

412. Paramonova, Ugolovnaja Jurisdikzija v Internet-prostranstve, p. 84.

413. Paramonova, Challenges for Criminal Law and International Criminal Law in Cyberspace. In: Justice Report. Canadian Criminal Justice Association. 2014, Issue/Volume 29, N 4, pp. 26–29.

414. Lebedev, Kommentarii k UK RF, pp. 23–26.

Russian law (requirement of double criminality). Concerning the terms of punishment that should be served, Russian courts are allowed to determine the type of punishment and the maximum term for committing the respective crime within limits provided for by the Russian Criminal Code irrespective of the inflicted punishment by the foreign state. Where the sentence passed by a foreign state´s court concerns two or several acts, not all of which are crimes under Russian law, the Russian court shall determine which part of the punishment inflicted under the sentence shall apply to the act which is considered criminal (Article 472, paragraphs 2–5 UPKR).

308. On the ground of the regulations of, Article 472, paragraph 6 UPKR, any further changing of a sentence passed by a foreign state (dismissal, pardon, amnesty, etc.) in respect of a person serving punishment in Russia is taken into consideration within the Russian legal system. The changed foreign judgment is treated as if it was a new decision of a foreign court and should be analyzed by a Russian court within a new procedure.

309. According to Article 472, paragraph 2, No. 5 UPKR credit for the time already served in a foreign country is given to convicted offenders that serve their sentence in the Russian Federation. Article 72 UKR lays down the rules for the calculation of the terms of different types of punishment.[415]

§3. Principles Concerning the Applicability of Criminal Statutes with Respect to Persons

I. Immunities Based on National Public Law

310. National public law provides immunity to some groups of persons. The main criterion for granting immunity is the continuous, stable and sustainable functioning of the state institutions and authorities. Granted immunity excludes criminal punishability, however, not the fact of committing an offense.

311. Criminal prosecution with regard to the person who has been granted immunity can be started if the immunity is deprived or the prosecution authorized by the entitled body.

312. According to Russian public law, immunity is granted to the President of the Russian Federation (Article 91 Const.), to the members of both chambers of the Federal Assembly (Russian Parliament,[416] Article 98 Const.), i.e., to the members of the Council of the Federation and the deputies of the State Duma, to the judges of all courts (Article 122 Const.), to the members of regional parliaments, to the

415. Paramonova, Extraterritorial jurisdiction in Russia. In: Sieber, U. / Forster, S. / Jarvers, K. (ed(s).): National Criminal Law in a Comparative Legal Context. Volume 2.1: General limitations on the application of criminal law. Berlin, Duncker & Humblot, 2011, pp. 301–303.

416. For political and administrative structure, *see* General Introduction, §1, IV, paras. 11–20.

ombudsman for human rights in the Russian Federation (Article 1 "On the Ombudsman for Human Rights in the Russian Federation"[417]), to the prosecutors (Article 39 of the Federal Law on the Prosecutor's Office[418]).

313. The issue of depriving immunity shall be solved by the authorized body. The President of the Russian Federation may, for example, be impeached by the Council of the Federation only on the basis of charges of high treason or another grave crime, advanced by the State Duma and confirmed by the conclusion of the Supreme Court of the Russian Federation (Article 93, paragraph 1 Const.). The issue of depriving the immunity of deputies of the Federal Parliament shall be solved upon the proposal of the Procurator General of the Russian Federation to the corresponding chamber of the Federal Assembly (Article 98, paragraph 2 Const.). As to the ombudsman, it's upon the authorization of the State Duma (Article 12 "On the Ombudsman for Human Rights in the Russian Federation"). The suspension of immunity with regard to judges and prosecutors is decided on the basis of the respective Federal Laws. For instance, procedural measures against a public prosecutor can be undertaken only with the consent of the superior prosecutor (Article 39 of the Federal Law on the Prosecutor's Office).

314. The rule of the granted immunity has a general exception: the case when the person granted immunity was caught red-handed. Article 98 Const., e.g., sets out this exception regarding deputies of the Federal Assembly of the Russian Federation: federal deputies possess immunity during the whole term of their mandate; they may not be detained, arrested, searched, except for cases of being caught at the site of crime.

II. Immunities Based on International Public Law

315. In compliance with Article 11, paragraph 4 UKR, the question concerning criminal responsibility of diplomatic representatives of foreign States and other individuals who enjoy immunity, if these persons have committed crimes on the territory of the Russian Federation, are settled in conformity with the standards of international law.

316. The Code of Criminal Procedure of the Russian Federation provides additionally for the rule that criminal procedural measures stipulated by the UPKR against persons granted immunity can be undertaken with the consent of the foreign state in whose service the person granted immunity is or was or the international organization a member of which staff he/she is or was. The Ministry of Foreign Affairs of the Russian Federation gives information on whether the person enjoys immunity and the extent of such immunity (Article 3, paragraph 2 UPKR).

417. Federal Law on the Ombudsman for Human Rights in the Russian Federation, Feb. 26, 1997, N 1-FKZ.
418. Federal Law on the Prosecutor's Office of the Russian Federation, Jan. 17, 1992, N 2202.

Chapter 3. General Principles of Criminal Liability

§1. Introduction: The Basic Elements of Criminal Offenses

I. The Concept of the Offense in Russian Criminal Law

317. The current legal definition of the **criminal offense** *(преступление)* is found in Article 14 of the **Criminal Code of the Russian Federation**. This definition is regarded as a formal-substantive one.

Art. 14 UKR (Concept of Crime)

(1) A socially dangerous act committed with guilt and prohibited by this Code under threat of punishment shall be deemed to be a criminal offense.
(2) An action (or omission), although formally containing the indicia of any act provided for by the present Code but by virtue of insignificance does not represent a social danger, shall not be a criminal offense.

318. The term act has a broader meaning, including both positive acts (action/commission, *действие)* and negative acts (omission, *бездействие)* (Article 14 UKR).[419]

319. These terms are not defined by the law. In the doctrine, "action" is considered to be a socially dangerous[420] willed conduct actively pursued by an individual. "Omission" refers to passivity: failure to act freely and consciously regardless of the duty and possibility to act in order to prevent criminal consequences.[421]

320. In contemporary doctrine, there are four main indicators of the criminal offense: a **socially dangerous act or omission** *(общественно опасное деяние)*, which is prohibited by means of criminal law regulations—**illegality** *(противоправность)* under threat of punishment—**punishability** *(наказуемость)* and committed culpably—**culpability** *(виновность)*.[422]

321. The concept of a criminal offense has been systematically discussed in Russian criminal law literature.[423] It is conventional to distinguish between three types of definitions of the criminal offense: **formal** *(формальное)*, **substantive** *(материальное)* and **formal-substantive** *(формально- материальное)*.[424] All

419. For action and omission crimes, *see* Part I, Chapter 3, §2, paras. 345–356
420. For the concept of the criminal offense, *see* Part I, Chapter 3, §1, paras. 317–321.
421. Naumov, Rossiiskoe ugolovnoe pravo, p. 316; Zhuravlev, Ugolovnoe pravo, p. 83.
422. Lebedev, Kommentarii k UK RF, p.54; Kropachev, Ugolovnoe pravo Rossii, p. 334.
423. Kistyakovskij, Obschee ugolovnoe pravo, p. 59; Spasovich, Ugolovnoe pravo, p. 60; Taganzev, Kurs ugolovnogo prava, pp. 45–46; Kropachev, Ugolovnoe pravo Rossii, pp. 325–349.
424. Lebedev, Kommentarii k UK RF, p. 56.

the definitions were used in the former Russian legislation, although the concept had been changed according to the political and ideological background.[425]

A. Formal Concept of the Criminal Offense

322. The **formal** concept is found in the prohibition of certain behaviors by legal provisions, under threat of punishment.[426] The reason behind the use of the formal concept is that it is impossible to give a permanent substantive definition of the criminal offense because social danger, which is the substantive indicator of the criminal offense, is a historically changing phenomenon and can be broadly interpreted.[427] On the other hand, the purely formal concept of the criminal offense has been criticized in Russian literature for the reason that it does not accord with social reality: an act may be criminal regardless of whether it is actually socially dangerous.[428] For instance, during the czar's times, "the disobedience to the Czar's will and violation of the legal provisions"[429] was considered criminal. So, even less dangerous matters were criminalized: cutting down of a rare tree or a murder could be of the same importance, and both were worthy of the death penalty.[430]

B. Substantive Concept of the Criminal Offense

323. When the legislature explains why a particular conduct is dangerous (a threat against the State, society or individuals), the definition of the criminal offense acquires a **substantive** (social) nature.[431] In other words, the substantive component shows what kind of behavior is deemed "socially dangerous" in a particular society.

324. "Social danger" has been understood differently depending on the historical context. In the **Czar's Russia,** as mentioned above, it was a violation of the Czar's will. The perception of the Czar as the protector of the whole nation and the ambassador of God on Earth has existed throughout Russian history.[432] Nevertheless, from 1649,[433] all criminal offenses had to be legislatively determined. In the

425. Paramonova, Concept and systematization of the criminal offense in Russia, 2011, pp. 86–89.
426. Naumov, Rossiiskoe ugolovnoe pravo, p. 155.
427. Gontar´, Prestuplenie i sostav prestupleniya, p. 20; Spasovich, Ugolovnoe pravo, p. 60.
428. Taganzev, Kurs ugolovnogo prava, p. 5; Spasovich, Ugolovnoe pravo, p. 60; Durmanov, Ponyatie prestupleniya, p. 259.
429. Council Code of Czar Alexej Romanov, 1649: Russian legislation from X till XX centuries in 9 volumes. vol. 6, 1988, p. 174.
430. Military Articles of Peter the Great, 1714: Russian legislation from X till XX centuries in 9 volumes, vol. 4, 1988, p. 320.
431. Kropachev, Ugolovnoe pravo Rossii, p.328.
432. Karamzin, Istoriya Gosudarstva Rossiiskogo: http://bibliotekar.ru/karamzin/index.htm.
433. Council Code of Czar Alexej Romanov, 1649: Russian legislation from X till XX centuries in 9 volumes. vol. 6, 1988, p. 174.

Soviet time, the social danger was measured in terms of "threatening the fundamentals and principles of the worker-peasants' Soviet order."[434] The formal indicator of the crime—the provision by law—did not have any importance because the courts had the legislative authority to create new crimes through reasoning by analogy. The concept of social danger in **contemporary** Russia leans toward individual and non-class-specific interests. The protection of the rights and freedoms of man and citizens is prioritized over public order and security.

325. According to the prevailing doctrine, "social danger" as a substantive indicator of the criminal offense has qualitative and quantitative characteristics.[435] Different types of criminal offenses are distinguished by means of the degree of social danger.[436] The qualitative feature is determined by the targeting of different groups of legally protected interests (compare, e.g., crimes against life and against ownership). Quantitative characteristics demarcate the difference between criminal offenses targeting the same group of legally protected interests (compare, e.g., homicide of one person and two or more persons).

C. Formal-Substantive Concept of the Criminal Offense

326. The existence of both, a formal indicator (illegality) and a substantive one (a reference to the social danger of the criminal offense), characterizes the **formal-substantive** concept of the criminal offense. Thus, the criminal offense is a behavior, which is illegal in its form and socially dangerous in its content.[437] The current legal definition of the criminal offense (Article 14 UKR) corresponds to this concept. First, it contains the requirement of legal form: all criminal offenses shall be determined only by the UKR. Second, an act should meet a certain degree of social danger in order for it to be a criminal offense.[438]

327. The extent of the **social danger** determines the **distinction between criminal, administrative and civil offenses**. For instance, hooliganism, targeting the same group of legally protected interests, can be a criminal as well as an administrative offense. The administrative offense of hooliganism is defined as an "insignificant violation of public order,"[439] whereas the criminal offense has additional "socially dangerous" characteristics and is determined as "the flagrant violation of public order with the application of weapons or for reasons of racial hatred … ."

434. Leading principles in criminal law of RSFSR of 12.12.1919 (Rukovodyaschie nachala po ugolovnomu pravu RSFSR); Criminal Code of the Russian Soviet Federative Socialist Republic 01.06.1922 (Ugolovnij Kodeks RSFSR, VCIK-resolution), Criminal Code of the Russian Soviet Federative Socialist Republic 22.11.1926 (Ugolovnij Kodeks RSFSR, VCIK- resolution).

435. Georgievskij, Obschee ponyatie prestupleniya, p. 3; Kuznecova, Prestuplenie i prestupnost´, p. 72.

436. On the division of crimes into categories, *see* paras. 34, 638–646.

437. Kropachev, Ugolovnoe pravo Rossii, p. 326.

438. Military Articles of Peter the Great, 1714: Russian legislation from X till XX centuries in 9 volumes, vol. 4, 1988, p. 320.

439. Art. 20.1 of the Code of Administrative Offenses of the Russian Federation, 30.12.2001, N 195—FZ (Kodeks RF ob administrativnih pravonarusheniyah).

328. Another significant distinguishing criterion for criminal, administrative and civil offenses lies in the presence of **guilt.**[440] In order to be classified as a criminal or administrative offense, an act (or omission) should be committed guiltily: with intent or negligence. Committing civil wrongs without guilt still entails responsibility.

329. The next distinguishing criterion is **illegality.** All criminal offenses are determined only by the UKR and not by any additional legal regulations. The principle of legality prohibits the application of analogy in criminal and administrative law. Analogy can, however, be used in the case of civil offenses.[441]

330. The degree of social danger is also used to distinguish between **criminal offenses** and **insignificant acts**, which are formally regarded as criminal offenses, but by virtue of **insignificance** *(малозначительность)* do not represent a social danger and are therefore not deemed to be criminal offenses (Article 14, paragraph 2 UKR), e.g., theft of RUB 2.

II. General Requirements of Criminal Liability: Methodological System

331. In order to describe the method of determining basic requirements of criminal liability, it is essential to mention that traditionally, Russian criminal law distinguishes between '**crime**' *(преступление)* and '**elements of crime**' *(состав преступления).*[442] The distinction was made in order to determine the grounds for criminal responsibility. In accordance with Article 8 UKR, "the ground for criminal responsibility is the **commission of an act containing all the indicia of the 'elements of crime'** provided for by the present Code." The only function of the term 'crime' in the sense of Article 14 UKR is to differentiate between criminal and noncriminal offenses. The systematization of criminal liability is done through the means of doctrinal abstraction—the "elements of crime."[443]

332. The definition of the "elements of crime" started to be used after many years of discussion in the criminal law doctrine[444] and consists of a theoretical **quadripartite system** of objective and subjective elements of criminal liability, which are provided for in the criminal law legislation.[445] Before the appearance of this quadripartite system, only objective (external) elements of the crime were taken

440. On the subjective aspects of the offense, *see* Part I, Chapter 3, §4, paras. 383–428.

441. For the principle of legality, *see* Part I, Chapter 1, paras. 197–226; Paramonova, Concept and systematization of the criminal offense in Russia, 2011, pp. 87–89.

442. Kuznecova, Kurs ugolovnogo prava, p. 175; Kropachev, Ugolovnoe pravo Rossii, p. 367; Taganzev, Kurs ugolovnogo prava, p. 5; Kistyakovskij, Obschee ugolovnoe pravo, p. 59; Piontkovskij, Sovetskoe ugolovnoe pravo, p. 241.

443. Kuznecova, Kurs ugolovnogo prava, p. 176; Zhuravlev, Ugolovnoe pravo, p. 63.

444. Kistyakovskij, Obschee ugolovnoe pravo, p. 59; Piontkovskij Sovetskoe ugolovnoe pravo, p. 241; Trainin, Sostav prestupleniya, pp. 59–60.

445. Kuznecova, Kurs ugolovnogo prava, p. 164; Kudryavzev, Ugolovnoe pravo Rossii, p. 98.

into account.[446] The appearance of the "elements of crime"—system in Russian criminal law goes back to the classical school of criminal law (18th–19th centuries). Traditionally, German criminal law had a significant influence on the Russian legal system since many Russian lawyers were educated in the German legal system.[447] However, the German tripartite interpretation of the "elements of crime" was not adopted by Russian criminal law. Throughout Russian legal history, the quadripartite model of analysis remained unchanged at the core.

333. Originally, the "elements of crime" had a purely **procedural role.** Before a case could be brought to court, the "elements of crime" had to be satisfied.[448] Now it serves as a theoretical scheme for the analysis of crimes as well as a scheme that is used by the prosecuting authorities for elements of crime that need to be proven.

334. Taking into consideration the indicators of the criminal offense and the regulations of Article 8 UKR, the following mode **of analysis of criminal liability** is currently applicable:[449]

"Elements of crime" *(элементы состава преступления)*	**Obligatory indicia of "elements of crime"** *(обязательные признаки состава преступления)* Elements that need to be proven by the prosecuting authorities
Object of crime	– legally protected interests: – generic; – specific; – direct
Objective side of crime (*cf. actus reus*)	– socially dangerous act (action or omission); – consequences *(последствия)* of the crime; – causality *(причинно-следственная связь)* between an action and the consequences; – methods, background, means, place, time
Subjective side of crime (*cf. mens rea*)	– intent (direct; indirect) – negligence (mindlessness; carelessness)
Subject of crime	– natural person – imputability – age

446. Kudryavzev, Ugolovnoe pravo Rossii, p. 98.
447. Kuznecova, Kurs ugolovnogo prava, p. 166.
448. Kuznecova, Kurs ugolovnogo prava, p. 166.
449. Kuznecova, Kurs ugolovnogo prava, 166; Kudryavzev, Ugolovnoe pravo Rossii, p. 98; Kropachev, Ugolovnoe pravo Rossii, p. 364.

Additional (facultative indicia) of "elements of crime" *(факультативные признаки состава преступления; квалифицированные составы преступлений)*, e.g., special motives, purposes or consequences of a crime

– obligatory element only for some crimes

Circumstances excluding criminal responsibility (excuses)

335. The first element of the "elements of crime" is the **object of crime** *(объект преступления)* —that is, legally protected interests that are infringed.[450] These can be subdivided into generic *(родовой)*, specific *(видовой)* and direct *(непосредственный)* objects. The first is the most general one, for instance, the interests of the economy. The specific object is an object within the generic one, e.g., personal property. The direct one is an immediate object of infringement, e.g., money.

336. The second feature of criminal liability is the **objective side of crime** *(объективная сторона преступления).* [451] This is an external element: the criminal conduct of the offender (in the form of action or omission) has its impact on other individuals.[452] **Consequences** *(последствия)* of the crime and **causality** *(причинно-следственная связь)* between a certain crime and results of this crime are among the features of the objective side.

337. The **subjective side of crime** *(субъективная сторона преступления)* is an internal characteristic which determines the mental (intellectual, cognitive and emotional) processes of the offender toward his unlawful actions.[453] The intellectual and cognitive elements are analyzed within the "**forms of guilt**" *(формы вины)* following Article 24 UKR: **intent** *(умысел)* and **negligence** *(неосторожность).* In compliance with Articles 25 and 26 UKR, depending on the different variations of the combination of the intellectual and cognitive elements, the relevant mental state can be classified as **direct intent** *(прямой умысел)*, **indirect intent** *(косвенный умысел)*, **mindlessness** *(легкомыслие)* or **carelessness** *(небрежность)*.[454] For instance, a crime shall be deemed to be committed with direct intent if a person was aware (intellectual element) of the social danger of his conduct and wished that socially dangerous consequences ensued (cognitive element).

450. Kropachev, Ugolovnoe pravo Rossii, p. 371.
451. On the objective aspects of the offense, *see* Part I, Chapter 3, §2, paras. 342–371.
452. Zhuravlev, Ugolovnoe pravo, p. 60; Kropachev, Ugolovnoe pravo Rossii, p. 371. *See also* discussion on the objective aspects of the offense, *see* Part I, Chapter 3, §2, paras. 342–371.
453. Kropachev, Ugolovnoe pravo Rossii, p. 372; *See* chapter 3, §3.
454. Kropachev, Ugolovnoe pravo Rossii, p. 373; on the subjective aspects of the offense, *see* Part I, Chapter 3, §4, paras. 383–428.

338. The **subject of crime** *(субъект преступления)* is a person who can be criminally liable according to the UKR. In compliance with Articles 19, 20, paragraphs 1 and 2 UKR, only a natural person (Russian citizen, a foreign citizen or stateless person) of sound mind, who has attained the age of 16 or 14, shall be subject to criminal responsibility.[455]

339. The abovementioned indicia of the **"elements of crime"** *(обязательные признаки)* are obligatory indicia and must be present in every committed crime.

340. According to the structure of the offense, the object of crime, as well as the subject of crime, are regarded as separate elements, belonging neither to the objective side nor to the subjective side of crime.

341. In addition, **additional or facultative characteristics** *(факультативные признаки)*[456] are called this way since they are not present in all crimes, such as special motive.[457] These are obligatory requirements only for those crimes for which these indicia are provided for by law, e.g., mercenary purpose or hooligan-like motives. Hooligan-like motives, for instance, should be included in the analysis of the subjective side of crime. Another example is Article 285 UKR (abuse of official power): the "special subject of crime" *(специальный субъект преступления)* in this case requires the additional characteristic that the perpetrator has to be a public official.

§2. Objective Side: The Material or Physical Element (*Actus Reus*)

I. Description

342. The **objective side of crime** *(объективная сторона преступления)*[458] or material element of crime (*actus reus*) is considered to be an aggregation of the legally defined features characterizing the external aspects of the criminal offense.

343. According to the prevailing doctrine,[459] and as mentioned before, the following characteristics should be included in the analysis of the objective side of crime: socially dangerous act (action or omission); **consequences**

455. On the objective aspects of the offense, *see* Part I, Chapter 3, §2, paras. 342–371.
456. For the difference with the notion of "aggravating circumstances," *see* Part I, Chapter 3, §2, paras. 363–371.
457. Kropachev, Ugolovnoe pravo Rossii, p. 375.
458. Paramonova, Objective aspects of the offense in Russia. In: Sieber, U. / Forster, S. / Jarvers, K. (ed(s).): National Criminal Law in a Comparative Legal Context. Volume 3.1: Defining criminal conduct. Berlin, Duncker & Humblot, 2011, p. 239–254.
459. Kovalev, Ob´ektivnaya storona sostava prestupleniya, p. 145; Kropachev, Ugolovnoe pravo Rossii, p. 403; Kuznecova, Kurs ugolovnogo prava, p. 213; Naumov, Rossiiskoe ugolovnoe pravo, p. 313; Trainin, Obschee uchenie o sostave prestupleniya, p. 132.

(последствия) of the crime; **causality** ***(причинно-следственная связь)*** between an action and the consequences; methods, background, means, place, time.

344. It is disputable which features are obligatory and which are optional. According to the prevailing opinion, only the socially dangerous act or omission is always necessary for the analysis of the objective side of crime.[460] The other features are optional unless they are specified in the legal provisions. For instance, the violation of secrecy of correspondence (Article 138 UKR) will entail criminal responsibility even in the absence of further consequences or special methods (formal crime: "non-result crime"). On the other hand, intentional causing of minor harm to health (Article 115 UKR) requires additional characteristics as particular consequences—a short-term impairment of health or insignificant, persistent loss of general physical capacity (material crime: "harmful result crime").

II. Actions Omissions, and Causation

A. *Concept of Criminal Act*

345. An act is the most important element of the objective side of crime. It has two forms: **action** ***(действие)*** and **omission** ***(бездействие)*** (Article 14 UKR). These terms are not defined by the law. In the doctrine, "action" is considered to be a socially dangerous[461] willed conduct actively pursued by an individual. "Omission"—in contrast—is a failure to act freely and consciously in spite of the duty and possibility to act in order to prevent harmful consequences.

346. According to the prevailing doctrine,[462] the **socially dangerous act** ***(общественно опасное деяние)*** is the only element of the objective side of crime that should be present for all types of crimes. **Social danger** ***(общественная опасность)***[463] is the main characteristic of a criminal act. An insignificant act, formally containing the indicia of the crime, is not deemed to be criminal (Article 14 UKR).

347. Furthermore, an act should be **externally identifiable** ***(внешнее проявление действия)*** in the form of action or omission; that is, it should entail some change in the world that can be perceived by the senses. Contemporary Russian criminal law is namely based on the postulate *cogitationis poenam nemo patitur*—no one can be punished for their thoughts. It emphasizes that

---

460. Ignatov/Krasikov, Kurs rossijskogo ugolovnogo prava, pp. 132–133; Kropachev, Ugolovnoe pravo Rossii, p. 405; Naumov, Rossiiskoe ugolovnoe pravo, p. 314.
461. For the concept of the criminal offense, *see* Part I, Chapter 3, §1, paras. 317–321.
462. Kovalev, Ob´ektivnaya storona sostava prestupleniya, p. 145; Kropachev, Ugolovnoe pravo Rossii, p. 403; Kuznecova, Kurs ugolovnogo prava, p. 213; Naumov, Rossiiskoe ugolovnoe pravo, p. 313; Trainin, Obschee uchenie o sostave prestupleniya, p. 132.
463. For the concept of the criminal offense, *see* Part I, Chapter 3, §1, paras. 317–321.

the only basis for criminal punishment can be criminal behavior, in the form of perceivable conduct and not mere convictions and views.[464] Attempted crime, as well as the preparation for crime (Article 30 UKR) are, on the contrary, criminalized by reason of the fact that these acts have already entered the domain of external perception.[465]

348. The next feature of the act is a **will** *(воля)*. The will is regarded as the ability to react freely and consciously in relation to external factors.[466] Hence, an act committed, for example, under physical or mental coercion,[467] irresistible force (natural catastrophes, disasters, and emergency cases) or pursuant to an order,[468] does not have a criminal character by virtue of failure of will. Reflex actions (e.g., damaging one's property by falling down) are also not considered as actions of will. However, not every physical or mental coercion or acting pursuant to an order (Article 42 UKR) excludes criminal responsibility, although they are always regarded as circumstances mitigating punishment (Article 61, paragraph 1UKR). For instance, after minor beatings, one can still control his conduct; therefore, his act is still willed. In the case of intoxication (Article 23 UKR), it is presumed that the offender puts himself freely and consciously into this state and is, therefore, not excused from criminal responsibility.[469]

349. The abovementioned obligatory features of an act represent the concept of a criminal act in criminal law as a combination of "social theory" (socially meaningful human action), "teleological theory" (goal-directed theory of human act), and "causal theory" (act as a result of will).[470]

B. Offenses of Omission

350. "Omission" refers to passivity but has, apart from that, the same features as "action."[471] Nevertheless, the criterion by which omission is distinguished from neutral acting is passivity that possesses the socially dangerous features relevant for the criminal law: failure to act freely and consciously regardless of the duty and possibility to act in order to prevent criminal consequences (e.g., doctors). This kind of "non-doing" is not necessarily characterized by a purely physical passivity. In a physical sense, one can be active but still act passively in the context of criminal

464. Lebedev, Kommentarii k UK RF, p. 27.
465. On attempt, *see* Part I, Chapter 5, paras. 544–589.
466. Lebedev, Kommentarii k UK RF, p. 27; Zhuravlev, Ugolovnoe pravo, p. 83.
467. On justification, excuse, and other grounds of impunity, *see* Part I, Chapter 4, paras. 429–528.
468. On justification, excuse, and other grounds of impunity, *see* Part I, Chapter 4, paras. 429–528.
469. Lebedev, Kommentarii k UK RF, p. 47.
470. Paramonova, Objective aspects of the offense in Russia. In: Sieber, U. / Forster, S. / Jarvers, K. (ed(s).): National Criminal Law in a Comparative Legal Context. Volume 3.1: Defining criminal conduct. Berlin, Duncker & Humblot, 2011, p. 241–242; Naumov, Rossiiskoe ugolovnoe pravo, pp. 316–317.
471. Naumov, Rossiiskoe ugolovnoe pravo, p. 316; Zhuravlev, Ugolovnoe pravo, p. 83.

law.[472] For instance, an individual who is working in his garden watches a child drowning (Article 125 UKR, failure to give assistance to persons in mortal danger). The omitting to act can be as dangerous as action and therefore is as relevant for criminal law.[473]

351. In Russian criminal law, there are two classifications of crime that are related to omission.

352. The first group focuses on the form of a commission of the crime. Within this category, three types of crimes can be distinguished: **crimes of "pure" action** *(преступления, совершаемые только путем действия)*—can be committed only by acting (e.g., theft), **crimes of "pure" omission** *("чистое" преступное бездействие)*—can be committed through non-acting (e.g., failure to render help), and **composite-crimes** *(смешанные деяния)*—can be committed by both action and (or) omission (e.g., abuse of official powers).[474]

C. Determining Criminal Responsibility for Omissions

353. In order to determine criminal responsibility for omissions, the following requirements should be considered:[475]

– A legal **duty to act** *(обязанность действовать)* under certain circumstances.

Offenses of "pure" omission, as well as composite-crimes that have been committed by omitting to act, can entail criminal responsibility only when a person has the legal duty to act. It is not sufficient to have only a moral duty to act.[476] The basis for the legal duty can be different. According to prevailing doctrine, the following three main groups are distinguished on the basis of the obligation to act:[477]

– *By virtue of legal provisions other than criminal norms*

These legal provisions are not restricted to criminal law but also refer, e.g., to civil or administrative law regulations. For instance, the duty of care of parents

472. Naumov, Rossiiskoe ugolovnoe pravo, pp. 317–318.
473. Paramonova, Objective aspects of the offense in Russia. In: Sieber, U. / Forster, S. / Jarvers, K. (ed(s).): National Criminal Law in a Comparative Legal Context. Volume 3.1: Defining criminal conduct. Berlin, Duncker & Humblot, 2011, p. 242.
474. Krasikov, Kurs rossijskogo ugolovnogo prava, p. 143; Kropachev, Ugolovnoe pravo Rossii, pp. 334, 416; Lebedev, Kommentarii k UK RF, p. 27; Naumov, Rossiiskoe ugolovnoe pravo, pp. 318–319; Zhuravlev, Ugolovnoe pravo, p. 83;.
475. Kropachev, Ugolovnoe pravo Rossii, p. 416; Kudryavzev, Ugolovnoe pravo Rossii, p. 133; Lebedev, Kommentarii k UK RF, p. 29; Naumov, Rossiiskoe ugolovnoe pravo, p. 319; Zhuravlev, Ugolovnoe pravo, pp. 84–85.
476. Krasikov, Kurs rossijskogo ugolovnogo prava, pp. 140–141.
477. Gercenzon, Ugolovnoe pravo. Obschaya Chast, p. 293; Kropachev, Ugolovnoe pravo Rossii, p. 416; Kuznezova, Objektivnaya storona prestupleniya, p. 223; Naumov, Rossiiskoe ugolovnoe pravo, p. 318; Piontkovskij, Sovetskoe ugolovnoe pravo, pp. 178–179; Zhuravlev, Ugolovnoe pravo, p. 85.

toward their children is provided for by the Family Code of the Russian Federation.[478] Omission, in the form of the nonpayment of maintenance (Article 157 UKR), entails criminal responsibility.

– *On the basis of profession required by the criminal provisions*

Certain professional positions or skills require a person to act within the sphere of his specific duties. So, a physician should render aid to a sick person. Otherwise, it leads to criminal responsibility (Article 124 UKR, failure to render aid). The captain of a vessel has the responsibility to help people suffering a disaster at sea (Article 270 UKR). A firefighter, having extended professional experience and skills, compared to a layman, can take a person out of the fire. In the literature, there is also discussion about whether people of some professions should be obliged to act only while on duty according to their work schedule.[479]

– *On the basis of the previous conduct*

For example, one has decided to help a blind person to cross a dangerous road, although in the middle of the street, has left him alone, when seeing a nice girl.[480] Even if a person takes on the responsibilities voluntarily (irrespective of whether it is a "neutral" or dangerous type of conduct), he has to fulfill them in order not to cause socially harmful consequences. In this case, failure to help entails criminal responsibility according to Article 125 UKR (leaving in danger).

354. The possibility to act is assessed by taking into account several criteria. First, the objective aspects of a certain situation. For example, a security guard who was tied up and on the ground of physical coercion[481] did not prevent the robbery of a bank (Article 40, paragraph 1 UKR).[482] Second, the personal (subjective) characteristics of the offender should be considered: his professionalism, practical experience, etc. The same circumstance can exclude or create criminal responsibility depending on the different personal skills and responsibilities. For instance, a physician could not get to his patient and render help because of the overflow of a river. However, under the same circumstances, a military man has the responsibility to overcome difficulties by fulfilling his military duties. Another example is that a fire is an irresistible force (or force majeure that is beyond the control of a layman) for a normal person, in contrast to a firefighter, who has special skills, equipment, and experience.

355. Criminal acts in the form of omission can be intentional as well as negligent.[483] This is based on the provisions regarding forms of guilt of Articles 14 and 24–28 UKR, which contain the same requirements for action and omission.

478. Sobranie Zakonodatel´stva RF, Jan. 1, 1996, N 1, Art. 16.
479. Naumov, Rossiiskoe ugolovnoe pravo, pp. 318–319; Zhuravlev, Ugolovnoe pravo, pp. 85–86.
480. Krasikov, Kurs rossijskogo ugolovnogo prava, p. 140.
481. On justification, excuse, and other grounds of impunity, *see* Part I, Chapter 4, paras. 429–528.
482. Zhuravlev, Ugolovnoe pravo, p. 84.
483. On the subjective aspects of the offense, *see* Part I, Chapter 3, §4, paras. 383–428.

356. However, according to Article 30 UKR and legal practice, incomplete crimes (at the stage of preparation[484] or attempt[485]) in both forms, action and omission, must be committed with direct intent (Article 30, paragraphs 1, 3 UKR) and not, by negligence, in order to be punishable by the criminal law.[486]

D. Causation

357. **Causality** ***(причинно-следственная связь)*** is the subtype of the objective side of crime. It literally means "connection between causations (acts) and consequences." In Russian criminal law doctrine, the problems of both causation and objective attribution belong to the topic of causality.[487] Thus, an individual is held accountable for the occurrence of harm if causality (the connection between his acts and consequences) is affirmed.

– Theories of Causation

The main theories that are presented in legal doctrine are the following:

– The **theory of the equivalence of conditions** *(теория эквивалентности: conditio sine qua non)* was historically the first (since the middle of the 19th till the beginning of the 20th century), and the prevailing theory in the doctrine and in judicial practice.[488] According to this theory, all conditions that occasioned the harmful result are equally relevant for determining criminal liability.

358. For example, A hit B slightly with a stick. However, A did not know that the stick was infected with tetanus (an infectious disease of the central nervous system). B died after one month because of the infection. In this case, A would be held liable for negligent homicide because his strike with the stick was causal.

359. The disadvantage of the theory is its broadness in relation to the relevant conditions. The other theories take different criteria as a basis in order to limit these conditions.

– **Theory of distinguishing between causations and conditions** *(теория разграничения причин и условий)* or the theory of adequate causation. The idea of this theory is to differentiate between causations (that are determining for

484. On attempt, *see* Part I, Chapter 5, paras. 544–589.
485. On attempt, *see* Part I, Chapter 5, paras. 544–589.
486. Postanovlenie Plenuma Verhovnogo Suda RF (Supreme Court of the Russian Federation), Jan. 27, 1999, N 1, para. 2; Paramonova, Objective aspects of the offense in Russia. In: Sieber, U. / Forster, S. / Jarvers, K. (ed(s).): National Criminal Law in a Comparative Legal Context. Volume 3.1: Defining criminal conduct. Berlin, Duncker & Humblot, 2011, pp. 243–245.
487. Kovalev, Ob´ektivnaya storona sostava prestupleniya, p. 145; Kropachev, Ugolovnoe pravo Rossii, p. 403; Kuznecova, Kurs ugolovnogo prava, p. 213; Trainin, Obschee uchenie o sostave prestupleniya, p. 132; Naumov, Rossiiskoe ugolovnoe pravo, p. 313.
488. Naumov, Rossiiskoe ugolovnoe pravo, p. 323.

the occurrence of the harmful consequences) and conditions (that are necessary but not decisive for the harmful result).[489] Hence, only causations should be taken into account for criminal liability.

The criteria that are suggested to distinguish between causations and conditions are the following:

– **facilitating (promoting) cause** *(теория степени способствования наступления результата)* : the determining factors here are those that facilitated the occurrence of the harm.[490]
– **"degree of harmfulness" of criminal conduct** *(теория степени причинения)* : some authors propose a distinction between more harmful (main conditions) and less harmful conditions. Only the first should be decisive for criminal liability.[491]
– **proximate cause** *(теория ближайшей причины)* : a term which is taken from the common law. The time boundaries regarding the harmful result cannot be unlimited, and only the latest should be taken into account.[492]
– **real opportunity** *(теория реальной возможности)*: to be considered as causation and thus imply criminal liability, an act should create a real opportunity for the occurrence of the harmful consequences.[493] For instance, if someone starts to shoot chaotically in a crowd.

– According to the **theory of the adequate cause** *(теория адекватной причинности)*,[494] there is causality if the harmful consequences are typical for the act. For example, C hit D slightly on the head with his arm. D died because of the complications this hit caused after his, at the time of the strike, recent brain surgery operation (which C did not know about). Death is not a typical consequence of a slight hit. Hence, C cannot be held liable for the death-consequence. In the tetanus case above,[495] A could be held liable only for causing light (slight) harm to health according to this theory.
– The **theory of the necessary cause** *(теория необходимого причинения)* appeared first in the Soviet doctrine.[496] The basis for this theory is the difference between **accidental** *(случайности)* and **necessary** *(необходимости)* conditions relating to consequences. Only the necessary conditions can be accountable. The necessary result belongs to the essence of a certain phenomenon, to its natural development. An accidental result—in contrast to the necessary result—occurs with the interference of additional factors or circumstances and is not derived from the essence of the phenomenon.[497]

360. In the "brain surgery case," the slight hit itself cannot be the only condition for the cause of death. The death only occurred together with additional factors

489. Pozdnischev, Osnovnie nachala nauki ugolovnogo prava, p. 320.
490. Taganzev, Russkoe ugolovnoe pravo, p. 672.
491. Kudryavzev, Ugolovnoe pravo Rossii, p. 144.
492. Kenii, Osnovi ugolovnogo prava, p. 139.
493. Cereteli, Prichinnaya svyaz´v ugolovnom prave, p. 131.
494. Ignatov/Krasikov, Kurs rossijskogo ugolovnogo prava, pp. 132–133.
495. For the tetanus case, *see* para. 358.
496. Piontkovskij, Ugolovnoe pravo, p. 304.
497. Kovalev/Vas´kov, Prichinnaya svyaz v sovetskom prave, p. 62.

(accidental conditions). Here, these are the complications of recent brain surgery. So, according to this theory, C cannot be held responsible for D's death. The same logic is applicable for the tetanus case: A cannot be responsible for B's death.

– Scheme for the Analysis of Causality

The prevailing doctrine uses a schema for the analysis of causality, which is based on diverse theories. It includes the following requirements:

- Sequence of the development: the socially dangerous criminal act (action or omission) must occur before the harmful consequences.
- An act (action or omission) should be the necessary condition in regard to the socially dangerous consequences. Without this condition, the occurrence of the consequences would not have been possible.
- An act should create the real opportunity for the occurrence of the socially dangerous consequences (in A's case: usually, a slight hit with a stick does not create a real opportunity for death).[498]

– Intervening Factors

361. In the doctrine and in the judicial practice, unforeseeable intervening factors, such as peculiarities of the victim's organism in connection with causality, is a controversial topic. Depending on the specific case, they can be held either for the necessary or for the accidental conditions described above.[499] However, if the causality is affirmed, criminal responsibility for a certain crime can be denied by the analysis of subjective factors (the subjective side).[500] For instance, if in the tetanus case, the causality was affirmed, but A was not aware of the fact that the stick was infected with tetanus, he could not have been held guilty for the homicide. Under the same circumstances, but in the case of awareness of A of the infected stick, he would have been found guilty of intentional homicide.[501]

III. Classification of Offenses from the Point of View of the Material Element

362. From the point of view of the material or objective element of the crime, there are several offense types.

---

498. Paramonova, Objective aspects of the offense in Russia. In: Sieber, U. / Forster, S. / Jarvers, K. (ed(s).): National Criminal Law in a Comparative Legal Context. Volume 3.1: Defining criminal conduct. Berlin, Duncker & Humblot, 2011, p. 251
499. Naumov, Rossiiskoe ugolovnoe pravo, p. 334.
500. On the subjective aspects of the offense, *see* Part I, Chapter 3, §4, paras. 383–428.
501. Paramonova, Objective aspects of the offense in Russia. In: Sieber, U. / Forster, S. / Jarvers, K. (ed(s).): National Criminal Law in a Comparative Legal Context. Volume 3.1: Defining criminal conduct. Berlin, Duncker & Humblot, 2011, pp. 249–251.

363. Russian criminal law distinguishes between **result (substantial)** *(материальный состав преступления)* and **formal** *(формальный состав преступления)* crimes.[502]

364. All crimes are considered to have harmful consequences; however, only the occurrence of certain results is relevant for criminal law.[503] In some crimes, certain conduct is already dangerous, regardless of the consequences.

365. Result crimes require a certain result provided for by legal provisions in order to entail criminal responsibility. For instance, homicide by the mother of a newborn child (Article 106 UKR) can be punishable only under the condition of the child's death. Another example is the criminalization of infecting with venereal disease (Article 121 UKR); an act of infection is considered to be a harmful result.

366. In contrast, formal or conduct crimes do not connect criminal responsibility with any concrete harmful results (consequences in a narrow sense). An act is already criminal, regardless of its consequences. An example is slander (Article 128.1 UKR).

367. In the case of result crimes, the consequences are an essential element (*conditione sine qua non*) of the crime in order to be punishable. However, some (initially formal) crimes can be aggravated by **facultative (additional) indicia** *(квалифицированные составы преступлений)*, which are specifically defined by the legal provisions. For instance, more severe punishment is foreseen for the kidnapping of a person, which entailed the death of the victim (Article 126, paragraph 3 UKR), rather than for the same crime without this consequence: Article 126, paragraph 1 UKR.[504] In contrast, the list of aggravating circumstances[505] is non-exhaustive, Article 63 UKR, and can be applied to any crime. Thus, the crime of the kidnapping of a person, which entailed the death of the victim (Article 126, paragraph 3 UKR), can be aggravated (on top of the facultative indicia) with the aggravating circumstances of Article 63 UKR, e.g., using the especially cruel method of killing.

368. With regard to formal crimes, there are no concrete consequences required by the legal provisions. However, if these types of crimes have caused harmful results, they should be taken into account for sentencing (Article 60, paragraph 3 UKR) as aggravating (or mitigating) circumstances (Articles 61, 63 UKR). An example is a slander (Article 128.1 UKR) that entails, for instance, the suicide of the victim. The suicide of the victim is a harmful result of a formal crime and an aggravating circumstance that is applicable on the basis of Article 63 UKR.

---

502. Kuznezova, Objektivnaya storona prestupleniya, pp. 237–238; Naumov, Rossiiskoe ugolovnoe pravo, p. 319.
503. Naumov, Rossiiskoe ugolovnoe pravo, p. 320.
504. On the subjective aspects of the offense, *see* Part I, Chapter 3, §4, paras. 383–428.
505. For aggravating circumstances, *see* Chapter 7, § 6, paras. 753–756.

369. Russian criminal law distinguishes furthermore between two different types of **crimes that provide for the possibility of causing danger** *(деликты создания опасности)*. These are **crimes of real endangerment** *(деликты реальной опасности)* and **crimes of abstract endangerment** *(деликты абстрактной опасности)*.[506]

370. Crimes of real endangerment are so referred to because the consequences of such a crime (action or omission) create a concrete (or real) danger to the legally protected interests. The occurrence of the harmful consequences is possible, and more than likely, without any additional factors.[507] An example can be leaving an unconscious person in a room which is full of propane gas (Article 125 UKR, failure to render help). The concrete consequences can be specifically provided for by the legal provisions. For instance, according to Article 217 UKR, the violation of safety rules mentioned on explosive objects is penalized under specific circumstances, namely "if this could entail the death of a person or entailed the causing of large-scale damage."

371. Crimes of abstract endangerment are criminalized because of their general dangerousness to the legally protected interests. The protected interests could possibly be infringed in the present dangerous situation; however, only in connection with additional factors.[508] For example, as to drunk driving, the danger of the occurrence of harmful results is, in itself, relatively high. However, the concrete infringement occurs only under the influence of additional circumstances (e.g., a pedestrian crossing the street who is run over by a drunk driver).

§3. Subject of Crime and Object of Crime

I. Object of Crime

372. As mentioned before, along with the objective side of crime and the subjective side of crime, the subject of crime and the **object of crime** *(объект преступления)* are also components of a crime.[509]

373. The Russian criminal law system distinguishes between the "**object of crime**" *(объект преступления)*—legally protected social relationships that are infringed and classified according to a certain criterion (e.g., ownership)—and the "**object**" *(предмет преступления)*—material items which are impacted by an offender (e.g., a ring).[510] Pure conduct offenses do not have an object, for instance, desertion (Article 338 UKR).

---

506. Kropachev, Ugolovnoe pravo Rossii, p. 420; Kudryavzev, Ugolovnoe pravo Rossii, pp. 138–139; Zhuravlev, Ugolovnoe pravo, p. 89.
507. Kudryavzev, Ugolovnoe pravo Rossii, p. 138.
508. Kropachev, Ugolovnoe pravo Rossii, p. 420; Kudryavzev, Ugolovnoe pravo Rossii, pp. 138–139.
509. For the concept of the criminal offense, *see* Part I, Chapter 3, §1, paras. 317–321.
510. Kropachev, Ugolovnoe pravo Rossii, p. 371.

374. The objects of crime are classified as follows: **general** *(общий)*, **generic** *(родовой)*, **specific** *(видовой)*, and **direct** *(непосредственный)* .[511]

375. The general object of crime represents the whole amount of legally protected social relationships in criminal law. The generic object of crime represents the group of certain legally protected interests or homogenous social relationships protected by the provisions of sections of the Special Part of the UKR (e.g., section 10, state power; section 8, economic crimes).

376. The specific objects of crime are different groups of protected interests within the generic object, which are found in the chapters of the Special Part (e.g., the foundations of the constitutional system or fundamentals of justice).

377. The direct object of crime—the most specific one—represents a protected legal interest infringed on a concrete crime. For instance, personal property can be the direct object of different crimes: theft, fraud, or robbery.[512]

II. Subject of Crime

378. The following components are included within the analysis of the **subject of crime** *(субъект преступления)*: **age of criminal responsibility** *(возраст уголовной ответственности)*,[513] **mental disturbance** *(психическое расстройство)*, *and* **committing a crime in a state of intoxication** *(совершение преступления в состоянии опьянения)*. Mental disturbance and committing a crime in a state of intoxication are discussed within **imputability** *(вменяемость)*—mental capacity.[514]

379. Hence, according to Articles 19–23 UKR, only a natural person (Russian citizen, foreign citizen, or stateless person) of sound mind (imputable), who has attained the age of 16 or 14 (in some cases), shall be subject to criminal responsibility. This legal doctrine is based on the principle of individual responsibility.[515] However, the problem of criminal liability of legal persons has been discussed in Russian criminal law doctrine.[516]

380. Furthermore, certain offenses can be committed only by a defined group of individuals—by "**special subjects of crime**" *(специальный субъект преступления)*.

511. Zhuravlev, Ugolovnoe pravo, pp. 76–78.
512. For the concept of the criminal offense, *see* Part I, Chapter 3, §1, paras. 317–321.
513. On justification, excuse, and other grounds of impunity, *see* Part I, Chapter 4, paras. 429–528.
514. On justification, excuse, and other grounds of impunity, *see* Part I, Chapter 4, paras. 429–528.
515. Naumov, Rossiiskoe ugolovnoe pravo, p. 345.
516. For the the difference between criminal and administrative law, *see* paras. 218, 327–330. Legal persons are punished under administrative (quasi criminal law) for criminal liability of legal persons, *see* paras. 112, 379.

381. The first type of these offenses indicates the special qualifications of the perpetrator that establish criminal liability.[517] These qualifications are obligatory in order for an act to be a crime. For instance, violation of rules regarding combat duty can be committed only by military servicemen (Article 340 UKR), failure to render aid by physicians (Article 124 UKR) and official forgery is only criminal if it is committed by civil servants (Article 292 UKR).

382. The second group of offenses consists of acts that would be criminal regardless of the perpetrator's qualifications. However, the latter act as aggravating or mitigating circumstances for the purposes of punishment. For example, fraud or smuggling committed as an employee of an organization (Articles 159, paragraph 3, 188, paragraph 3 UKR) entails a more severe punishment compared to the same offense committed by an outsider.[518]

§4. The Moral or Mental Element (*Mens Rea*)

I. Subjective Guilt or Culpability

383. The **mental element or subjective side of crime** ***(субъективная сторона преступления)***, also referred to as *mens rea*, is regarded as an internal characteristic of the criminal offense which determines the mental (intellectual, volitional, and emotional) processes of the offender toward his unlawful conduct and its criminal consequences.[519]

384. The subjective side of a crime contains the following elements:

– culpability (in the form of intent or negligence);
– motives and goals of the crime;
– the emotional condition of the offender during the commission of a crime.

385. **Culpability** ***(вина)*** is an essential condition for criminal liability and the central characteristic of the subjective side of crime. In the criminal law doctrine, "culpability" is described as the mental attitude of the offender in the form of intent or negligence in regard to his criminal behavior and its consequences.[520]

386. Within "culpability," two components of the mental processes of the offender are analyzed: an **intellectual component** ***(интеллектуальный)*** —awareness of the social danger of his conduct—and a **volitional** one

517. Naumov, Rossiiskoe ugolovnoe pravo, p. 362; Zhuravlev, Ugolovnoe pravo, p. 105.
518. Paramonova, Objective aspects of the offense in Russia. In: Sieber, U. / Forster, S. / Jarvers, K. (ed(s).): National Criminal Law in a Comparative Legal Context. Volume 3.1: Defining criminal conduct. Berlin, Duncker & Humblot, 2011, p. 239–241.
519. Paramonova, Subjective aspects of the offense in Russia, 2011, p. 436; Kropachev, Ugolovnoe pravo Rossii, p. 372; Kudryavzev, Ugolovnoe pravo Rossii, p. 192; Naumov, Rossiiskoe ugolovnoe pravo, p. 364.
520. Lebedev, Kommentarii k UK RF, p. 48; Naumov, Rossiiskoe ugolovnoe pravo, p. 365.

(волевой)—the conscious concentration of mental and physical efforts on the achievement of certain goals (in other words, wishing or permitting the occurrence of socially dangerous results, or the confidence that all socially dangerous results can be prevented).[521]

387. Basically, objectively illegal behavior and harmful results cannot be considered criminal without the will (volitional component) and understanding (intellectual component) of them by the offender.

388. The **principle of culpability** *(принцип вины)*, which is legally defined in the Criminal Code of the Russian Federation, prohibits objective imputability or liability (Article 5 UKR).[522] According to the principle of culpability, a person shall be subject to criminal responsibility only for those criminalized socially dangerous acts and consequences which ensued, and with respect to which his guilt has been established (Article 5 UKR).

Art. 5 UKR (Principle of Culpability)

1. A person shall be subject to criminal responsibility only for those socially dangerous actions (or omissions), and the socially dangerous consequences which ensued, with respect to which guilt has been established.
2. Objective imputability, that is, criminal responsibility for the causing of harm without guilt, shall not be permitted.

Art. 28 UKR (Infliction of Harm without Guilt)

1. An act shall be deemed to be committed without guilt if the person who has committed it has not realized and could not realize the social danger of his action (omission) due to the circumstances of the case, or has not foreseen the possibility of the occurrence of socially dangerous consequences, and could not or should not foresee them due to the circumstances of the case.
2. An act shall be deemed to be committed without guilt if the person who has committed it, although having foreseen the possibility of the occurrence of the socially dangerous consequences of his actions (omission), could not prevent these consequences because of an inconformity of his psycho-physiological abilities which has arisen due to the extreme conditions, or nervous and psychic stresses, which comprise it.

389. Chapter 5 UKR (Articles 24–28) is completely devoted to the concept of "culpability." According to Articles 24–26 UKR, the division of "**culpability**" into

521. Kudryavzev, Ugolovnoe pravo Rossii, p. 199; Lebedev, Kommentarii k UK RF, p. 49.
522. For the principle of culpability and principles of criminal law, *see* Part I, Chapter 1, paras. 194–196.

two **forms** ***(формы вины)***, **intent** ***(умысел)*** and **negligence** ***(неосторожность)***, is based on the differing content and combination of the intellectual and the volitional elements.

390. As a general rule, **motives** ***(мотив)*** and goals ***(цель)*** of the crime, as well as the **emotional condition** ***(эмоциональное состояние)*** of the offender are optional features of the subjective side of crime. They can be taken into consideration, for instance, as mitigating or aggravating circumstances. However, these characteristics can become obligatory if they are explicitly defined by the UKR as a feature of a certain crime. For example, homicide with motives of racial or religious hatred (Article 105, paragraph 2, item k UKR) is a self-contained crime along with homicide (Article 105, paragraph 1 UKR).

391. In the doctrine, the issue of whether motives and goals are always included within "culpability" is disputed. In contrast to the psychological view where motives and goals are an inherent part of "culpability," the formal juridical concept regards them as separate elements of the subjective side of crime.[523]

II. Intent

A. Definition and Elements of Intent

392. The main theoretical aspects of "**intent**" ***(умысел)*** are legally defined in the present Criminal Code (Article 25 UKR).

Art. 25 UKR (Crime Committed Intentionally)

(1) An act committed with direct intent or indirect intent shall be deemed to be a crime committed intentionally.
(2) A crime shall be deemed to be committed with direct intent if the person was aware of the social danger of his actions (omissions), foresaw the possibility or inevitability of socially dangerous consequences ensuing from them, and wished for these consequences to ensue.
(3) A crime shall be committed with indirect intent if the person was aware of the social danger of his actions (omissions), foresaw the possibility of socially dangerous consequences ensuing, and did not wish them, but consciously permitted these consequences, or was indifferent to them.

393. In the doctrine, "intent" is represented through a combination of intellectual and volitional elements. It is regarded as the mental attitude of the offender who was aware of the social danger of his actions (omissions), foresaw the possibility or

523. Paramonova, Subjective aspects of the offense in Russia, 2011, pp. 436–437; Kudryavzev, Ugolovnoe pravo Rossii, pp. 194, 195; Lebedev, Kommentarii k UK RF, p. 50.

inevitability of the ensuing of socially dangerous consequences (intellectual element) and wished the ensuing thereof, or consciously permitted these consequences, or was indifferent to them (volitional element).[524]

394. The "intent" applies to the objective offense elements (social danger, causality, and socially dangerous consequences).[525] Meaning that the offender has to commit criminal acts with intent (one of its forms) and at least take into consideration relevant harmful consequences. His/her intent has to include causality between his/her criminal behavior and the consequences.

395. Within the **intellectual element**, the following components refer to the objective offense elements:

- The **consciousness of social danger** *(осознание общественной опасности)* by the offender of his conduct in general features (i.e., in factual and social aspects) is sufficient for "intent."[526] For instance, by committing a theft, the offender is aware that he is stealing property belonging to someone else (factual aspect) as well as that he is infringing proprietary rights with his action (social aspect).[527]
- By foresight of the **inevitability** *(неизбежность)* of the ensuing of socially dangerous consequences (only by direct intent), the offender consciously excludes any factors that could influence intended causality: meaning that—according to the offender—socially dangerous consequences will occur for sure.
- The foresight of the **possibility** *(возможность)* of the ensuing of socially dangerous consequences means that the offender admits that the consequences may, for some reason, not occur. In this case, the offender is not sure whether harmful results will occur or not.

396. To illustrate the intellectual element, the following two situations can be considered:

1. M, who is physically strong, threw B (after a quarrel with him) out of the window from the 14th floor, and B died.
2. In the same situation, M threw B out of the window of the second-floor apartment, and B died.

397. In the first situation, the offender foresaw the inevitability of the occurrence of death. However, in the case of the second-floor apartment incident, the offender regarded death only as a possible harmful result, which would depend on additional factors (e.g., whether B fell onto grass or onto a heap of bricks, etc.).

524. Paramonova, Subjective aspects of the offense in Russia, 2011, pp. 438–439.
525. On the objective aspects of the offense, *see* Part I, Chapter 3, §2, paras. 342–371.
526. Lebedev, Kommentarii k UK RF, p. 51.
527. Naumov, Rossiiskoe ugolovnoe pravo, p. 373.

398. The **volitional content** of the intent refers to either wishing the ensuing of socially dangerous consequences, or to consciously allowing them, or indifference toward them.[528] Hence, the volitional content of the intent refers to the wish or "want," whereas the intellectual component refers to "know." The wish is characterized as striving for certain results that appear as a final goal or as an intermediate stage of the conduct. The wish can include means to achieve criminal goals.

399. The intent of the offender refers to different objective offense elements. It can either include harmful (or socially dangerous) consequences as an element or not. It depends on the construction of the crime (classification of material or result and formal crimes[529]). In formal crimes, which do not require certain harmful results, the intent refers only to the socially dangerous action (omission), for example, perjury is punishable as such independently, whether further harmful circumstances occur (Article 307 UKR). Hence, intent in the cases of formal crimes does not require harmful consequences as an objective element of offense. In result crimes, intent should encompass all three obligatory elements: socially dangerous action/omission, causality, and socially dangerous consequences, for instance, intent in homicide.

400. The intent encompasses the present and future circumstances of the case. However, intent also referring to the future circumstances should exist at the time of the commission of a crime. In conduct crimes, such as slander without aggravating circumstances, it is sufficient that the intent encompasses the present socially dangerous conduct. However, if, as a result of this crime, certain grave circumstances have occurred, e.g., the suicide of the victim, there are two possibilities to qualify this criminal behavior. The qualification depends on whether intent encompassed the occurred socially dangerous consequences at the time of the commission of a crime or not. If it did encompass, then it is considered to be slander with aggravating circumstances. If it did not, it is qualified as a criminal behavior conducted with two forms of culpability: an intentional form of guilt for criminal conduct and negligent form of culpability for the undesired consequences, Article 27 UKR.[530] In result crimes with a later ensuing of the socially dangerous consequences, the intent of the offender at the time of the commission of the crime should refer first to the present criminal behavior and second to the future harmful results. Result crimes can be committed with two forms of culpability.[531]

528. Naumov, Rossiiskoe ugolovnoe pravo, p. 374.

529. On the objective aspects of the offense, *see* Part I, Chapter 3, §2, paras. 342–371.

530. For types of intent, *see* paras. 401–408.

531. For types of intent, *see* paras. 401–408; Paramonova, Subjective aspects of the offense in Russia, 2011, pp. 438–439.

B. Types of Intent

1. Direct Intent (Dolus Directus)

401. According to Article 25 UKR, intent has been classified into two types: direct and indirect intent. The main difference between these two types of intent lies in the volitional element. With regard to direct intent—in contrast to indirect intent—an offender must wish that socially dangerous consequences ensue.[532]

402. **Direct intent** ***(прямой умысел)*** has three features that are legally defined (Article 25, paragraph 2 UKR). In the doctrine, these features are analyzed within the intellectual and volitional elements. The following requirements should be fulfilled in order to affirm direct intent:

- consciousness of social danger (intellectual element);
- foresight of the inevitability or possibility of the ensuing of socially dangerous consequences (intellectual element);
- wishing of the ensuing of the socially dangerous consequences (volitional element).[533]

403. An example of the direct intent is the following situation: hitting another person into the heart with a knife.

2. Indirect Intent

404. The **indirect intent** ***(косвенный умысел)*** consists of the following features (Article 25, paragraph 3 UKR):

- consciousness of social danger (intellectual element);
- foresight of the possibility of the ensuing of socially dangerous consequences (intellectual element);
- not wishing the ensuing of socially dangerous consequences, but a conscious allowance of them, or indifference to them (volitional element).[534]

405. An example of indifference: two robbers, B and F, beat up an old lady and leave her alone unconscious in her apartment. She dies. In this case, B and F foresaw the possibility of the ensuing death but were indifferent to this fact.

532. Paramonova, Subjective aspects of the offense in Russia, 2011, p. 440.
533. Ignatov/Krasikov, Kurs rossijskogo ugolovnogo prava, p. 212; Naumov, Rossiiskoe ugolovnoe pravo, pp. 373–374.
534. Ignatov/Krasikov, Kurs rossijskogo ugolovnogo prava, pp. 212–217; Naumov, Rossiiskoe ugolovnoe pravo, pp. 375–379.

406. Hence, the deciding difference between direct and indirect intent is rooted in the volitional element: wishing of the harmful results (direct intent) and not wishing but conscious permission thereof or indifference to them (indirect intent). Therefore, the offender having indirect intent, has a passive attitude toward socially dangerous consequences. For this reason, indirect intent is regarded as less dangerous than a direct intent.[535]

3. Other Classifications of Intent

407. In Russian criminal law doctrine, there are further classifications of types of intent. However, they do not create new forms of culpability. In judicial practice and doctrine, they serve to create a better understanding of the intellectual and volitional content of intent. The two-type classification into direct and indirect intent is the only determining differentiation for culpability.[536]

408. There are further classifications of types of intent in the doctrine:

Within the first group, two types of intent are distinguished depending on the time of the forming of intent: **deliberate intent** ***(заранее обдуманный умысел)*** and **spontaneously formed intent** ***(внезапно возникший умысел)***. The first type is considered to be (the) more dangerous one: the intention to commit a crime and the crime itself are separated temporally. Within this period of time, the offender becomes more assured in his decision to commit the crime. The second type refers to the intent to commit a crime that is executed immediately after it is formed (e.g., A sees a banknote sticking out of somebody's pocket and steels it: "saw-stole"-model).[537]
In the second group, the classification of intent is characterized by the level of awareness of the offender of socially dangerous results being caused by his acts. This classification distinguishes determined and undetermined intent.
Determined intent ***(определенный умысел)*** requires a precise vision by the offender of the harmful result1s. It can be of two forms: **simple** ***(простой умысел)*** and **alternative** ***(альтернативный умысел)***. In the simple form, the offender foresees one harmful result, for example, the death of a victim by striking him in the heart with a knife. In the alternative form, the offender takes two or more socially dangerous consequences into account (e.g., death or grave harm to health by striking a victim with a knife into the stomach).
Undetermined intent ***(неопределенный умысел)*** is characterized by the awareness of the offender of socially dangerous conduct and results. However, this view of the harmful consequences is not concrete. The offender accepts a whole variety of possible ensuing results from his/her conduct. For instance, in hitting someone on the head with a stick, the offender accepts a range of consequences from light to

535. Paramonova, Subjective aspects of the offense in Russia, 2011, p. 440.
536. Paramonova, Subjective aspects of the offense in Russia, 2011, p. 441; Naumov, Rossiiskoe ugolovnoe pravo, p. 379.
537. Lebedev, Kommentarii k UK RF, p. 54; Naumov, Rossiiskoe ugolovnoe pravo, p. 379.

grave harm to the health of the victim. In accordance with the judicial practice in the case of undetermined intent, criminal responsibility depends on the factually caused harmful results because the offender foresaw and permitted any of these consequences to ensue.[538]

III. Negligence/Recklessness

A. *Definition*

409. "**Negligence**" ***(неосторожность)*** is another and less grave than the intent form of culpability. Negligence is defined through a combination of intellectual and volitional elements and is considered as the negative mental attitude of the offender toward the ensuing of socially dangerous consequences (intellectual element), the occurrence of which he does not consider possible and does not wish (volitional element).[539]

B. *The Criminalization of Negligence*

410. As a form of culpability, negligence is legally defined in the Criminal Code (Article 26 UKR).

411. Furthermore, negligent action is deemed to be a crime only when it is specially provided for by the respective article of the UKR (Article 24, paragraph 2 UKR).[540]

> Art. 24 UKR (Forms of Culpability)
>
> (1) […]
> (2) An act committed negligently shall be recognized as a crime only in cases where this is specially provided for by the relevant Article of the Special Part of this code.

538. Lebedev, Kommentarii k UK RF, p. 54; Naumov, Rossiiskoe ugolovnoe pravo, pp. 380–381; Paramonova, Subjective aspects of the offense in Russia, 2011, pp. 440–441.
539. Lebedev, Kommentarii k UK RF, p. 57; Ignatov/Krasikov, Kurs rossijskogo ugolovnogo prava, p. 217; Paramonova, Subjective aspects of the offense in Russia, 2011, p. 442.
540. Paramonova, Subjective aspects of the offense in Russia, 2011, p. 442.

Art. 26 UKR (Crime Committed through Negligence)

(1) An act committed through mindlessness or carelessness shall be deemed to be a crime committed through negligence.
(2) A crime shall be deemed to be committed through mindlessness if the person foresaw the possibility of the ensuing of the socially dangerous consequences of his actions (or omissions) but, without sufficient grounds, self-confidently counted on the prevention of these consequences.
(3) A crime shall be committed through carelessness if the person did not foresee the possibility of the ensuing of the socially dangerous consequences of his actions (omissions), although with necessary attentiveness and prudence these consequences should and could have been foreseen.

412. The legal definition of negligence is constructed for result crimes.[541] In this case, negligence refers to the following objective offense elements: socially dangerous conduct, causality, and socially dangerous consequences. Meaning that the attitude of the offender shall be negligent toward his criminal conduct, harmful consequences, and the causality between them. Thus, in the case of mindlessness (if the offender counted on the prevention of the harmful consequences), he should have foreseen not only the occurrence of the socially dangerous consequences but also the causality between his conduct and the consequences. For example, a bus driver overtakes a car on a dangerous segment of a high-speed highway relying on his professional skills. However, with regard to carelessness, even if the offender did not foresee the possibility of the occurrence of the negative results, he would still be liable if he could be expected to have predicted the situation, at least to some extent, according to objective and subjective criteria.

413. In the case of formal crimes, so-called conduct crimes, negligence can be applied merely to socially dangerous behavior; the occurrence of the harmful consequences is irrelevant for criminal liability. However, whether formal crimes, in general, can be committed with negligence is a controversial issue in the doctrine.[542] According to the majority opinion, they cannot be committed with negligence by reason that "conduct crimes," as such, implicate the intentional commission (e.g., contempt of court, Article 297 UKR).[543]

414. Negligence, as well as intent, refers to the present and future circumstances of the situation, which the offender realizes (or should and could realize) at the time of committing a crime.[544]

541. On the result crime, *see* para. 399; on the objective aspects of the offense, *see* Part I, Chapter 3, §2, paras. 342–371.
542. Kropachev, Ugolovnoe pravo Rossii, p. 482.
543. Lebedev, Kommentarii k UK RF, p. 57; Naumov, Rossiiskoe ugolovnoe pravo, p. 381.
544. Paramonova, Subjective aspects of the offense in Russia, 2011, pp. 442–443.

C. Types of Negligence

415. Article 26 of the Russian Criminal Code provides for two forms of negligence: mindlessness and carelessness. Both forms are compounded by the intellectual and volitional elements.[545]

416. **Mindlessness** *(легкомыслие)* as the mental attitude of the offender toward his action must satisfy the following requirements:

- foresight of the possibility of the ensuing of socially dangerous consequences (intellectual element);
- self-confidently counting on the prevention of the harmful consequences without sufficient grounds (volitional element).[546]

417. The legal formulation of the intellectual element of mindlessness and indirect intent is the same: "foresight of the possibility of the ensuing of socially dangerous consequences." However, the character of the intellectual element (of foresight) is different. With regard to indirect intent, it has more concrete features. For instance, the offender striking a victim with a knife in the stomach foresees that the harmful result will be caused by his concrete act. In contrast, in the case of mindlessness, the individual has only a vague perception of the possibly ensuing dangerous consequences. For example, a bus driver overtaking a car on a dangerous segment of a high-speed highway could foresee a possible accident with a suddenly appearing third car that he could not initially see.

418. The main difference between mindlessness and intent (direct and indirect) lies in the volitional element. With regard to mindlessness (as distinct from intent), the will of the offender is directed to the prevention of the harmful consequences: he counts on certain circumstances, which are sufficient, to his mind, to prevent the harmful results. For example, in the last-mentioned case, the bus driver counted on his professional skills, driving experience, the good technical condition of the bus, etc. Unfortunately, his estimations were wrong because of the suddenly changed circumstances; he could have predicted the consequences. However, he did not necessarily approve of these consequences and did not want them to happen.[547]

419. **Carelessness** *(небрежность)* has the following features:

- non-foresight of the possibility of the ensuing of socially dangerous consequences (intellectual element);
- possibility of the foresight (should and could) of the socially dangerous results with necessary attentiveness and prudence (volitional element).[548]

545. Paramonova, Subjective aspects of the offense in Russia, 2011, p. 443.
546. Naumov, Rossiiskoe ugolovnoe pravo, pp. 382–384.
547. Paramonova, Subjective aspects of the offense in Russia, 2011, p. 444.
548. Naumov, Rossiiskoe ugolovnoe pravo, pp. 384–388.

420. The intellectual element of carelessness is strongly differentiated from the intellectual element of both intent (direct and indirect) and mindlessness. In committing a crime with carelessness, the offender does not foresee the possibility of the ensuing socially dangerous consequences. Hence, the consciousness of social danger does not exist. Accordingly, culpability is founded in the volitional element of carelessness and not in the intellectual element.

421. The volitional element has two criteria: objective (should have foreseen) and subjective (could have foreseen the socially dangerous consequences).

422. The doctrine and judicial practice connect the **objective criterion** ***(объективный критерий)*** with the responsibilities of individuals by way of legal provisions and generally accepted rules, as well as their profession. The responsibilities that are placed on an individual as a consequence of the following considerations require that he/she is able to foresee the ensuing socially dangerous consequences. For example, an engineer has to act according to the safety guidelines and professional standards of which he is deemed to be aware.

423. The **subjective criterion** ***(субъективный критерий)*** refers to the individual person himself by reference to his personal skills, qualifications, knowledge, health condition, etc., and based on this, his ability to foresee the harmful results ("could have foreseen").

424. For instance, an experienced fisherman who knew the river well pushed his friend into the river from a small bridge as a joke, thinking the river was deep enough. The latter struck the bottom of the river and drowned. In this case, the fisherman should have (objectively) and could have foreseen (subjectively) the socially dangerous consequences. First, according to generally accepted rules of human behavior, pushing somebody into the water can cause harm. Second, by virtue of his additional experience of fishing in the river for a long time, he could have known that the river was not deep enough at that place.[549]

IV. Principle of Culpability

425. The principle of culpability is one of the central criteria of Russian criminal law and is found in the prohibition of criminal liability without guilt (Articles 5, 28 UKR). Hence, an act, in order to be qualified as a criminal act, must be committed either intentionally or negligently.[550]

549. Paramonova, Subjective aspects of the offense in Russia, 2011, pp. 444–445.
550. Paramonova, Subjective aspects of the offense in Russia, 2011, p. 445.

Art. 5 UKR (Principle of Culpability)

1. A person shall be subject to criminal responsibility only for those socially dangerous actions (or omissions), and the socially dangerous consequences which ensued, with respect to which guilt has been established.
2. Objective imputability, that is, criminal responsibility for the causing of harm without guilt, shall not be permitted.

Art. 28 UKR (Infliction of Harm without Guilt)

1. An act shall be deemed to be committed without guilt if the person who has committed it has not realized and could not realize the social danger of his action (omission) due to the circumstances of the case, or has not foreseen the possibility of the occurrence of socially dangerous consequences, and could not or should not foresee them due to the circumstances of the case.
2. An act shall be deemed to be committed without guilt if the person who has committed it, although having foreseen the possibility of the occurrence of the socially dangerous consequences of his actions (omission), could not prevent these consequences because of an inconformity of his psycho-physiological abilities which has arisen due to the extreme conditions, or nervous and psychic stresses, which comprise it.

V. Criminal Liability with Two Forms of Culpability

426. Besides intent and negligence, contemporary Russian criminal law (Article 27 UKR) contains the construction "**criminal responsibility with two forms of culpability**" *(ответственность за преступление с двумя формами вины).*[551]

Art. 27 UKR (Responsibility for Crime Committed with Two Forms of Culpability)
If as a result of the commission of an intentional crime grave consequences are caused which, according to a law entail a more severe punishment, and which were not encompassed by the intent of the person, criminal responsibility for such consequences shall ensue only in the case where the person foresaw the possibility of their ensuing but without sufficient grounds self-confidently counted on the prevention thereof, or in the event the person did not foresee, but should and could have foreseen the possibility of the ensuing of these consequences. As a whole, such crime shall be deemed to have been committed intentionally.

427. According to this construction, one form of culpability refers to socially dangerous conduct and another to the socially dangerous consequences of the act.

551. Naumov, Rossiiskoe ugolovnoe pravo, pp. 388–390; Lebedev, Kommentarii k UK RF, pp. 60–61.

However, this scheme is applicable only when the main crime has been committed intentionally (direct or indirect intent), and the mental attitude toward the ensued consequences is stated in the form of negligence (mindlessness or carelessness). Examples of these crimes are the illegal performance of abortion (with direct or indirect intent), death of the victim through negligence (Article 123, paragraph 3 UKR) and intentional causing of grave harm to health (with direct or indirect intent), which entailed the death of the victim through negligence (Article 111, paragraph 4 UKR). This construction serves the precise qualification of crimes, especially of contiguous crimes. For instance, in the case of, Article 111, paragraph 4 UKR (intentional causing of grave harm to health, which entailed the death of the victim through negligence), the "two forms of culpability"—construction allows this crime to be distinguished from similar crimes: namely, intentional homicide and causing death through negligence.

428. Although the crimes committed with two forms of culpability are deemed to be intentional, this form of culpability is less dangerous than that of both direct and indirect intent. The reason is that the offender's intent did not exist with respect to socially dangerous consequences. As a result, criminal punishment is less severe.[552]

552. Paramonova, Subjective aspects of the offense in Russia, 2011, pp. 445–446.

Chapter 4. Justification, Excuse, and Other Grounds of Impunity

§1. General Principles

I. Overview: Grounds for Excluding Criminal Liability

429. Grounds for excluding criminal liability arise when a conduct that is formally a crime is committed under such circumstances that it is not regarded as socially dangerous and, therefore, not deserving of criminalization. For example, acting in necessary defense (Article 37 UKR) and causing harm to a detained person who has committed a crime (Article 38 UKR) are recognized as conducts that are socially useful and appropriate despite the fact that they may cause harm to a legally protected interest. With a view toward the safeguarding of social values, other legally protected interests—those that are more highly valued— are given priority.[553]

430. Due to the fact that the grounds listed above nullify the social danger of the conduct at issue, instead imbue it with characteristics of a socially useful nature, these norms are sometimes called **inciting or stimulating** ***(поощрительные или стимулирующие нормы)***. This is because the aim of these rules is to improve the social activity of citizens and law enforcement officials in certain situations in the performance of their civil and/or official duties, while they at the same time prevent crime and eliminate imminent danger to the legally protected interests of the individual, society, and the state.[554]

431. Russian criminal law, strictly speaking, does not differentiate between justifications and excuses. According to both legislation and jurisprudence, the following are the main **grounds**[555] **for excluding criminal liability** ***(обстоятельства, исключающие преступность деяния)*** that can be referred to as "justifications": necessary defense (Article 37 UKR), causing harm to a detained person who has committed a crime (Article 38 UKR), extreme necessity (Article 39 UKR), physical or mental coercion (Article 40 UKR), justified risk (Article 41 UKR), carrying out of order or instruction (Article 42 UKR),[556] and insignificance. Such justification as **"insignificance"** ***(малозначительность)*** descends from the definition of crime and applies to the acts that are formally regarded as criminal offenses but by virtue of their insignificance do not represent a social danger, for example, a theft of RUB 2 (Article 14, paragraph 2 UKR).[557]

553. Naumov, Rossiiskoe ugolovnoe pravo, p. 485; Komissarov/Krilova/Tyazhkova, Ugolovnoe pravo RF, pp. 450–453.
554. Revin, Ugolovnoe pravo Rossii, pp. 170–172.
555. *See* Plenum of the Highest Court of the Russian Federation, Sep. 27, 2012.
556. Paramonova, Grounds for excluding criminal liability in Russia. In: Sieber, U. / Jarvers, K. /Silverman, E. (ed(s).): Grounds for excluding criminal liability. Berlin, Duncker & Humblot, 2016, pp.129–131.
557. For the concept of the criminal offense, *see* Part I, Chapter 3, §1 paras. 317–321; Paramonova, Grounds for excluding criminal liability in Russia. In: Sieber, U. / Jarvers, K. /Silverman, E. (ed(s).): Grounds for excluding criminal liability. Berlin, Duncker & Humblot, 2016, pp.129–131.

432. Additional grounds excluding criminal liability—that can be referred to as 'excuses'—are based on the following two criteria: age and health.[558] The first category applies to individuals who are not subject to criminal liability due to their failure to fulfill an obligatory criterion of criminal liability: age. The second major category applies to individuals who are not subject to criminal liability due to the criterion of health. Insanity, for example, defined as the suspect's inability to understand or govern his or her actions due to a number of listed conditions, may exclude criminal liability (Article 21, paragraph 1 UKR).

433. According to the **formal-substantive concept of the criminal offense** *(формально-материальное определение)* as recognized by legal provisions, jurisprudence, and legal scholarship, in order to be considered criminal, an act has to be illegal in form (i.e., criminalized by the UKR)[559] and socially dangerous in content (Article 14 UKR).[560] This concept encompasses the four main definitional elements (indicators) of a criminal offense: a criminal offense is, first, a **socially dangerous act or omission** *(общественно опасное деяние)* second, prohibited by means of a provision of criminal law (**illegality**, *противоправность*) under threat of, third, punishment (**punishability**, *наказуемость*) and, fourth, committed culpably (**culpability**, *виновность*).[561] If an act fails to fulfill even one of these four criteria, it does not entail criminal liability.

434. In the legal literature, it is disputed whether conduct that does not entail criminal liability due to one of the grounds for excluding criminal responsibility fails to fulfill only one criterion of Article 14 UKR or all four.[562] One group of authors argues that such conduct does not comply with the substantive criterion, that is, is not considered socially dangerous. It means that the conduct fails to conform to the other criteria, namely, illegality, punishability, and culpability, as well. As a result, the conduct fails to fulfill all four criteria by missing one.[563]

435. A second group of authors takes the view that depending on the particular ground for excluding criminal liability, one of the four criteria is not fulfilled.[564] For example, in the case of necessary defense (Article 37 UKR), social dangerousness (Article 14, paragraph 1 UKR) is absent, although other elements—according to these authors—are present. As far as the offense of carrying out an order or instruction (Article 42 UKR) is concerned, intent as the necessary element of the subjective side of the offense and, hence, culpability, is absent. Thus, in this context,

558. Komissarov/Krilova/Tyazhkova, Ugolovnoe pravo RF, pp. 273–296.
559. For the principle of legality, *see* Part I, Chapter 1, paras. 197–226; for a discussion of the formal-substantive concept of the criminal offense, *see* Part I, Chapter 3, §1, paras. 326–330.
560. Kropachev, Ugolovnoe pravo Rossii, p. 326. On the concept of social danger, *see* Part I, Chapter 3, §1, paras. 317–321.
561. Lebedev, Kommentarii k UK RF, p. 54; Kropachev, Ugolovnoe pravo Rossii, p. 334; for the concept of the criminal offense, *see* Part I, Chapter 3, §1, paras. 317–321.
562. Ragog, Ugolovnoe pravo, p. 259; Komissarov/Krilova/Tyazhkova, Ugolovnoe pravo RF, p. 452.
563. Naumov, Rossiiskoe ugolovnoe pravo, p. 485.
564. Ragog, Ugolovnoe pravo, p. 259.

objectively illegal behavior and socially dangerous results are not considered criminal if the offender acts without the necessary will and understanding. This is due to the **principle of culpability** ***(принцип вины)***, which is defined in the Criminal Code and which prohibits objective (strict) imputability (Article 5 UKR).[565]

436. This discussion regarding the relationship of the various grounds for excluding criminal liability to the necessary definitional elements (indicators) of the criminal offense is theoretical in nature. Regardless of the theory applied, the legal consequence, that is, the exclusion of criminal liability, is the same.[566]

437. If there is a ground for excluding criminal liability but its prerequisites are only partially fulfilled, the situation can be treated by the court as a circumstance mitigating punishment. Similarly, in the case of excess, the court could still consider mitigating the punishment, even if the conditions for the ground, excluding criminal liability, are not met.

438. This rule applies with regard to any ground for excluding criminal liability (Article 61, paragraph 1, item f and g UKR). For example, in a situation where the limits of extreme necessity are exceeded, it can be regarded as a circumstance in which punishment should be mitigated (Article 61, paragraph 1, item g UKR). Provocative or immoral conduct on the part of the victim, which is not recognized as a ground for excluding criminal liability, also leads to a mitigated punishment (Article 61, paragraph 1, item h UKR). Punishment imposed for a crime that was committed out of compassion can also be mitigated (Article 61, paragraph 1, item e UKR). Consent of the victim does not, however, exclude the criminality of the act.[567]

II. Grounds for Excluding Criminal Liability, Grounds for Terminating Criminal Liability, Grounds Hindering Criminal Liability, and Other Similar Grounds

439. It is necessary to differentiate between grounds for excluding criminal liability, grounds for terminating criminal liability,[568] grounds hindering criminal liability, and other similar grounds, for example, abandonment of attempt.

440. In the context of the grounds **for excluding criminal responsibility** ***(обстоятельства, исключающие преступность деяния)***, which include acting in necessary defense (Article 37 UKR), acting under physical or mental coercion (Article 40 UKR), and carrying out an order or instruction (Article 42 UKR),

565. On the principles of criminal law, *see* Part I, Chapter 1, paras. 194–196; on the subjective aspects of the offense, *see* Part I, Chapter 3, §4, paras. 383–428.
566. Paramonova, Grounds for excluding criminal liability in Russia. In: Sieber, U. / Jarvers, K. /Silverman, E. (ed(s).): Grounds for excluding criminal liability. Berlin, Duncker & Humblot, 2015, pp. 126–134.
567. Komissarov/Krilova/Tyazhkova, Ugolovnoe pravo RF, p. 455.
568. For extinction of criminal liability, *see* Part III, Chapter 4, paras. 1456–1483.

one or more of the definitional elements of a criminal offense are changed or not fulfilled. For instance, in a case of physical coercion, social danger and/or "culpability" as a characteristic of the subjective side of crime are absent. As a result, an act carried out under such circumstances is not considered criminal. Certain grounds for excluding criminal liability have additional prerequisites with regard to relevant elements of a criminal offense. For example, in order to exclude criminal liability for carrying out an order or instruction (Article 42 UKR), the additional criterion of the "**special subject of crime**" ***(специальный субъект преступления)***, namely, the subordinate who carries out the order or instruction being in a hierarchical relationship with the person who gives the order/instruction, must be fulfilled.

441. It is important to distinguish between grounds for excluding criminal liability and grounds for terminating criminal liability.[569] In the case of excluded criminal liability, conduct is deemed not to be criminal. In contrast, in the case of termination of criminal liability, an act fulfills all the requirements of criminal liability and is thus regarded as criminal, but, due to certain provisions or further decisions, the act does not give rise to criminal liability and, as a result, punishment (or continued punishment) need not be served. For instance, a person may be convicted of a crime, but the criminal liability may be terminated due to the fact that he or she has reconciled with the victim (Article 76 UKR), or the person may be released from serving punishment due to a pardon (Article 85 UKR).[570] Grounds for terminating criminal liability are divided into two major groups: relief from criminal liability (Articles 75, 76, 78, 84, 90 UKR) and relief from (serving) criminal punishment (Articles 79–85 UKR).[571]

442. Grounds hindering criminal liability, such as immunity of members of both chambers of the Federal Assembly (Russian Parliament) (Article 98 of the Constitution of the Russian Federation of 1993, *Konstitucija Rossijskoj Federacii*, Const.[572]),[573] exclude criminal liability due to the absence of an obligatory element of crime—in this example, there is no proper **subject of crime** ***(субъект преступления)***.[574]

443. Abandonment of attempt is one of the grounds that, under certain circumstances, has the same legal consequences as a ground leading to relief from criminal liability.[575] However, abandonment of attempt can be regarded, as such, a ground only to a limited extent. For example, a person who voluntarily refuses to

569. For extinction of criminal liability, *see* Part III, Chapter 4, paras. 1456–1483.

570. On pardon, *see* Paramonova, Grounds for excluding criminal liability in Russia. In: Sieber, U. / Forster, S. / Jarvers, K. (ed(s).): National Criminal Law in a Comparative Legal Context. Berlin, Duncker & Humblot, 2016, pp.344–345.

571. On grounds for terminating or expunging criminal liability, *see* Paramonova, Grounds for excluding criminal liability in Russia. In: Sieber, U. / Forster, S. / Jarvers, K. (ed(s).): National Criminal Law in a Comparative Legal Context. Berlin, Duncker & Humblot, 2016, pp. 343–344.

572. Constitution of the Russian Federation, Dec. 12, 1993.

573. On the system of government, *see* General Introduction, §1, IV, paras. 11–20.

574. For elements of crime, *see* Part I, Chapter 3, §1 paras. 331–341, 2, 3.

575. For abandonment of attempt, *see* Part I, Chapter 5, paras. 580–589.

complete a crime (abandonment of attempt) is still subject to criminal liability if the act committed by him or her factually fulfills the requirements of another crime (Article 31, paragraph 3 UKR). Take, for example, offender A, who puts poison into B's glass but then changes his or her mind and gets rid of the glass (abandonment of attempt); if, however, another person, C, drinks from the glass before A gets rid of it, A is criminally liable for the negligent homicide of C, despite having abandoned the attempt to kill B.

§2. Grounds of Justification

I. Necessary Defense

A. General Characterization

444. A harmful act is considered to be an act of **necessary defense** ***(необходимая оборона)*** if it is carried out in the course of protecting the defending person and its rights or the rights of other persons or the legally protected interests of society or the state against a socially dangerous infringement if the infringement involves violence that threatens the defending person's or another person's life or involves a direct threat of the use of such violence (Article 37, paragraph 1 UKR).[576]

Art. 37 UKR (Necessary Defense)[577]

(1) It shall not be deemed as a crime when harm is inflicted in the state of necessary defense to an attacking person, that is, in the case of protection of the person and the rights of the defending person or other persons, the law-protected interests of the society or the state against a socially dangerous infringement, if such an infringement involved a violence threatening life of the defending person or another person or a direct threat of use of such a violence.

(2) Defense against an attack not involving a violence that is threatening life of the defending person or another person or not involving a direct threat of use of such a violence is legal if in this case the limits of necessary defense have not been exceeded, that is, intentional actions that have been committed which clearly do not correspond to the character and danger of the infringement.

(2.1.) Actions of a defending person shall not be deemed as exceeding the limits of necessary defense, if this person due to the unexpectedness of the infringement could not objectively assess the degree and nature of the threat.

---

576. Paramonova, Grounds for excluding criminal liability in Russia. In: Sieber, U. / Jarvers, K. /Silverman, E. (ed(s).): Grounds for excluding criminal liability. Berlin, Duncker & Humblot, 2015, pp.134–138.

577. All translations of the UKR in this chapter (revised by the author) are taken from Butler, Criminal Code of the Russian Federation.

(3) Legal provisions of this article are equally applied to all persons irrespectively of their professional or other special training background and employment position, as well as irrespectively of the possibility of evading a socially dangerous infringement or asking other persons or authorities for help.

445. Necessary defense is a subjective natural right enjoyed by each and every person: "Everyone shall have the right to protect his rights and freedoms by all means not prohibited by law" (Article 45 Const.). Article 45 UKR legitimizes the institution of necessary defense. The idea behind the non-criminalization in this context is the lack of social danger exhibited by an act of necessary defense if the act does not exceed established limits. Intentional actions that, for example, clearly do not correspond to the character and danger of the attack, exceed the limits of necessary defense (Article 37, paragraph 2 UKR). The essence and nature of this defense are manifested in an active form of conduct (actions) that are carried out in order to prevent or repel an attack, and that infringes upon the protected legal interests of the attacker.[578]

B. Requirements

446. The prerequisites for an act to qualify as an act of necessary defense are divided into two groups: those associated with the infringement of protected legal interests by the attacker and those associated with protection.[579]

1. Requirements Relating to the Attack

447. In order for an act to qualify as an act of necessary defense, the following prerequisites associated with the infringement of protected legal interests by the attacker must be met:

- social danger of the infringement;
- imminence of the infringement;
- existence in fact of the infringement.

448. An **attack** ***(посягательство)*** that causes or threatens to cause harm to specific legally protected public and state interests (life, health, public safety, property rights, etc.), for example, an attempt to commit a crime, is considered a socially

578. Revin, Ugolovnoe pravo Rossii, pp. 173–175.
579. Paramonova, Grounds for excluding criminal liability in Russia. In: Sieber, U. / Jarvers, K. /Silverman, E. (ed(s).): Grounds for excluding criminal liability. Berlin, Duncker & Humblot, 2015, pp.135–136.

dangerous infringement.[580] In order to be considered socially dangerous, infringements, as such, do not have to be criminally punishable. An (unpunishable) attack carried out by a mentally ill person who does not have the criminal capacity, for example, may be deemed socially dangerous.[581] It is sufficient that the infringement can be perceived as a criminal attack by means of objective indicators.

449. In the case of a sudden attack, the limits of the necessary defense are expanded: actions of a defending person do not exceed the limits of necessary defense if, due to the unexpectedness of the infringement, the defending person could not objectively assess the degree and nature of the threat (Article 37, paragraph 2.1 UKR).[582]

450. Acts of the original attacker undertaken in response to acts of necessary defense undertaken by the original victim are not regarded as a necessary defense.[583] For instance, if a person committing a robbery is strongly rebuffed by the victim, the putative robber cannot claim that the injury he or she inflicted upon the victim was carried out in order to avoid harm to him- or herself. In other words, the actions of someone who, by his or her own unlawful actions, provokes violent behavior toward him- or herself are not considered acts of necessary defense.[584]

451. The second prerequisite associated with the infringement of protected legal interests by an attacker is the imminence of the attack. An attack is considered imminent if an infringement has begun or, according to emerging conditions, will inevitably begin (e.g., a thief puts a hand into someone's pocket) but has not yet actually ended at the time the act of necessary defense is carried out.

452. The third prerequisite of necessary defense with regard to the infringement of protected legal interests is the objective existence of the infringement. Thus, an infringing attack must exist not only in the mind of the defending person but must also exist objectively and must have the potential to cause harm to legally protected interests.[585]

2. Requirements Relating to the Defense (Protection)

453. In order for an act to qualify as an act of necessary defense, the following prerequisites associated with **protection** *(защита)*—response to the infringement of protected legal interests by an attacker—must be met:[586]

---

580. On social dangerousness, *see* Part I, Chapter 3, §1, paras. 317–321; on attempt, *see* Part I, Chapter 5, paras. 544–589.
581. Naumov, Rossiiskoe ugolovnoe pravo, pp. 488–489.
582. *See* Plenum of the Highest Court of the Russian Federation, Sep. 27, 2012.
583. Naumov, Rossiiskoe ugolovnoe pravo, p. 490; Batichko, Uglovnoe pravo.
584. Revin, Ugolovnoe pravo Rossii, pp. 174–175; Naumov, Rossiiskoe ugolovnoe pravo, p. 490.
585. *See* Plenum of the Highest Court of the Russian Federation, Sep. 27, 2012.
586. *See* Plenum of the Highest Court of the Russian Federation, Sep. 27, 2012.

- proper object of protection;
- proper target of the defensive act;
- timeliness of the defensive act;
- proportionality of the defensive act.

454. The first prerequisite refers to the objects—legally protected social relationships or interests—that can be protected according to the rules of necessary defense. These objects include all legally protected interests (Article 37, paragraph 1 UKR): individual rights and legitimate interests of the defending person; individual rights and legitimate interests of other persons; legally protected interests of society; and legally protected interests of the state.

455. The second prerequisite involves the target of the defensive act: the act must be directed against the attacker (his or her life, health, property, etc.), not against third persons.

456. The third feature is the timeliness of the defensive act. The defensive act is considered timely if it is carried out during the actual infringement of protected legal interests by the attacker, that is, if it is carried out after the socially dangerous attack has begun and before it has ended. Actions of the defending person cannot be considered acts of necessary defense if they are carried out after the infringing attack has been prevented or completed and the defensive act is no longer needed. However, a defensive act is considered an act of necessary defense if, due to the circumstances, the time of completion of the infringing act was not clear to the defending person, and it is carried out immediately after the infringing act is completed. In judicial practice, for instance, it is generally accepted that the infringement does not immediately end when the defending person gains possession of weapons or other items used in the infringing attack.[587]

457. Under the fourth prerequisite, the defensive action may not exceed established limits of necessary defense; that is, the defensive action must be proportional. This is the case if no intentional actions are committed that clearly do not correspond to the character and danger of the attack (Article 37, paragraph 2 UKR).[588] Negligent acts that exceed the limits of necessary defense do not entail criminal responsibility.[589] Although the question of proportionality is an issue for the courts to decide on a case-by-case basis, the limits are determined by the interrelation between the defensive action and the danger posed by the infringing attack. A defensive action is considered excessive if the discrepancy between the danger it poses and the danger posed by the infringing attack is obvious. This discrepancy can be expressed, for example, in the intensity of the attack and the defensive act, in the

587. Naumov, Rossiiskoe ugolovnoe pravo, pp. 491–493; Bulleten Verhovnogo Suda RF, 1993, N 5, pp. 13–14.

588. On the definition and forms of intent, *see* Part I, Chapter 3, §3, II, paras. 392–408.

589. Batichko, Uglovnoe pravo. For definition and forms of negligence, *see* Part I, Chapter 3, §3, III, paras. 409–424.

number of attacking persons, or in the means of defense chosen in response to a particular attack. For instance, it is disproportionate for a victim to shoot a thief who steals an apple from the victim's garden. However, the harm caused to the attacker by a defensive act may be greater than the harm prevented since it is not always possible to prevent an infringement by means of a lesser harm.[590] For instance, in the case of endangerment of health as a protected legal interest, defensive action directed at the life of the attacker may be justified.[591]

458. The defending person must have an advantage over the attacker. This position is reflected in Article 37, paragraph 2.1 UKR, which states that in the case of a sudden attack, actions of a defending person are not deemed in excess of the limits of necessary defense if, due to the unexpectedness of the infringing attack, the defending person could not objectively assess the degree and nature of the threat.

459. Moreover, all persons have the right to necessary defense, regardless of whether it would be possible for them to avoid a socially dangerous attack (e.g., by retreating) or to seek the assistance of other persons or authorities (Article 37, paragraph 3 UKR).[592]

460. Necessary defense excludes criminal liability. In general, the legal consequences of the necessary defense depend on a combination of subjective and objective circumstances. In a situation in which there is reason to believe, objectively, that an infringement of protected legal interests by an attacker is actually taking place but the defending person, subjectively, is not aware of this and could not possibly realize the error of his or her assumptions (intellectual component), a defensive act engaged in by the defending person is considered to be committed under the circumstances of necessary defense.[593] In this case, criminal liability is excluded (Article 37, paragraph 1 UKR). In a situation in which, objectively speaking, the defending person could and should realize (intellectual component) that an alleged attacker poses no real threat of harm and, despite this, the defending person causes harm to the alleged attacker, he or she incurs liability for the commission of a crime of negligence (imaginary defense, see *infra* C.).[594]

590. *See* Plenum of the Highest Court of the Russian Federation, Sep. 27, 2012.
591. Naumov, Rossiiskoe ugolovnoe pravo, pp. 495–496.
592. *See* Plenum of the Highest Court of the Russian Federation, Sep. 27, 2012.
593. *See* Plenum of the Highest Court of the Russian Federation, Sep. 27, 2012; Naumov, Rossiiskoe ugolovnoe pravo, p. 494.
594. Naumov, Rossiiskoe ugolovnoe pravo, p. 494; Plenum of the Highest Court of the Russian Federation, Sep. 27, 2012. For definition and forms of negligence, *see* Part I, Chapter 3, §3, III, paras. 409–424; Paramonova, Grounds for excluding criminal liability in Russia. In: Sieber, U. / Jarvers, K. /Silverman, E. (ed(s).): Grounds for excluding criminal liability. Berlin, Duncker & Humblot, 2015, pp.136–138.

C. Putative Necessary Defense and Other Problems in Relation to Mistake

461. In the theory of criminal law and in judicial practice, necessary defense should be distinguished from the so-called imaginary defense. The latter differs from necessary defense in that the infringement exists only according to the subjective perception of the defendant. In judicial practice, cases involving imaginary defense are solved with the help of the rules that apply in the context of mistakes of fact and mistakes of law.[595]

II. Causing Harm to a Person Who Has Committed a Crime While Detaining the Person

462. A ground for excluding criminal liability that refers to the avoidance of the consequences of (present/future) offenses is, under certain circumstances, **causing harm to a detainee who has committed a crime** *(причинение вреда при задержании лица, совершившего преступление)* (Article 38 UKR). This ground was first added to the Criminal Code in 1996.[596]

> Art. 38 UKR (Causing Harm to a Person Who Has Committed a Crime While Detaining the Person)
>
> (1) Causing harm to a person who has committed a crime while detaining this person in order to deliver him or her to the authorities and to prevent the possibility of the commission by him or her of further offenses, shall not be deemed a crime, if other means to detain this person were not possible and the use of measures needed for this detention were not excessive.
>
> (2) An excess of the use of measures needed for the detention of the person who has committed a crime shall be deemed to be their obvious discrepancy with the character and degree of the social danger of the offense committed by the detained person and the circumstances of the detention, when the harm was caused to the person which was clearly excessive and not called for by the situation. Such excess shall entail criminal responsibility only in cases of intentional causing of harm.

463. Detaining a person who has committed a crime is a legal right and, in some cases, a moral obligation, regardless of the detaining person's official status and duties with regard to the prevention of unlawful acts. For some officials, however, detaining offenders is a legal obligation.[597]

---

595. For mistakes of fact and mistakes of law, *see* Part I, Chapter 4, §3, paras. 525–528.
596. Paramonova, Grounds for excluding criminal liability in Russia. In: Sieber, U. / Jarvers, K. /Silverman, E. (ed(s).): Grounds for excluding criminal liability. Berlin, Duncker & Humblot, 2015, pp.160–163.
597. For official duties, *see* paras. 498–508.

464. The following prerequisites determine the legitimacy of the conduct of a person who causes harm to another whom he or she has detained on the grounds that the detainee has committed a crime (Article 38 UKR):[598]

- the reason for the detention;
- the purpose of the detention;
- the proportionality of the detaining act as compared to the harm caused and the danger prevented.

465. The first prerequisite involves the reason for the detention. Harm may only be caused during the detention of a person who has committed a criminal offense[599] (Article 14 UKR). This ground for excluding criminal liability does not apply to harm caused during the detention of a person who has committed an administrative or disciplinary offense or a tort. The detaining person should have a strong belief that he or she is detaining someone who is committing or has just committed a crime. For instance, the arrest should be made when witnesses or victims point out the person who committed the crime or if there are clear traces of the crime.[600] Cases of harm caused to detainees who were mistakenly taken for criminals—so-called imaginary criminals—are decided on the basis of the general rules governing mistakes of fact.[601] In cases where it is impossible for the detaining person to realize the error of his or her perception regarding the identity of the victim and the grounds for detention (intellectual element) and if he or she does not wish for or permit the occurrence of socially dangerous results (volitional element), criminal liability is excluded due to the absence of culpability.[602] In this situation, the use of measures necessary for the detention of a person who has committed a crime (even though the detainee has not, in fact, committed a crime) is not considered exceeded.

466. The second condition involves the purpose of the detention. Harm to a person who has committed a crime can be caused solely for the purpose of detaining and delivering him or her to the competent authorities. Causing harm to a detainee for any other purpose is illegal and entails criminal responsibility.

467. In order to fulfill the third prerequisite—proportionality of the act of detention to the harm caused and danger prevented—the detaining act may not exceed the established limits of the use of measures needed for the detention of the person who has committed a crime. The question of proportionality is to be decided by the courts on a case-by-case basis. A detaining act is considered excessive if the discrepancy between the use of measures needed for the detention and the character and degree of the social danger of the offense committed by the detainee is obvious (Article 38, paragraph 2 UKR). This discrepancy can be expressed in inappropriate means used for detention. This would be the case, for example, if someone shot a

---

598. *See* Plenum of the Highest Court of the Russian Federation, Sep. 27, 2012.
599. For the concept of the criminal offense, *see* Part I, Chapter 3, §1, paras. 317–321.
600. *See* Plenum of the Highest Court of the Russian Federation, Sep. 27, 2012.
601. On mistakes of fact, *see* Part I, Chapter 4, §3, paras. 525–526.
602. On the principle of culpability, *see* paras. 194–195, 388, 425.

thief who was stealing an apple from a neighbor's garden. However, with respect to the proportionality of the act of detention, the harm caused to the offender may be greater than the harm prevented since causing less harm does not always allow an infringement to be prevented.[603] For instance, in the case of endangerment of health as a protected legal interest, the act of detention directed at the life of the attacker is justified.[604] It should be borne in mind that persons who detain offenders are not always able to choose means that are absolutely proportionate (which is objectively not always possible) to the danger posed by the committed crime. The means chosen by the detaining persons depend on various factors: strong emotion; a rapidly changing environment; time and place of detention, etc. Therefore, the harm caused to the offender when detaining, and that is greater than the damage that the offender would otherwise have caused, may be considered proportional.[605] Also, negligent acts that exceed the limits of the use of measures needed for the detention do not entail criminal liability.[606] In contrast and as already mentioned, the intentional commission by the detaining person of acts that clearly do not correspond to the character and danger of the infringement is not allowed and will result in criminal liability (Article 38, paragraph 2 UKR).[607]

468. In general, if the prerequisites of the grounds for excluding criminal liability are fulfilled, causing harm while detaining a person who has committed a crime in order to deliver him or her to the authorities and to prevent the commission of (additional) offenses is not criminally punishable (Article 38, paragraph 1 UKR).[608]

III. Extreme Necessity

A. Necessity as a Justification

469. Choice of evils, better known under the name **extreme necessity** (***крайняя необходимость***, Article 39, paragraph 1 UKR), occurs when, in order to eliminate a direct danger to his or her individual rights or to the rights of other persons or to legally protected interests of society and the state, a person causes harm to the interests of third persons under circumstances that prevent him or her from eliminating this danger by other means. In so doing, the person may not exceed the established limits of extreme necessity.[609]

---

603. *See* Plenum of the Highest Court of the Russian Federation, Sep. 27, 2012.
604. Naumov, Rossiiskoe ugolovnoe pravo, pp. 495–496.
605. *See* Plenum of the Highest Court of the Russian Federation, Sep. 27, 2012.
606. Batichko, Uglovnoe pravo; Plenum of the Highest Court of the Russian Federation, Sep. 27, 2012. For definition and forms of negligence, *see* Part I, Chapter 3, §3, III, paras. 409–424.
607. For definition and forms of intent, *see* Part I, Chapter 3, §3, II, paras. 392–408.
608. Paramonova, Grounds for excluding criminal liability in Russia. In: Sieber, U. / Jarvers, K. /Silverman, E. (ed(s).): Grounds for excluding criminal liability. Berlin, Duncker & Humblot, 2015, pp.163.
609. Batichko, Uglovnoe pravo; Naumov, Rossiiskoe ugolovnoe pravo, pp. 503–504; Paramonova, Grounds for excluding criminal liability in Russia. In: Sieber, U. / Jarvers, K. /Silverman, E. (ed(s).): Grounds for excluding criminal liability. Berlin, Duncker & Humblot, 2015, pp.138–139.

Art. 39 UKR (Extreme Necessity)

(1) The causing of harm to interests protected by a criminal law in a state of extreme necessity, that is, for the purpose of eliminating a danger directly threatening the person or his or her rights, or the rights of other persons, the legally protected interests of the society or the state, shall not be deemed to be a crime, if this danger could not be removed by other means and if there was no exceeding the limits of extreme necessity.
(2) The infliction of harm that obviously does not correspond to the character and the degree of the threatening danger, nor to the circumstances under which the danger was eliminated, when harm that was caused to the mentioned interests was equal or more significant than the prevented harm, shall be deemed to be exceeding the limits of extreme necessity. Such exceeding shall entail criminal responsibility only in cases of intentional causing of harm.

470. Extreme necessity always involves a collision of two groups of legally protected interests and a situation in which it is possible to prevent the infringement of one of the groups of interests only by causing harm to the other group. A person who finds him- or herself in a state of extreme necessity must choose between two evils. The person must avoid the greater evil by engaging in the conscious violation of interests considered less significant. Take, for instance, a witness who does not appear at trial to give testimony because he/she cannot leave his or her injured father at home alone. In this example, the legally protected interest in the administration of justice collides with the legally protected interest in life and health. Acts committed in a state of extreme necessity are recognized as useful to society, morally justified, and legitimate.[610]

B. Requirements

471. Prerequisites for qualification as an act of extreme necessity are divided into two groups: those associated with danger and those associated with protection.[611]

1. Requirements Relating to the Danger

472. The following are prerequisites associated with **danger** ***(опасность)***:

– the character of the source of danger must create a state of extreme necessity;
– the danger must be imminent;

610. Naumov, Rossiiskoe ugolovnoe pravo, p. 503.
611. Paramonova, Grounds for excluding criminal liability in Russia. In: Sieber, U. / Jarvers, K. /Silverman, E. (ed(s).): Grounds for excluding criminal liability. Berlin, Duncker & Humblot, 2015, pp.139 .

– the danger must exist objectively (imaginary danger is insufficient);

473. In order to satisfy the first prerequisite, the character of the source of danger must create a state of extreme necessity. Various sources of danger are possible: natural, technological, industrial, pathological, and physiological. An example of a source of danger that satisfies this prerequisite is being lost in the jungle. Thus, a person who is lost in the jungle does not incur criminal liability for killing a protected animal.

474. The danger must be imminent. Danger is considered imminent beginning at the moment when the threat of harm as such appears (e.g., there is a risk of flooding, fire, accident, death, etc.) and not only when it takes on a concrete shape. Thus, there is a legal basis for the application of extreme necessity from the moment when the threat of danger appears, through the time it lasts, and continuing until the moment of its actual termination.[612] If the danger has not yet appeared and there is no threat to legally protected interests or, in contrast, if the danger has already succeeded in causing harm, there is no legal basis for the application of extreme necessity.[613]

475. The danger must also exist objectively. If a person mistakenly believes, subjectively, that a danger exists, but in fact, objectively, it does not, the situation is governed by the rules applicable to the imaginary necessary defense.

2. Requirements Relating to the Protection

476. The following are prerequisites associated with **protection** ***(защита)***:

- the object of protection must be proper;
- the target of protection (third persons or other protected interests) must be proper;
- the danger cannot be eliminated by means that would not cause harm to third-party interests;
- the protection must be proportional.

477. The first prerequisite has to do with the objects of protection, namely, legally protected social relationships or interests that fall under protection according to the rules of extreme necessity (Article 39, paragraph 1 UKR). The following interests are considered proper objects of protection: individual rights and legitimate interests of the person who eliminates the danger; individual rights and legitimate interests of other persons; legally protected interests of society; legally protected interests of the state.

---

612. *See* Plenum of the Highest Court of the Russian Federation, Jul. 9, 2013, N 24.
613. Batichko, Uglovnoe pravo; Naumov, Rossiiskoe ugolovnoe pravo, p. 505.

478. Another obligatory characteristic has to do with the target of the protection in a state of extreme necessity. In contrast to the necessary defense, the damage caused by the actions of extreme necessity must be directed solely toward third persons, that is, persons who are not responsible for creating the socially dangerous situation, or to other legally protected interests of the society or the state.

479. The factual basis for the application of extreme necessity is the impossibility in the current situation of eliminating the imminent danger by means other than those that infringe upon legally protected interests.[614] For instance, in order to avoid being attacked by an angry bull, it is possible to run away. The state of extreme necessity is only justified if the application of other means is impossible, or their application is not sufficient for the successful aversion of the danger.[615] Referring again to the angry bull, for example, this would be the case if it was not possible to run away. The state of necessary defense, in contrast, allows the use of other means that infringe upon legally protected interests regardless of the possibility of evading a socially dangerous infringement or asking other persons or authorities for help (Article 37, paragraph 3 UKR).

480. In order to satisfy the prerequisite of proportionality of the protection, the harm caused by the prevention of the danger must not exceed the established limits of extreme necessity; that is, the harm caused must be smaller than the harm prevented.[616] Even the causing of harm equal to the harm prevented is considered in excess of the limits of extreme necessity (Article 39, paragraph 2 UKR). This is one of the major differences from the necessary defense, according to which even the causing of greater harm is justified. In each concrete case, the limits of the proportional protection as an adequate response to the danger are determined by the relationship between the legally protected interests that have been harmed (harm caused) and the interests, the infringement of which has been prevented by the protection act (harm prevented).[617] For instance, interests in life and health are considered more important than property interests. Hence, in the following situation, the state of extreme necessity is justified: A cuts down the only tree nearby, which is growing in the garden of B, in order to make a fire so as to survive a cold winter night. Here, life and health have priority over property interests. However, if A cuts down the tree in B's garden (realizing that he is damaging private property) despite the fact that there is a public forest full of trees adjacent to the garden, the prerequisite of proportionality is not fulfilled.[618]

481. If all the prerequisites of extreme necessity are satisfied, criminal liability is excluded. Criminal liability for acts in excess of the limits of extreme necessity

614. *See* Plenum of the Highest Court of the Russian Federation, Jul. 9, 2013, N 24.
615. Batichko, Uglovnoe pravo.
616. *See* Plenum of the Highest Court of the Russian Federation, Oct. 16, 2009.
617. Naumov, Rossiiskoe ugolovnoe pravo, pp. 506–507.
618. Paramonova, Grounds for excluding criminal liability in Russia. In: Sieber, U. / Jarvers, K. /Silverman, E. (ed(s).): Grounds for excluding criminal liability. Berlin, Duncker & Humblot, 2015, pp.139–142.

is incurred only if the harm to legally protected interests is caused intentionally;[619] no criminal liability is incurred for the negligent infliction of harm in such cases (Article 39, paragraph 2 UKR).[620] For instance, A, being in the woods, cuts down a tree on territory belonging to B in order to build a fire so as to survive a cold winter night. A does not incur criminal liability for this negligent act. In this case, it is most probable that A does not realize that he is on private territory (e.g., there is no fence like in the garden; moreover, he is there at night). However, B has the right to compensation for damages under private law. The prerequisites of extreme necessity would not be satisfied, and thus, criminal liability would not be excluded if A caused damage to B's tree even though there was a public forest full of trees adjacent to B's garden and A realized that the tree in question was situated on B's property (indirect intent).[621]

IV. Physical or Mental Coercion

482. Another ground for excluding criminal liability is **physical or mental coercion** ***(физическое или психическое принуждение)***. Physical or mental coercion, also known as duress, is conduct directed toward a person that is designed to deprive that person of his or her possibility of free choice and induce that person to cause damage to legally protected interests.[622] It can be expressed in terms of physical violence (beatings, torture, injuries, illegal imprisonment, etc.) or psychological (mental) violence (various threats to life, health, honor, dignity, property interests, etc.).[623]

Art. 40 UKR (Physical or Mental Coercion)

(1) The causing of harm to the interests protected by a criminal law as a result of physical coercion, if in consequence of such coercion the person could not control his or her actions (omissions), shall not be a crime.
(2) The question of criminal responsibility for the causing of harm to the interests protected by a criminal law as a result of mental coercion, and also as a result of physical coercion, in consequence of which the person has retained the possibility of controlling his or her actions, shall be decided by taking into account the provisions of article 39 of the present Code.

483. There are two major constellations of physical or mental coercion. They are reflected in Article 40 UKR. The first is when a person cannot control his or her behavior, and the second is when a person retains control over his or her actions.

---

619. For definition and forms of intent, *see* Part I, Chapter 3, §3, II, paras. 392–408.
620. For definition and forms of negligence, *see* Part I, Chapter 3, §3, III, paras. 409–424.
621. For definition and forms of intent, *see* Part I, Chapter 3, §3, II, paras. 392–408.
622. Paramonova, Grounds for excluding criminal liability in Russia. In: Sieber, U. / Jarvers, K. /Silverman, E. (ed(s).): Grounds for excluding criminal liability. Berlin, Duncker & Humblot, 2015, pp.142–144.
623. Batichko, Uglovnoe pravo; *see* Plenum of the Highest Court of the Russian Federation, Jul. 9, 2013, N 24.

484. A person who, as a result of coercion, cannot control his or her behavior and causes damage to legally protected interests will not incur criminal liability (Article 40, paragraph 1 UKR). For example, if A and B are in a museum and B by threatening A with a gun makes him break an expensive vase, A will not incur criminal liability.

485. However, if a coerced person retains the ability to control his or her actions (omissions), prerequisites for the exclusion of criminal liability due to physical or mental coercion are similar to those for extreme necessity (Articles 40, paragraph 2, 39 UKR).[624] If the prerequisites of extreme necessity are fulfilled, criminal liability is excluded. If extreme necessity is not applicable as a ground for excluding criminal liability or if the limits of extreme necessity are exceeded, physical or mental coercion can still be regarded as a circumstance mitigating punishment (Article 61, paragraph 1 item f UKR).

486. The prerequisites of extreme necessity are associated with danger and protection, as mentioned in Chapter 4, §2, III. Prerequisites associated with **danger** ***(опасность)*** are the following: the character of the source of danger must create a state of extreme necessity; the danger must be imminent; and it must exist objectively (imaginary danger is insufficient). Prerequisites associated with **protection** ***(защита)*** are the following: the object of protection must be proper; the target of protection (third persons or other protected interests) must be proper; it must be impossible to eliminate the danger by means that would not cause harm to third-party interests; and, finally, the protection must be proportional.

487. Nonetheless, there are a number of significant differences between the prerequisites for the defense of physical or mental coercion (concerning persons that retain the ability to control his or her actions (omissions)) and those for the defense of extreme necessity, including the following:

- the objective side (*actus reus*) of the defensive act can be expressed not only in action, as in the case of extreme necessity, but also in omission;
- if a person subject to coercion retains the ability to control his or her behavior and has the possibility of appealing to the appropriate authorities for assistance and if the person does not make use of this possibility, criminal liability for crimes committed due to the physical or mental coercion is not excluded.

488. However, if the harm caused by coerced behavior is less than the harm prevented, it is not considered a crime. For example, a notary who records an illegal contract while under the threat of being killed will not incur criminal liability. In the case of equivalent harm, it is decided by the courts on a case-by-case basis.

---

624. For a discussion of extreme necessity (also known as choice of evils), *see* paras. 469–481.

V. Justified Risk

489. According to Russian criminal law, **justified or substantiated risk** ***(обоснованный риск)*** is recognized as a ground for excluding criminal liability. Justified risk refers to the risk of causing harm to legally protected interests in the pursuit of a socially useful purpose.[625]

Art. 41 UKR (Justified Risk)

(1) No criminal responsibility shall ensue for the infliction of harm to legally protected interests provided the risk is justified by attaining a socially useful goal.
(2) Risk shall be regarded as justified unless the said purpose could have been attained through other actions (omissions) not connected with the risk and provided that a person who committed the risk has undertaken all measures sufficient to prevent causing harm to legally protected interests.
(3) Risk shall not be deemed to be justified if it was knowingly accompanied by a threat to the life of many people, or a threat of environmental or societal catastrophe.

490. The development of new technologies and the improvement of manufacturing processes often involve a certain risk of harm. Justified risk, namely, one that poses a possible danger to legally protected interests in order to achieve socially beneficial results that could not otherwise be obtained, is recognized by the criminal law as a ground for excluding criminal liability.

491. The prerequisites for the exclusion of criminal liability on the basis of justified risk are the following:

- harm is caused to legally protected interests;
- a socially useful purpose is pursued;
- the socially useful purpose cannot be achieved by means of actions (omissions) that do not pose a risk;
- the person who takes the risk undertakes all sufficient measures to prevent harm to legally protected interests;
- the risk posed does not involve an obvious threat to the lives of numerous or a threat of environmental catastrophe or public calamity.

492. Justified risk is connected with the causing of harm to legally protected interests. Justified or substantiated risk is possible in any area of activity—scientific, technical, military, medical, environmental, legal, etc. Justified risk may involve the threat of harm to a person (life, health, rights) or to property, public safety, industrial activity, or nature.

625. Paramonova, Grounds for excluding criminal liability in Russia. In: Sieber, U. / Jarvers, K. /Silverman, E. (ed(s).): Grounds for excluding criminal liability. Berlin, Duncker & Humblot, 2015, pp.151–153.

493. Justified risk arises in the context of conduct carried out in pursuit of socially useful purposes, that is, conduct aimed at the public good. The development of space exploration and space travel, for example, is hard to imagine without risk. Developments in medicine, such as organ transplants, are also associated with the risk to the patient.

494. The prerequisite of the impossibility of achieving a socially useful purpose by means of risk-free actions (omissions) requires the chosen conduct to be the sole means of achieving a socially useful purpose. If there are other means of achieving the purpose that do not cause a risk of harm to legally protected interests, they should be used. For example, if it is possible to apprehend an armed criminal in a remote place, police should not arrest him or her in a public place.

495. The person who takes the risk is obliged to undertake sufficient measures to prevent harm to legally protected interests. This means that any harm caused occurs against the will of the risk-taker. If there was a possibility of avoiding the risk, but the person did not take it into account and preferred to take the risk, and as a result caused harm to legally protected interests, the risk would be unjustified, and the conduct would entail criminal liability.[626]

496. Risk is not justified if the related conduct involves the intentional causing of harm. Also, if it is certain that harm will be caused, the risk is not justified; risk can only be justified if there is some likelihood that no harm will be caused.

497. Risk that involves a threat to the lives of many people, a threat of environmental catastrophe, or a threat of public calamity is never justified (Article 41, paragraph 3 UKR).[627]

VI. Fulfillment of the Official Order or Instruction

498. Neither the Criminal Code nor the jurisprudence recognizes the carrying out of official duties as a specific, independent ground for excluding criminal liability in cases where the duties engaged in infringe on legally protected interests.[628] However, in legal scholarship, some authors regard conduct based on official duties as a possible ground for excluding criminal liability.[629]

499. Provisions that address the exclusion of criminal liability for harm caused in the course of executing a lawful superior order are based on the document entitled

626. For the different constellation of the case, *see* para. 494.
627. Revin, Ugolovnoe pravo Rossii, pp. 182–183.
628. Paramonova, Grounds for excluding criminal liability in Russia. In: Sieber, U. / Forster, S. / Jarvers, K. (ed(s).): National Criminal Law in a Comparative Legal Context. Berlin, Duncker & Humblot, 2016, pp. 145–149.
629. Batichko, Uglovnoe pravo.

"Principles of International Law Recognized in the Charter of the Nürnberg Tribunal and in the Judgment of the Tribunal."[630]

500. This principle is reflected in Article 42 UKR: harm caused to legally protected interests in the course of executing a superior order or instruction that is binding on a subordinate is not considered to be a crime unless it is caused by someone who intentionally carries out an obviously unlawful order or instruction. A person who carries out an obviously unlawful order will, under normal circumstances, incur criminal liability.[631]

Art. 42 UKR (Execution of Order or Instruction)

(1) Causing harm to the interests protected by the criminal law shall not be deemed a crime if it was committed by a person acting in execution of an order or instruction that was binding on him or her. Criminal responsibility for causing such harm shall be borne by a person who gave the unlawful order or instruction.

(2) A person who committed an intentional offense in execution of an obviously unlawful order or instruction shall be criminally liable under usual terms. The failure to execute an obviously unlawful order or instruction shall exclude criminal liability.

501. There is a presumption that official duties are carried out within the legitimate limits provided by law. Thus, carrying out official duties in an appropriate, legitimate way does not require justification by means of criminal law provisions. Certain categories of persons, for example, police officers, firefighters, and soldiers have a legal obligation to carry out their duties under extreme conditions. For instance, in breaking into a burning dwelling, a firefighter is saving a person's life and not infringing on a legally protected interest, for example, private property. In this situation, the applicable grounds for excluding criminal liability are the six general grounds recognized by the Criminal Code (Articles 37–42 UKR). Apart from these circumstances, any criminally relevant infringement of legally protected interests caused by improper performance of official duties entails ordinary criminal responsibility in accordance with the provisions of the Criminal Code.[632]

502. The scope of the official duties of certain categories of authorized persons, such as police officers and firefighters, is regulated by law, for example, the Federal Law on the Police[633] and the Federal Law on Fire Safety.[634] However, due to the

630. Nyurnbergskiy prozess, p. 16; Naumov, Rossiiskoe ugolovnoe pravo, p. 511; http://legal.un.org/ilc/texts/instruments/english/draft%20articles/7_1_1950.pdf [last visited Dec. 18, 2019].

631. Paramonova, Grounds for excluding criminal liability in Russia. In: Sieber, U. / Jarvers, K. /Silverman, E. (ed(s).): Grounds for excluding criminal liability. Berlin, Duncker & Humblot, 2015, pp. 148–149.

632. *See* Plenum of the Highest Court of the Russian Federation, Oct. 16, 2009.

633. Federal Law on the Police, Feb. 7, 2011, N 3-FZ.

634. Federal Law on Fire Safety, Dec. 21, 1994, N 69-FZ.

principle of legality, these special legal provisions cannot offer any grounds for excluding criminal liability beyond those found in the Criminal Code.[635]

503. The exclusion of criminal liability for the execution of a binding superior order or instruction (Article 42 UKR) applies to all legal regulations and to all categories of persons, for example, civil servants, police officers, soldiers, and different kinds of subordinates in hierarchical relationships under private or labor law.[636] There is no special rule for particular groups of persons with respect to this issue.[637]

504. Orders in the sense of this provision are organizational-administrative (documented) decisions that refer to subordinates of different kinds in hierarchical relationships.[638]

505. There are two groups of prerequisites that must be fulfilled in order for the execution of a superior order to serve as a ground, excluding criminal responsibility (within Article 42, paragraph 1).[639]

506. The first group refers to the *legitimacy of the order*. In this context, the legal literature has developed the following prerequisites.[640]

507. First, the order must be given by a person who has the right to give orders in the respective field. Such rights may be conferred by legal provisions, for example, those governing the activities of prosecutors (Federal Law on the Prosecutor's Office of the Russian Federation[641]). Second, it must be given within the framework of the competence of the person giving the order. Orders that go beyond the boundaries of the superior's rights and duties are considered unlawful. Third, the order must be given in an appropriate form (written or oral) and must be clear to the subordinate. Fourth, it must be possible for the order to be carried out under the circumstances and with the resources available to the person to whom it is given without causing damage to legally protected interests.[642]

---

635. For constitutional parameters of criminal law and for national sources of criminal law, *see* General Introduction, §5, II, paras. 145–181; for a definition and a discussion of the principle of legality, *see* Part I, Chapter 1, paras. 197–226; for the concept of the criminal offense, *see* Part I, Chapter 3, §1, paras. 317–321.
636. In the following text, the term "order" includes both orders and instructions.
637. Batichko, Uglovnoe pravo.
638. Batichko, Uglovnoe pravo.
639. Oreshkina, Prichineniye vreda pri ispolnenii prikaza, p. 24; Paramonova, Grounds for excluding criminal liability in Russia. In: Sieber, U. / Jarvers, K. /Silverman, E. (ed(s).): Grounds for excluding criminal liability. Berlin, Duncker & Humblot, 2015, pp.147–149.
640. Batichko, Uglovnoe pravo; Oreshkina, Prichineniye vreda pri ispolnenii prikaza, p. 24.
641. Federal Law on the Prosecutor's Office of the Russian Federation, Jan. 17, 1992, N 2202.
642. Komissarov/Krilova/Tyazhkova, Ugolovnoe pravo RF, p. 503; Naumov, Rossiiskoe ugolovnoe pravo, pp. 511–512.

508. The second group addresses the *behavior of the subordinate*:

First, the subordinate must not have had an opportunity to refuse to carry out the illegal order that was obligatory for him or her to execute. A second requirement is that he or she did not and could not realize that the order was unlawful.[643]
Causing harm to legally protected interests in the course of executing a lawful and binding superior order is thus not considered a crime; hence, criminal liability for such harm is excluded for the subordinate (Article 42 UKR).
In contrast, by carrying out an obviously unlawful order, a subordinate exposes him- or herself to criminal liability under normal circumstances, whereby courts can treat the execution of unlawful superior orders as a circumstance mitigating punishment (Article 61, paragraph 1 item g UKR).
On the other hand, if, for example, in the context of the military, the subordinate's failure to execute a lawful superior order causes substantial harm to the interests of the military, the subordinate will incur criminal liability (Article 332 UKR). In contrast, the failure by a subordinate to execute an obviously unlawful order or instruction is not a crime (Article 42, paragraph 2 UKR).
Article 42 UKR differentiates between "unlawful orders and instructions," of whose unlawfulness the superior knew and the subordinate did not and could not have known (Article 42, paragraph 1 UKR), and "obviously unlawful orders and instructions" (Article 42, paragraph 2 UKR). The legal consequences for a subordinate subject to these orders differ accordingly.
The first case (Article 42, paragraph 1 UKR) excludes the criminal liability of the subordinate if the subordinate was executing a binding order and did not have the opportunity to refuse to carry it out. The subordinate is not criminally liable under these circumstances if he or she could not have known. For instance, he/she did not know that the order was unlawful due to the fact that the document containing the orders satisfied all the prerequisites of a legitimate order. The superior who gave the unlawful order is, however, criminally liable for the harm caused. This is the case, for example, if the superior gives the order to arrest someone on the basis of a forged document, and the subordinate who carries out the arrest does not and could not know about the forgery. The superior's conduct is dealt with in accordance with the rules governing perpetration by means (Article 33, paragraph 2 UKR).
The second constellation addresses cases in which the orders are "obviously unlawful" to both the superior and the subordinate (Article 42, paragraph 2 UKR). In this situation, there are two prerequisites that must be fulfilled in order for the subordinate to incur criminal liability: first, he or she must commit an intentional crime in carrying out the order, and second, in doing so, the subordinate must know that the order is unlawful, that is, it does not fulfill one of four prerequisites of the legitimacy of the order. If these two prerequisites are fulfilled, the subordinate is criminally liable, under normal circumstances, as a perpetrator (Article 33, paragraph 2 UKR in conjunction with the respective criminal offense definition). The superior in this constellation is criminally liable as an instigator (Article 33, paragraph 4 UKR in conjunction with the respective criminal offense definition). If, however, in

643. Komissarov/Krilova/Tyazhkova, Ugolovnoe pravo RF, p. 503; Oreshkina, Prichineniye vreda pri ispolnenii prikaza, p. 24.

carrying out the unlawful order, the subordinate commits an offense of negligence, he or she will not incur criminal liability for this act since Article 42, paragraph 2 UKR criminalizes only intentional form of culpability of the commission of the crime[644]

VII. Insignificance

509. **'Insignificance'** ***(малозначительность)*** applies to the acts that are formally regarded as criminal offenses but by virtue of their insignificance do not represent a social danger. This ground of justification originates from the definition of crime, Article 14 UKR. For example, a theft of RUB 2 does not entail criminal liability (Article 14, paragraph 2 UKR).[645]

Art. 14 UKR (Concept of Crime)[646]

(2) An action (or omission), although formally containing the indicia of any act provided for by the present Code but by virtue of insignificance does not represent a social danger, shall not be a criminal offense.

VIII. Other Means Not Prohibited by Law

510. Everyone is free to protect his or her rights and freedoms by all means not prohibited by law (Article 45 Const.). **Self-help or self-protection (самозащита)** is allowed by Article 14 of the Civil Code of the Russian Federation (*Grazhdanskij Kodeks RF*, GKR[647]) as long as it does not entail any criminally-relevant consequences. However, in order to be justified, conduct undertaken in the course of exercising private rights (for example, self-help or the right of a rightful possessor to recover possession) that causes consequences prohibited by criminal law provisions (for example, damaging private property) must satisfy the prerequisites of one of the six recognized grounds for excluding criminal liability (Articles 37–42 UKR). Furthermore, even if certain conduct is justified in accordance with one of the six grounds, this does not preclude a civil lawsuit for compensation for harm. For example, A, who is in a forest on a cold winter night, cuts down a tree on

644. For definition and forms of negligence, *see* Part I, Chapter 3, §3, III, paras. 409–424.
645. For insignificant acts and discussion of the concept of criminal offense, *see* Part I, Chapter 3, §1, paras. 317–321,; Paramonova, Grounds for excluding criminal liability in Russia. In: Sieber, U. / Jarvers, K. /Silverman, E. (ed(s).): Grounds for excluding criminal liability. Berlin, Duncker & Humblot, 2015, pp. 130.
646. All translations (revised by the author) of the UKR in this chapter are taken from Butler, Criminal Code of the Russian Federation.
647. Civil Code of the Russian Federation, Nov. 28, 2001.

land belonging to B in order to build a fire so as to survive the night. While A's conduct does not entail criminal liability since A was acting negligently (extreme necessity), B has the right of redress for property damage under private law.[648]

511. In legal literature, self-help and the protection of private rights are suggested as grounds for excluding criminal liability.[649]

§3. Grounds of Excuse

I. Introduction

512. Additional grounds that exclude criminal liability (excuses) are based on the following criteria: age, health, and social danger.[650] The first category applies to individuals who are not subject to criminal liability due to their failure to fulfill an obligatory criterion of criminal liability: age. The second major category applies to individuals who are not subject to criminal liability due to the criterion of health. Insanity, for example, defined as the suspect's inability to understand or govern his or her actions due to a number of listed conditions, may exclude criminal liability (Article 21, paragraph 1 UKR). Finally, social danger is regarded as an additional criterion for the first two (age and health). For instance, a minor and an insane do not (fully) realize the social danger of their actions (omissions). However, some authors consider social danger as a third separate criterion. This way, they regard insignificance ***(малозначительность)*** as a ground for excuse and for justification (Article 14, paragraph 2 UKR).[651]

II. Minority

513. A person who can incur criminal liability according to the Criminal Code can function as the so-called **subject of crime** ***(субъект преступления)***.[652] Only natural persons (Russian citizens, foreign citizens, or stateless persons) of sound mind who have attained the age of 16 or, in the case of certain listed offenses, 14, can incur criminal liability (also referred to as criminal capacity) and thus can be considered as a subject of crime (Articles 19–20 UKR).[653]

---

648. Naumov, Rossiiskoe ugolovnoe pravo, p. 486; Paramonova, Grounds for excluding criminal liability in Russia. In: Sieber, U. / Jarvers, K. /Silverman, E. (ed(s).): Grounds for excluding criminal liability. Berlin, Duncker & Humblot, 2015, pp.150.
649. Piontkovkij, Sovetskoe ugolovnoe pravo, p. 342.
650. Komissarov/Krilova/Tyazhkova, Ugolovnoe pravo RF, pp. 273–296.
651. For a discussion of the concept of criminal offense, *see* Part I, Chapter 3, §1, paras. 317–321; Paramonova, Grounds for excluding criminal liability in Russia. In: Sieber, U. / Jarvers, K. /Silverman, E. (ed(s).): Grounds for excluding criminal liability. Berlin, Duncker & Humblot, 2015, pp.130.
652. On the concept of the criminal offense, *see* Part I, Chapter 3, §1, paras. 317–321.
653. On the objective aspects of the offense, *see* Part I, Chapter 3, §2, paras. 342–371.

Art. 20 UKR (Age of Criminal Responsibility)

(1) A person who has attained sixteen years of age at the time of commission of a crime shall be subject to criminal responsibility.
(2) Persons who have attained fourteen years of age at the time of commission of a crime shall be subject to criminal responsibility for homicide (Article 105), intentional causing of grave harm to health (Article 111), intentional causing of average gravity of harm to health (Article 112), kidnapping (Article 126), rape (Article 131), forcible sexual actions (Article 132), theft (Article 158), robbery (Article 161), assault with intent to rob (Article 162), extortion (Article 163), […].
(3) If a minor has attained the age provided for the first or second parts of this Article, but as a consequence of mental retardation not associated with mental derangement could not fully realize while committing a socially dangerous act the factual side and social danger of his or her actions (omissions) or could not control these acts, he or she shall not be subject to criminal responsibility.

Art. 87 UKR (The Criminal Responsibility of Juveniles)

(1) Persons who at the time of the commission of a crime have reached the age of fourteen but not yet the age of eighteen shall be deemed to be juveniles.
(2) […]

514. There are two major categories of grounds excluding criminal liability that are based on the criterion of age.[654]

515. The first category is made up of individuals who cannot incur criminal liability due to the failure to fulfill one specific obligatory criterion of criminal capacity: age. Children (persons under the age of 14 years) and juveniles that have not attained 16 years of age at the time of the commission of a crime are not criminally liable. However, for some crimes (e.g., homicide) provided for by Article 20, paragraph 2 UKR, juveniles can incur criminal liability if they have reached the age of 14 years at the time the offense is committed.

516. Subject to special provisions are juveniles aged 16 and 17 that are, as a rule, subject to criminal liability (Chapter 14 UKR).[655] However, a juvenile aged 16 and 17 who commits a crime of small or average gravity (Article 15 UKR)[656] may be

654. Komissarov/Krilova/Tyazhkova, Ugolovnoe pravo RF, pp. 273–296.
655. For special regimes connected to the status of the offender, *see* Part I, Chapter 7, §6, paras. 762–774.
656. On the concept of the criminal offense, *see* Part I, Chapter 3, §1, paras. 317–321.

relieved of criminal liability if the court finds that his or her reformation can be achieved by applying compulsory measures of an educational nature (Articles 90, paragraph 1, 92 UKR).[657]

517. The second major category encompasses individuals who are not subject to criminal liability due to the criterion of age, coupled with an additional prerequisite. Juveniles who have reached the age of criminal responsibility (generally speaking 16 or 14 for some crimes) but have not yet reached the age of 18 and who commit an offense as a consequence of mental retardation unconnected with mental insanity are not considered capable of fully realizing the actual character or social danger of their behavior; thus, they are not subject to criminal liability (Article 20, paragraph 3 UKR).[658]

518. The advanced age of an accused can be considered by the court as a circumstance mitigating criminal punishment (Article 61, paragraph 2 UKR).[659]

III. Insanity

519. The health of the offender is also one of the criteria that is important with respect to the determination of criminal liability. Persons who at the time of the commission of a crime are, for example, insane, defined as the suspect's inability to understand or govern his or her actions due to a number of listed conditions, may be considered not criminally liable.[660]

520. Insanity encompasses two obligatory elements. The first is the legal criterion: the suspect must lack the capacity to understand the actual character or social danger of his criminal behavior or must lack the capacity to control his behavior. The second criterion is the medical criterion: at the time of the commission of the socially dangerous act, the suspect must have had a chronic or temporary mental derangement, mental deficiency, or other mental condition.[661]

Art. 21 UKR Insanity

(1) A person who at the time of the commission of a socially dangerous act was insane, that is, was unable to understand the actual character or social

---

657. For special regimes connected to the status of the offender, *see* Part I, Chapter 7, §6, paras. 762–774.
658. Komissarov/Krilova/Tyazhkova, Ugolovnoe pravo RF, pp. 273–296.
659. Paramonova, Grounds for excluding criminal liability in Russia. In: Sieber, U. / Jarvers, K. /Silverman, E. (ed(s).): Grounds for excluding criminal liability. Berlin, Duncker & Humblot, 2015, pp.153–154.
660. Paramonova, Grounds for excluding criminal liability in Russia. In: Sieber, U. / Jarvers, K. /Silverman, E. (ed(s).): Grounds for excluding criminal liability. Berlin, Duncker & Humblot, 2015, pp.155–156.
661. Komissarov/Krilova/Tyazhkova, Ugolovnoe pravo RF, p. 285.

danger of his actions (omissions) or to control them due to chronic or temporary mental derangement, mental deficiency or any other mental condition, shall not be subject to criminal responsibility.

(2) Compulsory medical treatment provided for in this Code may be imposed by a court on a person, who has committed a socially dangerous act in a state of insanity.

521. In the case of a suspect with a permanent mental disorder/abnormality, criminal liability is excluded due to the failure of the conduct of mentally disturbed people to satisfy culpability (subjective side) requirements.[662] Insanity is a ground for the imposition of **compulsory measures of a medical nature** ***(принудительные меры медицинского характера)***, which are issued by the court in lieu of criminal punishment on the basis of a report issued by a medical expert (Articles 97–104 UKR).[663]

522. Special rules with regard to the question of criminal liability apply to offenders with a temporary mental disturbance that does not equal insanity.

Art. 22 UKR Criminal Responsibility of Individuals with Mental Derangement That Does Not Equal Insanity

(1) A person of sound mind who, while committing a crime, by virtue of mental derangement could not fully comprehend the actual character and social danger of his acts (omissions), or control them, shall be subject to criminal responsibility.

(2) Mental derangement that does not exclude sanity shall be taken into consideration by a court when imposing punishment, and may serve as a ground for the imposition of compulsory medical treatment.

523. As mentioned above, individuals who commit a crime in a state of insanity do not incur criminal liability (Article 21, paragraph 1 UKR). However, criminal liability may be incurred if the mental derangement suffered from does not exclude sanity (Article 22, paragraph 1 UKR), such as, for instance, heat of passion, nervous shock, or epileptic seizure.[664] The presence of mental and intellectual diseases that do not exclude sanity is a ground for the imposition of compulsory medical treatment. Compulsory medical treatment, in addition to punishment, is imposed by the court on the basis of a report issued by a medical expert (Articles 22, paragraph 2, 97, 99 UKR).

524. A grave illness (including mental diseases) can also be a ground for release from criminal punishment. Thus, if, after committing a crime, a person becomes ill with a grave illness that prevents him or her from realizing the social danger of his

662. On the subjective aspects of the offense, *see* Part I, Chapter 3, §4, paras. 383–428.
663. For compulsory measures of medical nature, *see* Part I, Chapter 7, §6, paras. 762–764.
664. Komissarov/Krilova/Tyazhkova, Ugolovnoe pravo RF, p. 286.

or her acts (Article 81, paragraph 1 UKR) or that prevents the serving of punishment (Article 81, paragraph 2 UKR), the person may be relieved by a court from serving punishment (Article 81, paragraphs 1 and 2 UKR). In this case, compulsory medical treatment can be imposed by the court (Article 81, paragraph 1 UKR).[665]

IV. Ignorance or Mistake

A. Mistake of Fact

525. The rules concerning both factual mistakes and mistakes of law are not legally defined in Russian criminal law and are formulated in the doctrine only.

526. The general rule for factual mistakes is that criminal responsibility is determined by the degree of culpability: namely, by what the offender took into account and what he should and could have been aware of at the moment of committing the crime.[666] A **factual mistake** ***(фактическая ошибка)*** is characterized as a false perception by the offender of the factual circumstances which refer to the following elements of an offense: the object (and subject-matter) of crime, the objective side of crime, or the subject of crime.[667] In this way, the following types of factual mistakes can be distinguished:

- **Mistake in relation to the "object of crime"** ***(ошибка в объекте)*** does not change the form but changes the content of culpability. The "object of crime" is considered to be the legally protected social relationship classified according to a certain criterion (e.g., property or public security). It can primarily be identified by the specific "objects" (material items) that fall under the relevant "object of crime." For instance, A stole a box ("object") from the weapons' storage, thinking it contained guns. In reality, it was a box with shoes. The factually infringed object is private property (Chapter 21 "crimes against ownership," Article 158 UKR—theft), and the imagined one is public security (Chapter 24 "crimes against public security," Article 226 UKR—theft of weapon, ammunition, and explosive substances). Juridically, these "objects of crime" are not equal: criminal punishment is more severe for the second "object of crime." So the scope of criminal responsibility will be decided upon the actual intent of the offender: in this case, attempted theft of weapons (pa. 3 Articles 30 and 226 UKR).[668] In cases where the "nature" of the "object of crime" is equal (e.g., the infringement object is private property), the rule of determining criminal responsibility according to the actual intent is also applicable. For example, where A intended to steal a box

665. Paramonova, Grounds for excluding criminal liability in Russia. In: Sieber, U. / Jarvers, K. /Silverman, E. (ed(s).): Grounds for excluding criminal liability. Berlin, Duncker & Humblot, 2015, pp.156.
666. Lebedev, Kommentarii k UK RF, p. 56; Paramonova, Subjective aspects of the offense in Russia, 2011, p. 446.
667. On the objective aspects of the offense, *see* Part I, Chapter 3, §2, paras. 342–371.
668. Naumov, Rossiiskoe ugolovnoe pravo, p. 398.

with socks but stole, in fact, a box with shoes, his act will be qualified as theft of socks (Article 158 UKR). In this case, it will be a theft of private property.

- **Mistake in relation to the "object"**[669] ***(ошибка в предмете)*** is subdivided into two groups: mistake about the "object" (material items) and mistake as regards the person (as the central protected "object" of criminal law).

  Mistakes in relation to "object" refer to the mistakes within the same "object of crime" (legally protected social relationship classified according to a certain criterion, e.g., property). In the example of stealing a car: 'car' refers to "object," and "stealing a car" is considered an infringement of the legally protected interests in such an "object of crime" as private property.

  The factual mistakes belonging to the first group do not influence the qualification of the crime as long as the "objects" (both infringed and imagined) are protected to the same degree and within the same "object of crime"—the protected legal interests.[670] For example, B stole somebody's wallet, thinking there was approximately 100 € in it. In reality, he stole the wallet with about the same sum in Yuan. The difference in types of currency does not play a role in the qualification of the offense: the kind and degree of infringement are comparable. In both cases, the crime is qualified as theft (Article 158, paragraph 1 UKR).

  However, the qualification of a crime can be changed if the intent of the offender encompasses aggravating (or mitigating) circumstances referring to the crime. For instance, consider the situation where B stole the wallet, being sure that it contained USD 8,500 (1st case)/USD 50 (2nd case), but in reality, there were USD 50 (1st case)/USD 8,500 (2nd case) in it. In the first case, the offender is responsible for the attempted theft of a high degree—USD 8,500 (Articles 30, paragraph 3, item c, 158, paragraph 3 UKR). In the second situation, criminal responsibility is limited by the extent of culpability of the offender on the basis of the principle of culpability (Article 5 UKR). As a result, he can be held liable only for the theft of USD 50 (Article 158, paragraph 1 UKR).

- The factual **mistake in a person (subject of crime)** ***(ошибка в личности потерпевшего)*** belongs to the group of mistake in the "object." It has basically no influence on the qualification of the crime because the same legally protected interests are infringed (e.g., life or health).[671] If, for example, G targeted H but erroneously (in the darkness) shot K, he would still be responsible for homicide (Article 105, paragraph 1 UKR). However, there are cases when some characteristics of the person can be relevant for the qualification of the crime. For example, L threatened a judge with the goal that the judge decides his case in his favor. In reality, he threatened a person who looked very much like the judge. The factually infringed object (life and health: Article 119 UKR—the threat of murder or infliction of grave injury to health) and the imagined object (justice: Article 296 UKR—threats or violent actions in connection with the administration of justice or a preliminary investigation) are different. According to the logic that the offender can be held liable only for those socially dangerous acts (omissions) that

---

669. On the objective aspects of the offense, *see* Part I, Chapter 3, §2, paras. 342–371.
670. Lebedev, Kommentarii k UK RF, p. 48; Naumov, Rossiiskoe ugolovnoe pravo, pp. 398–400.
671. Kropachev, Ugolovnoe pravo Rossii, pp. 504–509; Lebedev, Kommentarii k UK RF, p. 48; Naumov, Rossiiskoe ugolovnoe pravo, pp. 398–399.

his culpability was directed to, L is responsible for the attempted threat to obstruct the course of justice (Article 296 UKR). In addition, he would be liable for the completed offense of threat to a person.

- **Mistake regarding the social danger of the conduct** *(ошибка относительно общественной опасности)* refers to unawareness by the offender of this fact.[672] Hence, this mistake can be made only with negligence (carelessness). Negligent crimes do not entail criminal responsibility unless it is specified in a legal provision (Article 24, paragraph 2 UKR). For instance, O is not aware that the banknote he used as payment was forged. O is not responsible for the sale of forged money (Article 186 UKR) because the respective criminal provision criminalizes only an intentional form of this kind of crime. In the next case, however, a nurse is held liable for causing death through negligence by reason of the improper performance of her professional duties (pa. 2 Article 109 UKR). Here, the nurse (N) gave an injection containing the wrong medicine to a patient, not being aware of that fact. As a result, the patient died. N did not foresee the socially dangerous situation; nevertheless, due to her professional position, she should and could have foreseen it.[673]
- **Mistake with regard to socially dangerous consequences** *(ошибка относительно общественно опасных последствий)* is characterized as the false perception by the offender of the amount of the caused harm.[674] For example, A broke a safe with the intent to steal antique jewelry. In reality, he stole inexpensive accessories (the caused harm is less than the offender imagined). A has done everything to achieve the desired result, which did not occur due to circumstances independent of A's will. Hence, A is responsible for the attempted theft of a high degree (Articles 30, paragraph 3, item c, 158, paragraph 3 UKR) and for a completed theft of fake jewelry (i.e., what he in fact stole) (Article 158, paragraph 2 UKR). Another example: a punch in the face in a fight from which the victim falls and hits his head against a stone, it results in death. The consequences are graver than the perpetrator imagined; therefore, the crime is to qualify as causing death by negligence, Article 109, paragraph 1 UKR.
- **Mistake regarding causality** *(ошибка в оценке развития причинной связи)* refers to the offender's wrong perception of the development of causality. The first group of these mistakes deals with the offender's false perception of the causality, which leads to different harmful results. This is the ground for another qualification of the crime. For instance, P hit G several times on the head with a hammer with the intent to kill him. Thinking that G was dead, P threw him into the river. The death, however, occurred due to drowning. P would be held liable for attempted homicide (P did everything he could to kill G) and causing death through negligence (P did not foresee, by throwing G into the river, that G would die from drowning).[675]

672. Kropachev, Ugolovnoe pravo Rossii, p. 509.
673. Naumov, Rossiiskoe ugolovnoe pravo, p. 399.
674. Naumov, Rossiiskoe ugolovnoe pravo, p. 400; Kropachev, Ugolovnoe pravo Rossii, pp. 514–515.
675. Naumov, Rossiiskoe ugolovnoe pravo, p. 400; Kropachev, Ugolovnoe pravo Rossii, p. 511; Lebedev, Kommentarii k UK RF, p. 56.

The second group of mistakes comprises so-called technical mistakes *(технические ошибки)*: the wrong perception of causality leads to juridically equal consequences. For example, Z shot U, targeting the heart with the intent to kill him, but hit U's head instead. U died. In both cases (heart and head shooting), Z is responsible for the intentional homicide.[676]

– **Mistake regarding means of committing a crime** *(ошибка в средствах совершения преступления)* takes place when the offender uses different means (from which he originally planned) not being aware of that fact.[677] Criminal responsibility will be assigned according to the extent of the intent. For example, if somebody used salt to commit a homicide, thinking it was poison, he would be held liable for attempted homicide. However, the use of means like devotions, hexes, and exorcisms for committing a crime would not entail criminal responsibility. It would be qualified as an **attempt with ineligible means** *(покушение с ничтожными средствами)*.

It is disputable whether mistakes regarding aggravating (mitigating) circumstances are a separate group of mistakes. According to the majority opinion, these mistakes can fall under any category of the abovementioned mistakes (for example, with a box of shoes/weapons or threatening a judge or a "normal" person).[678]

B. *Mistake of Law*

527. A **mistake of law** *(юридическая ошибка)* is the wrong perception by an individual of criminalization (prohibition) of certain conduct, its qualification, as well as the type and severity of criminal punishment that follows from it.[679] Russian criminal law scholarship distinguishes among the following four forms of avoidable mistakes of law:

– A **mistake involving a misperception of the criminalized conduct** *(ошибочное представление лица о преступности деяния)* takes place when the individual considers his or her behavior to be criminal when in reality it is not, for example, sneezing on the street. This kind of conduct, which is called **"imaginary crime"** *(мнимое преступление)*, does not entail criminal liability due to the principle of legality: according to the principle *nullum crimen sine lege scripta*, criminal liability can only be incurred for the commission of a socially dangerous act that is explicitly forbidden by written criminal law.[680] An individual who does not incur criminal liability due to this kind of mistake may, however, incur another kind of liability if his or her conduct infringes upon the norms

676. Naumov, Rossiiskoe ugolovnoe pravo, p. 401.
677. Naumov, Rossiiskoe ugolovnoe pravo, pp. 400–401.
678. Paramonova, Subjective aspects of the offense in Russia, 2011, p. 446–449; Lebedev, Kommentarii k UK RF, p. 56; Naumov, Rossiiskoe ugolovnoe pravo, p. 402.
679. Paramonova, Subjective aspects of the offense in Russia, 2011, pp. 446–450; Kropachev, Ugolovnoe pravo Rossii, p. 515; Lebedev, Kommentarii k UK RF, p. 55; Naumov, Rossiiskoe ugolovnoe pravo, p. 395.
680. For the principle of legality, *see* Part I, Chapter 1, paras. 197–226.

of another branch of law. If, for example, someone who intends to commit a crime engages in an act (omission) that, in fact, amounts only to an administrative offense, he or she is subject to legal consequences under the relevant administrative law.[681]

- A **mistake involving a misperception of the non-criminalization of the conduct** *(ошибочное представление лица о непреступности деяния)* at issue is made when an individual realizes the social danger of his or her behavior but believes that it does not entail criminal liability, for example, honor killing. In this situation, the generally recognized presumption of knowing the law applies; hence, the person incurs criminal liability. Exceptions connected with newly enforceable legal provisions are possible. For instance, if it can be established that a person did not and could not know about new criminal prohibitions, the person cannot be held liable under the criminal law since he or she was acting without culpability (Article 5 UKR, principle of culpability).[682]
- In the case of a mistake involving a misperception of the legal norms relevant to the **application of a criminal provision** *(ошибочное представление лица о юридической квалификации)* the offender is held liable for the crime actually committed and not for the crime the offender thought he or she had committed. For example, even if a person thinks that by destroying a neighbor's rare plant, he or she has committed murder, the person is criminally liable only for damaging private property.[683]
- **Mistakes involving a misperception of the type and severity of criminal punishment** *(ошибочное представление лица о виде и размере наказания)* do not have any influence on the legal consequences of the crime because these circumstances are irrelevant with regard to the required elements of the subjective side of the offense. For example, regardless of A's belief that the punishment for destroying a neighbor's rare plant is the death penalty, A's destruction of the neighbor's plant fulfills the definitional elements of the offense of damaging private property.[684] Thus, A's conviction will be for damaging private property, and the criminal punishment imposed by the court will be determined in accordance with the legal provisions governing that offense.[685]

528. There are four forms of avoidable mistakes of law (e.g., misperception of the non-criminalization of the conduct). Thus, the legal consequences of a particular mistake depend on which one it is.[686] In the case of unavoidable mistakes of law—such as might arise in the context of the publication of a newly enacted law with incorrect information about the decriminalization of a certain act—a committed act is not considered criminal due to the principle of legality (Article 3

681. Naumov, Rossiiskoe ugolovnoe pravo, pp. 395–396.
682. Lebedev, Kommentarii k UK RF, p. 48; Naumov, Rossiiskoe ugolovnoe pravo, p. 396.
683. Lebedev, Kommentarii k UK RF, p. 48; Naumov, Rossiiskoe ugolovnoe pravo, p. 397.
684. Naumov, Rossiiskoe ugolovnoe pravo, p. 397.
685. Paramonova, Subjective aspects of the offense in Russia, 2011, p. 450.
686. For the legal consequences of mistakes of fact, *see* Part I, Chapter 4, §3, paras. 525–526.

UKR).[687] One of the formal requirements of the principle of legality is *nullum crimen sine lege scripta*,[688] according to which legal provisions must be officially published. The main idea of this formal requirement is to enable citizens to be aware of their rights and obligations. Thus, if a law is not published in the form in which it is enacted by the legislature, the rule of *nullum crimen sine lege scripta* and, consequently, the principle of legality are infringed. As a result, in such a situation, a mistake of law is unavoidable and criminal liability is excluded.

§4. Grounds That Are Regarded Neither as Justifications Nor as Excuses

I. Consent of the Victim

529. Consent of the victim to (criminal) harm caused to him or her is regarded as a ground for excluding criminal liability in legal scholarship;[689] it is, however, not regarded as such in the Criminal Code or in case law.

530. At one time, the Criminal Code of the Russian Soviet Federal Socialist Republic had a norm (although only for six months) that excluded criminal liability for a homicide committed out of compassion on the basis of the express consent of the victim (Article 143 UKR of 1922).[690] Due to the difficulty of proving *ex post facto* whether or not the victim's consent was genuine, under current law, consent has no effect on the criminality of the act.[691]

531. However, the commission of a crime with the consent of the victim and/or out of compassion can be considered by the court as a mitigating circumstance (Article 61, paragraph 2 UKR).

532. Euthanasia in any form is forbidden in Russia by the Federal Law on the Basis of Health Protection of the Citizens of the Russian Federation[692] and is regarded as homicide (Article 105 UKR).

533. There is one exception in the criminal law legislation that is considered by some scholars to be an independent ground for excluding criminal responsibility due to the consent of the victim. Article 122 UKR (infection with HIV) states that an accused person who threatened to infect another person or who in fact infected

687. For the principle of legality, *see* Part I, Chapter 1, paras. 197–226.
688. On *nullum crimen sine lege scripta*, *see* Part I, Chapter 1, paras. 161–167.
689. Batichko, Uglovnoe pravo.
690. Criminal Code of the Russian Soviet Federal Socialist Republic, May 26, 1922, N 15, (Ugolovnij Kodeks RSFSR); Paramonova, Grounds for excluding criminal liability in Russia. In: Sieber, U. / Jarvers, K. /Silverman, E. (ed(s).): Grounds for excluding criminal liability. Berlin, Duncker & Humblot, 2015, pp.150–160.
691. Komissarov/Krilova/Tyazhkova, Ugolovnoe pravo RF, p. 455.
692. Federal law on the Basis of Health Protection of the Citizens of the Russian Federation, Nov. 21, 2011, N 323-FZ.

another person with HIV must be released from criminal liability if the threatened or infected person was warned in due time about such a disease and agreed voluntarily to perform the actions that created the danger of infection.[693]

II. The Effect of Confession to the Authorities

534. Confession to the authorities after committing a crime is not recognized as a ground for excluding criminal liability. However, the situation of acknowledgment of guilt, actively assisting in investigating crime, catching of other parties to crime, and search of property acquired as a result of the crime can be treated by the court as a circumstance mitigating punishment (Article 61, paragraph 1, item i UKR).

III. Family Relationships

535. There are no specific grounds stipulated in the Criminal Code regarding the disciplinary rights of parents and educators.[694] In general, in order to be justified, any harm caused by a parent or educator in the course of carrying out his or her disciplinary rights must satisfy the prerequisites of one of the six legally recognized grounds for excluding criminal liability. There are no special rights for parents or educators that would allow them, for instance, to use violence for the sake of nurturing or education. For instance, a parent who beats his or her child in a state of necessary defense must fulfill all the prerequisites of this ground of excluding criminal responsibility.

536. A hierarchical relationship between parties to a crime may, however, have an effect (aggravating or mitigating) on criminal punishment. These relationships include familial (parents, children, other relatives) and other relationships (guardian, dependence of the victim on the offender, etc.). For example, parents, teachers, and guardians who involve minors in their care in the commission of a crime are punished more severely than an adult who involves an unrelated minor in the commission of a crime (Article 150, paras1 and 2 UKR). On the other hand, children and minors who commit crimes as a result of physical or mental coercion or by reason of material, official, or any other dependence (parent-child or educator-child) are entitled to a ground of justification or to the mitigation of punishment (Article 61, paragraph 1, item f UKR).

---

693. Paramonova, Revista Penal, 2014, pp. 267–270; Komissarov/Krilova/Tyazhkova, Ugolovnoe pravo RF, p. 456; for grounds for terminating criminal liability, *see* Paramonova, Grounds for excluding criminal liability in Russia, 2016, pp. 151.

694. Paramonova, Grounds for excluding criminal liability in Russia. In: Sieber, U. / Jarvers, K. /Silverman, E. (ed(s).): Grounds for excluding criminal liability. Berlin, Duncker & Humblot, 2015, pp.149–150.

IV. Intoxication and Withdrawal Symptoms

A. Intoxication

537. Offenders who commit crimes in a state of intoxication caused by the consumption of alcohol, drugs, or other stupefying substances are subject to criminal liability (Article 23 UKR).

> Art. 23 UKR (The Criminal Responsibility of Persons Who Have Committed Crimes in a State of Intoxication)
> A person who has committed a crime in a state of intoxication, caused by the use of alcoholic drinks, narcotics, or other stupefying substances, shall be subject to criminal responsibility.

538. The fact that somebody deliberately or inadvertently puts him- or herself into a state of intoxication through alcoholic drinks, narcotics, or other stupefying substances (*actiones liberae in causa*) does not influence the legal consequence of his or her conduct: the person is subject to criminal liability. Indeed, in imposing punishment—which takes into consideration the character and degree of the social danger of the offense, the circumstances of the case, and the personality of the accused—the court can regard the commission of a crime in a state of intoxication as an aggravating circumstance (Article 63, paragraph 1.1 UKR).[695] The Criminal Code of the Russian Soviet Federative Socialist Republic, 1960, regarded a "state of intoxication" as an aggravating circumstance (Article 39, item 10).[696]

539. If a person deliberately puts someone else into a state of intoxication in order to make him or her commit a crime, the person who initiated the state of intoxication bears criminal liability. His or her conduct is dealt with in accordance with the rules governing perpetration by means (Article 33, paragraph 2 UKR).[697]

540. Another issue in this context arises when alcohol or drugs cause diseases that lead to insanity. In this situation, criminal liability is excluded (Article 21 UKR).[698]

B. Withdrawal Symptoms and the Regulation of Drug Addiction

541. Offenders who have committed a crime in a state of intoxication caused by consuming alcohol, drugs, or other stupefying substances, are subject to criminal responsibility within the regular criminal procedure scheme (Article 23 UKR). It is

---

695. Federal Law on Changes to the Criminal Code, Oct. 21, 2013, N 270-FZ.
696. Criminal Code of the Russian Soviet Federative Socialist Republic, Oct. 27, 1960 (Ugolovnij Kodeks RSFSR).
697. For parties to crime, *see* Part I, Chapter 5, §2, paras. 590–634.
698. Paramonova, Grounds for excluding criminal liability in Russia. In: Sieber, U. / Jarvers, K. /Silverman, E. (ed(s).): Grounds for excluding criminal liability. Berlin, Duncker & Humblot, 2015, pp.156–157.

another question, however, whether alcohol or drugs can, for instance, cause diseases that lead to insanity and thereby exclude criminal responsibility (Article 21 UKR).

542. There are special rules with regard to offenders dependent on drugs. A court can suspend the enforcement of a sentence of a drug addict for up to five years if he/she has committed the narcotic and psychotropic substance-related crimes that are set out in Articles 228, paragraph 1, 231, paragraph 1, and 233 UKR for the first time. The offender must, in this case, show a willingness to undergo drug addiction treatment, as well as medical and social reformation that can be imposed by the court in addition to criminal punishment (Article 82.1 UKR).[699]

V. Insurmountable Fear

543. Insurmountable fear is not regarded as a separate ground for excluding criminal liability according to Russian criminal law. However, there are cases where other grounds for excluding criminal liability are applicable. For instance, if insurmountable fear results in mental abnormality,[700] it incurs legal consequences of this particular ground for excluding criminal liability.

699. Federal Law on Changes to the Criminal Code and Other Legal Provisions, Dec. 7, 2011, N 420-FZ; Paramonova, National characteristics, fundamental principles, and history of criminal law in Russia, 2014, p. 248.
700. *See* paras. 762–764.

Chapter 5. Inchoate Offenses and Parties to Crime

§1. Criminal Preparation and Attempt

I. Overview of Criminal Liability for Inchoate Offenses and Legal Framework

544. The general idea behind the criminalization of conduct prior to the completion of a target offense is that inchoate criminal activity (preparation and attempt) is already socially harmful and dangerous with regard to legally protected interests. Even though in an inchoate offense, the objective elements of the target crime have not all been fulfilled, the volitional and cognitive requirements (intent) with regard to the infringement of the relevant protected interests have been subjectively expressed.[701]

545. Another rationale behind the criminalization of conduct that has not yet led to a "criminal success" derives from the protective and preventive function of criminal law.[702] Thus, a possible violation of legally protected interests (if a "criminal success" takes place) opens the door to intervention by mechanisms of the criminal justice system. In the case of inchoate offenses, this means that law enforcement bodies are authorized to intervene at an early stage (preparation, attempt) in order to prevent graver consequences (target crime).[703]

546. Chapter 6 (Articles 29–31) of the Criminal Code of the Russian Federation is devoted to inchoate offenses.

547. Article 29 UKR gives the legal definition of both **completed and inchoate offenses** ***(неоконченное преступление)***.

Art. 29 UKR (Completed and inchoate offenses)[704]

(1) An offense is deemed to be completed if an act committed by a person contains all indicia of "elements of crime" provided for by this Code.
(2) Preparation for a crime and an attempt to commit a crime shall be deemed to be an inchoate offense.
(3) Criminal responsibility for an inchoate offense shall ensue according to the Article of this Code that enshrines responsibility for the completed crime, with reference to Article 30 of this Code.

---

701. For a discussion of intent, *see* Part I, Chapter 3, §3, II, paras. 392–408.
702. Naumov, Rossiiskoe ugolovnoe pravo, p. 24.
703. Paramonova, Punishable conduct prior to the completion of an offense in Russia. In: Sieber, U. / Jarvers, K. /Silverman, E. (ed(s).): Special forms of criminal liability. Berlin, Duncker & Humblot, 2015, pp.46–47.
704. All translations of the UKR in this chapter (revised by the author) are taken from Butler, Criminal Code of the Russian Federation.

548. A crime is a complex social phenomenon expressed in a certain action (omission) whose execution often proceeds through several stages of development. In the legal literature, these stages are called **stages of committing a crime** *(стадии совершения преступления)*.[705] The stages can be distinguished according to the extent to which objective as well as subjective aspects of the target crime[706] have been fulfilled.[707] The various stages serve as indicators of the extent to which the social danger has been realized: the closer to the completed target crime, the more deeply the committed act has infringed upon legally protected interests and the more socially dangerous the behavior.[708]

549. In compliance with the statutory definition, the legal literature[709] distinguishes between the following three stages: **preparation of a crime** *(приготовление к преступлению)*; **attempt to commit a crime** *(покушение на преступление)*, and **completed crime** *(оконченное преступление)*

550. The first two stages represent forms of inchoate criminal activity. With regard to preparation and attempt, certain obligatory indicia of elements of the target crime are lacking. This might be, for example, the objective elements of criminal liability (e.g., harmful consequences). A crime is deemed to be completed (third stage) if an act fulfills all the indicia of the elements of crime required by the offense definition: object of crime; objective side of crime; subjective side of crime; subject of crime.[710]

551. When the commission of a target crime takes place in stages, only the most advanced of the stages achieved by the actor en route to completion is of significance for criminal prosecution: previous stages are merged or superseded by the subsequent (more criminally dangerous) stage.[711] Thus, the conviction of the completed target crime precludes conviction for both attempt and preparation, and conviction for attempt precludes conviction for preparation.

552. Conduct prior to the completion of a (target) crime is considered less socially dangerous[712] since the target crime has not yet been consummated. This

---

705. Komissarov/Krilova/Tyazhkova, Ugolovnoe pravo RF, pp. 358–367; Naumov, Rossiiskoe ugolovnoe pravo, p. 421; Zhuravlev/Nikulin. Ugolovnoe pravo, p. 128; Paramonova, Punishable conduct prior to the completion of an offense in Russia. In: Sieber, U. / Jarvers, K. /Silverman, E. (ed(s).): Special forms of criminal liability. Berlin, Duncker & Humblot, 2015, pp.46.
706. Komissarov/Krilova/Tyazhkova, Ugolovnoe pravo RF, pp. 358–367; Naumov, Rossiiskoe ugolovnoe pravo, p. 421.
707. On the objective aspects of the offense, *see* Part I, Chapter 3, §2, paras. 342–371; on the subjective aspects of the offense, *see* Part I, Chapter 3, §4, paras. 383–428.
708. Revin, Ugolovnoe pravo Rossii, pp. 54–64; Naumov, Rossiiskoe ugolovnoe pravo, p. 424; Batichko, Uglovnoe pravo; Komissarov/Krilova/Tyazhkova, Ugolovnoe pravo RF, pp. 366–367.
709. Naumov, Rossiiskoe ugolovnoe pravo, p. 421; Komissarov/Krilova/Tyazhkova, Ugolovnoe pravo RF, pp. 364–367; Batichko, Uglovnoe pravo; Revin, Ugolovnoe pravo Rossii, pp. 54–64.
710. On the internal structure of the criminal offense, *see* Part I, Chapter 3, §1, paras. 331–341.
711. Naumov, Rossiiskoe ugolovnoe pravo, p. 424.
712. For discussion of the "social danger" concept, *see* Part I, Chapter 3, §1, paras. 317–330.

lower degree of social dangerousness is taken into consideration when the punishment for inchoate criminal activity is imposed.

553. Based on the postulate *cogitationis poenam nemo patitur* (no one can be punished for his or her thoughts or views), Russian criminal law does not punish mere criminal intent—expressed, for example, in diary entries—if it is not in some way coupled with an act.[713]

554. It must also be emphasized that, from the perspective of the subjective aspects of an offense, inchoate activity is criminalized only with regard to intentional behavior (Article 30, paragraphs 1 and 3 UKR).[714]

II. Preparation

555. Preparation, defined as the "intentional creation of conditions to commit a crime" (Article 30, paragraph 1 UKR), is a stage in the commission of a target crime that precedes attempt. Preparation can be committed at a considerable distance from the locus of commission of the offense,[715] and there can be a significant time gap between the preparation stage and the act of committing a crime.[716]

Art. 30 UKR (Preparation for crime and attempted crime)

(1) Preparation for a crime shall be deemed to be the finding, manufacturing, or adapting by a person of means or instruments for committing a crime, the finding of accomplices to a crime, the conspiracy to commit a crime, or any other intentional creation of conditions to commit a crime, if in so doing the crime has not been brought to the end due to circumstances beyond the control of this person.

(2) Criminal responsibility shall ensue only for preparation to commit grave or (and) especially grave crime.

---

713. *See* Naumov, Rossiiskoe ugolovnoe pravo, p. 422–423; Kudryavzev, Ugolovnoe pravo Rossii, pp. 239–243; Komissarov/Krilova/Tyazhkova, Ugolovnoe pravo RF, p. 362; Plenum of the Highest Court of the Russian Federation, 10.01.2000, N 6; On the objective aspects of the offense, *see* Part I, Chapter 3, §2, paras. 342–371.

714. Paramonova, Punishable conduct prior to the completion of an offense in Russia. In: Sieber, U. / Jarvers, K. /Silverman, E. (ed(s).): Special forms of criminal liability. Berlin, Duncker & Humblot, 2015, pp.47.

715. Paramonova, Internationales Strafrecht im Cyberspace, pp. 130–158; Revin, Ugolovnoe pravo Rossii, pp. 54–64.

716. Kudryavzev, Ugolovnoe pravo Rossii, pp. 243–247; Komissarov/Krilova/Tyazhkova, Ugolovnoe pravo RF, pp. 364–365; for extraterritorial jurisdiction, *see* paras. 282–303.

556. In the legal literature and in case law, the following elements of "preparation" have been elaborated. All requirements must be fulfilled in order for an actor to incur preparation liability:[717]

- conditions favorable for the commission of the crime—such as the elimination of obstacles to achieving the criminal result and/or the concoction of difficulties to hinder identification of the perpetrator, for example, the provision of a false alibi—must be created (objective criterion);
- preparatory criminal behavior must have been interrupted due to reasons beyond the control of the offender (objective criterion);[718] and
- preparatory activities must be undertaken with direct intent (subjective criterion).[719]

557. As a general rule, criminal liability is only incurred for completed and attempted crimes. As the preparation stage is regarded as remote from the completion of the offense, preparation as a form of inchoate criminal activity leads to criminal liability only in the context of grave or especially grave crimes such as homicide (Articles 30, paragraph 2, 105 UKR). Preparation for crimes of small and average gravity[720] is not criminalized.

558. Among other actions, the Criminal Code recognizes the following activities as forms of preparation (Article 30, paragraph 1 UKR): the **finding** ***(приискание)***, **manufacturing** ***(изготовление)***, or **adapting** ***(приспособление)*** of means or weapons/instruments for committing a crime, the **finding of accomplices to a crime** ***(приискание соучастников преступления)***, and **conspiracy to commit a crime** ***(сговор на совершение преступления)***.[721]

III. Attempt

559. The objective and subjective requirements of attempt liability, as reflected in its legal definition (Article 30, paragraph 3 UKR), have been developed and

717. Lebedev, Kommentarii k UK RF, pp. 64–70; Komissarov/Krilova/Tyazhkova, Ugolovnoe pravo RF, pp. 373 and 370–380; Zhuravlev/Nikulin, Ugolovnoe pravo, pp. 135–138; Kropachev/Volzhenkin/Orechov, Ugolovnoe pravo Rossii, pp. 534–540; Naumov, Rossiiskoe ugolovnoe pravo, pp. 424–430.
718. Kropachev/Volzhenkin/Orechov, Ugolovnoe pravo Rossii, p. 539.
719. On direct intent, *see* Part I, Chapter 3, §3, II, paras. 392–408. *See also* Bulletin of the Supreme Court RF (Бюллетень Верховного Суда РФ) 1996, N 8, p. 13; Komissarov/Krilova/Tyazhkova, Ugolovnoe pravo RF, pp. 377–378.
720. On the division of crimes into categories, *see* paras. 34, 638–646.
721. Komissarov/Krilova/Tyazhkova, Ugolovnoe pravo RF, pp. 373–377.

stated more precisely in case law and legal literature.[722] The distinction between preparation, attempt, and completion of the offense is made according to objective and subjective criteria.[723]

Art. 30 UKR (Preparation for crime and attempted crime)

(1)–(2) […]
An attempted crime shall be deemed to be intentional actions (omissions) of a person directly aimed towards the commission of a crime, if in so doing the crime has not been brought to the end due to circumstances beyond the control of this person.

A. *Objective Requirements of Attempt Liability*

560. The following three objective requirements must be fulfilled in order for an actor to incur attempt liability: the act must be directly aimed at the commission of a (target) crime; the target **crime** must be **incomplete** ***(незавершенность деяния)***; and the fact that the target crime was not completed must be due to circumstances beyond the control of the offender (Article 30, paragraph 3 UKR).[724]

561. The first requirement—the direct aim at the commission of a (target) crime—serves as a means of distinguishing between preparation and attempt. Whereas preparation involves the creation of conditions conducive to the commission of a crime, such as researching means and gathering instrumentalities (Article 30, paragraph 1 UKR), an attempt presents a real danger to the protected legal interest (Article 30, paragraph 3 UKR).[725] For example, someone who buys a gun in order to shoot another person has engaged in preparation, whereas someone who shoots at another person with a gun but misses has engaged in attempt.

562. With regard to this first requirement, it is important to note that incomplete criminal actions or omissions are classified according to the legally protected interest aimed at by the offender.[726] This way, one and the same act can be regarded as an attempt in the context of one target crime but as preparation in the context of another. For instance, breaking into a dwelling place with the goal of committing theft is regarded as attempted theft, whereas the same act (breaking into a dwelling

722. Blagov, Journal of Russian Law 2005 no. 8, 71–76; Kudryavzev, Ugolovnoe pravo Rossii, pp. 247–253; Komissarov/Krilova/Tyazhkova, Ugolovnoe pravo RF, pp. 380–389; Zhuravlev/Nikulin, Ugolovnoe pravo, pp. 132–135.
723. Paramonova, Punishable conduct prior to the completion of an offense in Russia. In: Sieber, U. / Jarvers, K. /Silverman, E. (ed(s).): Special forms of criminal liability. Berlin, Duncker & Humblot, 2015, pp.48–49.
724. Komissarov/Krilova/Tyazhkova, Ugolovnoe pravo RF, pp. 382–384.
725. Plenum of the Highest Court of the Russian Federation, 10.01.2000, N 6; Lebedev, Kommentarii k UK RF, p. 66.
726. Naumov, Rossiiskoe ugolovnoe pravo, pp. 432–434.

place) committed with the goal of committing homicide is considered as a preparation for the commission of homicide.[727]

563. Incompleteness of the target crime—the second requirement—is the main criterion for distinguishing between an inchoate offense and a completed target crime. An offense is deemed to be completed if an actor fulfills all indicia of elements of crime provided for by the Criminal Code (Article 29, paragraph 1 UKR). However, determining the moment when the target crime can be considered completed depends on the objective side of the relevant offense definition. Substantive (or result) crimes, for example, require a certain tangible result in order to reach the stage of "completed crime" (e.g., homicide, Article 105 UKR). Thus, in the case of result crimes, it is relatively easy to distinguish between attempt and completion. In contrast, formal (or conduct) crimes do not connect completion of the offense with any concrete harmful results (consequences in a narrow sense).[728] Some conduct crimes committed in the form of action can be regarded as attempted offenses. For example, the would-be rapist was not able to complete the crime. Nonetheless, with regard to most conduct crimes committed in the form of action (e.g., slander, Article 130 UKR) or omission (e.g., abandoning an endangered person, Article 125 UKR)—in contrast to result crimes—an attempt is indistinguishable.[729] A criminal action (omission) is already completed regardless of the consequences.[730]

564. The third objective requirement addresses the reason or reasons why the actor did not succeed in completing the offense. According to the Criminal Code, the target crime must remain incomplete due to circumstances beyond the actor's control (Article 30, paragraph 3 UKR). In other words, the criminal act remains incomplete despite the fact that the actor did everything in his or her power to complete it.[731] For example, the actor intended to break into a house but did not succeed because he or she did not manage to break the lock on the door.

565. Attempted crime is furthermore divided into two groups: **incomplete attempts** *(неоконченное покушение)* and **complete attempts** *(оконченное покушение)*.[732] An attempt is considered incomplete if the offender did not fulfill all planned and necessary actions (omissions) for the completion of the target crime and thus did not achieve the strived-for criminal result. An example of an incomplete attempt is a would-be hijacker who, while attempting to hijack an aircraft, is stopped by the aircraft crew (Articles 30, paragraph 3 and 211, paragraph 1 UKR). In contrast, an attempt is deemed complete if the actor fulfilled all acts that he or

727. Naumov, Rossiiskoe ugolovnoe pravo, p. 432.
728. On the distinction between conduct and result crimes, *see* Part I, Chapter 3, §2, paras. 252, 253, 363–368.
729. Naumov, Rossiiskoe ugolovnoe pravo, p. 433.
730. *See* Lebedev, Kommentarii k UK RF, pp. 62–63.
731. *See* Plenum of the Highest Court of the Russian Federation, 10.01.2000, N 6.
732. Komissarov/Krilova/Tyazhkova, Ugolovnoe pravo RF, pp. 386–388. On the role of distinction between complete and incomplete attempt in the context of abandonment of attempt, *see* Part I, Chapter 5, paras. 580–589.

she considered necessary, but the criminal "success" was not achieved due to circumstances beyond the actor's control. An example is a would-be terrorist who carries out all necessary acts in order to bomb a building, but the bomb is defused by law enforcement agents before it can explode (Articles 30, paragraph 3 and 205 UKR).

B. Subjective Requirements of Attempt Liability

566. Inchoate activity is criminalized only with regard to **intentional crimes** (*умышленные преступления*, Article 30, paragraphs 1 and 3 UKR).[733] While the Criminal Code itself contains no provisions specifying the type of intent sufficient for attempt liability, the prevailing opinion in both legal literature and case law is that indirect intent is insufficient while direct intent will suffice.[734]

567. The possibility of incurring attempt liability on the basis of indirect intent is excluded because, in cases of indirect intent, only so-called side effects of the criminal actions (omissions) are covered by the mental attitude of the offender: he or she "did not wish socially dangerous consequences, but consciously permitted them, or was indifferent to them" (Article 25, paragraph 3 UKR). Therefore, a person acting with indirect intent does not satisfy the criterion of Article 30, paragraph 3 UKR, according to which "an action (omission) must be directly aimed at the commission of a crime."

568. In contrast, persons acting with direct intent engage in intentional acts that are directly aimed at the completion of the offense: "the person was aware of the social danger of his actions (omissions), foresaw the possibility or inevitability of socially dangerous consequences ensuing from them, and wished for these consequences to ensue" (Article 25, paragraph 2 UKR). Thus, an attempted homicide is only possible in the context of direct intent, that is, when the offender was aware of the social danger of his or her actions (omissions), foresaw the possibility or inevitability of the death of another person, and wished that person's death. Attempt liability may be incurred for such conduct if a fatal consequence did not ensue due to the circumstances beyond the control of the offender, such as the victim's resistance, the intervention of others, etc.[735]

569. With respect to crimes of negligence,[736] the various stages of commission are not relevant from the criminal law perspective since there is no intent to commit

733. Komissarov/Krilova/Tyazhkova, Ugolovnoe pravo RF, pp. 385–386.
734. On direct and indirect intent, *see* Part I, Chapter 3, §3, II, paras. 392–408; Plenum of the Highest Court of the Russian Federation, 27.1.1999, N 1; Naumov, Rossiiskoe ugolovnoe pravo, p. 434; Blagov, Journal of Russian Law 2005 no. 8, 71–76.
735. Plenum of the Highest Court of the Russian Federation, 27.1.1999, N 1.
736. On negligence, *see* Part I, Chapter 3, §3, III, paras. 409–424.

a criminal act and thus no possibility of incurring inchoate liability. Criminal liability can be incurred for a negligent act only when criminalization is explicitly provided for in the Special Part of the Criminal Code (Article 24 UKR).[737]

IV. Attempting the Impossible and Other Specific Issues

A. *Attempting the Impossible*

570. In accordance with both case law and the prevailing scholarly opinion,[738] the two types of "complete attempts"—inchoate offenses in the form of an **attempt on an insufficient object** ***(покушение на негодный объект)*** and inchoate offenses in the form of an **attempt with insufficient means** ***(покушение с негодными средствами)***[739]—are treated like regular attempts.

571. No provisions in the Criminal Code expressly regulate this issue. Impossibility of the infringement of the legally protected interest is not regarded as a mitigating factor since in such case, the offender does everything in his or her power to obtain criminal "success," but the target crime remains incomplete due to circumstances beyond the offender's control (Article 30, paragraph 3 UKR).[740]

572. An **attempt on an insufficient object** occurs when the offender commits an error with regard to the object of an infringement. In such cases, no real danger or harm to the legally protected interest arises from the act. An offender who steals a coin purse in which there is no money, for example, commits such an attempt. Although the legally protected interest of property has not, in fact, been infringed upon, the act is nonetheless criminally punishable as an attempted theft (Articles 30, paragraph 3 and 158 UKR).

573. An **attempt with insufficient means** occurs when an actor chooses to carry out the target offense with means (i.e., tools, weapons, methods, processes, etc.) that he or she considers suitable for the fulfillment of the target offense but which could not allow him to possibly succeed in completing the offense due to the objective characteristics of the chosen means. An example of such an attempt is an offender who shoots at a person with an unloaded rifle, thinking that the weapon was loaded. This act is treated as an attempted homicide (Articles 30, paragraph 3, 105 UKR)

---

737. Paramonova, Punishable conduct prior to the completion of an offense in Russia. In: Sieber, U. / Jarvers, K. /Silverman, E. (ed(s).): Special forms of criminal liability. Berlin, Duncker & Humblot, 2015, pp.48–52.
738. Plenum of the Highest Court of the Russian Federation, 12.3.2002, N 5; Naumov, Rossiiskoe ugolovnoe pravo, p. 437; Batichko, Uglovnoe pravo; Komissarov/Krilova/Tyazhkova, Ugolovnoe pravo RF, p. 389.
739. Naumov, Rossiiskoe ugolovnoe pravo, pp. 435–437; Komissarov/Krilova/Tyazhkova, Ugolovnoe pravo RF, pp. 387–389.
740. Paramonova, Punishable conduct prior to the completion of an offense in Russia. In: Sieber, U. / Jarvers, K. /Silverman, E. (ed(s).): Special forms of criminal liability. Berlin, Duncker & Humblot, 2015, pp.52–53.

even though the legally protected interest of life is unharmed. This approach complies with the general rule for factual mistakes adopted in Russian criminal law: criminal responsibility is determined by the degree of culpability, namely, what the offender took into account and what he or she should and could have been aware of at the moment of committing the crime.[741]

574. The use of **obviously insufficient means** ***(очевидно непригодных средств)*** to commit a criminal offense—such as utilizing supernatural powers, spells, or incantations in order to kill someone—does, however, not lead to criminal attempt liability.[742]

B. Attempt and Complicity

575. The Criminal Code contains the following provisions with regard to attempt and complicity.[743]

Art. 34 UKR (Responsibility of parties to crime)

(1) The responsibility of parties to crime shall be determined by the character and the degree of the actual participation of each of them in the commission of the crime.

(2)–(4) […]

(5) If the perpetrator of a crime fails to bring a crime to the end due to the circumstances beyond his control, the remaining parties to crime shall bear criminal responsibility for preparation of a crime or for attempted crime. A person who has not succeeded in abetting other persons in committing a crime due to the circumstances beyond his control shall also bear criminal responsibility for preparation of the crime.

576. Participants in crime bear criminal responsibility for preparation or attempt if the perpetrator does not complete the crime due to circumstances beyond his or her control (Article 34, paragraph 5 UKR). In such cases, a so-called **unsuccessful participation** ***(неоконченное или неудавшееся соучастие)*** or attempted participation takes place.[744] The following is an example of unsuccessful participation: Perpetrator A, organizer B, and accessory C plan to commit a robbery. A is caught red-handed. A's actions are treated as an attempted crime. The actions of B and C

---

741. On mistakes of fact, *see* Part I, Chapter 4, §3, paras. 525–526; Lebedev, Kommentarii k UK RF, pp. 64–70; Paramonova, Punishable conduct prior to the completion of an offense in Russia. In: Sieber, U. / Jarvers, K. /Silverman, E. (ed(s).): Special forms of criminal liability. Berlin, Duncker & Humblot, 2015, pp. 53.
742. Kropachev/Volzhenkin/Orechov, Ugolovnoe pravo Rossii, p. 547.
743. For parties to crime, *see* Part I, Chapter 5, §2, paras. 590–634.
744. For a discussion on attempt, *see* Part I, Chapter 5, paras. 544–589; Komissarov/Krilova/Tyazhkova, Ugolovnoe pravo RF, pp. 444–446.

are regarded as participation in an attempted crime (Articles 161 and 30, paragraph 3 UKR in conjunction with Article 33, paragraphs 3 and 5 UKR, respectively).[745]

C. *Other*

577. Within the analysis of liability for criminal attempt, it is important to consider the following issues:

The first issue involves attempts in which the results of the crime actually committed are less serious than those of the intended crime. The general rule concerning the scope of the offender's intent in the determination of criminal responsibility is also applicable here.[746] If, for example, instead of stealing an original painting by a famous artist, the offender steals a copy of the painting (stealing of articles of special historical, scientific, or cultural value is criminalized by Article 164 UKR), the act is treated as an attempt to steal the intended items (Articles 30, paragraph 3 and 164 UKR); it is not regarded as a (completed) regular theft (Article 158 UKR). Hence, the intent of the offender (subjective side) and not the legally protected interest actually infringed upon is decisive.
The second issue refers to conduct involving crimes with unintentionally serious results.[747] In Russia, this situation is analyzed within the subjective side of the criminal offense (not within the framework of inchoate criminal activity). The intentional causing of grave harm to health, which leads to the death of the victim through negligence (Article 111, paragraph 4 UKR), is, for example, not regarded as an attempt of any kind but rather as a crime committed with two forms of culpability.[748] According to the construction "criminal responsibility with two forms of culpability," one form of culpability refers to socially dangerous conduct and another to the socially dangerous consequences of the act. This scheme is applicable only when the basic offense is committed intentionally, and the mental attitude toward the ensuing consequences is manifested, at least in the form of negligence (Article 27 UKR).

578. As already mentioned before, according to Article 30 UKR, incomplete crimes (preparation and attempt) in both forms (commission and omission, Article 14, paragraph 2 UKR) must be committed with direct intent (Article 30, paragraphs 1 and 3 UKR)—and not, for example, committed negligently—in order to be punishable by criminal law.[749]

---

745. Paramonova, Punishable conduct prior to the completion of an offense in Russia. In: Sieber, U. / Jarvers, K. /Silverman, E. (ed(s).): Special forms of criminal liability. Berlin, Duncker & Humblot, 2015, pp.53–54.
746. Kropachev/Volzhenkin/Orechov, Ugolovnoe pravo Rossii, p. 546.
747. On the subjective aspects of the offense, *see* Part I, Chapter 3, §4, paras. 383–428, and for the concept of "consequences of the offense," *see* Part I, Chapter 3, §2, paras. 342–361.
748. Naumov, Rossiiskoe ugolovnoe pravo, pp. 388–390; Lebedev, Kommentarii k UK RF, pp. 60–61.
749. Postanovlenie Plenuma Verhovnogo Suda RF (Supreme Court of Russian Federation), 27.01.1999, N 1, para. 2; for crimes of omission, *see* Part I, Chapter 3, §2, paras. 345–356.

579. The commission of so-called illusion offenses—offenses a person thinks are criminally prohibited, but that are, in fact, not criminal offenses—does not lead to criminal liability. This is due to the concept of crime (Article 14, paragraph 1 UKR)[750] and the principle of legality[751] (Article 3, paragraph 1 UKR), according to which only conduct that is prohibited by the criminal code is subject to punishment.[752]

V. Abandonment of Attempt

580. In the process of realizing a criminal plan, new circumstances may arise, and an actor may experience new motivations that conflict with the previously formed intention to commit a crime. Under the influence of such factors, an actor may not only change his or her initial criminal plan but may also abandon the attempt to commit a crime entirely, thus avoiding harmful consequences connected with criminal activity.[753] In order to encourage such behavior, Russian criminal law has provided a related ground for excluding criminal liability, namely, **voluntary refusal to commit a crime** ***(добровольный отказ от преступления).***[754]

581. The criminal law provision that regulates issues surrounding voluntary refusal (which can also be referred to as "abandonment of preparation and attempt") is Article 31 UKR.

Art. 31 UKR (Voluntary refusal to commit a crime)

(1) The voluntary refusal to commit a crime shall be deemed to be the termination by the person of preparation of a crime or the termination of actions (omissions) directly aimed at the commission of the crime, if the person was aware of the possibility of the crime being brought to the end.
(2) A person shall not be subject to criminal responsibility for a crime if he or she voluntarily and completely refused to bring this crime to the end.
(3) A person who has voluntarily refused to bring a crime to the end shall be subject to criminal responsibility if the act committed by him or her factually contains another "*corpus delicti.*"
(4)–(5) […]

750. On the concept of crime, *see* Part I, Chapter 3, §1, paras. 317–321.
751. For the principle of legality, *see* Part I, Chapter 1, paras. 197–226.
752. Paramonova, Punishable conduct prior to the completion of an offense in Russia. In: Sieber, U. / Jarvers, K. /Silverman, E. (ed(s).): Special forms of criminal liability. Berlin, Duncker & Humblot, 2015, pp.54–56.
753. Paramonova, Punishable conduct prior to the completion of an offense in Russia. In: Sieber, U. / Jarvers, K. /Silverman, E. (ed(s).): Special forms of criminal liability. Berlin, Duncker & Humblot, 2015, pp.56.
754. For grounds for excluding criminal liability, *see* Part I, Chapter 4, paras. 429–443; Zhuravlev/ Nikulin, Ugolovnoe pravo, pp. 138–141.

582. The three core requirements of "voluntary refusal to commit a crime"—as reflected in Article 31 UKR—have been developed and made more precise in case law and legal literature.[755] The requirements are as follows: **voluntary abandonment** *(добровольность отказа)*; **awareness of the possibility of bringing a crime to an end** *(осознание возможности доведения преступления до конца)* and **finality of abandonment** *(окончательность отказа)*.

583. Abandonment is considered to be voluntary if the person who has commenced committing a crime discontinues further criminal conduct out of his or her own free will—and not as a consequence of any formidable external obstacles (Article 31, paragraph 1 UKR).[756] Various motives for withdrawal are possible: remorse, compassion for the victim, fear of possible punishment, awareness of immorality of their behavior, etc.[757]

584. Another very important indicator of voluntary refusal is "awareness of the possibility of bringing a crime to an end." This awareness is based on the full confidence of the actor that there is nothing preventing him or her from completing the target crime. Even if the person choosing voluntary refusal was sure that he or she could successfully complete the target crime, although in fact there was no such possibility (something the person was not aware of), the person's behavior is still considered a "voluntary refusal to commit a crime."[758]

585. "Finality of abandonment" means that the person who has started committing an offense abandons commission completely and irrevocably—not temporarily—with no intention of resuming commission in the future. In contrast, if a person only suspends continuation of the commission of the already started crime—in order, for instance, to complete it when conditions are more favorable—he or she cannot be considered having engaged in a voluntary refusal to commit a crime (Article 31 UKR).[759]

586. There are two forms of voluntary abandonment: **active abandonment** *(добровольный отказ, выраженный в активных действиях)* and **passive abandonment** *(добровольный отказ, выраженный в пассивных действиях)*. They depend on the nature of the commenced criminal activity.

587. In the case of a complete attempt, voluntary abandonment is manifested in active behavior aimed at preventing the possible criminal result. An example is an offender who puts poison into the victim's glass but then changes his or her mind and gets rid of the glass.

755. Komissarov/Krilova/Tyazhkova, Ugolovnoe pravo RF, pp. 389–395.
756. Blagov, Journal of Russian Law 2005 no. 8, 71–76; Komissarov/Krilova/Tyazhkova, Ugolovnoe pravo RF, p. 391.
757. Plenum of the Highest Court of the Russian Federation, 12.3.2001, N 5.
758. Komissarov/Krilova/Tyazhkova, Ugolovnoe pravo RF, p. 392.
759. Komissarov/Krilova/Tyazhkova, Ugolovnoe pravo RF, p. 392; Kropachev/Volzhenkin/Orechov, Ugolovnoe pravo Rossii, p. 551.

588. In the cases of preparation of a crime and incomplete attempt, voluntary abandonment may be expressed through both active as well as passive withdrawal from continuing the commission of the criminal act. An example of active abandonment is when A, an organizer of a crime, hits B, a perpetrator, in order to prevent B from committing the crime. An example of passive abandonment is when C, the organizer of a crime, does not give the planned sign to perpetrator D so that D does not arrive on time to commit the crime.

589. Voluntary abandonment of completion of the target crime must be distinguished from **active repentance** (*деятельного раскаяния*, Article 75 UKR). For example, compensation for the damage inflicted by the crime or giving oneself up after committing a crime are forms of active repentance. The following are three differences between voluntary abandonment and active repentance: First, voluntary abandonment is only possible before the completion of the target crime; active repentance is possible only after its completion. Second, voluntary abandonment may be manifested by means of passive behavior (discontinuing the commission of a crime); active repentance requires active behavior. Finally, voluntary abandonment negates criminal liability; active repentance is a circumstance that leads to the mitigation of punishment.[760]

§2. Parties to Criminal Offenses

I. Introduction

590. One of the most complex and important aspects of the theory of criminal law is the institution of complicity. Criminal activity can, in fact, be carried out not only by a single person but also by a group of persons and even by an organized group of persons with a complex hierarchical structure.[761]

591. **Complicity or participation in a crime** *(соучастие в преступлении)* is recognized in the legal scholarship as a special type of criminal activity that differs from the prototype situation in which a crime is carried out by a single perpetrator acting alone.[762] Participation in crime is defined by law as "an intentional joint participation of two or more persons in the commission of an intentional crime" (Article 32 UKR).

760. Paramonova, Punishable conduct prior to the completion of an offense in Russia. In: Sieber, U. / Jarvers, K. /Silverman, E. (ed(s).): Special forms of criminal liability. Berlin, Duncker & Humblot, 2015, pp.56–61.

761. Komissarov/Krilova/Tyazhkova, Ugolovnoe pravo RF, pp. 397–398; Paramonova, Parties to Crime in Russia. In: Sieber, U. / Jarvers, K. /Silverman, E. (ed(s).): Special forms of criminal liability. Berlin, Duncker & Humblot, 2015, pp. 185–186.

762. Naumov, Rossiiskoe ugolovnoe pravo, p. 445; Komissarov/Krilova/Tyazhkova, Ugolovnoe pravo RF, pp. 397–399.

592. According to the legal scholarship, when committed by multiple parties,[763] the objective side of the offense is characterized by the following two elements: quantity, that is, the participation of more than one person with criminal capacity,[764] and **causality** ***(причинно-следственная связь)***,[765] namely, a causal relationship between an act and the consequences.[766]

593. The criminal liability of parties to crime is governed by the **principle of individual responsibility** (***принцип индивидуальной ответственности***, Article 34, paragraph 1 UKR);[767] the liability of each party is determined by the character and the degree of that person's actual contribution to the commission of the crime.

594. The institution "participation in crime" was established as a result of the need to legitimate the attribution of criminal liability to persons—such as instigators—who have made a causal contribution to a criminal act but whose contribution is not made through direct performance or through the physical commission of an act.[768]

595. The approach taken by the Russian legal system on this subject is two-pronged. First, it recognizes various **types of participation** ***(виды соучастников преступления)***, and second, it recognizes various **types of collaboration** ***(формы соучастия)***. The four types of participation focus on the nature of an individual participant's contribution (Article 33 UKR). The four types of collaboration, which are analyzed in legal scholarship and defined in the law (Article 35 UKR), center on the degree of concurrence of behavior of the parties to crime and on the level and the quality of organization and collaboration of the participants.

596. At this point, it is important to mention that a number of different approaches are taken into account in legal scholarship with regard to the criminal liability of parties to crime. The theory based on the accessory nature of participation, that is, on the idea that the criminal liability of parties to crime derives from or is dependent on the responsibility of the perpetrator (i.e., the person who fulfills

---

763. On the concept of the criminal offense, *see* Part I, Chapter 3, §1, paras. 317–321; on objective aspects of the offense, *see* Part I, Chapter 3, §2, paras. 342–371.
764. For a discussion of criminal capacity, *see* Part I, Chapter 3, §1 paras. 317–321.
765. For causality, *see* Part I, Chapter 3, §2, paras. 357–361.
766. Ignatov/Krasikov, Kurs rossijskogo ugolovnogo prava, pp. 254–258; Naumov, Rossiiskoe ugolovnoe pravo, p. 446; on causality, *see* Part I, Chapter 3, §2, paras. 357–361.
767. For the principles of criminal law, *see* Part I, Chapter 1, paras. 194–196.
768. Komissarov/Krilova/Tyazhkova, Ugolovnoe pravo RF, p. 398.

the objective side of the crime),[769] is reflected in criminal law provisions and followed in the case law. According to this theory, a perpetrator must be found guilty in order for other parties to crime to incur criminal liability.[770]

II. Legal Rules on Parties to Crime

597. Issues involving parties to crime are regulated in provisions of both the General and the Special Parts of the Criminal Code.

598. The General Part of the Criminal Code addresses the following issues: definition of complicity (Article 32 UKR), types of participation (Article 33 UKR), and types of collaboration (Article 35 UKR). In addition, all types of multi-party collaboration (Article 63, paragraph 1, item c UKR), as well as the playing of an especially active role in the commission of a crime (Article 63, paragraph 1, item d UKR), are considered circumstances aggravating punishment with regard to any crime committed in complicity (independent of the type of participation or collaboration).[771]

> Art. 32 UKR (The concept of complicity in a crime)[772]
> The intentional joint participation of two or more persons in the commission of an intentional crime shall be deemed to be complicity in a crime.
>
> Art. 33 UKR (Types of parties to a crime)
>
> (1) Organizer, instigator, and accessory shall, together with the perpetrator, be deemed to be parties to crime.
> (2) A person who has actually committed a crime or who directly participated in its commission together with other persons (co-perpetrators), and also a person who has committed a crime by means of the use of other persons who are not subject to criminal responsibility by virtue of age, insanity, or other circumstances provided for by this Code, shall be deemed to be a perpetrator.
> (3) A person who has organized the commission of a crime or has directed its commission, and also a person who has created an organized group or a criminal community (criminal organization) or has guided them, shall be deemed to be an organizer.
> (4) A person who has abetted another person in committing a crime by persuasion, bribery, threat, or by any other method shall be deemed to be an instigator.

---

769. On the objective aspects of the offense, *see* Part I, Chapter 3, §2, paras. 342–371.
770. Naumov, Rossiiskoe ugolovnoe pravo, pp. 464–468; Paramonova, Parties to Crime in Russia. In: Sieber, U. / Jarvers, K. /Silverman, E. (ed(s).): Special forms of criminal liability. Berlin, Duncker & Humblot, 2015, pp. 186.
771. Paramonova, Parties to Crime in Russia. In: Sieber, U. / Jarvers, K. /Silverman, E. (ed(s).): Special forms of criminal liability. Berlin, Duncker & Humblot, 2015, pp. 187–188.
772. All translations of the UKR in this chapter (revised by the author) are taken from Butler, Criminal Code of the Russian Federation.

(5) A person who has assisted in the commission of a crime by advice, instructions, the granting of information, means, or implements for commission of the crime, or by elimination of obstacles, and also a person who has promised beforehand to conceal the criminal, means, or implements for commission of the crime, traces of the crime, or objects obtained by criminal means, and equally a person who has promised beforehand to acquire or sell such objects, shall be deemed to be an accessory.

Art. 35 UKR (The commission of a crime by a group of persons, by a group of persons with a prior agreement, by an organized group, or by a criminal community [criminal organization])

(1) A crime shall be deemed to be committed by a group of persons if two or more perpetrators have jointly participated in its commission without a prior agreement.
(2) A crime shall be deemed to be committed by a group of persons with a prior agreement, if the persons who agreed beforehand to the joint commission of the crime participated therein.
(3) A crime shall be deemed to be committed by an organized group, if it has been committed by a stable group of persons who in advance united for the commission of one or more offenses.
(4) A crime shall be deemed to be committed by a criminal community (criminal organization), if it has been committed by a structured organized group or by an association of organized groups, that operate under the unified leadership, whose members are united with the goal of jointly commission of one or more grave or especially grave crimes in order to obtain, directly or indirectly, a financial or other material benefits.
(5) A person who has created an organized group or a criminal community, or has had a leadership over them, shall be subject to criminal responsibility for the organization and direction thereof in the cases provided for by the Articles 208, 209, 210 and 282.1 of the present Code, and also for all the offenses committed by the organized group or the criminal community (criminal organization), if they have been covered by his/her intent. Other participants of the organized group or criminal community (criminal organization) shall bear criminal responsibility for their participation in cases provided for by Articles 205.4, 208, 209, 210, and 282.1 of the present Code, and also for the crimes, in the preparation or commission of which they have participated.[773]
(6) The creation of an organized group in cases which are not provided for by articles of the Special Part of the present Code shall entail criminal responsibility for the preparation of those offenses for the commission of which it was created.

---

773. Federal Law on Changes to Criminal Code, Nov. 30. 2009, N 245-FZ and Nov. 2, 2014, N 302-FZ.

(7) The commission of a crime by a group of persons, by a group of persons with a prior agreement, by an organized group, or by a criminal community (criminal organization) shall entail a more severe punishment on the basis and within the limits provided for by the present Code.

Art. 63 UKR (Circumstances aggravating punishment)

1. The following circumstances shall be deemed to be aggravating circumstances:

   […]

   c) commission of a crime by a group of persons or a group of persons as a result of a prior agreement, by an organized group, or by a criminal community (criminal organization);
   d) especially active role played in the commission of a crime;

   […].

599. In addition to the provisions located in the General Part, there are also provisions in the Special Part of the Criminal Code that are relevant to the multi-party commission of crime. These norms address specific types of multi-party collaboration that differ from the groups or organizations mentioned in Article 34 UKR. The organization and creation of a terrorist community (Article 205.4 UKR) and the organization and creation of an extremist community (Article 282.1 UKR) are, for example, criminalized by norms in the Special Part of the Criminal Code.

III. Forms of Multi-party Commission

600. In legal scholarship, there are different classifications of complicity.

601. First, depending on the combination of the joint efforts of parties to crime, the legal scholarship divides all manifestations of participation in crime into two categories: **simple complicity** *(простое соучастие)* and **complex complicity** *(сложное соучастие)*.[774]

602. **Simple complicity**, or so-called **co-perpetration** *(соисполнительство)*, is characterized by multi-party participation in crime with no difference between the roles or qualities of the contribution of each party to the offense. An example of simple complicity is two persons beating up a third person, with their conduct bringing about grave harm to the third person's health.[775]

603. **Complex complicity** involves distinct roles in and/or various qualities of contributions to the commission of the crime. Thus, in addition to a perpetrator,

774. Paramonova, Parties to Crime in Russia. In: Sieber, U. / Jarvers, K. /Silverman, E. (ed(s).): Special forms of criminal liability. Berlin, Duncker & Humblot, 2015, pp. 189–190.
775. Ignatov/Krasikov, Kurs rossijskogo ugolovnogo prava, pp. 260–261.

complex complicity requires the involvement of at least one other type of participant, such as an organizer, instigator, or an accessory.[776]

604. Second and third classifications refer to different types of participation and collaboration. In the legal scholarship, complicity is divided into various **types of participation in crime or qualities of contributions** ***(виды соучастников преступления)*** and various **types of collaboration** ***(формы соучастия)***. The types of participation are relevant for identifying the degree of contribution of each individual participant, whereas the types of collaboration reflect the level of organization of the participants involved. Therefore, the various types are combinable.[777]

A. *Types of Participation*

605. Depending on the character and the degree of the actual contribution, the objective role, and the function of each participant in the commission of the crime, the legal scholarship recognizes four **types of participation in crime** ***(виды соучастников преступления)***. The Criminal Code provides for all four of these types.

606. The various types of participation in crime (Article 33 UKR) are characterized as follows:

607. A **perpetrator** (***исполнитель***, Article 33, paragraph 2 UKR) is someone who fulfills the objective side[778] of a target crime by him- or herself or someone who directly participates in the commission of a target crime together with another person or persons (co-perpetrator[s]). The term also applies to someone, the so-called perpetrator by means, who commits a crime by means of another person who is not subject to criminal liability by virtue of age, insanity, or other circumstances. There can be more than one perpetrator per crime. In order for participants to be recognized as co-perpetrators, their acts need not be factually identical but, taken together, the acts must fulfill the objective side of the target crime. For instance, during the commission of a robbery, perpetrator A threatens the victim with a gun while co-perpetrator B takes away the victim's bag. In this example, the acts of the two co-perpetrators, taken together, fulfill the objective side of the crime.[779]

---

776. Naumov, Rossiiskoe ugolovnoe pravo, p. 455; Komissarov/Krilova/Tyazhkova, Ugolovnoe pravo RF, pp. 424–425.
777. Paramonova, Parties to Crime in Russia. In: Sieber, U. / Jarvers, K. /Silverman, E. (ed(s).): Special forms of criminal liability. Berlin, Duncker & Humblot, 2015, pp. 189.
778. On the objective aspects of the offense, *see* Part I, Chapter 3, §2, paras. 342–371.
779. Ignatov/Krasikov, Kurs rossijskogo ugolovnogo prava, pp. 267–270.

608. An **organizer** (*организатор*, Article 33, paragraph 3 UKR) organizes the commission of a crime or directs its commission. Someone who creates an organized group or a criminal community (criminal organization) or who guides such a group or organization is also an organizer.

609. An **instigator** (*подстрекатель*, Article 33, paragraph 4 UKR) abets another person in the commission of a crime by persuasion, bribery, threat, or any other method. Abetting means creating or generating in another person the intent to commit a crime. There are different forms of instigation, including promising, incitement to hatred, and deception.[780]

610. An **accessory** (*пособник*, Article 33, paragraph 5 UKR) facilitates the commission of a crime by means of advice, instructions, the granting of information, means, or implements for committing the crime, or by eliminating obstacles. Persons who promise beforehand to conceal the perpetrator, the means or implements for commission of the crime, traces of the crime, or objects obtained by criminal means, as well as persons who promise beforehand to acquire or sell such objects are also accessories. The facilitation can be material (e.g., transportation, weapons, or money) or intellectual (e.g., advice, support, or instructions).[781]

611. Among the four types of participants in crime, only the perpetrator (Article 33, paragraph 2 UKR) actually commits the crime by carrying out an act that forms an objective side[782] of the crime or by directly participating in its commission together with other persons (co-perpetrators). Hence, (co)perpetrator(s) are immediately involved in the commission of crime. In contrast, organizers, instigators, as well as accessories (Article 33, paragraphs 3–5 UKR) participate in the commission of a crime indirectly by contributing, by organizing, or by abetting and aiding. They do not directly fulfill the objective side of the crime.[783]

B. Types of Collaboration

612. The **types of collaboration** ***(формы соучастия)*** recognized by the legal scholarship and defined in Article 35 UKR are classified into the following four groups, depending on the absence or presence of a **prior agreement** ***(предварительный сговор)*** between participants and on the level or degree of organization:

– **group of persons without a prior agreement** (*группа лиц без предварительного сговора*, Article 35, paragraph 1 UKR);

780. Ignatov/Krasikov, Kurs rossijskogo ugolovnogo prava, pp. 271–274; Naumov, Rossiiskoe ugolovnoe pravo, p. 452.
781. Ignatov/Krasikov, Kurs rossijskogo ugolovnogo prava, pp. 274–277.
782. On the objective aspects of the offense, *see* Part I, Chapter 3, §2, paras. 342–371.
783. Naumov, Rossiiskoe ugolovnoe pravo, p. 451.

- **group of persons with a prior agreement** (*группа лиц по предварительному сговор*, Article 35, paragraph 2 UKR);
- **organized group** (*организованная группа*, Article 35, paragraph 3 UKR);
- **criminal community or criminal organization** (*преступное сообщество или преступная организация*, Article 35, paragraph 4 UKR).

613. Within every type of criminal collaboration, there can be different combinations of participants in crime. An exception is the first type: group of persons without prior agreement (Article 35, paragraph 1 UKR). It requires the participation of at least two perpetrators. Criminal collaboration in the form of groups of persons with a prior agreement, organized groups, and criminal community or organization can be committed by perpetrators, organizers, instigators, and accessories (in various combinations).[784]

IV. Requirements of Complicity

614. In accordance with the legal norms, objective and subjective requirements for criminal complicity that are applicable to all types of participation and collaboration in crime have been developed by the legal scholarship. These requirements make it possible to distinguish between criminal complicity and the coincidental overlapping of criminal activity of persons who objectively infringe upon the same legally protected interests but who act independently of one another and who are not united by the same intent.[785] An example of the latter is when goods are stolen from a store that happened not to be locked by random passers-by who did not agree in advance to engage in stealing.

A. Objective Requirements of Criminal Complicity

615. According to the legal scholarship, the objective side of the offense when committed by multiple parties[786] is characterized by the following two elements: quantity[787] (participation of more than one person with criminal capacity) and **causality**[788] ***(причинно-следственная связь)***, namely, a causal relationship between an act and the consequences.[789]

784. Paramonova, Parties to Crime in Russia. In: Sieber, U. / Jarvers, K. /Silverman, E. (ed(s).): Special forms of criminal liability. Berlin, Duncker & Humblot, 2015, pp.190–202.
785. Taganzev, Russkoe ugolovnoe pravo, p. 329; Naumov, Rossiiskoe ugolovnoe pravo, p. 445.
786. On the concept of the criminal offense, *see* Part I, Chapter 3, §1, paras. 317–321; for a discussion of objective aspects of the offense, *see* Part I, Chapter 3, §2, paras. 342–371.
787. For a discussion of criminal capacity and for elements of crime, *see* Part I, Chapter 3, §1 paras. 331–341.
788. On causality, *see* Part I, Chapter 3, §2, paras. 357–361.
789. Ignatov/Krasikov, Kurs rossijskogo ugolovnogo prava, pp. 254–258; Naumov, Rossiiskoe ugolovnoe pravo, p. 446; on the concept of the criminal offense, *see* Part I, Chapter 3, §1, paras. 317–321; for a discussion of objective aspects of the offense, *see* Part I, Chapter 3, §2, paras. 342–371.

616. The first—the quantity characteristic—requires the participation of two or more persons with criminal capacity.[790] If a perpetrator uses, for instance, a minor or an insane person in order to commit a crime, only the perpetrator—who has criminal capacity—is criminally liable. However, liability for complicity may be incurred even if one or more participants with criminal capacity are released from criminal liability on the basis of one of the grounds provided for by law, for example, by virtue of active repentance or reconciliation with the victim (Articles 75, 76 UKR).[791]

617. The second objective requirement is a causal relationship between the acts of each participant and the criminal result.[792] As mentioned before, the criminal activity of the participants can be divided into four groups: actions directly aimed at achieving the criminal result (perpetrator), actions connected with organizing the commission of a crime (organizer), actions facilitating the commission of a crime or concealing its traces (accessory), and actions associated with participation in an organized group or criminal community. The key condition for causality is that the acts or omissions of each participant are directed toward committing the same crime and achieving a common criminal result.

618. In determining whether or not a causal relationship exists, it is essential to consider the objective side of the crime at issue,[793] namely, whether it is a formal ("non-result") crime or a substantive, so-called material ("harmful result") crime.[794] In the case of formal crimes, it is sufficient to establish causality between the behavior of a participant and the acts of the perpetrator(s), for example, giving a bribe (Article 291 UKR), whereas with regard to substantive crimes, for example, homicide, there must be a causal relationship between the acts of the participant and the harmful consequences that were the result of the perpetrator's behavior.[795]

B. Subjective Requirements of Criminal Complicity

619. Only intentional acts or omissions can form the basis of criminal complicity. Hence, criminal participation is only possible for intentional crimes.[796]

620. Intent in the context of criminal complicity is manifested in the mutual awareness of each party regarding the commission of an offense and the coherence

790. For a discussion of objective aspects of the offense, *see* Part I, Chapter 3, §2, paras. 342–371.
791. On the grounds for terminating or expunging criminal liability, *see* Paramonova, Grounds for excluding criminal liability in Russia, 2016, pp.353–354.
792. For a discussion of the objective side of the crime, *see* Part I, Chapter 3, §2, paras. 342–371.
793. For a discussion of the objective side of the crime, *see* Part I, Chapter 3, §2, paras. 342–371.
794. For a discussion of the objective side of the crime, *see* Part I, Chapter 3, §2, paras. 342–371; Naumov, Rossiiskoe ugolovnoe pravo, p. 447.
795. Paramonova, Parties to Crime in Russia. In: Sieber, U. / Jarvers, K. /Silverman, E. (ed(s).): Special forms of criminal liability. Berlin, Duncker & Humblot, 2015, pp. 195–196.
796. On the subjective aspects of the offense, *see* Part I, Chapter 3, §4, paras. 383–428.

of their acts.[797] Mutual awareness is reflected in the fact that each participant is aware (intellectual element)[798] and wishes (volitional element)[799] that his or her acts or omissions are of a joint nature in committing a certain crime and that they aim at achieving a common criminal result.[800] The presence of these intellectual and volitional elements expresses the necessary psychological connection between the participants, which determines the compatibility of their activities in fulfilling the common goal.

621. Negligence does not require mutual awareness and willingness directed toward the achievement of a mutual criminal goal,[801] and criminal participation is excluded in crimes of negligence.[802]

622. There are two kinds of intent: direct (awareness and foresight of the inevitability or possibility of the onset of socially dangerous consequences and wishing for the onset of the socially dangerous consequences, Article 25, paragraph 2 UKR) and indirect (awareness and foresight of the inevitability or possibility of the onset of socially dangerous consequences and not wishing the onset of these consequences, but the conscious allowance of them or indifference to them, Article 25, paragraph 3 UKR).[803] In the legal scholarship there is a discussion on the question of whether direct and/or indirect intent is required for criminal participation. One group of authors considers complicity to be possible only in the case of crimes committed with direct intent.[804] Another group takes the position that participation in crime is possible in cases of both direct and indirect intent.[805] Judicial practice follows the second position.[806] According to this position, mental attitude (type of intent) is determined in two steps: first, with regard to the criminal conduct, and second, with regard to the consequences of this conduct. The mental attitude of the participants with regard to both criminal conduct and harmful consequences must be manifested in some form of intent.

623. As far as criminal conduct in the context of multi-party commission of crime (e.g., abetting or organizing committing crimes) is concerned, the mental attitude of the participants must be manifested in the form of direct intent. For instance,

797. On the subjective aspects of the offense, *see* Part I Chapter 3, §4, paras. 383–428.
798. On the subjective aspects of the offense, *see* Part I Chapter 3, §4, paras. 383–428.
799. On the subjective aspects of the offense, *see* Part I Chapter 3, §4, paras. 383–428.
800. Komissarov/Krilova/Tyazhkova, Ugolovnoe pravo RF, p. 409–410; Naumov, Rossiiskoe ugolovnoe pravo, pp. 447–448.
801. On the subjective aspects of the offense, *see* Part I Chapter 3, §4, paras. 383–428.
802. Naumov, Rossiiskoe ugolovnoe pravo, p. 448.
803. On the subjective aspects of the offense, *see* Part I Chapter 3, §4, paras. 383–428.
804. On the subjective aspects of the offense, *see* Part I, Chapter 3, §4, paras. 383–428; Burchak, Uchenie o souchastii, pp. 119–122; Komissarov/Krilova/Tyazhkova, Ugolovnoe pravo RF, pp. 407–410.
805. On the subjective aspects of the offense, *see* Part I, Chapter 3, §4, paras. 383–428; Naumov, Rossiiskoe ugolovnoe pravo, p. 447–449.
806. Plenum of the Highest Court of the Russian Federation, Dec. 28, 1999, N 1.

in the case of participation in a formal ("non-result") crime,[807] parties to crime incur criminal liability only if they act with direct intent. For instance, a slander one cannot commit without direct intent.

624. As far as the harmful consequences that result from the perpetrator's behavior are concerned, the mental attitude of the participant can be manifested in the form of indirect intent.[808] For instance, an instigator must have at least an indirect intent toward the harmful result of the criminal behavior of the perpetrator. For example, if G mentions in a conversation with four people that G's friend F's expensive paintings are not locked one day, as they usually are, in a safe, and the next day, one of the four people steals F's paintings, G's conduct can be classified as instigation due to a presence of indirect intent. However, if G mentions in a conversation with four people that his friend F possesses expensive paintings, and the next day one of the four people steals F's paintings because F forgets to lock his safe, G's conduct cannot be classified as instigation due to a lack of intent.

625. In sum, direct intent regarding criminal behavior and indirect intent with regard to harmful consequences are the minimum subjective requirements of guilt for all four types of participation in crime (Article 33 UKR).[809]

V. Criminal Liability of Parties to Crime

626. There are two major theories in legal scholarship regarding the criminal liability of parties to crime. The first theory is based on the independence of the criminal liability of participants from the acts of the perpetrator. The second theory—which is reflected in legal provisions and followed by the judicial practice—is based on the accessory nature of participation, that is, the criminal liability of participants is considered derivative or dependent on the liability of the perpetrator.[810] Due to the fact that the objective side of the crime is fulfilled by the perpetrator, the liability of the other participants is dependent on the perpetrator's acts.

627. Nonetheless, the criminal liability of participants is not fully accessorial. For instance, the principle of individual responsibility (Article 34, paragraph 1 UKR) requires the criminal liability of a participant to be determined according to his or her actual role and the quality of his or her contribution to the commission of the crime. At the same time, this principle has an accessory side as well since the criminal liability of participants derives from the behavior of a perpetrator.

807. For a discussion of the objective side of the crime, *see* Part I, Chapter 3, §2, paras. 342–371; Naumov, Rossiiskoe ugolovnoe pravo, p. 447.
808. Ignatov/Krasikov, Kurs rossijskogo ugolovnogo prava, pp. 212–217; Naumov, Rossiiskoe ugolovnoe pravo, pp. 375–379.
809. On the subjective aspects of the offense, *see* Part I, Chapter 3, §4, paras. 383–428; Paramonova, Parties to Crime in Russia. In: Sieber, U. / Jarvers, K. /Silverman, E. (ed(s).): Special forms of criminal liability. Berlin, Duncker & Humblot, 2015, pp.196–198.
810. Naumov, Rossiiskoe ugolovnoe pravo, pp. 464–468.

Art. 34 UKR (Responsibility of parties to crime)

(1) The responsibility of accomplices in a crime shall be determined by the character and the degree of the actual participation of each of them in the commission of the crime.
(2) Co-perpetrators shall be responsible under the Article of the Special Part of this Code for a crime committed by them jointly, without reference to Article 33 of this Code.
(3) The criminal responsibility of an organizer, instigator, and accessory shall ensue under the Article that provides for punishment for the crime committed, with reference to Article 33 of this Code, except for in cases when they simultaneously were co-perpetrators of the crime.
(4) A person who is not a participant in a crime specially indicated in the relevant Article of the Special Part of this Code and who has taken part in the commission of the crime, stipulated by this Article, shall bear criminal responsibility for the given offense as its organizer, instigator, or accessory.
(5) If the perpetrator of a crime fails to carry out the crime due to the circumstances beyond his/her control, then other participants shall bear criminal responsibility for preparations for a crime or attempted crime. A person who did not succeed in abetting other persons to commit a crime due to the circumstances beyond his/her control shall also bear criminal responsibility for preparations for the crime.

VI. Special Cases

A. Excessive Acts of the Perpetrator

628.

Art. 36 UKR (Excessive act of the perpetrator)
The commission of a crime that is not embraced by the intent of other parties to a crime shall be deemed to be an excessive act of the perpetrator. Other parties to the crime shall not be subject to criminal responsibility for the excessive act of the perpetrator.

629. The rule that a party to a crime is not subject to criminal liability for acts of the perpetrator not encompassed by his or her intent (Article 36 UKR) is based on the principle of culpability (Article 14, paragraph 1 UKR)[811] and on the principle of individual responsibility (Article 34, paragraph 1 UKR). Parties to a crime are criminally liable only to the extent of their mutual agreement or plan. In order to incur criminal liability for a crime committed by a perpetrator, a party to a crime must be aware of the perpetrator's criminal intentions.

811. For the principles of criminal law, *see* Part I, Chapter 1, paras. 194–196.

630. The two types of **excessive acts** *(эксцесс исполнителя преступления)* that a perpetrator can commit, quantitative and qualitative, are dealt with differently in legal scholarship. This difference has a certain practical value as it affects the classification of the criminal acts of parties to a crime, in particular, the acts of the perpetrator.

631. **Quantitative excess** *(количественный эксцесс)* takes place when a perpetrator commits acts of the same nature as all parties to a crime agreed upon, but with more serious consequences.[812] For example, an accessory, instigator, and perpetrator agree to beat up a victim in order to cause light harm to his or her health; however, the perpetrator causes grave harm to the victim's health. In this example, the perpetrator is held responsible for the more serious crime that he or she actually committed, namely, intentional causing of grave harm to health (Article 111 UKR). Other parties to the crime are responsible only for participation in intentional causing of light harm to health (Article 115 UKR in conjunction with Article 33 UKR, if necessary Article 27 UKR).

632. **Qualitative excess** *(качественный эксцесс)* occurs where a perpetrator commits an act of a different character than the act agreed upon by the parties.[813] For example, an accessory, instigator, and perpetrator agree to beat up a victim in order to cause light harm to his or her health; the perpetrator, however, kills the victim.[814] In this example, the perpetrator is held responsible for homicide (Article 105 UKR). As in the case of quantitative excess, the other parties are criminally liable only within the scope of their intent (Article 115 UKR in conjunction with Article 33 UKR, if necessary Article 27 UKR).[815]

B. Participation and Omission

633. The commission of a crime by omission is possible for perpetrators, instigators, and accessories (Articles 14, paragraph 2, 33 UKR). The exception is the organizer, whose role always requires positive action (Article 33, paragraph 3 UKR).[816]

634. The perpetrator can be subject to criminal liability by actually committing a crime of omission if he or she has a legal duty and possibility to act.[817] For

812. Ignatov/Krasikov, Kurs rossijskogo ugolovnogo prava, pp. 281–282; Komissarov/Krilova/Tyazhkova, Ugolovnoe pravo RF, p. 444; Naumov, Rossiiskoe ugolovnoe pravo, p. 468.
813. Naumov, Rossiiskoe ugolovnoe pravo, p. 469; Komissarov/Krilova/Tyazhkova, Ugolovnoe pravo RF, p. 444.
814. Ignatov/Krasikov, Kurs rossijskogo ugolovnogo prava, p. 282.
815. Paramonova, Parties to Crime in Russia. In: Sieber, U. / Jarvers, K. /Silverman, E. (ed(s).): Special forms of criminal liability. Berlin, Duncker & Humblot, 2015, pp.199–200.
816. For a discussion of the objective side of the crime, *see* Part I, Chapter 3, §2, paras. 342–371.
817. Kropachev, Ugolovnoe pravo Rossii, p. 416; Kudryavzev, Ugolovnoe pravo Rossii, p. 133; Lebedev, Kommentarii k UK RF, p. 29; Naumov, Rossiiskoe ugolovnoe pravo, p. 319; Zhuravlev, Ugolovnoe pravo, pp. 84–85.

instance, failure by physicians acting as co-perpetrators to render aid is considered criminal (Article 124 UKR).[818] In the case of instigation, the instigator can incite another person to commit a crime by failing to take appropriate action. An accessory is someone who facilitates the commission of crime not only by means of active conduct (advice, instructions, etc.) but also by helping to "eliminate the obstacles" (Article 33, paragraph 5 UKR). An example is an employee who does not report facts that he or she is aware of that might prevent a crime.[819] In another example, A plans a terrorist act with four other people. B knows about this but does not act (e.g., B does not report this knowledge to the police). Because of B's failure to act, B can be held criminally liable as an accessory to the perpetration of crime in the form of omission. An attempted crime is out of the question here due to the absence of "intentional acts directly aimed at the commission of a crime," an essential prerequisite of attempt liability (Article 30, paragraph 3 UKR).[820]

818. Komissarov/Krilova/Tyazhkova, Ugolovnoe pravo RF, p. 445.
819. Kuznezova, Objektivnaya storona prestupleniya, pp. 413–416.
820. For a discussion of the objective side of the crime, *see* Part I, Chapter 3, §2, paras. 342–371; for a discussion of attempt, *see* Part I, Chapter 5, paras. 544–589; Paramonova, Parties to Crime in Russia. In: Sieber, U. / Jarvers, K. /Silverman, E. (ed(s).): Special forms of criminal liability. Berlin, Duncker & Humblot, 2015, pp.201–202.

Chapter 6. Classification and Survey of Criminal Offenses

§1. General Classification of Criminal Offenses

635. Criminal offenses may be classified according to various criteria. For example, from the point of view of the objective element, crimes can be divided into substantial or result crimes and formal or non-result crimes, or into momentary and continuous offenses. Material crimes (result crimes) require that a certain result is provided for by the particular legal provision and criminal conduct leads to that harmful result in order to entail criminal responsibility. Formal crimes (conduct crimes)—in contrast—do not connect criminal responsibility with any concrete harmful results.[821] There can also be distinguished between two different types of crimes that provide for the possibility of causing danger: crimes of real endangerment and crimes of abstract endangerment.[822]

636. Crimes can furthermore be classified from the point of view of the subjective element, according to which offenses are divided, e.g., into negligent and intentional crimes.

637. The statutory classification that is provided for in the Russian Criminal Code is based on the criterium of gravity. This division into four categories entails concrete legal consequences, as will be explained below.

I. Statutory Classification of Criminal Offenses

638. The **categories of crimes** *(категории преступлений)* are represented in Article 15, paragraph 1 UKR.

639. The UKR distinguishes between the following categories of crimes: **crimes of small gravity** *(преступления небольшой тяжести)*, **crimes of average gravity** *(преступления средней тяжести)*, **grave crimes** *(тяжкие (тяжкие,* and **especially grave crimes** *(особо тяжкие преступления)*. Every criminal offense falls under one of these categories.[823]

640. The distinction is based on the substantive criterion of the crime—its "character and degree of social danger."[824] Another indicator is the severity of punishment: the more serious the crime, the greater is the degree of punishment. For instance, if the punishment for a criminal offense exceeds ten years of deprivation of freedom, it will fall under the category of especially grave crimes. If it does not

821. On the classification from the point of view of the objective element, *see* Part I, Chapter 3, §2, paras. 363–371.
822. On the classification from the point of view of the objective element, *see* Part I, Chapter 3, §2, paras. 363–371; Kropachev, Ugolovnoe pravo Rossii, p. 420; Kudryavzev, Ugolovnoe pravo Rossii, pp. 138–139; Zhuravlev, Ugolovnoe pravo, p. 89.
823. Paramonova, Subjective aspects of the offense in Russia, 2011, pp. 89–91.
824. Lebedev, Kommentarii k UK RF, p. 31.

exceed two years, it shall be deemed to be a crime of small gravity. All other basic forms of punishment, for example, the deprivation of the right to occupy determined posts, can be measured in terms of years as well (Article 72 UKR).

641. The difference between categories can also be seen in the subjective aspects of the offense: grave crimes and especially grave crimes can only be acts committed with intention, while crimes of small gravity and crimes of average gravity can be either intentional or negligent.

642. Article 15 UKR provides for the statutory classification of criminal offenses.

Art. 15 UKR (Categories of Crimes)

(1) Depending upon the character and degree of social danger, the acts provided for by the present Code shall be subdivided into crimes of small gravity, crimes of average gravity, grave crimes and especially grave crimes.
(2) Intentional and negligent acts, for the commission of which the maximum punishment provided for by the present Code does not exceed two years of deprivation of freedom, shall be deemed to be crimes of small gravity.
(3) Intentional acts for the commission of which the maximum punishment provided for by the present Code does not exceed five years of deprivation of freedom, and negligent acts for the commission of which the maximum punishment provided for by the present Code does not exceed two years freedom deprivation, shall be deemed to be crimes of average gravity.
(4) Intentional acts, for the commission of which the maximum punishment provided for by the present Code does not exceed ten years of deprivation of freedom, shall be deemed to be grave crimes.
(5) Intentional acts, for the commission of which punishment is provided for by the present Code in the form of deprivation of freedom for a term exceeding ten years or more severe punishment, shall be deemed to be especially grave crimes.

A. *Consequences of the Statutory Classification*

643. Every criminal offense in the Russian legal system belongs to one of the four legally determined categories.[825] Certain legal consequences result from this division.

644. This division is, for example, relevant for the **assignment of punishment and criminal responsibility**. A court can relieve the accused from criminal responsibility if a crime of small or average gravity has been committed for the first time

825. For the principle of legality, *see* Part I, Chapter 1, paras. 197–226.

if the accused voluntarily acknowledged his guilt and facilitated the investigation of the crime (Article 75, paragraph 1 UKR). However, in the case of grave or especially grave crimes, this would only be possible in instances specially provided for by the Special Part of the UKR.

645. A further consequence is that criminal responsibility shall ensue only for preparations to commit grave or especially grave crimes. In contrast, in terms of attempt, as a later stage in the commission of crime compared to preparation, criminal responsibility is attached to the attempt of all categories of crimes, provided that they are committed intentionally (Article 30, paragraph 3 UKR).

646. In the sphere of **criminal enforcement,** the type of imprisonment (colony-settlements, correctional colonies of the general, strict or special regime) corresponds to a certain category of crimes (Article 58, paragraph 1 UKR). For example, according to Article 58, paragraph 1, item c UKR, imprisonment in strict regime correctional facilities is reserved for males sentenced for the commission of especially grave crimes. Punishment for small and average gravity crimes is, however, to be served in colony-settlements.

II. Ordinary and Political Offenses

647. Political offenses that have certain political content are not treated in any special way in Russian criminal law. This means that the respective crimes that are provided for in the Special Part of the Criminal Code are subject to the same rules as ordinary offenses.

§2. Survey of Criminal Offenses

I. Criminal Offenses of the Penal Code

648. The Russian Criminal Code distinguishes between a **General** ***(общая часть)*** and a **Special** ***(особенная часть)*** **part**. These parts are further split into sections, chapters, articles, parts and items.

649. The General Part (Articles 1–104.3 UKR) consists of the following six sections: “criminal law” (Articles 1–13 UKR), “crime” (Articles 14–42 UKR), “punishment” (Articles 43–74 UKR), “relieving from criminal responsibility and from punishment” (Articles 75–86 UKR), “criminal responsibility of minors” (Articles 87–96), and “compulsory measures of medical character” (Articles 97–104.3 UKR). The sections are divided into sixteen chapters. These are, for instance, the principles of the criminal code (Chapter 1 UKR), the concept of crime and categories of crime (Chapter 3 UKR) and assignment of punishment (Chapter 10 UKR). The

General Part is an accumulation of the legally defined terms, categories and institutions that govern the interpretation of the Special Part.[826]

650. The Special Part (Articles 105–360 UKR) contains six sections and nineteen chapters. The sections are "crimes against the person," "crimes in sphere of economy," "crimes against public security and public order," "crimes against state power," "crimes against military service," and "crimes against peace and security mankind." The new systematization of the Special Part of the UKR 1996 shows a tendency to prioritize crimes against individual interests, rights and freedoms. The Special Part starts with section VII (crimes against the person), unlike all previous criminal codes of Russia,[827] which put crimes against public security first.

II. Criminal Offenses in Special Criminal Laws

651. Due to the principle of legality,[828] criminal responsibility occurs only on the basis of regulations codified in the UKR. Article 8 UKR states that "the ground for criminal responsibility is the commission of an act containing all indicia of the 'elements of crime'" provided for by the UKR (in the General and the Special Part of the UKR).[829] Some provisions of criminal law may require additional information in order to determine whether or how they apply to a particular conduct, for example, technical terms in the Federal Law about Weapons.[830]

652. However, in compliance with the norms provided for by the UKR (Articles 1, paragraph 1, 3, paragraph 1, and 14, paragraph 1), all criminal offenses, punishability, and other legal criminal consequences concerning the substantive criminal law shall be determined only by the UKR, not by any other federal or regional laws or normative legal provisions (e.g., administrative provisions).

826. Kropachev, Ugolovnoe pravo Rossii, pp. 230–240.
827. Criminal Code of the RSFSR 01.06.1922; Criminal Code of the RSFSR 22.11.1926.
828. For the principle of legality, *see* Part I, Chapter 1, paras. 197–226.
829. For elements of crime, *see* Part I, Chapter 3, §1 paras. 331–341.
830. Federal Law on weapons, Dec. 13, 1996, N 150-FZ.

Chapter 7. The Sanctioning System

§1. General Overview

I. Introduction

653. Russian criminal law provides a detailed and developed system of criminal punishment. It differentiates between **criminal penalties** and so-called **other measures of criminal-law nature** (Articles 97–104.3 UKR) that include compulsory medical measures (Chapter 15 UKR) and confiscation (Chapter 15.1 UKR).[831] 'Other measures of criminal-law nature' that partially fulfill the purposes of criminal punishment such as crime prevention (Article 98 UKR) are applicable fully or in part instead of criminal punishment or alongside with criminal sanctions.

654. The Criminal Code of 1996 introduced a new chapter (14) devoted to the criminal responsibility of **juveniles** and adopted a sanctioning system that allows imposing either criminal punishment or (and) compulsory measures of an educational nature on juveniles who have committed crimes (Article 87 UKR).

655. Furthermore, Russian criminal law distinguishes between **basic** penalties *(основные)*, **additional penalties** *(дополнительные виды наказаний)*, and those that can be applied as both basic and additional penalties.[832]

II. Purposes of Punishment

656. In previous criminal legislation, punishment was regarded as retribution—coercion with the goal of causing suffering—for the committed crime (e.g., Article 20 Criminal Code of RSFSR 1960).[833] In current Russian criminal law, retribution is not considered to be the purpose of punishment, neither by the legislator nor by the courts or by legal scholars.[834] The law does, however, not prohibit the application of coercion; this is consistent with the principle of justice, which serves as the basis for imposing punishment as a measure of state coercion.

657. The definition of punishment is set out in Article 43 UKR. The provision explicitly identifies the **purposes of punishment** *(цели наказания)*:

831. For confiscation, *see* paras. 734–736.
832. For additional punishment, *see* paras. 725–726.
833. Criminal Code of the Russian Soviet Federative Socialist Republic, Oct. 27, 1960 (Ugolovnij Kodeks RSFSR).
834. Ignatov/Krasikov, Kurs rossijskogo ugolovnogo prava, pp. 349–350; Korobeev, Polnij kurs ugolovnogo prava, pp. 740–741; Sundurov, Nakazanie i alternativnie meri v ugolovnom prave, pp. 32–36, 103; Mizkevich, Ugolovnoe nakazanie, pp. 3; Kruglikov, Kommentarij k ugolovnomu kodeksu RF, pp. 523–527.

Art. 43 UKR (The Concept and the Purposes of Punishment)

(1) Punishment is a measure of state compulsion assigned by a court's judgment. Punishment shall be applied to a person who has been found guilty of the commission of a crime, and shall consist of the deprivation or limitation of rights and freedoms of this person as provided for by the present Code.

(2) Punishment shall be applied for the purpose of restoring social justice, and also for the purpose of reformation of a convicted person and of preventing the commission of further crimes.

– Restoring Social Justice

658. According to academic opinion (as well as the Criminal Code), **restoring social justice** ***(восстановление социальной справедливости)*** is the main purpose of punishment.[835] "Social justice" is, however, a moral and inhomogeneous term, the content of which is primarily determined by the views and beliefs that prevail in a given society. The question of restoring social justice is the subject of theoretical analysis by criminal law scholars. This analysis includes numerous inevitably overlapping levels:

659. The first level reflects the requirements and expectations of justice in a given society with regard to criminal punishments. Legal provisions and sentencing practices that meet public expectations enhance the development of a respectful attitude toward the law.[836]

660. The second level represents the state's (legislative) requirements for imposing punishment. These are reflected in the relevant criminal provisions, in particular in the concrete sanctions for crimes. A sanction is considered fair if it reflects the gravity of the criminal act; sentencing provisions must leave the court a reasonable opportunity for differentiation and individualization of responsibility.[837]

661. The third level reflects the factors that the court must consider in order to impose a fair punishment. These are the nature and degree of the social danger of the offense, (mitigating or aggravating) circumstances of its commission, the personality of the accused, as well as the influence of the imposed penalty on the convicted person's reformation and his or her family (Articles 6, paragraph 1 and 60, paragraph 3 UKR).

835. Revin, Ugolovnoe pravo Rossii.
836. *Ibid.*
837. Korobeev, Polnij kurs ugolovnogo prava, pp. 741–743.

662. The fourth level involves the interests of the victim:

> Art. 52 Const.
> The rights of crime victims and of victims of abuse of office shall be protected by law. The state shall provide access to justice for them and compensation for sustained damage.

663. Finally, on the fifth level, the legitimate interests of the convicted person are taken into account. The fact that, as a rule, the public interest and the interests of the person who has committed a crime are diametrically opposed does not eliminate the convicted person's right to a just and appropriate punishment. Therefore, it is necessary to consider the following points: first, the double jeopardy prohibition (Article 50 Const., Article 6, paragraph 2 UKR); second, the fact that punishment and other measures of a criminal law character that may be imposed on a person who has committed a crime may not pursue the aim of causing physical suffering or demeaning human dignity (Article 21 Const., Article 7 UKR); and third, the effect of the imposed penalty on the convicted person (Articles 6, paragraph 1 and 60, paragraph 3 UKR).[838]

– Reformation of a Convicted Person

664. The next purpose of punishment provided for in Article 43 UKR is the **reformation of a convicted person** *(исправление осужденного)*. The term "reformation of convicts" is defined as "the formation of a respectful attitude toward persons, society, labor, norms, rules and traditions of human society and encouragement of law-abiding behavior" in Article 9, paragraph 1 Correctional Code of the Russian Federation (UIKR).

665. In legal literature, this purpose of punishment is regarded—in accordance with the definition of Article 9 UIKR—either in a broad sense, that is, including "moral" reformation of a convict, or in a narrow sense. The narrow sense represents the prevailing academic opinion and encompasses only the "legal" reformation of convicts: individual prevention as a goal of punishment is achieved when a person does not commit further crimes. The inward "moral" motivation behind law-abiding behavior is not taken into consideration.[839]

– Prevention of the Commission of Further Crimes

666. **Prevention of the commission of further crimes** *(предупреждение совершения новых преступлений)* is the third purpose of punishment established by Article 43 UKR. According to legal literature, this purpose encompasses two

838. Korobeev, Polnij kurs ugolovnogo prava, pp. 743–746; Revin, Ugolovnoe pravo Rossii; Ignatov/Krasikov, Kurs rossijskogo ugolovnogo prava, pp. 346–353.
839. Korobeev, Polnij kurs ugolovnogo prava, pp. 744, 746; Ignatov/Krasikov, ibid., pp. 348–350; Kruglikov, Kommentarij k UKR, pp. 530–531.

aspects: general prevention and specific or individual prevention. **General prevention** ***(общее предупреждение)*** means that crime is prevented by threatening with punishment, anyone who might commit an act that leads to criminal consequences. There is, however, an academic opinion that general prevention is a mechanism that applies only to "unstable" people, that is, those who tend to choose a criminal career path, rather than to other members of society.[840] **Specific or individual prevention** ***(специальное или частное предупреждение)*** is a mechanism that consists of deterring an offender who has been punished before from committing additional crimes in the future.[841]

§2. History of the Criminal Law Sanctioning System

I. Ancient Rus'

667. The Russian Truth of 1016 provided for the first mechanism of punishment for socially dangerous behavior.[842] The right to punish, that is, to avenge an offender for an "insult," belonged to the damaged party and his/her close relatives, rather than state authority. The rule of blood feuds in the Russian Truth was amended in 1072. Blood revenge for murder was now prohibited and replaced by a monetary payment to the victim/victim's family (**wergild**, ***вира***). Since the concept of the state as an interested party had not yet been developed, it was up to the injured party to exact punishment and collect payment for the damage caused.

668. From the beginning of the 14th century, however, the state began strengthening its influence with regard to serious violations of public order. The Dvina Charters, for example, prohibited punishment by lynching and, in the case of murder, required that wergild be paid to state authorities.

II. Russian Centralized State

669. The period of centralization of the Russian State (**Law Codes of 1497 and 1550**) was characterized by the broad use of corporal punishment as well as the death penalty. The death penalty was carried out in public and accompanied by torture, especially for political crimes, for example, rebellion.[843] According to some historical data, 4,000 people were executed during the reign of *Ivan IV (Ivan the Terrible)*.[844]

---

840. For further information, *see* Ignatov/Krasikov, *ibid.*, p. 353.
841. Revin, Ugolovnoe pravo Rossii; Naumov, Rossiiskoe ugolovnoe pravo, p. 25; Schedrin, Meri bezopasnosti kak sredstvo preduprezhdeniya prestupnosti, p. 3.
842. Kropachev/Volzhenkin/Orechova, Ugolovnoe pravo Rossii, pp. 117–121; Komissarov/Krilova/Tyazhkova, Ugolovnoe pravo, p. 53.
843. Kropachev/Volzhenkin/Orechova, Ugolovnoe pravo Rossii, pp. 117–121.
844. Smertnaya kazn': istoriya i statistika (Death penalty: history and statistics), http://ria.ru/spravka [last visited Dec. 18, 2019]; Paramonova, Death Penalty in Russia, forthcoming.

670. The main purpose of punishment established by the **Council Code of 1649** was deterrence.[845] The types of penalties (e.g., cutting off limbs, ears, nose, etc.) showed the brutality of Russia's punitive policies in the Middle Ages. Sanctions for concrete crimes were often not determined. Thus, for the purpose of deterrence, an offender may have been subjected to several different penalties. Archaic institutions such as collective responsibility of relatives and *lex talionis* were retained. Sentencing also took account of the offender's social status; punishments for members of the feudal nobility were softer. The Council Code was furthermore the first legislative act to introduce the use of prisoners' labor as well as the deportation of criminals to remote cities and jails (Articles 9, 10, 16 Council Code).[846]

III. Russian Empire

671. The **Military Code of 1716,** enacted by *Peter I,* provided for the death penalty for 123 various offenses. The forms of execution were very cruel, including drowning, burying the prisoner alive, and forcing liquid metal down the prisoner's throat. However, the execution was actually carried out only in cases of sedition, murder, and treason. Corporal punishment and/or deportation with hard labor were imposed on offenders convicted of other offenses.[847] The main purpose of punishment remained deterrence and retribution.

672. The trend toward the extensive use of cruel corporal punishments and the death penalty that characterized the epoch of *Peter I* subsided after his reign.

673. During the reign of *Catherine II,* the death penalty was applied only for crimes committed against the state rather than ordinary crimes. Special workhouses, namely houses for correction of the mischievous and insane, were established.[848]

674. The **Code on Criminal and Correctional Punishments of 1845** represented the most detailed codification of a system for the imposition of criminal punishment. It established three key components for determining one of 52 levels of criminal punishment: the degree of damage to the rights of the prisoner (entire loss of rights, e.g., loss of rank, property, or limited loss of rights), the period of deprivation of freedom, and the type of incarceration or forced labor (arrest; confinement in a fortress, prison, or workhouse; deportation to remote regions; hard labor in exile, etc.). According to the Criminal Code of 1845, capital punishment could be imposed on military and political crimes.[849] Nonetheless, in the 19th century, the actual carrying out of the death penalty was relatively rare: in the period from 1805

845. Rossijskoe zakonodatelstvo X-XX vekov: v 9 tomach. Tom 4. Moscow 1986.
846. Kropachev/Volzhenkin/Orechova, Ugolovnoe pravo Rossii, p. 128.
847. Paramonova, Death Penalty in Russia, forthcoming; Kropachev/Volzhenkin/Orechova, Ugolovnoe pravo Rossii, pp. 128–134.
848. Kropachev/Volzhenkin/Orechova, Ugolovnoe pravo Rossii, p. 129.
849. Smertnaya kazn', istoriya i statistika, http://ria.ru/spravka [last visited Dec. 18, 2019].

to 1891, approximately 300 people were executed (less than three persons per year), and from 1891 to 1905, capital punishment was not carried out even once.[850]

675. With the progressive judicial reforms of the liberal *Alexander II*, corporal punishment of women was repealed, and branding and the application of birches fell into limited use. In addition to retribution and the restoring of social justice, the reformation became a new purpose of criminal punishment.[851]

IV. Soviet Period

676. The criminal law of the Soviet period, in general, and the system of imposition of criminal punishment, in particular, were shaped by the ideology of the prevalence of executive power over the rule of law. The legislature and the judiciary were de facto merged with the executive. Another characteristic of Soviet criminal justice was the broad application of criminal sanctions such as deprivation of freedom and the death penalty.[852]

677. The first Soviet Criminal Code (**Criminal Code of the Russian Soviet Federal Socialist Republic, 1922**) allowed the application of analogy in the imposition of criminal punishment (Articles 7, 10 Criminal Code RSFSR). It is an extensive interpretation of the law that allows ruling a case that is not explicitly considered by a legal provision. Among all, it includes the imposition of criminal punishment that is not provided by a legal provision.[853] A rule enacted by the executive was a sufficient "legal" ground for the imposition of criminal sanction(s). A special Regulation "On State Crimes (Counterrevolutionary and Specially Dangerous Crimes Against Administrative Order)," of 1927[854] and the Decree of the Central Executive Committee of 1934[855] introduced, for example, criminal punishments that included deprivation of freedom and the death penalty. These and other decrees and regulations were in force parallel to the Criminal Codes. The Criminal Code of 1922 included the types of penalties that were characteristic of Soviet class-determined criminal law, for example, expulsion from the territory of the RSFSR and public censure.[856]

678. The same kinds of punishment were provided for by the **Criminal Code of 1926**. It is interesting to observe that this Code did not use the term "criminal punishment," but instead referred to **"measures of social defense"** (*меры социальной защиты*, Article 20 Criminal Code of 1926). However, these

850. Kozachenko, Criminal law, p. 507; Pristavkin, Death Penalty in Russia.
851. Kropachev/Volzhenkin/Orechova, Ugolovnoe pravo Rossii, p. 141.
852. *Ibid.*, p. 147–166; Komissarov/Krilova/Tyazhkova, Ugolovnoe pravo, pp. 63–72.
853. Kropachev/Volzhenkin/Orechova, ibid., p. 129.
854. Regulation "On the State Crimes (Counterrevolutionary and Especially Dangerous Crimes Against the Governmental Order)," Feb. 25, 1927; Kropachev/Volzhenkin/Orechova, Ugolovnoe pravo Rossii, p. 155.
855. Decree of the Central Executive Committee, Jul. 8, 1934; Kropachev/Volzhenkin/Orechova, *ibid.*
856. Kropachev/Volzhenkin/Orechova, ibid., p. 148.

were de facto criminal punishments as they included, for instance, corrective labor without (or with) deprivation of liberty, the extinction of political and other civil rights, and a proclamation that the accused was an enemy of the working class. According to the Criminal Code of 1926,[857] the death penalty could be imposed for 42 crimes (e.g., large-scale theft of state or public property).[858]

679. The abolition of the death penalty in 1947 by *Stalin* was merely an empty formality. The NKVD—which carried out mass extra-judicial executions—was prospering,[859] and in 1950, the death penalty was reintroduced de jure, for example, for espionage and treason to the motherland.[860]

680. The third and last **Soviet Criminal Code of 1960** represented a milder criminal policy. This policy was manifested in a decrease in (political) repression, the release of thousands of political prisoners from forced labor camps, the prohibition of nonjudicial imposition of criminal punishment, and the introduction of institutions such as the suspended sentence and the conditional sentence.[861]

681. In the Soviet period, the proclaimed purposes of criminal punishment were general and individual prevention, retribution, and reformation. Another purpose was the adjustment of the perpetrator to the socialist values and rules of the community.[862]

§3. Penalties

I. Administrative and Criminal Sanctions

682. One of the most controversial issues in the Russian legal system is the question of the distinction between criminal law and administrative penal law.

683. Despite the authority of administrative penal law to impose punitive sanctions, the majority of scholars do not regard it as a branch of law with a quasi-criminal function but rather considers it as being noncriminal in nature. Only a minority emphasizes its criminal nature and argues that the guarantees provided for by the criminal (procedural) law should also apply in the context of the administrative penal law.[863]

857. Criminal Code of the RSFSR. 1926.
858. Paramonova, Death Penalty in Russia, forthcoming.
859. Shishov, Smertnaya kazn' v Rossii.
860. Decree of the Highest Council of the USSR "On the Application of the Death Penalty to the Traitor, Spies, Saboteurs," Dec. 12, 1950; Paramonova, Death Penalty in Russia, forthcoming.
861. Kropachev/Volzhenkin/Orechova, Ugolovnoe pravo Rossii, p. 158.
862. *Ibid.*, pp. 150, 151, 158, 159; e.g., Criminal Code RSFSR 1922 or Criminal Code RSFSR 1960.
863. Golovko, Sootnoshenie ugolovnih prestuplenij i administrativnih pravonarushenij, http://ilpp.ru/ [last visited Dec. 18, 2019].

684. The minority approach is in compliance with the position of the ECtHR, whose decisions—due to the international obligations of the Russian Federation—are binding on domestic courts.[864] With reference to the nature of administrative offenses in the Russian legal system, the ECHR has explicitly stated that a number of administrative offenses with punitive sanctions are part of the "criminal matter,"[865] and therefore belong to criminal and not to administrative law. This is primarily due to the similarity between severe punitive sanctions of administrative law (sanctions associated with the deprivation of liberty) and criminal sanctions.[866] Nonetheless, all administrative offenses in the Russian legal system still remain in the realm of the administrative penal law.

II. Distinction Between Criminal and Administrative Law Based on the Three-Elements Methodology

685. At the present time, the distinction between criminal law and other areas of law, including administrative law, is drawn at the substantive level by means of theoretical (doctrinal) concepts. The spheres of the interests protected by, e.g., criminal, administrative, and civil areas of law overlap, but, substantively, the difference is defined by the extent of the social danger or harm posed.[867] For example, both criminal and civil law protect property. Criminal law is applied in the case of more severe infringements, administrative or civil law in the case of less severe infringements. In legal scholarship, the distinction made by this substantive rationale is based on the methodology for distinguishing between branches of law, which involves an analysis of three elements with regard to a relevant branch of law: subject-matter, method, and functions/tasks. According to this methodology, an aggregate of legal norms is considered to be an independent branch of law if it has a specific **subject-matter** ***(предмет)***, a specific **method** ***(метод)***, and specific **functions/tasks** ***(функции/задачи)***.[868] Some scholars regard the third element as optional.[869]

---

864. For further information on the international sources of criminal law, *see* paras. 116–144; Paramonova, KritVj 2013, 188–211; treaties of Council of Europe, http://conventions.coe.int/treaty/ [last visited Dec. 18, 2019]; Art. 1 Federal Law on Ratification of the ECHR, Mar. 30, 1998, N 54-FZ; http://www.echr.ru/convention/protocols.htm [last visited Dec. 18, 2019]; Resolution of the Supreme Court of the Russian Federation, Oct. 10, 2003 N 5; for national sources of criminal law, *see* General Introduction, §5, II, paras. 145–181.

865. *See* Menesheva v. Russia, Mar. 9, 2006, App. No. 59261/00 (ECtHR).

866. *Ibid.*; Engel v. Netherlands, Jun. 8, 1976, App. No. 5100/71 (ECtHR).

867. On the concept of social danger, *see* Part I, Chapter 3, §1, paras. 317–330; Mizkevich, Ugolovnoe nakazanie, p. 1.

868. *See also* Matuzov, Teorija gosudarstva i prava, pp. 406–410; Naumov, Rossiiskoe ugolovnoe pravo, pp. 1–36; Kropachev, Ugolovnoe pravo Rossii, pp. 15–62.

869. Komissarov/Krilova/Tyazhkova, Ugolovnoe pravo RF, p. 13.

A. Subject-Matter of Regulation

686. Criminal law regulations address the social relationships that arise due to the commission of the most socially dangerous acts—criminal offenses. Administrative penal law, which regulates some of the same legally protected interests—for example, property and health—deals with less serious acts.[870]

687. For this distinction between the scope of criminal and administrative law, the source of the offense/sanction is decisive: Criminal Code or Administrative Offenses Code. Unlike criminal law,[871] administrative (penal) law lies within the joint jurisdiction of the Russian Federation and the regions (Article 72, item k Constitution of the Russian Federation).[872] Administrative offenses/sanctions are provided for by the Federal Law—the **Administrative Offenses Code of the Russian Federation** (*Kodeks RF ob administrativnih pravonarusheniyah*, KoAPR)[873]—and regional administrative offenses codes, such as the Law of the Krasnoyarsk Region "On Administrative Offenses"[874] (Article 2.1 KoAPR). The regional laws governing administrative offenses must, however, comply with the federal Administrative Offenses Code.

688. In order to demarcate the difference between criminal and administrative offenses targeting the same group of legally protected interests, various quantitative characteristics are used, for example, the extent of monetary damage or the occurrence of particular harmful consequences. These criteria allow measurement of the "degree of social danger" and answer the question of whether an act falls within the scope of the criminal or the administrative law.[875]

689. For example, criminal and administrative law both protect property relationships and both criminalize theft: Article 7.27 KoAPR (petty theft) and Article 158 UKR (theft). However, Article 7.27 KoAPR defines theft as "petty" if the damage caused does not exceed RUB 1000 (about USD 28). Where the harm goes above this level, the theft is classified as a criminal offense.

690. Another example shows that the harmful consequences actually brought about in a particular case serve as a distinguishing criterion. According to both the Criminal Code and the Administrative Code, the "violation of the rules of the use of air space of the Russian Federation" is punishable (Article 271.1 UKR and Article

870. Matuzov, Teorija gosudarstva i prava, pp. 406–410; for the principle of legality, *see* Part I, Chapter 1, paras 197–226.
871. For the principle of legality, *see* Part I, Chapter 1, paras. 197–226; Komissarov/Krilova/Tyazhkova, Ugolovnoe pravo RF, p. 24.
872. Constitution of the Russian Federation (Konstitucija Rossijskoj Federacii, Const.), Dec. 12, 1993.
873. Code of Administrative Offenses of the Russian Federation, Dec. 30, 2001, N 195-FZ (Kodeks RF ob administrativnih pravonarusheniyah, KoAPR).
874. Law of the Krasnoyarsk Region "On Administrative Offenses," Oct. 2, 2008, N 7-2161: Krasnoyarsk Region Legislation, http://www.krskstate.ru/docs/0/doc/1877 [last visited Dec. 18, 2019].
875. On the concept of social danger, *see* Part I, Chapter 3, §1, paras. 317 330.

11.4 KoAPR).[876] However, criminal punishment is envisaged only for the more "socially dangerous" form of this violation In this case, the criminal offense is designed from the perspective of the **objective side** *(actus reus)*[877] as a substantive crime ("harmful result crime"), and a concrete result in the form of infliction of death or grave harm to the health of a person is required. Administrative law, in contrast, covers less dangerous forms of the analyzed conduct: the conduct is punishable as an administrative violation if the aforementioned consequences do not occur.

B. Methods of Regulation

691. Among the three primary methods of legal regulation that scholars agree on—**permission** ***(дозволение)***, **authoritative order** ***(предписание)***, and **prohibition** ***(запрет)***—the method of prohibition is central to criminal law, which creates models of forbidden social behavior.[878]

692. In contrast, the main method of legal regulation employed by administrative law in the broad sense (tax law, police law, etc.), which prescribes certain rules and requirements, is the method of authoritative order. As far as sanctions are concerned (administrative penal law), however, the method of prohibition is also dominant. This situation militates against the adoption of this criterion as a standard for differentiating between criminal law and administrative penal law.

693. Criminal law mainly uses compulsory methods.[879] Sanctions reserved for the criminal law always involve more serious infringements than those in administrative penal law (Articles 3.1–3.13 KoAPR and Articles 44–59 UKR). Administrative penal law also employs compulsory methods but with less severe punitive consequences.[880]

694. Certain sanctions are imposed by both administrative and criminal law as, for example, arrest, fine or compulsory work. Administrative arrest—the only administrative punishment connected with a deprivation of liberty—can be imposed for a maximum of 30 days (Article 3.9 KoAPR). Arrest as a criminal punishment can be imposed for a term of from one to six months (Article 54 UKR). Finally, the deprivation of liberty as punishment in the context of the criminal law can be imposed for a term of life (Article 57 UKR).

695. Nonetheless, problematic in this context—as already mentioned above—is the fact that administrative penal law, which may impose sanctions comparable with

876. Paramonova, Revista Penal 2012, 252–254.
877. On the objective aspects of the offense, *see* Part I, Chapter 3, §2, paras. 342–371.
878. Matuzov, Teorija gosudarstva i prava, pp. 394–403; Naumov, Rossiiskoe ugolovnoe pravo, pp. 13–16.
879. Korobeev, Polnij kurs ugolovnogo prava, pp. 19–2[illegible].
880. Matuzov, Teorija gosudarstva i prava, pp. 406–410; for the principle of legality, *see* Part I, Chapter 1, paras. 197 –226.

those of the criminal law (including punishments connected with the deprivation of liberty), does not provide the same rights and due process safeguards as criminal (procedural) law.[881]

696. For instance, the presumption of innocence is not applicable in the context of administrative offenses (Article 1.5 KoAPR). Similarly, a problem arises with regard to the prohibition of double jeopardy (or *ne bis in idem*). There is a legislative gap with respect to a person who has served an administrative punishment, as he/she can still be charged with a criminal offense for the same act for which punishment has already been served. There is no explicit requirement in any of the relevant legal provisions that the administrative punishment has to be taken into account (Article 50 Const. paragraph 1, Article 6, paragraph 2 UKR, Article 4.1, paragraph 5 KoAPR).[882] According to Article 50, paragraph 1 Const: "No one may be convicted twice for one and the same crime." This was double jeopardy prohibition refers only to criminal, not to administrative acts. As for the case law of the ECtHR, the Court's decisions that are to be executed at the national level do not necessarily lead to the relevant changes in the domestic criminal/administrative law for various financial, political or/and procedural (such as changing the Constitution) reasons.[883]

C. *Functions of Regulation*

697. The functions of criminal and administrative law also differ. The key functions of these two branches of law are the protection of individual rights, public order, and security (Article 2, paragraph 1 UKR and Article 1.2 KoAPR). The difference is again demarcated by means of the "social danger" substantive rationale: within the same group of legally protected interests, the sphere of criminal law protection encompasses more serious infringements than does administrative law.

698. In order to fulfill their functions, administrative, as well as criminal law have certain fundamental principles. However, some principles differ in scope depending on whether they are applied in the criminal or in the administrative law context.[884]

699. This is true with regard to the principle of equality before the law. Administrative law—unlike criminal law—applies not only to natural persons but also to legal entities that can be subject to administrative responsibility (Article 4 UKR, Article 1.4 KoAPR).[885] For that matter, the principle of culpability is applicable

881. Paramonova, Revista Penal 2012, 264–268.
882. Anganzanov, Zakonnost', N 2, 2009, 56; for the principle of legality, *see* Part I, Chapter 1, paras. 197–226.
883. *See* Sergey Zolotukhin v. Russia [GC]—14939/03. Judgment 10.2.2009 [GC].
884. For the principle of legality and other principles of criminal law, *see* Part I, Chapter 1, paras. 194–226.
885. On the concept of social danger, *see* Part I, Chapter 3, §1, paras. 317–330.

within criminal law only to natural persons (Article 24 UKR).[886] In administrative penal law, the principle applies to both natural persons and legal entities (Article 2.2 KoAPR). As far as legal entities are concerned, the question as to whether the legal entity at issue can act in compliance with the respective regulations must be taken into account (Article 2.1, paragraph 2 KoAPR): A legal entity shall be found guilty of an administrative offense if it had the opportunity to comply with the rules and norms, but it has not taken all measures depending on it to comply with the rules.

III. The Basic Penalties

700. As explained above, according to the current criminal legislation (Articles 44–59 UKR), the 13 penal sanctions can be divided into **basic penalties** *(основные)*, **additional types of penalties** *(дополнительные виды наказаний)*, and those that can be applied both as basic and additional penalties.

701. The following penal sanctions are applicable only as main or as **basic penalties** (Article 45, paragraph 1 UKR): **compulsory works** *(обязательные работы)*; **correctional labor** *(исправительные работы)*; **restriction in military service** *(ограничение по военной службе)*; **compulsory labor** *(принудительные работы)* **arrest** *(арест)* for a term of one to six months; **service in a disciplinary military unit** *(содержание в дисциплинарной воинской части)* for a term of three months to two years; deprivation of freedom (imprisonment) for a definite term, namely for a term of two months to twenty years with a maximum of thirty years due to the cumulation of sentences *(совокупность приговоров)*;[887] **life imprisonment** *(пожизненное лишение свободы)*; and **capital punishment** *(смертная казнь)*.

702. Main or basic penalties can be combined with additional types of penalties, e.g., arrest with deprivation of a military rank. Additional types of sanctions can be imposed only together with the main types of penalties. For instance, deprivation of a military rank (additional penalty) cannot be imposed on its own. The third type can be applied both as basic and additional penalties. For instance, a fine is possible to impose as a basic (main) sanction or to combine it with deprivation of state award (additional penalty). According to the statistics, custodial penalties, such as deprivation of freedom, are imposed more often than any other type of punishment.[888] This is due to various factors, such as the undeveloped infrastructure for alternative types of penalties as well as the long history of prisons.[889] In 2017, imprisonment was imposed in 28.7% of criminal cases. Other types of penal sanctions were imposed as follows: suspended sentences of imprisonment (27.2%); fine (14.7%); compulsory community service (18.4%), fines (13%), correctional labor (7.9%);

886. On subjective aspects of offense, *see* Part I, Chapter 3, §4, paras. 383–428.
887. For the principles and rules concerning sentencing, *see* paras. 747–776.
888. Ambamkin, Sokraschenie chislennosti tuyremnogo naseleniya; Paramonova, National characteristics, fundamental principles, and history of criminal law in Russia, 2014, pp. 195–196.
889. Gernet, Istoriya zarskoj tuyrmi, vol. 2, pp. 459–470.

other penalties (4.8%).[890] However, in the period from 2012 to 2017, a clear tendency toward the reduction of the imposition of imprisonment, in general, can be observed: from approx. 31% to 28%.[891]

A. Compulsory Community Service

703. Compulsory work or compulsory community service is a criminal punishment that consists of the performance of free socially useful work by the convict during his/her spare time. The type of compulsory work (e.g., cleaning work) and the places (e.g., hospitals, private companies) where it is to be served are determined by local self-government bodies (Article 49, paragraph 1 UKR). Compulsory work shall be served for not more than four hours a day.

704. Compulsory work may not be imposed upon persons who are deemed to have a disability of the first degree (the most serious disabilities; the list of disabilities is defined by the Government), pregnant women, women with children of less than 3 years of age, military servicemen undergoing military service after call-up, or military servicemen undergoing military service on a contractual basis in the capacity of soldiers and sergeants (Article 49, paragraph 4 UKR).

B. Correctional Labor

705. Correctional labor shall be imposed upon both convicts who do and do not have a principal place of work. The punishment shall be served at a principal place of work or at a place determined by a local self-government body in the area of a convicted person's permanent residence accordingly (Article 50, paragraph 1 UKR). For instance, if a convict works as cleaning staff in a company, he may perform correctional labor there or in a different place determined by a local self-government body, e.g., in a supermarket. Corrective labor shall be imposed for a term of from two months to two years.

706. Deductions for the benefit of the state shall be made from the earnings of the person sentenced to corrective labor in the amount fixed by the court's judgment within limits from five to 20 percent (Article 50, paragraph 3 UKR).

707. As it is the case for compulsory community service, correctional labor shall not be imposed upon persons who are deemed to have a serious disability, pregnant women, women with children of less than 3 years of age, military servicemen undergoing military service after call-up, or military servicemen undergoing military service on a contractual basis in the capacity of soldiers and sergeants (Article 50, paragraph 5 UKR).

890. FSSS, state of 2017.
891. FSSS, state of 2017.

C. Restriction in Military Service

708. Restriction in military service shall be imposed upon convicted servicemen/women undergoing military service under a contract for the commission of offenses against military service for a term of three months to two years. This punishment may be imposed upon convicted servicemen/women in a place of corrective labor.

709. Deductions for the benefit of the state shall be made from the allowance of a convict in the amount fixed by the court's judgment, however, of not more than 20 percent. During the serving of this punishment, the convicted person may not be promoted in his post or in military rank, and the period of punishment shall not be counted in the period of seniority for purposes of promotion in rank (Article 51 UKR).

D. Compulsory Labor

710. Compulsory labor is a relatively new type of criminal punishment. It was introduced in 2011 and is used as an alternative to imprisonment.[892] This penalty may be imposed in the cases stipulated by the relevant articles of the Special Part of the Criminal Code for the commission of crimes of small and average gravity for the first time (Article 53.1, paragraph 1 UKR).

711. If the court that has sentenced a person to imprisonment comes to the conclusion that there is a possibility of reformation of the convicted person without serving a sentence in prison, it decides to replace the custodial penalty with compulsory labor.

712. The punishment shall be served at the place determined by the institutions and bodies of the correctional system and shall be assigned for a term of two months to five years. From the salary of the sentenced to compulsory labor, the state withholds up to 25 percent.

713. Similar to compulsory work and correctional labor, compulsory labor may not be imposed upon certain social groups, such as minors, persons recognized as those having disability of the first or second group, pregnant women, women with children under 3 years old, women who have attained the age of 50, men who have attained the age of 60, and military personnel (Article 53.1, paragraph 7 UKR).

892. Federal Law Dec. 7, 2011, N 420-FZ.

E. Arrest

714. Arrest consists of the maintenance of a convicted person in the conditions of strict isolation from society (Article 54, paragraph 1 UKR). Arrest shall be assigned for a term of one to six months.[893] Arrest shall not be imposed on persons who have not reached 16 years of age by the time of adjudication, nor upon pregnant women or women who have children of less than 14 years of age.

715. The arrest is being served in the arrest houses. The conditions are similar to the prison camps of a general regime[894] of detention in which are established, as in the general regime in prison. Servicemen shall be taken into custody in the military detention facilities.

F. Service in a Disciplinary Military Unit

716. Service in a disciplinary military unit shall be imposed upon servicemen undergoing military service after call-up as well as upon servicemen undergoing military service under contract if he commits a crime. This punishment shall be assigned for a term of three months to two years in cases provided for by the pertinent articles of the Special Part of the Criminal Code for the commission of crimes against military service (Article 55, paragraph 1 UKR). This punishment may be imposed in place of imprisonment (deprivation of freedom) if the court considers that the nature of the crime and the personality of the guilty person allow the replacement.

G. Deprivation of Freedom

717. Deprivation of freedom is one of the basic criminal penalties that is defined as "an isolation of the convict from society by sending him/her to a settlement colony, placing him/her into an educational colony, into a medical treatment and reformatory institution or into a reformatory colony of the general, strict or special regime, or into prison"[895] (Article 56, paragraph 1 UKR). Deprivation of liberty shall be assigned for a minimum term of two months and for a maximum term of 20 years.

718. Due to quite frequent use of the deprivation of freedom by the courts in 2011, several restrictions were put on the imposition of this type of penalty. According to the introduced rule, in force today, punishment in the form of imprisonment may be imposed upon a convict who has committed an offense of small gravity[896]

893. Paramonova, National characteristics, fundamental principles, and history of criminal law in Russia, 2014, pp. 193–195.
894. For the aspects of living conditions in prison, *see* paras. 1392–1425.
895. For the types of correctional facilities, *see* paras. 57–59, 1388.
896. For the categories of crimes, *see* paras. 34, 638–646.

for the first time only with the presence of the aggravating circumstances provided for in Article 63 UKR (except for some offenses, such as drug dealing, Article 228 UKR). Another possibility for assigning deprivation of freedom is if this form of punishment is the only alternative provided for by the Special Part of the Criminal Code (the case only for grave crimes).[897]

719. With partial or full addition of terms of imprisonment through **cumulation of crimes** (*совокупность преступлений*),[898] the maximum term of imprisonment may not be more than twenty-five years and through **cumulation of sentences** (*совокупность приговоров*)[899]—over thirty years (Article 56, paragraph 4 UKR).

720. Imposition of punishment with regard to crimes of terroristic nature, e.g., Article 205 UKR (terroristic act), has some exceptions: through the imposition of punishment by cumulation of crimes, the maximum term of imprisonment encompasses thirty years, and by cumulation of sentences, the maximum term cannot exceed thirty-five years.[900]

H. Life Imprisonment

721. Deprivation of freedom for life or life imprisonment may be imposed exclusively for the commission of especially grave crimes (Article 15, paragraph 1 UKR) against human life as well as for commission of especially grave crimes against public health and morality, public security, sexual inviolability of minors who have not attained the age of 14.

722. Life imprisonment shall not be imposed upon women, nor upon persons who have committed crimes at ages below 18 years, nor upon men who have reached 65 years of age by the time of adjudication (Article 57 UKR).

I. Capital Punishment

723. Capital punishment has not been carried out in Russia since 1996. Capital punishment is, however, provided for in the Constitution as a measure of temporary character, that is, according to Article 20 Const., "capital punishment until its complete abolition may be established by Federal Law as an exclusive form of punishment for particularly grave crimes against life." In accordance with this constitutional provision, the Criminal Code, the Code of Criminal Procedure, and the Correctional Code of the Russian Federation provide for the necessary substantial and procedural rules for imposing the death penalty.

---

897. Federal Law, Mar. 9, 2001, N 25-FZ and Federal Law Dec. 7, 2011, N 420-FZ.
898. For the principles and rules concerning sentencing, *see* paras. 747–776.
899. For the principles and rules concerning sentencing, *see* paras. 747–776.
900. Federal Law May 5, 2014, N 130-FZ.

724. According to the prevailing opinion, the death penalty in Russia has been abolished de facto. However, in compliance with the minority opinion, which is based on the systematic interpretation of Russian legislation, de facto abolition has already been turned into de jure prohibition.[901] First, since signing Protocol No. 6 to the ECHR on April 16, 1997,[902] the Russian Federation has been obligated, as required by Article 18 Vienna Convention on the Law of Treaties, "to refrain from acts which would defeat the object and purpose of a treaty when it has signed the treaty […] until it shall have made its intention clear not to become a party to the treaty."[903] According to the Constitution, "the universally recognized principles and the standards of international law and the international agreements of the Russian Federation form an integral part of its legal system" (Article 15, paragraph 4 Const.). Second, the abolition of capital punishment was confirmed in 2009[904] by the Constitutional Court (whose decisions, de facto, have the same legal effect as legal provisions).[905] On the one hand, the decision was primarily determined by international obligations based on the ECHR, and, on the other hand, the decision was determined by the "legitimate constitutional regime" of non-application of the death penalty that had developed during the last 14 years.[906]

IV. The Additional Penalties

725. Additional penalties—in contrast to the basic ones—may be applied only in addition to basic criminal sanctions. **Deprivation of a special or military rank, honorary title, class rank, or governmental award** ***(лишение специального, воинского или почетного звания, классного чина и государственных наград)*** is imposed as an **additional type of penalty** (Article 45, paragraph 3 UKR).

726. According to Article 48 UKR, these additional penalties may be imposed by courts when convicting for a grave or especially grave crime with due account of the personality of the convicted person.

---

901. Paramonova, Death penalty in Russia, forthcoming.
902. Federal Law on the Entry of the Russian Federation into the Council of Europe, Feb. 23, 1996, N 19-FZ.
903. Vienna Convention on the Law of Treaties, May 23, 1969. Ratified by the Russian Federation on Apr. 29, 1986, http://treaties.un.org [last visited Dec. 18, 2019].
904. Decision of the Constitutional Court of the Russian Federation, Nov. 19, 2009, N 1344-O-P, http://www.ksrf.ru [last visited Dec. 18, 2019].
905. On death penalty in Russia, *see* Part I. Chapter 7, paras. 723–724, 1283–1285; Constitutional Court of the Russian Federation. Decisions, http://www.ksrf.ru/ru/Decision [last visited Dec. 18, 2019]; Paramonova, Russia's Constitutional Court and the Death Penalty, pp. 167–175; on death penalty in Russia, *see* Part I. Chapter 7, paras. 723–724, 1283–1285.
906. Paramonova, in: Arroyo/Biglino/Schabas (eds.), Hacia la Abolición Universal de la pena capital, pp. 195–197; for a discussion of the abolition of the death penalty in Russia, *see* Part I. Chapter 7, paras. 723–724, 1283–1285.

V. The Group of Penalties Applicable as Basic and Additional Penalties

727. In addition to basic penalties and additional penalties, there are penalties which can be applied as **both basic and additional penalties** (Article 45, paragraph 2 UKR): **fines** *(штраф)* and **deprivation of the right to hold selected posts or to engage in selected activities** *(лишение права занимать определенные должности или заниматься определенной деятельностью).*

A. *Fine*

728. A fine is a monetary penalty imposed within limits provided by the criminal law provisions (Article 46 UKR). A fine as a penalty can be imposed both as basic and additional punishment. As a basic penalty, it can be imposed as the only punishment. However, as an additional penalty, a fine may be imposed only in cases provided for by the pertinent articles of the Special Part of the Russian Criminal Code, e.g., embezzlement, Article 160 UKR (Articles 45, paragraph 2 and 46, paragraph 4 UKR).

729. When determining the amount of the fine, the court shall take into consideration the gravity of the crime as well as the property status of the convict and his/her family. The court shall also consider the ability of the convict to receive a wage or any other income. Considering the same circumstances, a court may impose a fine payable in installments for a term of up to five years (Article 46, paragraph 4 UKR).

B. *Deprivation of the Right to Hold Selected Posts or to Engage in Selected Activities*

730. Deprivation of the right to hold selected posts or to engage in selected activities consists of the prohibition to hold certain posts in the civil service and local self-government bodies or to engage in a professional or any other activity. This penalty may be imposed for a term of one year to five years as a basic penalty or for a term of six months to three years as an additional penalty. In the special cases provided for by the relevant articles of the Special Part of the Russian Criminal Code, the punishment may be imposed for a term of up to twenty years as an additional penalty (Article 47 UKR).

731. Deprivation of the right to hold selected posts or to engage in certain activities may be assigned as an additional form of punishment even if it not provided for by a pertinent article of the Special Part of the Russian Criminal Code if considering the nature and degree of social danger of the crime committed and the identity of the perpetrator; the court finds it impossible to maintain his/her right to hold certain posts or engage in selected posts.

§4. Other Measures of Criminal-Law Nature (Articles 97–104.3 UKR)

I. Compulsory Medical Measures

732. Compulsory medical measures may be assigned by the court upon the following groups of persons (Article 97, paragraph 1 UKR):

- persons who have committed crime(s) in a state of insanity;
- persons who became mentally deranged after they have committed crime(s);
- persons who have committed crime(s) with mental disorders that do not exclude sanity;
- persons over the age of eighteen who have committed crime(s) against the sexual inviolability of minors under 14 years of age and who suffer from a disorder of sexual preference (pedophilia) that does not exclude sanity.

733. These groups of persons can be divided into the categories, such as offenders with mental disorders, alcoholics and drug addicts, and sex offenders (*see* for details below).[907]

II. Confiscation

734. According to art 104.1 UKR, confiscation is a measure of criminal-law nature that is applicable in addition to criminal penalties for the commission of certain crimes.

735. Confiscation presupposes compulsory gratuitous withdrawal of property on the basis of a conviction so that the state becomes its owner. This property includes money, valuables and other property obtained from the commission of certain crimes, such as homicide, Article 105 UKR, or some economic crimes, as well as an income obtained from the commission of crimes that were partially or fully modified. Moreover, the money, valuables and other property that have been used or were intended to be used to finance terrorism, extremism, organized criminal groups or other illegal armed formations as well as weapons, equipment or other instrumentalities that have been used for committing a crime that belongs to the convict, may be confiscated (Article 104.1 UKR).

736. Besides other objectives of this criminal punishment, such as prevention of future crimes, especially economic crimes, one of the main goals of this measure is the compensation of damage caused to the victim (Article 104.3 UKR). Sometimes, the official incomes of a perpetrator do not allow to compensate material damage caused to the victim. Confiscation allows using other properties of the offender for this purpose.

907. For the imposition of compulsory measures, *see* paras. 762–764.

§5. Modes of Punishment

I. Conditional Sentence

737. The conditional sentence is one of the key criminal law measures in Russian law that is designed to fulfill the purposes of criminal punishment[908](restoring social justice, reformation of a convicted person, and prevention of the commission of further crimes, Article 43 UKR) without actual enforcement of criminal sanctions, for instance without isolating relatively undangerous convicts from society by imposing custodial penalties (Article 73 UKR). The actual application of the punishment is suspended as long as the convict complies with the behavioral rules prescribed, such as not to change his or her permanent place of residence, of work, or of study without notifying a specialized state authority engaged in the control of the correction of the convict, not to attend certain places, to undergo a course of treatment for alcoholism, drug addiction, toxicology, to work, to (continue) study, etc. (Article 73, paragraph 5 UKR).

738. By imposing a conditional sentence, the court shall take into account the nature and the degree of the social danger of the crime committed, the personality of the guilty person as well as mitigating and aggravating circumstances.

739. A conditional sentence can be imposed only if a criminal punishment imposed by the court does not exceed eight years, e.g., deprivation of freedom of maximum eight years, and only if the following types of punishment have been imposed by the court: correctional labor, restriction in military service, service in a disciplinary military unit or deprivation of freedom. Conditional sentences cannot be assigned in a number of cases, such as when the suspect was convicted of crimes against the sexual inviolability of minors under 14 years of age, when he/she has committed grave or especially grave crimes[909] during the probationary period under conditional sentence when he/she is a dangerous or particularly dangerous repeat offender, as well as in some other cases provided for by Article 73, paragraph 1 UKR.

740. By imposing a conditional sentence, the court fixes a **probationary period** (***испытательный срок***), during which the convict should prove his/her reformation through his/her behavior. Timewise the probation has a fixed term. In the case of the deprivation of freedom for a term of up to one year or a milder sentence, the probationary period shall not be less than six months and not more than three years. In the case of the deprivation of freedom for a term of more than one year, the probationary period shall be not less than six months and not more than five years (Article 73, paragraph 3 UKR). In the case of the imposition of punishment in the form of detention in a disciplinary military unit, a probationary period shall be established within the remaining military service on the day the sentence is announced (Article 73, paragraph 3.1 UKR).

---

908. For the purposes of criminal punishment, *see* paras. 656–666.
909. For the classification of criminal offenses, *see* Part I, Chapter 6, §1, paras. 635–637.

741. The court may assign the conditionally convicted person to perform different duties that contribute to his/her reformation, e.g., exercising control over the behavior of the conditionally convicted, do not visit certain places, undergo treatment for alcoholism, drug addiction, substance abuse or sexually transmitted diseases, work (find a job) or continue training in a general educational organization (Article 73, paragraph 5 UKR). If before the expiry of the probationary period, the conditionally convicted person has proved his/her reformation and additionally compensated for the damage completely or partially caused by the crime (if it is determined by the court), then the court may cancel the conditional sentence.

742. If a conditionally convicted person commits an administrative offense, a crime of negligence or an intentional crime of small or medium gravity during a probationary period, the question of canceling or maintaining a conditional conviction is decided by the court (Article 74, paragraph 3 and 4 UKR).

743. The conditional sentence should be revoked by the court if the conditionally convicted person during the probationary period has committed a grave or especially grave crime[910] (Article 74 paragraph 5 UKR).

II. Suspension of Serving Punishment

A. *Pregnant Women and Men with a Child under the Age of 14*

744. The court may suspend the actual serving of punishment for pregnant women and for women and men with a child under the age of 14 until the child reaches the age of 14. However, this provision does not apply to persons who have committed certain crimes, such as offenses against the sexual integrity of minors or crimes connected with terrorist activity (Article 82, paragraph 1 UKR).

745. The court, based on the proposal of the body responsible for the supervision of a convict, may decide to shorten the period of serving a sentence or to release the convicted person from serving a sentence partially or to release completely (Article 82, paragraph 4 UKR).[911] In order to do this, the court will take into consideration the behavior of the convict during the time of the suspension of the punishment based on a report of the authority responsible for his or her supervision (Article 82, paragraph 4 UKR).

B. *Alcoholics and Drug Addicts*

746. There are special rules of suspension of serving punishment with regard to offenders dependent on drugs stipulated in Article 82.1 UKR. A court can suspend

910. For the classification of criminal offenses, *see* Part I, Chapter 6, §1, paras. 635–647.
911. Lebedev, Kommentarii k UK RF, pp. 194–197.

the enforcement of a sentence of a drug addict for up to five years if he/she has committed the narcotic and psychotropic substance-related crimes for the first time. The offender, in this case, must show a willingness to undergo drug addiction treatment.[912]

§6. PRINCIPLES AND RULES CONCERNING SENTENCING

I. The General Principles

747. The framework for sentencing, based on the principle of legality, is provided for by the Criminal Code. The concrete criminal penalty has to be imposed by the judiciary within this legal framework.

748. The Russian sanctioning system determines the types of punishments,[913] the range of penalties applicable to a concrete offense, as well as a detailed set of rules concerning the imposition of a criminal sanction after declaring the defendant guilty (sentencing), (Chapter 11 UKR).

749. General principles of imposition of punishment are provided for by Article 60 UKR. Considering these legal provisions, the court shall impose a just punishment on a person who has been found guilty of the commission of a crime with due account to the limits stipulated by the relevant provisions of the Special and General Parts of the Criminal Code.

750. In conformity with the principles of proportionality and *ultimum remedium*, a **stricter penalty** than those provided for a certain crime shall be imposed only if a milder penalty cannot ensure the achievement of the purposes of punishment. The **grounds aggravating criminal** responsibility shall be taken into consideration (Article 63 UKR). Thereby, the imposition of a stricter punishment shall be precisely assigned within limits laid down by the rules of the **cumulation of crimes** (***совокупность преступлений***) (Article 69 UKR) and of the **cumulation of sentences** (***совокупность приговоров***) (Article 70 UKR). For example, the final punishment imposed through the cumulation of sentences must be greater than the punishment imposed for the newly committed crime, as well as the unserved part of the punishment according to the previous court verdict (Article 70, paragraph 4 UKR).

751. On the other hand, the **imposition of a softer punishment,** i.e., under the minimum limits imposed by the criminal law legislation, is possible considering special rules (Article 64 UKR). Moreover, the **grounds mitigating criminal punishment** shall be taken into consideration (Articles 61, 62 UKR). In general, there are no lower limits for punishment. The court may impose a milder punishment than

912. Federal Law on Changes to the Criminal Code and Other Legal Provisions, Dec. 7, 2011, N 420-FZ.
913. For the types of criminal punishment, *see* paras. 700–736.

provided for by the legal provision or decide not to apply the additional punishment (Article 64, paragraph 1 UKR). However, with regard to certain crimes, e.g., crimes of terroristic nature, a punishment below the lower limit or a milder punishment provided for by the legal provision cannot be imposed (Article 64, paragraph 3 UKR).

752. When imposing punishment, the character and the degree of the social danger of the crime and the personality of the convict shall be taken into consideration, including mitigating and aggravating circumstances, and also the influence of the imposed punishment on the reformation of the convicted person and on the conditions of life of his family.

II. Circumstances Modifying Criminal Punishment

A. Aggravating Circumstances

753. When imposing criminal punishment (sentencing), a court shall take into consideration various circumstances modifying criminal responsibility like, for example, circumstances aggravating criminal penalties. These are circumstances provided for in the Special Part of the Criminal Code, and they are applicable to all crimes. For example, "commission of a crime by abusing confidence placed in the guilty person by virtue of his official position or a contract," that is, abusing an official position (Article 63, paragraph 1, item m UKR), is an aggravating circumstance within the context of the commission of crimes by persons in leadership positions in collective legal entities.

754. According to Russian legislation, the following circumstances shall be deemed to be aggravating circumstances (Article 63 UKR):

- recidivism. According to Article 18 UKR, recidivism is the commission of an intentional crime by a person who has a criminal record for a previously committed intentional crime
- grave consequences of the commission of a crime;
- commission of a crime by a group of persons as a result of a prior agreement, by an organized group, or by a criminal community (criminal organization);
- an especially active role played in the commission of a crime;
- the involvement in the commission of the crime of the persons who suffer from heavy mental derangement or who are in a state of intoxication, or of persons who have not reached the age of criminal responsibility;
- the commission of a crime by the reasons of national, racial, or religious hatred or enmity as well as by the reasons of hatred or enmity regarding any other social group;
- the commission of a crime out of revenge for the lawful actions of other persons, or with the purpose of concealing or facilitating another crime;
- the commission of a crime against a person or his/her relatives in connection with his/her official activity or the discharge of his/her public duty;

- commission of a crime against a woman who is obviously in a state of pregnancy, or against a minor, another defenseless or helpless person, or a person who is dependent on the guilty person;
- the commission of a crime with especial brutality, sadism, or mockery, or involving torments for the victim;
- commission of a crime with the use of weapons, ammunition, explosives, fake explosives, specially manufactured technical means, poisonous or radioactive substances, etc., or with the use of physical or mental compulsion;
- the commission of a crime during a state of emergency, natural or social disaster, or during mass disturbances;
- the commission of a crime by abusing confidence placed in the guilty person by virtue of his/her official position or a contract
- the commission of a crime with the use of uniforms or documents of representatives of the state authorities;
- the commission of an intentional crime by an officer of the internal affairs;
- the commission of a crime against a minor by the parent or other person acting in loco parentis as well as pedagogical workers or other employees of educational, medical organizations, organizations providing social services, or other organization, obliged to supervise the minors;
- the commission of a crime to promote, justify and support terrorism.

755. Additionally, the court that imposes punishment and considers the nature and degree of social danger of the crime, the circumstances of its commission, and the identity of the perpetrator, may recognize commission of a crime in a state of intoxication caused by alcohol, drugs or other intoxicating substances as an aggravating circumstance (Article 63, paragraph 1.1. UKR).

756. Important is that in determining the appropriate sentence, an aggravating circumstance cannot be taken into consideration if the relevant offense definition in the Special Part already contains it as a **qualifying circumstance** (Article 63, paragraph 2 UKR). For example, Article 159, paragraph 3 UKR (fraud committed by virtue of abusing an official position) cannot be applied in conjunction with Article 63, paragraph 1, item m UKR ("commission of a crime by abusing confidence placed in the guilty person by virtue of his official position or a contract"). The maximum penalty, including criminal punishment with the aggravating circumstances, is provided for by the relevant article of the Special Part of the UKR.

B. Mitigating Circumstances

757. Mitigating circumstances belong to another group of essential factors that the court must consider in order to impose a fair punishment (Article 61 UKR).

758. The following circumstances shall be deemed to be mitigating circumstances:

- the commission of a crime of small or average gravity in consequence of a coincidence of circumstances;
- the age of minority of a guilty person;
- pregnancy;
- responsibility for young children;
- the commission of a crime in consequence of a coincidence of personal circumstances, or out of compassion;
- the commission of a crime as a result of physical or mental coercion, or by reason of material, official, or any other dependence;
- the commission of crime through a breach of the lawful conditions for necessary defense, the detention of a person who has committed a crime, extreme necessity, justified risk, or the execution of orders or instructions;
- the illegality or amorality of the victim's behavior, which served as a reason for commission of a crime;
- voluntarily surrendering or actively assisting in the exposure of a crime, catching other accomplices in a lie, or searching for property stolen as a result of committing a crime;
- rendering medical or other aid to the victim after the commission of the crime, voluntary compensation for material and mental damage caused as a result of the crime, and other actions directed on the smoothing down of damage caused to the victim.

759. By virtue of Article 61, paragraph 2 UKR, the list of these **circumstances is not limited**. Hence, a criminal court can take unlisted mitigating circumstances into account as well. For instance, as a general rule, motives and goals of the crime, as well as the emotional condition of the offender, are optional features of the subjective side of crime. They can be taken into consideration as mitigating circumstances. Another example can be an omission if it appears as a less dangerous form of committing a crime in a particular case. The commission of a crime with the consent of the victim and/or out of compassion can also be considered by the court as a mitigating circumstance.[914] The advanced age of an accused can be considered by the court as such a circumstance as well.

760. In situations where there are not sufficient grounds to exclude criminal liability, circumstances mitigating punishment can be applied. For instance, if the crime is not prevented despite measures undertaken by the organizer or instigator, the court may treat their efforts as mitigating circumstances when determining their punishment but may not view them as having satisfied the requirements of "voluntary refusal to commit a crime" (which negates criminal liability, Article 31 UKR). If **extreme necessity** is not applicable as a ground for excluding criminal liability or if the limits of extreme necessity are exceeded, physical or mental coercion can still be regarded as a circumstance mitigating punishment (Article 61, paragraph 1, item f UKR).

---

914. On justification, excuse, and other grounds of impunity, *see* Part I, Chapter 4, paras. 429–528.

761. A circumstance can be taken into consideration as a circumstance mitigating punishment only if the relevant offense definition in the Special Part **does not contain it as a qualifying circumstance** (Article 61, paragraph 3 UKR). For instance, if the illegality or immorality of the victim's conduct (e.g., grave insults on the part of the victim toward the offender) serves as a ground for the crime, this is deemed to be a circumstance mitigating punishment (Article 61, paragraph 1, item h UKR).

C. Circumstances Connected to the Status of Offenders

– Offenders with Mental Disorders

762. Persons who at the time of the commission of a crime were insane (Article 21, paragraph 1 UKR), for instance, suffered from oligophrenia (congenital mental retardation), belong to the group of criminally non-liable individuals.[915]

763. Insanity[916] is a ground for the imposition of **compulsory measures of a medical nature** *(принудительные меры медицинского характера)*, which are issued by a court in place of criminal punishment on the basis of medical expert reports (Articles 97–104 UKR). With regard to insane or other intellectually disabled or mentally ill individuals, these measures can be imposed only if the mental dysfunction threatens the individuals themselves or other persons with the possible infliction of further serious damage or danger (Article 97, paragraph 2 UKR). With respect to those who do not represent a danger due to their mental state, a court cannot impose compulsory measures of medical nature but can forward necessary materials to the public health bodies in order to settle the question of their medical treatment (Article 97, paragraph 4 UKR). The purposes of the application of compulsory medical measures are listed in Article 98 UKR: healing and medical treatment of insane persons and mentally disturbed individuals, improvement of their mental state, and crime prevention.

764. It should be noted that if the onset of a mental impairment that deprives an offender of awareness of the actual danger of his/her acts (or omissions) takes place after the commission of a crime, the offender must be released from punishment/ from the further serving of the sentence (Article 81, paragraph 1 UKR). In this case, however, a court can also impose compulsory medical measures under conditions provided for in Articles 97–104 UKR.

– Juveniles

765. One of the criteria for criminal responsibility is age (juvenile or adult).[917] Juvenile criminal law is not regarded as a separate branch of law.

915. On justification, excuse, and other grounds of impunity, *see* Part I, Chapter 4, paras. 429–528.
916. For insanity, *see* paras. 762–764.
917. On justification, excuse, and other grounds of impunity, *see* Part I, Chapter 4, paras. 429–528.

766. Chapter 14 UKR regulates the criminal responsibility and punishment of juveniles: types of penalties, imposition of punishments, application of compulsory measures of an educational nature, grounds for release of a minor from criminal punishment, etc.[918]

Art. 87 UKR (The Criminal Responsibility of Juveniles)

(1) Persons who at the time of the commission of a crime have reached the age of fourteen but not yet the age of eighteen shall be deemed to be juveniles.
(2) […].

767. Criminal law adopts a dual-track system with regard to juvenile offenders: "either punishment or compulsory measures of an educational nature" can be applied against juveniles who have committed crimes; "if released from punishment, a court may place a juvenile into a special closed-type educational institution under the authority of the relevant body in charge of education" (Article 87, paragraph 2 UKR). A juvenile who has committed a crime of small or average gravity (Article 15 UKR)[919] may be relieved from criminal responsibility if the court finds that his/her reformation can be achieved by applying compulsory measures of an educational nature (Articles 90, paragraph 1 and 92 UKR). The latter include warning surveillance by parents/ individuals acting *in loco parentis* or by a specialized state agency; redressing the damage caused by the crime; restriction of leisure activities; and establishment of special requirements for the behavior of the minor (Articles 90, paragraph 2 and 91 UKR).[920] The goals of the "multi-track" system regarding juveniles are education as well as general and specific prevention.[921]

– Alcoholics and Drug Addicts

768. Offenders who have committed a crime in a state of intoxication[922] caused by consuming alcohol, drugs, or other stupefying substances, are subject to criminal responsibility within the regular criminal procedure scheme (Article 23 UKR). It is another question, however, whether alcohol or drugs can, for instance, cause diseases that lead to insanity and thereby exclude criminal responsibility (Article 21 UKR).

769. There are special rules with regard to sentencing offenders dependent on drugs. A court can suspend the enforcement of a sentence of a drug addict for up to five years if he/she has committed the narcotic and psychotropic substance-related crimes for the first time that are set out in Articles 228, paragraph 1, 231, paragraph

918. Resolution of the Supreme Court's Plenary Assembly "On Judicial Practice on the Criminal Responsibility of Juveniles," Feb. 1, 2011, N 1.
919. For the categories of crimes, *see* paras. 34, 638–646.
920. Resolution of the Supreme Court's Plenary Assembly "On Judicial Practice on Conditional Release from Serving Punishment," Apr. 21, 2009, N 8.
921. Aktual'nie problemi juvenal'nogo prava. Conference materials, 2010, organized by the General Prosecutor's Office, http://rudocs.exdat.com/docs/index-443466.html [last visited Dec. 18, 2019].
922. For intoxication, *see* paras. 537–542-reference.

1, and 233 UKR. The offender, in this case, must show a willingness to undergo drug addiction treatment, as well as medical and social rehabilitation that can be imposed by the court in addition to criminal punishment (Article 82.1 UKR).[923]

– Sex Offenders

770. The situation with regard to compulsory measures and criminal punishment of sex offenders, especially pedophiles, has been a hotly debated topic over the past few years. Before major changes in this area were introduced with a Federal Law in 2012,[924] criminal punishment of child sex offenders was quite mild. Compulsory medical measures for pedophiles were introduced for the first time in 2012. As pedophiles are regarded as individuals who have committed a crime against the sexual integrity of a minor (a person under the age of 14) and who suffer from sexual preference disorder (pedophilia), they cannot be considered insane and treated accordingly (Article 97, paragraph 1, item e UKR). Rather, the new compulsory medical measure of chemical castration may be imposed, but only by a court, that bases its decision on a forensic expert report that confirms sexual preference disorder (pedophilia). With respect to individuals who have committed sex crimes against adolescents over 14 years of age, chemical castration is applied on a voluntary basis. The main goals of such "treatment," in addition to punishment, are to provide for the protection and security of potential victims as well as general and individual prevention.

– Recidivists

771. Recidivists were regarded in Soviet legal scholarship as a separate category of offenders, as a "special subject of crime" that could be characterized by the offender's immoral and antisocial appearance.[925] Since the Soviet period, the concept has shifted. At the present time, legal scholarship uses the term "recidivism" instead of the term "recidivist" and regards it as a feature that refers to the objective indicia of an act rather than to the personal characteristics of an offender.[926]

772. Article 18, paragraph 1 UKR defines recidivism as "the commission of an intentional crime by a person who has a record of conviction for the same or other intentional crimes." However, recidivism does not include, for example, convictions for intentional crimes of minor gravity as well as convictions for crimes committed by a person younger than 18 years of age (Article 18, paragraph 4 UKR). Recidivism is divided into "dangerous" (Article 18, paragraph 2 UKR) and "especially dangerous" recidivism. Recidivism is deemed to be especially dangerous if

923. Federal Law on Changes to the Criminal Code and Other Legal Provisions, Dec. 7, 2011, N 420-FZ.
924. Federal Law on Changes to the Criminal Code and Other Legislative Acts that Aggravate the Penalties for the Sexual Offenses Committed against Minors, Feb. 29, 2012, N 14-FZ.
925. Kafarov, Problemi recidiva pp. 8–9.
926. Komissarov/Krilova/Tyazhkova, Ugolovnoe pravo RF, pp. 298–299.

an offender has committed an especially grave crime and has previously been convicted either at least twice for grave crimes or for an especially grave crime (Article 18, paragraph 3 UKR).[927]

773. Recidivism is taken into consideration by the assignment of punishment and criminal responsibility (Article 68 UKR). According to Article 63, paragraph 1, item a UKR, recidivism is regarded as an aggravating circumstance. Thus, "recidivism involves a stricter punishment" than criminal responsibility on a regular basis (Article 18, paragraph 5 UKR). The general rule for the imposition of punishment in cases of recidivism is that, as long as it is within the limits of the sanction of the particular article of the Special Part of the Criminal Code, it may not be less than one-third of the maximum term of the most severe penalty provided for in relation to the offense (Article 68, paragraph 2 UKR).

774. Recidivism is relevant in the sphere of criminal enforcement with regard to the imposition of the type of imprisonment. For instance, according to Article 58, paragraph 1, item d UKR, imprisonment in special regime correctional facilities (the strictest type of imprisonment) is reserved for males sentenced for the commission of especially grave repeat crimes.

D. Other Circumstances Modifying Criminal Punishment

– Sentencing of Inchoate Offenses

775. Sentencing of **inchoate offenses** is carried out on the basis of the general rules contained in Article 60 UKR and in light of the specific legal provisions contained in Article 66 UKR.[928]

Art. 66 UKR (Imposition of punishment for inchoate offenses)

(1) When imposing punishment for an inchoate crime, the court shall take into consideration the circumstances by virtue of which the crime was not brought to an end.
(2) The term or the extent of punishment for preparation of a crime may not exceed half of the maximum term or extent of the most severe type of punishment provided for by the relevant Article of the Special Part of the present Code for a completed crime.
(3) The term or extent of punishment for an attempted crime may not exceed three-quarters of the maximum term or extent of the most severe type of punishment provided for by the relevant Article of the Special Part of the present Code for a completed crime.
(4) Neither capital punishment nor deprivation of freedom for life term shall be imposed for the preparation of a crime or for an attempted crime.

927. For the categories of crimes, *see* paras. 34, 638–646.
928. *See* Plenum of the Highest Court of the Russian Federation, 11.1.2007, N 2.

776. Conduct prior to the completion of a target crime is typically considered less socially dangerous than conduct that culminates in a completed target crime.[929] This determination is taken into consideration when imposing punishment. For example, the term or extent of punishment for preparation of a crime may not exceed half of the maximum term or extent of the most severe type of punishment provided for by the relevant article of the Special Part of the Criminal Code for a completed crime (Article 66, paragraph 2 UKR). In addition, the punishment of deprivation of freedom for life cannot be imposed for the preparation of a crime or for an attempted crime (Article 66, paragraph 4 UKR).

– *Imposition of Punishment for Crime Committed in Complicity*

Sentencing with regard to crimes committed by multiple parties is based on the principle of individual responsibility (Article 34, paragraph 1 UKR). When imposing criminal punishment, the degree and importance of the actual contribution of each individual participant, independent of the conduct of the perpetrator(s), is the most important consideration (Article 67, paragraph 1 UKR). This principle is also apparent in the fact that mitigating (Article 61 UKR) and aggravating circumstances (Article 63 UKR) can be taken into account with regard to each participant separately.

Art. 67 UKR (Imposition of punishment for crime committed in complicity)

(1) When imposing punishment for a crime committed in complicity, the character and degree of actual participation of the person in the commission thereof, the importance of this participation for the achievement of the purpose of the crime, and its influence on the character and on the amount of inflicted or possible damage, shall be taken into account.
(2) Mitigating or aggravating circumstances relating to the personality of one of the accomplices shall be taken into account when imposing punishment for this individual accomplice.

– *Relief from Criminal Responsibility for Crimes in the Economic Sphere*

In 2011, the institute of relief from criminal responsibility for most crimes in the economic sphere was introduced to the Criminal Code and the Code of Criminal Procedure (Article 76.1 UKR and Article 28.1 UPKR).[930] This way, a person, who has committed an economic crime for the first time, shall be relieved from criminal responsibility if he/she has compensated the damage to the federal budget (Article 76.1, paragraph 1 UKR); in some cases, under the condition of the compensation five times for the damage to the federal budget (Article 76.1, paragraph 2 UKR).

929. On the concept of social danger, *see* Part I, Chapter 3, §1, *see* paras. 317–330.
930. Federal Law on Changes to Criminal Code and Other Legal Provisions," Dec. 7, 2011, N 420-FZ.

– *Relief from Criminal Responsibility Due to Active Repentance*

A person who has committed a crime of small or average gravity may be released from criminal responsibility for active repentance if all of the following conditions are fulfilled: the person committed such a crime for the first time; after committing the offense, the person made a full confession; the person facilitated the investigation of the crime; the person compensated the damage caused as a result of the crime or in any other way effected compensation for it; and as a result of active repentance, the person ceased to be socially dangerous (Article 75 UKR).[931]

– *Relief from Criminal Responsibility Due to Reconciliation with Victim*

A person may be released from criminal responsibility due to reconciliation with the victim. A person who has committed a crime of small or average gravity for the first time may be released from criminal responsibility if he or she has reconciled with the victim and has compensated the damage caused by the crime to the victim (Article 76 UKR).[932]

III. Multiplicity of Offenses

A. Definition

777. Criminal liability in the event of **multiplicity of offenses** (***множественность преступлений***) has a number of significant features of theoretical and practical interest.[933]

778. In some cases, a crime that is made up of the commission of several acts (actions/omissions) and entails the occurrence of a range of consequences is considered to be one crime. On the other hand, one criminal act may contain 'elements of crime' of multiple offenses and represent several crimes. Thus, there is a problem of multiplicity of crimes, in particular, the determination of the limits of criminal liability in the case of various kinds of multiple offenses.

779. In legal scholarship, the multiplicity of crimes is defined as cases of commission by one person of two or more offenses by means of one or several criminal acts.[934] The following situations are covered by the problem of the multiplicity of offenses: A person commits two or more crimes before being convicted for these crimes and is prosecuted simultaneously for them (cumulation of crimes, Article 17 UKR). Another situation is that a person commits in one act two or more criminal

931. Lebedev, Kommentarii k UK RF, p. 179; Naumov, Rossiiskoe ugolovnoe pravo, pp. 607–612; Zhuravlev, Ugolovnoe pravo, pp. 240–242.
932. Lebedev, Kommentarii k UK RF, pp. 182–183; Komissarov/Krilova/Tyazhkova, Ugolovnoe pravo RF, pp. 687–690; Naumov, Rossiiskoe ugolovnoe pravo, pp. 612–614; Zhuravlev, Ugolovnoe pravo, p. 242.
933. Revin. Uchebnik Ugolovnoe Pravo.
934. Krivolapov, Multiplicity of Crimes under Soviet Criminal Law, pp. 10–19.

offenses falling under various articles of the Criminal Code. The problem of multiplicity of offenses is considered if a person has committed crime(s) after being convicted for the previous crimes upon condition that the criminal consequences of that crime(s) have not yet been expunged (cumulation of sentences) or he/she commits a new crime during the probationary period on conditional release and conditional conviction.[935] Hence, the multiplicity of crimes finds particular expression in the form of cumulation of sentences (in the case of recidivism, Article 18 UKR), and cumulation of crimes (*see infra*), Article 17 UKR.

B. Simple Single Crimes and Complex Single Crimes

780. In the context of multiplicity of crimes, it is essential to distinguish between multiple crimes and so-called **single crimes** (*единое преступление*). Single crimes are divided into two catergories: simple single crimes and complex single crimes.

781. A **simple single crime** (*простое единое преступление*) is committed by means of one act that qualifies as one crime, e.g., homicide, Article 105 UKR.[936] A **complex single crime** (*сложное единое преступление*) is recognized as an offense based on an alternative or/and repeated actions, for example, the illegal acquisition, storage, transportation, manufacture, processing of drugs, psychotropic substances or their analogs (Article 228 UKR). The commission by a person of each of these actions is already a sufficient basis for the recognition of the crime as completed, but at the same time, the commission of all actions together (or some of them) will be regarded as a single complex crime, without the formation of multiplicity.

782. The main distinguishing criterion between **multiple crimes** and so-called **complex single crimes** is the subjective side of crime (intent or negligence directed on commission of one crime). In contrast to a multiple crime (e.g., theft of weapons for the purpose of murder), a complex single crime, objectively consisting of several acts, however, subjectively directed on the commission of one crime, does not contain 'elements of crime' of different offenses, Article 228 UKR (illegal acquisition and storage of drugs).

783. In legal scholarship, complex single crimes are furthermore divided into three types: **compound** (*составные*), **lasting** (*длящиеся*) and **continued** crimes (*продолжаемые преступления*).

784. A **compound crime** is a crime that is composed of two or more separate offenses when considered in isolation. A compound crime refers to one offense qualification entailing the infringement of two (or more) legally protected interests. However, in the criminal law legislation, a compound crime qualifies as one crime,

935. Malkov/Timershin, Multiplicity of Crimes, p. 7.
936. Bazhanov, Sentencing for Cumulative Crimes and Cumulative Sentences, p. 3

for instance, robbery that encompasses violence threatening the life or health of a person and acquisition of another´s property, Article 162, paragraph 1 UKR. **Lasting crimes** are characterized by the feature that they are performed continuously for a longer or less long period of time. This type of complex single crime is not regarded as a separate one by all authors. However, most legal scholars recognize its complex nature due to its duration in time.[937] To such crimes belong, for example, the evasion of customs duties (Article 194 UKR) or failure to return to the territory of the Russian Federation objects of the artistic, historical and archeological heritage of the peoples of the Russian Federation and foreign countries (Article 190 UKR). Criminal responsibility occurs for one committed crime under the respective article or part of the article of the Criminal Code (Article 60, paragraph 1 UKR).

785. The third group of complex single crimes is related to **continued crimes**. The distinctive feature of this group manifests itself in the fact that such crimes are made up of a number of common acts directed toward a common goal, and all together, they constitute one offense. Such acts are committed continuously with renewable activities, maybe with certain interruptions. Separately, they are not regarded as crimes but a link or a continuing stage of the same crime. For example, within one year, a person had been stealing different parts of a TV from a factory (theft, Article 158, paragraph 1 UKR).[938] Hence, criminal punishment shall be imposed for the aggregate of continuously committed acts as for one crime. Continued crimes should be distinguished from cumulation crimes. The difficulty in distinguishing the cumulation of crimes from continued crimes lies in the fact that in their external features, they are largely the same. However, in the case of a continued crime, there is a subjective connection between separate acts. It is expressed in the fact that each subsequent act of the continued behavior is a link or stage in the person's unified criminal intent or is a continuation of imprudent activity caused by his/her unjustifiable mistake. In this case, the person bears criminal responsibility for one committed crime under the respective article or part of the article of the Criminal Code (Article 60, paragraph 1 UKR).

786. In contrast, in the case of the cumulation of crimes, every act is considered to be a separate crime by the criminal law provisions, e.g., theft of weapons with a purpose to commit a terrorist act (Articles 158 and 205 UKR). In the case of this form of multiplicity of offenses, the person shall bear criminal responsibility for each committed crime under the respective article or part of the article of the Criminal Code (Article 69, paragraph 1 UKR).

937. Malkov/Timershin, Multiplicity of Crimes, p. 19.
938. *Ibid.*

C. Cumulation of Crimes

– Definition

787. The multiplicity of crimes finds particular expression in the form of cumulation of crimes, Article 17 UKR.

788. "**Cumulation of crimes**" (*совокупность преступлений*) is defined as the commission of two or more different offenses, for none of which the person has been convicted, that are punishable under different articles or parts of articles of the Criminal Code. In case of this form of multiplicity of offenses, the person shall bear criminal responsibility for each committed crime under the respective article or part of the article of the Criminal Code (Articles 17, paragraphs 1 and 69, paragraph 1 UKR).

789. Legal scholarship classifies 'cumulation of crimes' into two types: **real cumulation of crimes** (*реальная совокупность преступлений*) and **ideal cumulation of crimes** (*идеальная совокупность преступлений*). The criterion for distinguishing between real and ideal cumulation of crimes is commission of several crimes either by multiple acts (actions or omissions) or by one act. In any case, 'cumulation of crimes' results in commission of two or more different offenses.

– Real Cumulation of Crimes

790. **Real cumulation of crimes** (*реальная совокупность преступлений*) presupposes that an offender **by performing multiple acts (two or more) commits several (two or more) different crimes**. An example of real cumulation of crime: a certain K., possessing a weapon without proper authorization (Article 222 UKR), caused bodily harm of average gravity to F. arising from a fight with this weapon (Article 112 UKR). Thus, the offender bears criminal responsibility for each committed crime (Articles 112 and 222 UKR). The punishment shall be imposed considering rules of Article 69 UKR, which will be explained below.

– Ideal Cumulation of Crimes

791. **Commission of several crimes through one act** (action or omission) is considered as **ideal cumulation of crimes** (*идеальная совокупность преступлений*) (Article 17, paragraph 2 UKR). This type of cumulation of crimes can form a combination of intentional and negligent offenses. For instance, an ideal cumulation of crimes occurs if an attempted murder of one person (Articles 105 paragraph 1 and 30 UKR) was committed alongside a negligent injury of another person (Article 118 UKR). The punishment for each crime shall be imposed considering rules of Article 69 UKR.

– Sentencing Rules for Cumulative Crimes

792. Article 69 UKR provides for the sentencing rules for cumulative crimes. According to these provisions, if crimes committed cumulatively only represent offenses of small or average gravity, or the preparation for grave or especially grave crime, or an attempt on a grave or especially grave crime, then final punishment shall be imposed by the **absorption** (*поглощение*) of the less severe penalty with a more severe one, or by partial or full **adding-up** (*сложения*) of penalties. It is up to the court to decide the sentencing option. The final punishment may, however, not exceed by more than half of the maximum term or scope of punishment provided for the gravest of the crimes committed. In the case where at least one of the crimes committed cumulatively is a grave or especially grave crime, then the final penalty shall be imposed by the partial or full adding-up of penalties.

793. Furthermore, in the case of cumulative crimes, additional penalties,[939] e.g., fine, Article 45 UKR, may be joined to the basic penalties.[940] Final additional punishment may not exceed the maximum term or scope prescribed for this type of additional punishment by the General Part of the UKR (Article 69, paragraph 4 UKR), e.g., the maximum term for the limitation of liberty as an additional penalty is two years (Article 53, paragraph 2 UKR).

D. Cumulation of Sentences

794. The multiplicity of crimes finds expression in the form of cumulation of sentences (Article UKR 18). Assignment of punishment by cumulative sentences is regulated in particular by Article 70 UKR. In imposing punishment by the cumulation of sentences, the court adds, partially or fully, the unserved part of the penalty under the court's previous sentence to the penalty imposed by the court's latest judgment.

795. The final punishment by cumulative sentences must be greater than either the punishment imposed for the new crime or the unserved part of the punishment under the previous court's judgment alone, Article 70, paragraph 4 UKR. However, the final punishment by cumulative sentences, if it is less strict than deprivation of freedom, may not exceed the maximum term or scope stipulated by the General Part of the Criminal Code for the given penalty. For instance, according to the rules laid down in the General Part, arrest as a criminal punishment cannot be imposed for longer than for a term of six months (Article 54, paragraph 1 UKR).

796. The final punishment by cumulative sentences in the form of deprivation of freedom may not exceed thirty years (Article 70, paragraph 3 UKR). Although

939. For additional penalties, *see* paras. 725–726.
940. For basic penalties, *see* paras. 700–725.

with regard to the crimes of terroristic nature, the maximum punishment can be thirty-five years (Article 56, paragraph 5 UKR).[941]

797. In the case of cumulative sentences, additional penalties may be imposed alongside the basic penalties according to the same rules as the imposition of punishment for cumulative crimes (Article 69, paragraph 4 UKR).

941. Federal Law, May 5, 2014, N130-FZ.

Part II. Criminal Procedure

Chapter 1. Principles, Institutions, and Stages

§1. Historical Overview

I. Ancient Rus'

798. The history of Russian criminal,[942] as well as of criminal procedural law, can be traced back to the Ancient Russian State *(Kievan Rus')*.[943] The first consolidated written source of legal rules of the *Kievan Rus'*, the "Russian Truth" of 1016 (including its further redactions) provided for an **accusatorial system of criminal justice** *(обвинительный процесс)*. The characteristic of this system was that a criminal case depended entirely on the accuser, who, at the same time, was a victim. Proceedings concerning any kind of offense—including the most serious crimes, for example, murder—were commenced only on the complaint of the victim. The latter, who was obliged to support the prosecution and to present evidence, could withdraw an action. There was no preliminary investigation as such. The main features of the accusatorial procedure were as follows: equality between the accuser and the accused, publicity of proceedings, as well as the use of ordeal (the so-called judgment of God—a trial by fire, water, etc.) to determine the guilt or innocence of the accused.[944]

799. In further legal sources such as the Dvina Charters of 1397 as well as the Pskov Judicial Charters of 1462, progressive growth of state control with regard to criminal procedure-related issues, for example, prohibition of vigilante justice, can be observed.[945] That trend continued and reached its apogee in the centralized Russian State.[946]

942. *See* General Introduction, §3. The Historical Background, p. 27.
943. Karamzin, Istoriya Gosudarstva Rossiiskogo, http://bibliotekar.ru/karamzin/index.htm [last visited Dec. 18, 2019]; Paramonova, National characteristics, fundamental principles, and history of criminal law in Russia, 2014, pp. 265–292.
944. Pikalov, Ugolovnij process; Russkaya Pravda, www.consultant.ru [last visited Dec. 18, 2019].
945. Rossijskoe zakonodatelstvo X-XX vekov: v 9 tomach. Tom 2. Moscow 1985.
946. Paramonova, National characteristics, fundamental principles, and history of criminal law in Russia, 2014, pp. 265–292.

II. Russian Centralized State

800. The development and strengthening of an inquisitorial criminal procedure, which indicates the growing role of the state in the regulation of social relations, took place during the time of the centralization of the Russian State (15th–16th centuries).[947] Certain behaviors were proclaimed harmful not only for private persons but also for the state.

801. Until the beginning of the 18th century, the inquisitorial criminal procedure existed alongside the accusatorial system of criminal justice. The first codified legal source of centralized Russia, the Law Code of Ivan III of 1497, defined the competence of state officials; it established the monopoly of the state to prosecute serious—in particular, political—crimes, for example, revolt. The Law Code of Ivan IV of 1550, continuing this trend, foresaw a more developed and far-reaching investigation system that involved the growth of the apparatus of the state. The Council Code of 1649 then provided for the possibility that certain cases could be considered within the inquisitorial procedure system, even if they were initially investigated under the system of accusatorial procedure.[948]

III. Russian Empire (1721–1917)

802. Following the reforms of *Peter I* (Military Statute of 1716; Naval Statute of 1720) in the 18th century and continuing until the liberal reforms of *Alexander II* (1864), the inquisitorial criminal procedure took a dominant position.[949] It was characterized by the growing control of the state in all procedural stages. The main features can be described as follows: separation of judicial power (the functions of investigator, prosecutor, and judge were merged in one entity) from the central government; complete lack of openness, publicity, and orality of proceedings; very limited rights of the accused; torture as a method of obtaining evidence; strict hierarchy of evidence; broad use of formal proofs (e.g., admission of guilt as "the queen of evidence," and the decisive role of the social status of the witnesses in the evaluation of evidence); no rule of *in dubio pro reo*. The defendant within the inquisitorial system of criminal justice was denied the opportunity to defend him- or herself and was considered the "object" of the procedure.[950] Torture was officially abolished in Russia in 1801 by the decree of *Alexander I*.[951]

803. The liberal reforms of *Alexander II* dating to the second half of the 19th century were the turning point in the law of criminal procedure. The Statute on Criminal Procedure of 1864 introduced the continental system of criminal justice,

947. Paramonova, National characteristics, fundamental principles, and history of criminal law in Russia, 2014, pp. 265–292.
948. Rossijskoe zakonodatelstvo X-XX vekov: v 9 tomach. Tom 4. Moscow 1986.
949. Paramonova, National characteristics, fundamental principles, and history of criminal law in Russia, 2014, pp. 265–292.
950. Bozhjev, Ugolovnij process, p. 16; Pikalov, Ugolovnij process.
951. Rossijskoe zakonodatelstvo X-XX vekov: v 9 tomach. Tom 4. Moscow 1986.

taking as a basis the French Code of Criminal Investigation *(Code d'instruction criminelle)* of 1808. It remained in force until the Revolution of 1917 and was applied in part even after 1917. The central element of the reform of the judicial system in 1864—which was based on the idea of the separation of powers—was the creation of a unified court system with fundamental changes in criminal trials.[952] The reform included the establishment of the independence of judges; free evaluation of evidence according to the personal conviction of the judges; the principle of equality of the parties involved; the introduction of such procedural guarantees as publicity, immediacy, and orality in criminal proceedings; and the establishment of elements of the adversarial system such as jury trial and the institution of professional advocacy (which had not previously existed in Russia). According to the Statute of 1864, these rules applied in criminal cases to persons of all social classes.[953]

804. These changes modified the existing inquisitorial criminal procedure into a hybrid system of criminal justice. It included elements of the inquisitorial procedure with respect to investigation (e.g., secrecy of preliminary investigation) and features of the adversarial system on the level of court proceedings (e.g., the jury).[954]

IV. Soviet Period (1917–1991)

805. The Revolution of 1917 that completely changed the political and social systems also inevitably influenced Russia's legal system and legal scholarship.[955] The result was the breakdown of knowledge accumulated and achievements gained over the several decades following the judicial reform in 1864. Ideas rejected by Soviet Russia included the following: independence of the judiciary, the priority of human rights over the state and public interests, and the possibility that adversarial elements, for example, the jury, could be used in criminal procedure.

806. With the Council of People's Commissars of the Russian Soviet Federative Socialist Republic's Decree, N 1 "On the judicial system" of 1917,[956] all institutions of the judicial system of czarist Russia were abolished. Among these were, for example, district courts, military and naval courts of all kinds, commercial courts, investigators, prosecutor's supervision, jury trials, and the professional bar association of attorneys.

---

952. Chelcov-Bebutov, Kurs ugolovno-processualnogo prava, p. 782.
953. Koni, Otzi i deti sudebnoj reformi, p. 352.
954. Paramonova, National characteristics, fundamental principles, and history of criminal law in Russia, 2014, pp. 265–292.
955. Paramonova, National characteristics, fundamental principles, and history of criminal law in Russia, 2014, pp. 265–292.
956. Decree N 1 "On judicial system" of the Council of People's Commissars of the RSFSR, Nov. 24, 1917.

807. Although the codes of criminal procedure of the Soviet period (Code of Criminal Procedure of the RSFSR of 1922[957] and Code of Criminal Procedure of the RSFSR of 1960[958]) retained considerable portions of the liberal-democratic rules from the Statute on Criminal Procedure of 1864, most of these rules were usually not applied in practice. Furthermore, during the years of repression (mainly the 1930s), large numbers of people were prosecuted without the application of any procedural safeguards. Criminal punishments, including capital punishment and deprivation of freedom, were imposed in extra-judicial procedures on the basis of executive decisions, that is, resolutions of two- or three-person committees (the so-called "special triples," "triples," and "twos" of the **People's Commissariat for Internal Affairs of the USSR** (*Народный Комиссариат Внутренних Дел* CCCP, NKVD).[959] Between 1934 and 1946, the NKVD was the central body of state administration of the USSR for fighting crime, maintaining public order, and ensuring public safety. Among other things, it conducted mass extrajudicial executions and ran the system of forced labor camps.[960]

808. The Code of Criminal Procedure of the RSFSR of 1960[961] was enacted during the "Khrushchev Thaw," a period characterized by more moderate criminal justice politics, and remained in force until the enactment of the new Code of Criminal Procedure in 2001. The criminal procedure embodied in the Code of 1960 followed the inquisitorial model. The dominance of state organs during the pretrial and trial stages, on the one hand, and the achievement of substantive truth, proclaimed as a goal of criminal procedure (which required comprehensive, full, and objective investigation of the circumstances of a case), on the other, formed the core of the criminal procedure. Investigators and judges, who worked closely together, had a monopoly on appraising evidence and on the application of procedural measures of coercion and decided on other relevant procedural issues.[962] For instance, Article 418, paragraphs 1 and 2 of the 1960 Code authorized judges in certain cases to initiate criminal prosecutions, to draft charging documents, and then to decide the case.[963]

---

957. Code of Criminal Procedure of the RSFSR, May 26, 1922, N 15, Art. 153 (Ugolovno-processualnij Kodeks RSFSR).
958. Code of Criminal Procedure of the RSFSR, Oct. 27, 1960, N 8, Art. 613 (Ugolovno-processualnij Kodeks RSFSR).
959. Kudryavcev, Rol' sudebnich i vnesudebnich organov v provedenii repressii; Shishov, smertnaya kazn' v Rossii; Yakovlev/Burtsov, Concentration Camps in the USSR, http://javot.net/arhiv/8.htm [last visited Dec. 18, 2019].
960. Yakovlev/Burtsov, ibid.
961. Code of Criminal Procedure of the RSFSR 1960.
962. For new developments in Russian criminal procedure, *see* Paramonova/Bogush, ZStW 125 (2013), 703–728.
963. Paramonova, National characteristics, fundamental principles, and history of criminal law in Russia, 2014, pp. 265–292.

§2. Contemporary Criminal Procedure

809. The complete political reorientation of the 1990s necessitated a reform of the entire system of criminal procedure. One of the most significant reforms was the introduction of adversarial principles into a traditionally inquisitorial system of criminal justice.[964] For the first time, the **principle of adversariness** ***(принцип состязательности)*** was anchored at the legislative level (Article 15 UPKR, Article 123, paragraph 3 Const.). The role of the judiciary was essentially reduced from that of the main decision maker in the criminal procedure system to that of a neutral arbitrator,[965] and jury trials—that were common practice in Czar´s Russia till 1917—were reintroduced.[966]

810. The special features of the new Code of Criminal Procedure were the expansion of judicial review of measures taken by investigative and prosecution authorities as well as the differentiation of procedural forms. For example, Chapter 40 UPKR introduced a special form of court procedure that applies if the defendant agrees with the indictment and wants to plead guilty.[967] In 2009,[968] the special procedure of pretrial cooperation between prosecution and defense (Chapter 40.1. UPKR)—an analog of *plea bargaining*[969]—was introduced. The purpose of the institution is to enhance the adversarial element of Russian criminal procedure. This issue, however, belongs to one of the most controversial legal discussions. Like other countries of continental Europe, Russia shows a more cautious approach to the application of plea bargaining than in some common law jurisdictions. The main reason for that is that traditionally in Russia, the pursuit of objective truth by punishing a guilty person is considered a goal of criminal procedure and not the outcome of better legal bargaining (Article 6 UPKR).[970]

811. Contemporary procedure is a compromise between new liberal legal ideas reflecting the principle of adversarial procedure proclaimed by the Constitution (Article 123, paragraph 3) and the inquisitorial model of criminal procedure of the Code of Criminal Procedure of 1960.[971] The procedure of the new Code of Criminal Procedure of 2001 represents a **"neo-inquisitorial" (mixed or hybrid) model** of criminal procedure.[972]

---

964. Petrukhin, Teoreticheskie osnowi reformi ugolovnogo prozessa; Kahn, Russia's Hybrid Code of Criminal Procedure.
965. Pomorski, Criminal Law Forum, 17 (2006), 130.
966. Paramonova/Bogush, ZStW 125 (2013), 703–728; Paramonova, National characteristics, fundamental principles, and history of criminal law in Russia, 2014, pp. 265–292.
967. Federal Law on Changes to Code of Criminal Procedure, Jul. 4, 2003, N 92-FZ.
968. Federal Law on Changes to Code of Criminal Procedure, Jun. 29, 2009, N 141-FZ.
969. For the special criminal procedures and for plea bargaining, *see* paras. 114, 961, 1273–1278.
970. For the more detailed information on the plea bargaining in Russia, *see* Paramonova, Revista Penal 2012, 264–268; Poznyshev, Russkij ugolovnij prozess, pp. 29–30; Petrukhin, Reforma ugolovnogo prozessa, p. 26. For plea bargaining, *see* paras. 114, 810, 961, 1273–1278.
971. Criminal-Procedural Code of the RSFSR 1960.
972. Bozhjev, Ugolovnij process, p. 16; Paramonova/Bogush, ZStW 125 (2013), 703–728.

812. On the one hand, the Code of Criminal Procedure proclaims the principle of adversarial procedure for both the investigation stage and the subsequent stage of court proceedings (Article 15 UPKR) as well as the rule of equality of arms: the prosecution and defense enjoy equal rights before the court (Articles 15, paragraph 4, 244 UPKR). On the other hand, due to the public interest of the state in criminal matters, investigation authorities are privileged over the defense, for example, by having full access to all relevant documents of a case.[973]

813. Another important factor is the influence of the ECtHR on contemporary criminal procedure. For instance, the reform of judicial remedies of 2016 is one of the measures undertaken in response to the case law of the ECtHR.[974] It began in 2010, and the latest amendments were introduced by the Federal Law in 2016.[975] The reform has changed the system of legal remedies in criminal cases fundamentally.[976] There have been changes in some principles of criminal procedure (see *infra* §3).

§3. Principles of Criminal Procedure

I. Definition of the Principles

814. The principles of criminal procedure are the guiding ideas provided for in legislation that define the essential features, nature, and characteristics of criminal procedure.[977] They determine the major procedural constructs and institutions, namely, the subject and method of procedural regulation, the forms of investigation, the quality of the preliminary investigation and the criminal trial procedure, as well as the major directions for development and implementation of the relevant legal provisions.[978] The influence of the case law of the ECtHR will be highlighted with regard to the principles that have undergone certain changes under this influence.

815. Chapter 2 of the Code of Criminal Procedure (Articles 6–19 UPKR[979]) is devoted to the **principles of criminal procedure** (*принципы уголовного судопроизводства*). According to this chapter, these principles serve to implement the aim of criminal procedure, which is defined as "protecting the rights and legitimate interests of the persons and organizations, who (which) have suffered

973. For the principles of criminal law, *see* Part I, Chapter 1, paras. 194–196.
974. *See* Ryabykh v. Russia, Jul. 24, 2003, App. No. 52854/99; Smarygin v. Russia, Dec. 1, 2005, App. No. 73203/01; Federal Law, Dec. 29, 2010, N 433-FZ. Paramonova, KritVj 2013, 207.
975. Federal Law, Jul. 6, 2016, N 375-FZ.
976. For the reform of judicial remedies, *see* Chapter 3, paras. 1303–1311; for a detailed analysis of the reform, *see* Paramonova/Bogush, ZStW 125 (2013), 703–728.
977. Paramonova, National characteristics, fundamental principles, and history of criminal law in Russia, 2014, pp. 175–292.
978. Bezlepkin, Kommentarij k UPKR; Radchenko, Kommentarij k UPKR.
979. Code of Criminal Procedure of the Russian Federation, Dec. 18, 2001 N 174-FZ (Ugolovno-prozessual´nij Kodeks RF).

from the crimes, and as protecting the person from unlawful and ungrounded accusations and conviction, and from the restriction of his/her rights and freedoms" (Article 6, paragraph 1 UPKR). The fundamental principles of criminal procedure are also reflected in other legal provisions, for example, in provisions of the Constitution and the Criminal Code.[980]

II. Classification of the Principles

816. In the literature, the principles of criminal procedure are usually classified according to various criteria. These include the legal source of the principle (e.g., Constitution or (and) Code of Criminal Procedure), the limits on the principle's regulatory scope (principles that are applicable to all aspects of criminal procedure are distinguished from those that apply only to the certain procedural stage(s) (e.g., the principle of immediacy with respect to evidence, Article 240 UPKR), and the content of the principle.[981] The classification based on content—which will be applied in the overview below—is considered the major one. With regard to content, the following distinctions are made: (1) basic principles; (2) principles concerning due process and procedural safeguards for participants in the criminal process, in particular for the accused; (3) principles concerning the judiciary and the administration of criminal justice; and (4) other principles of criminal justice.[982]

817. The various principles of criminal procedure—each with its own content—overlap, reinforce one another and are closely related. Together they form a unified legal framework.[983]

A. Basic Principles

818. **Respect for the person's honor and dignity** *(уважение чести и достоинства личности)* is one of the fundamental principles of criminal procedure and is based on the principle of humanity. It can be found in provisions that prohibit violence, torture, or other kinds of cruel or humiliating treatment in criminal proceedings (Article 21 Const., Article 9 UPKR, Article 302 UKR).

819. This principle is inextricably connected with another basic principle of criminal procedure, namely, the **protection of the rights and lawful interests of a person in criminal proceedings** *(охрана прав и свобод человека и гражданина в уголовном судопроизводстве)*, which encompasses the obligation of the court,

980. On the principles of criminal law, *see* Part I, Chapter 1, paras. 194–196; Paramonova, National characteristics, fundamental principles, and history of criminal law in Russia, 2014, pp. 175–292.
981. Bezlepkin, Kommentarij k UPKR; Radchenko, Kommentarij k UPKR, Lebedev, Nauchno-prakticheskij kommentarij k UPKR, 2016, p. 5.
982. Bezlepkin, Kommentarij k UPKR; Radchenko, Kommentarij k UPKR.
983. Paramonova, National characteristics, fundamental principles, and history of criminal law in Russia, 2014, pp. 175–292.

prosecutor, investigator, or inquirer to explain to the participants in the criminal proceedings their rights, responsibilities, and liabilities and to guarantee the possibility of exercising these rights (Article 45 Const., Articles 11 and 6, paragraph 1 UPKR). This includes, first, the right of a participant in the criminal process not to testify against him- or herself, his or her spouse and close relatives, and second, the obligation of the state authorities to take security measures with regard to endangered participants in criminal proceedings, e.g., witnesses (Article 51 Const., Article 11, paragraphs 2–3 UPKR).[984]

820. An inherent element of the aforementioned principle is the **right to rehabilitation**, which includes the right to compensation for property and intangible damages that result from a violation of human rights inflicted by a court or officials conducting the criminal prosecution, as well as the right to restoration of infringed rights, for example, employment rights (Article 53 Const., Articles 11, paragraph 4, 6, paragraph 2, and 133 UPKR). The rehabilitation of all those who have been groundlessly subjected to criminal prosecution, the non-prosecution of innocent persons, and the imposition of just punishment on guilty persons are the components of the **principle of justice** *(принцип справедливости)* according to both legal provisions (Article 6, paragraph 2 UPKR) and literature.

Art. 6 UPKR (Purpose of the Criminal Proceedings)

(1) […].
(2) The criminal prosecution and the imposition of just punishment on guilty persons shall be the purpose of the criminal proceedings to the same extent as the refusal from the criminal prosecution of innocent persons, their relief from punishment, and the rehabilitation of all those who have been groundlessly subjected to criminal prosecution.

821. Another basic principle that must be mentioned is the **principle of legality in criminal procedure** *(принцип законности при производстве по уголовному делу)*, a principle that is binding upon all state authorities, in particular courts, prosecutors, investigators, and inquirers (Article 7 UPKR).[985] None of these authorities may apply a Federal Law that contradicts the Code of Criminal Procedure because—as stated by the Constitutional Court of the Russian Federation—the Code of Criminal Procedure has priority over other relevant Federal Laws.[986] Evidence obtained in violation of provisions of the Code of Criminal Procedure is furthermore inadmissible (Article 7, paragraph 4 UPKR).[987]

---

984. For national sources of criminal law, *see* General Introduction, §5, II, paras. 145–181.
985. For the principle of legality, *see* Part I, Chapter 1, paras. 197–226.
986. Decision of the Constitutional Court of the RF, Jun. 29, 2004, N 13-II.
987. For inadmissible evidence, *see* para. 1029; Paramonova, National characteristics, fundamental principles, and history of criminal law in Russia, 2014, pp. 175–292.

B. Principles Concerning Due Process and Procedural Safeguards

822. The second group of maxims consists of principles concerning due process and procedural safeguards for participants in the process.[988] One of the most important of these procedural safeguards is the **principle of personal integrity** *(неприкосновенность личности)*. It is formulated in Article 22 Const. and Article 10 UPKR and is based on the principle of legality: No one can be detained on suspicion of committing a crime, placed into a medical or psychiatric hospital, or taken into custody except on the basis of legal grounds set out in the Code of Criminal Procedure. Pending a court decision, no one can be detained for a period longer than 48 hours.

823. The principle of the integrity of personality is closely connected with the right to qualified legal **assistance** *(право на получение квалифицированной юридической помощи)*. According to Article 48 Const. and Article 16 UPKR, everyone has the right to the assistance of a defense counsel from the moment of being detained, placed in custody, or accused of committing a crime. In the cases provided for by law, legal assistance must be provided free of charge, for example, for low-income individuals. The suspect or accused[989] may refuse to be assisted by a defense counsel and defend him- or herself (Article 52 UPKR). However, in certain circumstances, assistance by a defense counsel and/or of a legal representative is obligatory. This is the case, for instance, when the suspect or accused[990] is a minor, that is, under the age of 16 (Article 51, paragraph 1 UPKR, Article 20 UKR).

824. This principle has been modified under the influence of the ECtHR. In 2013, Federal Law[991] amended Articles 49 and 144 of the Code of Criminal Procedure to allow the defense counsel to participate in the criminal process from the moment when procedural actions of any kind affecting the rights and freedoms of the participant of the process have started. According to the previous legal provisions, the entry of a defense counsel into the criminal procedure was allowed from the moment a criminal investigation was launched officially. It did not always allow to comply with the principle of providing qualified legal assistance and, in some cases, created the basis for abuse of the law enforcement authorities. The ECtHR has repeatedly pointed out this problem in its decisions[992] that eventually led to the change of the Code of Criminal Procedure of Russia.

825. Now, the investigator (or inquirer)[993] is obliged from the moment of verifying the report of a crime to clarify the rights to all persons participating in the

988. Paramonova, National characteristics, fundamental principles, and history of criminal law in Russia, 2014, pp. 175–292.
989. For the difference in legal status of the suspect and accused, *see* paras. 928–943.
990. For the difference in legal status of the suspect and accused, *see* paras. 928–943.
991. Federal Law, Mar. 3, 2013, N 23-FZ.
992. E.g., *Mirilashvili v. Russia* (2008) ECHR 1669, para. 225.
993. For the preliminary investigation, *see* paras. 871–926.

criminal procedure in the manner provided for in Article 144 UPKR: not to testify against themselves, their spouse, and close relatives, as well as to make use of these rights.

826. The **presumption of innocence** (*in dubio pro reo, презумпция невиновности*) (Article 49 Const. and Article 14 UPKR) must be observed throughout the criminal process. This very significant procedural safeguard guarantees that an accused is regarded as innocent until guilt has been proved. The suspect or accused[994] is not obliged to prove his or her innocence: the burden of proving the charge lies on the prosecution. A verdict of guilt cannot be based on assumptions, and all doubts concerning the guilt of the accused must be interpreted in the accused's favor.

827. Another procedural safeguard—the **principle of a reasonable time period for criminal proceedings**—was introduced into the Code of Criminal Procedure in 2010 (Article 6.1).[995] This amendment—accompanied by a Federal Law on Compensation for a Violation of the Right to a Trial within a Reasonable Time[996]—was introduced primarily in response to the jurisprudence of the ECtHR. It included compulsory inclusion of effective remedies for violations of procedural deadlines in all stages of the criminal procedure.[997] According to the amended Article 6.1. UPKR, criminal proceedings must be conducted strictly within a reasonable time period for criminal proceedings and according to the procedure provided for by the UPKR. In determining a "reasonable time period," a combination of diverse factors must be taken into consideration, including the legal and factual complexity of the case, the behavior of the participants, and the adequacy and effectiveness of the court, prosecutor, and investigator.[998]

§4. The Legal Position of the Accused and the Victim

I. The Legal Position of the Suspect and Accused

A. Definitions

828. The problem of a reasonable time period for criminal proceedings raises the important issue of the **right to appeal** (*право на обжалование*) against actions and decisions of the court, prosecutor, investigator, body of inquiry, or inquirer[999] (Articles 46 and 50, paragraph 3 Const., Articles 19, 123–127 UPKR). This right is one of the core procedural guarantees and encompasses the right to appeal

994. For the difference in legal status of the suspect and accused, *see* paras. 928–943.
995. Federal Law on Changes to Code of Criminal Procedure, Apr. 30, 2010, N 69-FZ.
996. Federal Law on Compensation for a Violation of the Right to a Trial within a Reasonable Time or the Right to the Enforcement of a Judgment within a Reasonable Time, May 4, 2010, N 68-FZ.
997. Khudoyorov v. Russia, Nov. 8, 2005, Burdov v. Russia, Jan. 15, 2009; for international sources of criminal law, *see* General Introduction, §5, paras. 116–144.
998. *Khudoyorov v. Russia*, Nov. 8, 2005, *Burdov v. Russia*, Jan. 15, 2009.
999. For the preliminary investigation, *see* paras. 871–926.

against—among other things—imposed coercive measures (Article 101, paragraph 3 UPKR) as well as the right of a convicted person to a review of his or her sentence by a higher court (Article 19, paragraph 2 UPKR).[1000]

829. The right of accused persons in criminal proceedings to use their native language or a language of which they have a good command is guaranteed in criminal procedure. The **right to interpreter's services free of charge** also belongs to the key procedural guarantees (Article 18 UPKR).[1001]

B. Principles Concerning the Judiciary and the Administration of Criminal Justice

830. The third group consists of principles concerning the judiciary and the administration of criminal justice. Most of them, however, could also be classified as procedural safeguards.

831. According to the **principle of official investigation**, the investigation of criminal matters may only be conducted by public officials—namely, prosecutors, investigators, and inquirers[1002]—who represent and act on behalf of the state (Article 21 UPKR).[1003] The principle is not only one of the fundamental organizational maxims of criminal justice; it is also regarded as one of the most significant procedural safeguards for an accused.[1004]

832. The **principle of mandatory prosecution** *(обязанность осуществления уголовного преследования)* is also a procedural safeguard; it requires criminal prosecutions to be conducted independently of any expression of the victim's will (Article 21 UPKR). There are minor exceptions to this rule, including so-called **private prosecution** *(уголовные дела частного обвинения)* and **private-public prosecution cases** *(уголовные дела частно-публичного обвинения)*[1005] where the victim has suffered only a slight injury (e.g., Article 115 UKR) and prosecution may only be initiated upon application by the victim (Article 20, paragraphs 1 and 2 UPKR).

833. The **principle of conducting criminal justice only by a court** *(осуществление правосудия только судом)*, a procedural guarantee, determines the fundamental structures of the criminal justice process (Article 46 Const., Article 8 UPKR).[1006] It encompasses the right of an accused to have his or her case heard

1000. On the judicial system, *see* General Introduction, §1, paras. 21–23, 52–55.
1001. Paramonova, National characteristics, fundamental principles, and history of criminal law in Russia, 2014, pp. 175–292.
1002. For the preliminary investigation, *see* paras. 871–926.
1003. For the criminal procedure, *see* Part II, Chapter 1, §6, paras. 858–926.
1004. Radchenko, Kommentarij k UPKR; Barabash, Priroda rossijskogo ugolovnogo processa, 2005, pp. 3–10.
1005. On the legal position of the victim and the civil party (civil claimant), *see* paras. 944–960.
1006. *Ibid.*

in court by a judge assigned by law. It is expressed in the requirement that no one is to be subjected to criminal punishment except through a sentence imposed by a court (Article 47 Const., Article 8 UPKR).[1007] However, there is a difference between imposition of administrative and criminal sanctions: While criminal punishments can only be imposed by courts, administrative sanctions, for example, fines (Article 3.5 KoAPR), can be imposed by both judicial and executive authorities. An additional problem in this regard is that pecuniary administrative sanctions can be far heavier than those imposed by the criminal law: often, the smallest fine permitted as a criminal punishment is considerably less than the maximum permitted administrative fine. The lowest possible criminal fine is RUB 5,000 (about USD 140, Article 46, paragraph 2 UKR), whereas the maximum administrative fine is RUB 500,000 (about USD 14,000) for natural persons (Article 3.5 KoAPR). For instance, the notorious Federal Law that introduced amendments to the KoAPR in response to demonstrations during the presidential election campaign in 2012 raised administrative fines for the violation of law on demonstrations and rallies dramatically—fines for natural persons were increased by a factor of 200 (from RUB 100 to RUB 20,000).[1008]

834. Hence, severe—de facto criminal—punishments are often hidden under the veil of administrative sanctions and imposed in accordance with administrative procedures (by executive authorities). Even though all such executive decisions (in compliance with Article 6 ECHR) can be appealed to a court: "Decisions and actions (or inaction) of bodies of state authority and local self-government, public associations and officials may be appealed against in court" (Article 46, paragraph 2 Const.). Nonetheless, supporters of the designation of administrative offenses as "criminal matter" offenses regard the possibility of the imposition of severe (de facto criminal and de jure administrative) sanctions by executive authorities as "one of the deepest deformations inherited from Soviet law."[1009]

835. The **principle of judicial independence** is expressed in Article 8.1 Code of Criminal Procedure and Article 120 Const

Art. 120 Const.[1010]

(1) Judges shall be independent and are bound only by the Constitution and the Federal Law.
(2) […].

1007. On the judicial system, *see* General Introduction, §1, paras. 21–23, 52–55.

1008. Federal Law on Meetings, Rallies, Demonstrations, Marches and Pickets, Jun. 8, 2012, N 65-FZ, *see also* Human Rights Watch, Report 2012: http://www.hrw.org/sites/default/files/reports/wr2012.pdf [last visited Dec. 18, 2019]; Human Rights Watch nazvala 2012 god chudschim dlya prav cheloveka, http://rbcdaily.ru/society/562949985633902 [last visited Dec. 18, 2019].

1009. Golovko, Sootnoshenie ugolovnih prestuplenij i administrativnih pravonarushenij, http://ilpp.ru/ [last visited Dec. 18, 2019]; Federal Law on the Procedure of the Consideration of Appeals of Citizens of the Russian Federation, May 2, 2006, N 59-FZ.

1010. All translations of the provisions of the Constitution in this chapter are taken from http://www.constitution.ru/en/10003000-01.htm [last visited Dec. 18, 2019].

836. According to Article 8.1 Code of Criminal Procedure, judges consider and resolve criminal cases in conditions that exclude outside influence on them. The intervention of state bodies, local governments, other bodies, organizations, officials or citizens in the activities of judges in the administration of justice is prohibited and entails responsibility provided for by the law. However, not all judicial activities are linked to the just resolution of the case. State bodies may verify judicial decisions that do not affect the essence of the case. For example, tax authorities are entitled to control tax collection to the budget and therefore, e.g., the control accuracy of payments of state fees for concrete claims (Article 333.16 of the Tax Code of the Russian Federation).

837. Following **the principle of free evaluation of evidence**, judges, jurors, as well as prosecutors, investigators, and inquirers must assess the evidence in accordance with their "inner conviction" and based on the aggregate of the evidence presented in the case; they must rely on the law and their own consciences (principle of free evaluation of evidence). It follows that no aspect of evidence can be regarded, in advance of the proceedings, as having any pre-determined force (Article 17 UPKR).

838. The principles of judicial independence and the principle of free evaluation of evidence are determined by the concept of judicial power, which has been adopted by the current Code of Criminal Procedure. This concept underpins coercive measures (Article 101 UPKR) and investigative actions (Article 165 UPKR). It requires that, with regard to coercive and investigative measures provided for by Articles 101 and 165 UPKR, the decision of the prosecutor, inquirer, or investigator on the selection of a coercive measure be based on a judicial ruling, that is, a power that is vested only in a judge. Exceptions to the requirement of judicial power are provided for by the Code of Criminal Procedure.

> Art. 101 UPKR (Resolution and Ruling on the Selection of a Coercive Measure)
>
> (1) On the selection of a coercive measure the inquirer, the investigator, the prosecutor or the judge shall pass a resolution, and the court—a ruling, containing an indication of the crime of which the person is either suspected or accused, and the grounds for selecting this coercive measure.
>
> (2)–(3) […].

839. The inviolability of a dwelling (***неприкосновенность жилища***, Article 25 Const., Article 12 UPKR) as well as the right to privacy of correspondence, telephone conversations, and postal and other communications (***тайна переписки, телефонных переговоров, почтовых и иных сообщений***, Articles 23 and 24

Const., Article 13 UPKR) are also principles of criminal procedure that concern the judiciary and the administration of criminal justice.[1011]

C. Other Principles of Criminal Justice

840. The final group of principles is designated as general requirements for court proceedings by the Code of Criminal Procedure (*общие условия судебного разбирательства*, Chapter 35). In the literature, however, they are classified as principles concerning the judiciary and criminal justice administration or simply as procedural safeguards.[1012] These are the following maxims: principle of orality of criminal court proceedings (*устность судебного разбирательства*, Article 240 UPKR); principle of immediacy with respect to evidence (*непосредственность исследования доказательств*, Article 240 UPKR); principle of openness and transparency of criminal court proceedings (*гласность судебного разбирательства* Article 241 UPKR); principle of invariability of the court composition (*неизменность состава суда*, Article 241 UPKR); principle of adversarial procedure (*принцип состязательности*, Articles 15, paragraph 4 and 244 UPKR).[1013]

§5. THE JUDICIAL ORGANIZATION

841. An overview of the judicial system can be found in the General Introduction (see *supra*, §1, V *judicial system* and *trial jurisdictions*, §2, III, 4).[1014] Hereunder, the judicial competences and the composition of the courts are discussed in more details.

842. The organization of the judicial system is based on the principle of jurisdictional unity. **Magistrate courts** *(мировые судьи)*, **district courts** *(районные суды)*, courts of entities of the Russian Federation—**regional courts** *(суды субъектов Российской Федерации)*, and the **Supreme Court** *(Верховный Суд)*—the highest judicial body for criminal cases—constitute the criminal judicial system (for further details on the courts, *see infra*).[1015]

843. The jurisdiction of military courts, namely **military presidial courts** *(гарнизонные военные суды)* and **military district courts** *(военные окружные*

1011. Paramonova, National characteristics, fundamental principles, and history of criminal law in Russia, 2014, pp. 175–292.
1012. For the general requirements for the trial, *see* Chapter 3, paras. 1068–1191; Paramonova, National characteristics, fundamental principles, and history of criminal law in Russia, 2014, pp. 175–292; Barabash, Priroda rossijskogo ugolovnogo processa, 2005, pp. 3–257; Smirnov/ Kalinowski, Ugolovnij process: uchebnik, 2015, pp. 3.
1013. For the general requirements for the trial, *see* Chapter 3, paras. 1068–1191.
1014. For the trial jurisdictions, *see* paras. 52–55.
1015. For the trial jurisdictions, *see* paras. 52–55.

суды), is based on the territorial principle (Articles 19–22 Federal Law on the Judicial System of the Russian Federation).[1016] The **Military Panel of the Supreme Court** ***(Военная Коллегия Верховного Суда)*** is the final instance for the lower military (presidial and district) courts.

844. The least serious cases, which are listed in Article 31, paragraph 1 UPKR (e.g., tax evasion of small amounts), have a maximum punishment of three years' imprisonment and are heard in the magistrate courts.

845. District courts serving as first instance courts deal with more serious cases (provided for in Article 31, paragraph 2 UPKR), for example, theft on a large scale. District courts also serve as the Court of Second Instance for magistrate courts.

846. Regional courts, as second instance courts, have a supervisory function with regard to district courts. At the same time, regional courts can also adjudicate at first instance. As first instance courts, they decide cases that are more serious in nature than those heard in district courts (e.g., the murder of two and more persons) as well as cases involving crimes against state power (e.g., treason, Article 31, paragraph 3 UPKR). There is one regional court in every entity of the Federation (85 in total).

847. The Supreme Court is the Court of First Instance for criminal cases involving federal deputies or judges (Article 452 UPKR). At the same time, it serves as the Court of Second Instance for regional courts. It also supervises the activities of all judicial bodies and provides explanations on issues of court proceedings (Article 126 Const.). The Supreme Court consists of thirteen judges.

848. Thus, all criminal courts—except for magistrate courts—can serve as both first and second instance courts.

849. The **composition of the criminal courts** ***(состав суда по уголовным делам)*** depends on the instance and the stage of appeal. According to Article 30 UPKR, criminal cases are tried by the court either collectively or by one judge alone.

850. All the courts that sit in first instance try criminal cases in one of the following compositions: one federal judge, one federal judge and eight jurors, or a panel of three federal judges (regional court); one district judge (district court); one magistrate judge (magistrate court).

851. At the appeals stage (second instance), as far as appeals from magistrate courts to district courts are concerned, the case is heard by one district judge. All other appeals and cassations are examined by a panel of three federal judges. Cases (such as appeals from regional courts) under the judicial supervision procedure by

1016. Paramonova, National characteristics, fundamental principles, and history of criminal law in Russia, 2014, p. 190.

the Supreme Court are reexamined by a panel of at least three judges; one of the judges on the panel functions as the panel's chairman.

852. Although all judges have the same basic status,[1017] there are several differences between the magistrate and federal judges: First, all judges except for magistrate judges are federal judges. Second, magistrate judges are appointed and nominated by regional bodies (Article 6 Federal Law on Magistrate Judges[1018]) whereas federal judges are appointed by federal bodies (by the highest federal courts by means of resolution of the highest panel of judges of the Russian Federation) upon nomination by the president of Russia (Article 6 Federal Law on the Status of Judges). Supreme Court judges are appointed by the Council of the Federation (upper chamber of the Federal Assembly) upon the proposal of the president (Article 128 Const.).

853. Third, federal judges are appointed for a lifetime term. In contrast, the tenure of magistrate judges is provided for by regional laws, according to which their first term cannot exceed five years; subsequently, lifetime tenure is possible (Article 11 Federal Law on the Status of Judges).

854. The participation of **lay judges** ***(народные заседатели)*** in criminal trials, which was abolished with the introduction of the UPKR of 2001, has been a controversial issue in the literature.[1019] Nonetheless, the Russian criminal law system provides for the opportunity of a **jury trial** ***(суд с участием присяжных заседателей)*** with a professional judge as a chairman in criminal cases involving grave crimes against life (Article 20, paragraph 2 Const., Chapter 42 UPKR). Lay judges—in contrast to jurors—were not entitled to participate in resolving many issues arising from the criminal cases. Moreover, lay judges were elected from a number of candidates, whereas jurors receive their competences as a result of random sampling from the whole population.

855. According to statistics, however, only 8% of cases are heard by a jury. In 2008, through the adoption of the Federal Law on amendments in the Criminal Code, the kinds of cases that can be heard by a jury were reduced; for example, since then, cases involving terrorism can no longer be judged by a jury (Article 205 UKR). This was regarded as an invasion of the independence of trial, as in Russia, a jury trial is considered to be more independent than a trial with professional judges,[1020] professional judges (0.73%) hand down fewer acquittals than jurors (17%). Therefore, amendments of the Code of Criminal Procedure of 2016 in this field can be estimated as very positive: Amendments of the UPKR implied the expansion of the kinds of criminal cases that are considered by a jury while reducing the number of jurors from 12 to eight people. The number of jurors is provided

1017. For the judicial independence, *see* paras. 22, 835, 838, 1091, 1093.

1018. Federal Law on Magistrate Judges of the Russian Federation, Dec. 17, 1998, N 188-FZ.

1019. Rudnev, Narodnie zasedateli v otpravlenii pravosudiya, pp. 39–42.

1020. For the judicial independence, *see* paras. 22, 835, 838, 1091; Federal Law, Dec. 30, 2008, N 321-FZ; Golovko, Konstituzionnij sud vs sud prisyazhnich; *see also* Paramonova/Bogush, ZStW 125 (2013), 703–728; Paramonova, Revista Penal 2012, 264–268.

for by the Code of Criminal Procedure; judges cannot change this quantity. It made the procedure less complicated and provided more accused with the right to a jury trial.[1021]

856. At the present time, the jury panel in a criminal case is made up of eight jurors (Article 328 UPKR). A non-guilty verdict passed by the jurors is binding upon the judge and leads to an acquittal (Article 348 UPKR). A guilty verdict is not binding upon the judge.

857. According to Article 4 Federal Law on the Status of Judges of the Russian Federation,[1022] all **professional judges** *(профессиональные судьи)* must be at least 25 years of age and must hold a law degree. They may not have foreign citizenship, a criminal record, or suffer from an illness that will not allow them to perform their official duties properly. Eligibility requirements for judges vary furthermore depending on the judicial body. For instance, judges of the regional courts (federal judges) must be at least 30 years old and have not less than seven years' work experience in the legal field. Judges of the Supreme Court must be at least 35 years old and have not less than ten years' work experience in the legal field.[1023]

§6. The Stages of the Penal Process

I. Basic Distinctions

858. In compliance with the Code of Criminal Procedure and the Criminal Code of the Russian Federation, criminal procedure is divided into three **stages** (*стадии уголовного процесса*): the **pretrial stage** *(досудебное производство)*, the **court procedure** or the **trial** (*судебное производство*), and the **execution of the sentence**[1024] (*исполнение приговора*).

859. In legal scholarship, a stage of the criminal procedure is defined as a separate stage of the penal process. Each stage is characterized through its own objectives, content, beginning, ending, and its participants that are provided for by the legal provisions.[1025]

860. The aim of the **pretrial stage** (initiation of a criminal case and preliminary investigation) (Articles 140–226.9 UPKR) is to disclose the circumstances of the committed crime (time, place, method, and other circumstances of the offense) and

1021. Golubkova, Mariya/Kozlova, Natalya. Bud´te sudimi, Rossijskaya Gazeta 25.02.2016: http://rg.ru /2016/02/25/ks-rf-rasshiril-polnomochiia-prisiazhnyh-i-razreshil-im-sudit-zhenshchin.html.

1022. Federal Law on the Status of Judges of the Russian Federation, Jun. 26, 1992, N 3132-I.

1023. Paramonova, National characteristics, fundamental principles, and history of criminal law in Russia, 2014, pp. 190–193.

1024. For the general requirements for the execution of sanctions, *see* Part III, paras. 1365–1383.

1025. Smirnov/ Kalinowski, Ugolovnij process: uchebnik, 2015, pp. 10.

expose the person(s) responsible for the crime (Articles 21, paragraph 2, 140, paragraph 2 UPKR). The facts related to the crime shall be clarified to such an extent that it allows the public prosecutor to file the indictment to the court (Article 222 UPKR).

861. The key function of determining the truth is given to the court. The final establishment of the circumstances of the crime occurs in the course of the **trial** or **court procedure** (Articles 227–313 UPKR). In its decision about the indictment, the court answers the question, whether the accused is found guilty of the criminal offense(s) with which he/she is charged. The court also decides about the measure of punishment.

862. The criminal proceedings terminate when the judicial sentence comes into force. The **execution of sentence** (*see* below, Part III) is regarded as the final stage of the penal process.[1026]

863. Each stage includes a number of substages (*see* below). That said, some authors regard the substages as independent stages of the criminal process, which explains why, in legal theory, the number of the stages of the penal process sometimes varies.[1027]

864. In accordance with the prevailing opinion, the pretrial stage is a homogeneous and unified stage of the criminal procedure that commences from the moment of officially obtaining information on the crime to open a criminal case (Articles 140, 145 UPKR) and durations until the indictment has been filed in a court (Article 5, paragraph 9 UPKR).

865. The criminal process is characterized by a continuing investigation conducted initially by the police.[1028]

II. The Pretrial Stage

866. As mentioned above, the pretrial stage *(предварительное расследование)* is the first stage of the criminal process. It includes the following two substages: 1. The **initiation or opening of a criminal case** (*возбуждение уголовного дела*), and 2. The **preliminary investigation** (*предварительное расследование*). The latter can conducted in two forms: **pretrial investigation** *(предварительное следствие)* and **inquiry** *(дознание)*.[1029]

1026. For the general requirements for the execution of sanctions, *see* Part III, paras. 1365–1383.
1027. Radchenko, Kommentarij k UPKR.
1028. For the criminal procedure, *see* Part II, Chapter 1. §6, paras. 858–926.
1029. Paramonova, National characteristics, fundamental principles, and history of criminal law in Russia, 2014, pp. 185–186.

A. Initiation of a Criminal Case

867. The first substage of the pretrial stage is called "**initiation or opening of a criminal case**" (*возбуждение уголовного дела*) (Articles 140–149 UPKR).

868. In this phase, inquiring, investigating bodies and the prosecutor[1030] are obliged to verify the information received concerning committed crime(s), e.g., through reporting a crime by a victim or through confession of an offender (Article 140 UPKR).[1031] This rule is based on the principle mentioned above—the principle of mandatory prosecution (Article 144 UPKR).[1032]

869. This part of the criminal proceedings is aimed at the detection of sufficient evidence pointing to a criminal act (Articles 140, paragraph 2 and 146, paragraph 1 UPKR). It results either in the opening a criminal case or the refusal to institute criminal proceedings. The complainant is informed about this decision (Article 145 UPKR).

870. According to Article 148, paragraph 5 UPKR, the refusal to open a criminal case may be appealed to the prosecutor, the head of the investigative body or to the court.

B. Preliminary Investigation

1. Definition of the Preliminary Investigation

871. Once the criminal case has been opened, the criminal proceedings continue to the second substage of the pretrial stage, which is the "**preliminary investigation**" (*предварительное расследование*), Articles 150–226.9 UPKR. The essence of the preliminary investigation is the clearance of crime. It requires that investigating bodies take all necessary legal measures in order to substantiate the facts and circumstances of the committed crime.

872. During this stage, investigators and inquirers[1033] have an obligation to detect and preserve traces of the committed crime—evidence (Article 81 UPKR). By collecting the evidence, the circumstances of the committed crime that are subject to proof in the trial procedure have to be proved (Article 73 UPKR): such as the event of the crime (time, place, mode and the other circumstances of committing the crime), the accused of committing the crime, the form of his/her possible

1030. For the preliminary investigation, *see* paras. 871–926.
1031. For the different types of investigating bodies, *see* above General Introduction, §2, III, paras. 43–47.
1032. For the principles of the criminal procedure, *see* Part II, Chapter 1, §3, paras. 814–827.
1033. For the preliminary investigation, *see* paras. 871–926.

culpability (e.g., direct or indirect intent) and the motives, circumstances characterizing the personality of the accused, character and the scale of the damage caused by the crime, etc.[1034]

873. An indispensable condition for the completeness of the disclosure of the crime is a necessary and sufficient body of evidence. When the evidence and facts related to the crime that are subject to proof in the trial proceedings have been collected and clarified by the investigating authorities, the indictment is forwarded to the public prosecutor (Article 220 UPKR).

874. The preliminary investigation terminates when the indictment has been filed to the court by the public prosecutor (Article 222 UPKR).

2. Forms of the Preliminary Investigation

875. As mentioned above, there are two **forms of preliminary investigation** (*предварительное расследование*, Article 150 UPKR): **pretrial investigation** *(предварительное следствие)* and **inquiry** *(дознание)*.[1035]

876. Pretrial investigations are conducted by **investigating bodies or investigators** *(следователи)*, while inquiries are conducted by **inquiry bodies or inquirers** *(дознаватели)*.[1036] The investigating and inquiry bodies work under the supervision of the prosecutor (Article 37, paragraph 1 UPKR).

877. The form employed depends on the character and the gravity of the committed crime. In contrast to **investigating bodies**, which deal with serious crimes, such as homicide or fraud of a large scale, inquiry bodies deal only with minor criminal offenses (Articles 38, 40, 41, 150, paragraph 2, 223 UPKR), for example, Article 168 UKR (damage of property by negligence). Most of the inquirers are the **inquirers of the domestic affairs bodies** *(дознаватели органов внутренних дел)*—i.e., the **police** (*полиция*), but there are also inquirers in specialized areas, e.g., inquirers of the customs bodies, or inquirers of the state fire supervision, Article 40, paragraphs 3 and 4 UPKR.[1037]

878. With regard to the distribution of procedural competencies (Articles 38–41, 146 UPKR), investigators, as well as inquirers, are entitled to initiate criminal cases for offenses that fall within their competencies. They can direct on their own the course of the investigation and make decisions on the performance of procedural actions, some of which require a prosecutor's or court's authorization. For instance,

1034. On the rules of evidence, *see* Part II, Chapter 1, paras. 961–967.

1035. Paramonova, National characteristics, fundamental principles, and history of criminal law in Russia, 2014, pp. 185–186.

1036. For the different types of investigating bodies, *see* above General Introduction, §2, III, paras. 43–47.

1037. For the different types of investigating bodies, *see* above General Introduction, §2, III, paras. 43–47.

house arrest as a measure of restriction (Article 107 UPKR) must be authorized by a court. Investigators have the authority to oblige the bodies of inquiry to carry out certain procedural measures, for example, arrest or detention (Article 38, paragraph 4 UPKR).[1038]

3. Pretrial Investigation

879. The **pretrial investigation** *(предварительное следствие)* is the term employed for the investigation of almost all criminal cases unless it falls under inquiry.

880. The criminal procedure is called **inquiry** (*дознание*)[1039] if it falls under the investigative jurisdiction of the inquiry bodies that deal with investigating minor crimes (Articles 150, paragraph 3, 151 UPKR). The rules that apply to inquiry as the second form of preliminary investigation as well as to pretrial investigation are the same, however, with some exceptions that will be discussed below (Article 223, paragraph 1 UPKR).[1040]

a. Deadlines of the Pretrial Investigation

881. In general, criminal procedural provisions regarding deadlines of the pretrial investigation are based on the following procedural safeguard—the **principle of a reasonable time period for criminal proceedings.** It was introduced into the Code of Criminal Procedure in 2010 (Article 6.1) in response to the jurisprudence of the ECtHR.[1041] The timeframe of the pretrial investigation includes the period of time from the day of initiation of the criminal case until the day of forwarding it to the public prosecutor with the indictment or with the resolution on handing over the criminal case to the court for examining the question about the application of mandatory measures of the medical character, or until the day of adopting the resolution on the termination of the proceedings on the criminal case (Article 162, paragraph 2 UPKR). The investigator is the one who adopts the indictment (when all pretrial investigative measures were carried out and the evidence gathered is sufficient) or the resolution (Article 215 UPKR).

882. As a general rule, the pretrial investigation on a criminal case shall be completed within **two months** from the day of opening a criminal case (Article 162, paragraph 1 UPKR).

1038. For coercive measures, *see* Part II, Chapter 2, §1, paras. 1033–1066.
1039. For the rules on conducting the inquiry *see* paras. 1039–1059.
1040. For the rules on conducting the inquiry *see* paras. 1039–1059.
1041. Burdov v. Russia, Jan. 15, 2009; for international sources of criminal law, *see* General Introduction, §5, paras. 116–144; Federal Law on Changes to Code of Criminal Procedure, Apr. 30, 2010, N 69-FZ.

883. In the term of the pretrial investigation is not included the time during which the investigation was suspended (Articles 162, paragraph 3 and 208 UPKR). It can be suspended, e.g., if a serious temporary illness of a suspect, certified by a medical certificate, prevents him/her from participating in investigative and other procedural actions or if the suspect escaped from the investigation (Article 208 UPKR).

884. The period of two months (Article 162, paragraph 1 UPKR) may be **extended** in the manner provided for by Article 162 paragraphs 4–8 UPKR.

885. For instance, the term of the pretrial investigation, stipulated by Article 162, paragraph 1 UPKR (two months), may be extended by up to three months by the head of the investigative body (Article 162, paragraph 4 UPKR).

886. Particularly, in complicated cases, the term may be extended by the head of the investigative body of the federal entity or by his/her deputies by up to twelve months (Article 162, paragraph 5 UPKR).

887. Further extension of the term of the pretrial investigation may be made only in exceptional cases by the Chairman of the Investigative Committee of Russia, by the head of the federal investigative authority and by their deputies (Article 162, paragraph 5 UPKR).

b. Decisions Made During the Pretrial Investigation

(1) The Suspension and Resumption of the Pretrial Investigation

888. The procedure and the grounds for the **suspension and resumption of the pretrial investigation** (*приостановление и возобновление предварительного следствия*) are stipulated in Chapter 28 UPKR (Articles 208–211).[1042]

889. The pretrial investigation shall be suspended, if one of the following grounds is present and if the investigation—which can be renewed anytime—cannot move forward at the present moment according to the investigators of the case (Article 208, paragraph 1 UPKR):

- the person, subject to involvement in the capacity of the accused, has not been identified;
- suspect or accused[1043] have fled from the investigation, or his/her location has not been identified for other reasons;
- location of the suspect or accused is known, but there is no realistic possibility of his/her participation in the criminal proceedings, e.g., he/she cannot be extradited from a foreign country;

1042. *See* Smirnov/ Kalinowski, Ugolovnij process: uchebnik, 2015, pp. 30.
1043. For the difference in legal status of the suspect and accused, *see* paras. 928–943.

– a serious temporary illness of the suspect or accused certified with a medical report, which prevents his/her participation in the investigative or other procedural actions.

890. The pretrial investigation can be suspended according to the first two grounds solely after the deadlines of the investigation (Article 162 UPKR) have expired. On the contrary, in the case of the last two grounds, the pretrial investigation can be suspended before its terms expire (Article 208, paragraph 4 UPKR).

891. The investigator passes a resolution on the suspension of the pretrial investigation, a copy of which he/she directs to the public prosecutor.

892. The investigator is obliged to notify the victim and his/her representative, the civil claimant (party)[1044] and the defendant, including their representatives, about the suspension of the investigation. He also has an obligation to explain to them their right to appeal the decision (Article 209, paragraph 1 UPKR).

893. Before the suspension of the pretrial investigation, the investigator is obliged to undertake all possible measures to avoid its suspension, such as conducting investigative activities that can be performed in the absence of the suspect/accused, for instance, to identify his/her location or to conduct all possible measures for identification and search of the person who has committed the crime (Article 208, paragraph 5 UPKR).

894. When the grounds for the suspension do not concern all of the accused if two or more accused are involved in a criminal case, the investigator has the right to allocate the case into a separate procedure and to suspend the criminal case only with respect to some of the accused (Article 208, paragraph 4 UPKR).

895. After the pretrial investigation has been suspended, conducting investigative actions is inadmissible (Article 209, paragraph 3 UPKR). However, in the cases where a suspect/accused or his/her location have not been identified (Article 208, paragraph 1 UPKR), the investigator has to take all measures despite the suspension in order to identify the suspect/accused and his/her location and, e.g., to entrust the search for suspect/accused to the bodies of inquiry and, if possible, renew the investigation (Article 211 UPKR).

896. The pretrial investigation is renewed (resumed) on the basis of the investigator's resolution due to the grounds provided for by Article 211 UPKR:

– the grounds for the suspension of investigation have disappeared;
– the need for the conduction of investigative actions, which may be carried out without the participation of the suspect/accused, has arisen;
– the prosecutor or the head of the investigative body overruled the decision of suspension of the pretrial investigation.

1044. On the legal position of the victim and the civil party (civil claimant), *see* paras. 944–960.

897. All participants of the criminal proceedings have to be informed about the resumption of the pretrial investigation (Article 211, paragraph 3 UPKR).

(2) The Termination of the Investigation

898. The termination of the criminal investigation entails the termination of the criminal prosecution (Articles 24, paragraph 3, 212, 213, 214 UPRK).[1045]

899. The grounds for termination of the criminal proceedings and prosecution are stipulated by Articles 24–28.1 UPKR:

- absence of the event of a crime (Article 24, paragraph 1 UPKR);
- absence of the *corpus delicti*[1046] in the act (Article 24, paragraph 1 UPKR);
- expiration of the statute of limitations for criminal prosecution (Article 24, paragraph 1 UPKR);
- death of the suspect or accused,[1047] with the exception of the cases where the criminal proceedings on the case are necessary for the rehabilitation of the deceased (Article 24, paragraph 1 UPKR);
- absence of the victim´s application, if the criminal case belongs either to the private prosecution or private-public prosecution cases, in which prosecution may be instituted only upon application by the victim (Article 20, paragraphs 1, 2 and 4 UPKR) (Article 24, paragraph 1 UPKR);
- a lack in the court resolution of the elements of crime in the conduct of some special groups of persons (such as Prosecutor General of the Russian Federation, judges of the Constitutional Court, Article 448, paragraphs 2, 3 UPKR), or a lack of the approval of the relevant body, e.g. in respect of a judge of the Constitutional Court approval by the Chairman of the Investigative Committee of the Russian Federation with the consent of the Constitutional Court (Article 448, paragraphs 3–5 UPKR);
- termination of the criminal proceedings in connection with the parties′ reconciliation. The court, as well as the investigator with the consent of the head of the investigating body with the consent of the prosecutor, have the right to terminate criminal investigation upon an application, filed by the victim or by his/her legal representative, for the termination of the criminal case with respect to the person, suspected of or charged with committing a crime of a small or average gravity.[1048] It is required that the person has reconciled with the victim and has recompensed the damage he/she has inflicted (Article 25 UPKR);
- noninvolvement of the suspect or accused in the committed crime (Article 27, paragraph 1 UPKR);
- amnesty (Article 27, paragraph 3 UPKR);

1045. Radchenko, Kommentarij k UPKR; Lebedev, Nauchno-prakticheskij kommentarij k UPKR, 2016, pp. 5-1056.
1046. For the concept of the criminal offense, *see* Part I, Chapter 3, §1, paras. 317–321.
1047. For the difference in legal status of the suspect and accused, *see* paras. 928–943.
1048. For the categories of crimes, *see* paras. 34, 638–646.

- existence of a sentence on the same charge (e.g., ruled by a different court earlier) or a judge´s decision to terminate the criminal case on the same charge (e.g., the decision of a different judge earlier), which have entered into legal force, with respect to the suspect or accused (Article 27, paragraph 4 UPKR);
- refusal of the State Duma or/and of the Federal Council of the Federal Assembly of the Russian Federation to give its consent to the deprivation of the immunity of a former President of the Russian Federation (Article 27, paragraph 5 UPKR);
- termination of the criminal prosecution with respect to a person who has not reached, by the moment of committing the crime, the age of criminal liability (Article 20 UKR; Article 27, paragraph 3 UPKR);
- termination of the criminal prosecution with respect to a minor who has reached the age of criminal liability, however, did not due to his/her retardment in the psychological development, not connected with a mental disorder, fully realize the actual character and the social danger of his/her actions (omissions) and direct them at the moment of committing the act (Article 22 UKR; Article 27, paragraph 3 UPKR);
- termination of the criminal prosecution in connection with active repentance. The court, as well as the investigator with the consent of the head of the investigating body with the consent of the prosecutor, have the right to terminate the criminal investigation with respect to the person suspected of or charged with committing a crime of a small or average gravity[1049] (Article 28 UPKR). With regard to the graver crimes, the decision upon termination is made by the court, as well as by the investigator with the consent of the head of the investigative body with the consent of the prosecutor. However, only if such procedure (for grave crimes) is stipulated explicitly in the Criminal Code of the Russian Federation, i.e., provided for by the relevant articles of the Special Part of the Criminal Code (Article 28 UPKR);
- termination of criminal proceedings in cases involving crimes in the economic sphere, i.e., all crime of Chapter VIII of the UKR (Article 28.1 UPKR).[1050] Legislative changes of the criminal procedural provisions within the most far-reaching reforms (2009–2012) of criminal law since the existence of the Russian Criminal Code (1996) were primarily aimed at the recovery of the business environment and creating a more favorable investment climate in Russia.[1051] The criminal procedure provision of 2011[1052] introduced the institute of termination of criminal prosecution for most crimes in the economic sphere (Article 76.1 UKR and Article 28.1, paragraph 3 UPKR).[1053] Criminal charges regarding a person, who has committed an economic crime for the first time, can be dropped by

1049. For the categories of crimes, *see* paras. 34, 638–646.
1050. Paramonova, Recent Reforms of Criminal and Criminal Procedural Law in Russia, Revista Penal, 2012, Issue/Volume 30, pp. 264–268.
1051. Paramonova, Legal Guarantees for Investments: http://www.insor-russia.ru.
1052. Federal Law on Changes to Criminal Code and Other Legal Provisions, Dec. 7, 2011, N 420-FZ; *see* as well The Federal Law on Changes to Tax Law and Other Legal Provisions, Dec. 29, 2009, N 383-FZ.
1053. Federal Law on Changes to Criminal Code and Other Legal Provisions, Dec. 7, 2011, N 420-FZ.

the court as well as by the investigator with the consent of the head of the investigative body if he/she has fully compensated the damage to the federal budget (Article 28.1, paragraph 1 UPKR).[1054]

900. The public prosecutor has the competence to overrule the decision, which is not his/her own, on the termination of the criminal prosecution. If the resolution of the head of an investigating body or the investigator on the termination of criminal proceedings is considered illegal or unreasonable, the public prosecutor cancels it no later than fourteen days from the receipt of the case file. The prosecutor is obliged to make a reasoned resolution clarifying concrete circumstances that are subject to further investigation. The resolution, together with the case file, shall be immediately sent to the head of the investigating body (Article 214 UPKR).

c. Closing the Pretrial Investigation. Prosecutor´s Decisions on the Indictment and Filing the Indictment to the Court

901. The day of the **closing of the pretrial investigation** (*окончание предварительного следствия*) is the day when an investigator has filed the **indictment** (*обвинительное заключение*) to the public prosecutor or has filed the resolution to the court on the application of **compulsory measures of a medical nature** (*принудительные меры медицинского характера*) (Articles 97–104 UKR), which are issued by the court in lieu of criminal punishment on the basis of a report drafted by a medical expert (Articles 5, paragraph 9, 162, paragraph 2, 215, 222 UPKR). The pretrial investigation is also considered closed in the case of termination of criminal proceedings, Article 212 UPKR.

902. In order to file an indictment to the public prosecutor, the investigator has to clarify the facts related to the crime to a sufficient extent by conducting all necessary investigative activities on the criminal case and by collecting all available evidence for indicting an accused[1055] (Article 215, paragraphs 1, 2 UPKR).

903. The investigator is obliged to notify all the parties of the criminal proceedings on the closing of the pretrial investigation. The accused shall be informed on the closing procedure and shall be advised of his/her right to inspect all the materials of the criminal case, his/her right to make motions and remarks to the materials as well as on the right to make copies of the materials of the case, both personally and with the assistance of the defense counsel and/or his/her legal representative (Articles 215, paragraph 1, 217 UPKR).

904. If the defense counsel, the legal representative of the accused, the representative of the victim, or the representative of the civil claimant (party)[1056] or defendant cannot come and inspect the materials of the criminal case at the

1054. Paramonova, Recent Reforms of Criminal and Criminal Procedural Law in Russia, Revista Penal, 2012, Issue/Volume 30, pp. 264–268.
1055. For the difference in legal status of the suspect and accused, *see* paras. 928–943.
1056. On the legal position of the victim and the civil party (civil claimant), *see* paras. 944–960.

appointed time due to a legitimate reason, the investigator shall postpone it for a term of maximum five days (Article 215, paragraph 2 UPKR). If the accused, who is not held in custody, does not come for inspecting the materials of the criminal case or if he/she evades such inspection, the investigator shall compile the indictment and file it to the public prosecutor after expiration of five days from the day of announcing the closing of the conduction of the investigative activities or from the day, when the other participants of the criminal proceedings inspected the materials of the criminal case (Article 215, paragraph 5 UPKR).

905. After the investigator has signed the indictment and the head of the investigating authority has approved it, the indictment shall be immediately filed to the public prosecutor. If needed, the investigator shall provide for a translation of the indictment (Articles 18, 220, paragraph 6 UPKR).[1057]

906. The public prosecutor shall consider the indictment filed by the investigator and is obliged to take on it one of the following decisions within ten days:

- approval of the indictment and forwarding the criminal case to the court;
- returning the criminal case to the investigator for conducting an additional investigation, for changing the scope of charges or for providing a new formulation of the indictment by eliminating failures;
- forwarding the criminal case to a higher-ranking public prosecutor for approval of the indictment if the case is under the jurisdiction of the higher court (Article 221, paragraph 1 UPKR).

907. If the criminal case is complex or voluminous, the time period may be extended by a higher-ranking prosecutor up to 30 days upon a reasoned request of the prosecutor.

908. According to Article 221, paragraph 4 UPKR, the decision of the prosecutor to return the criminal case to the investigator may be appealed by the investigator (with the consent of the head of the investigative body) within 72 hours to the higher prosecutor. In case of disagreement with the decision of the latter, it can be appealed to the General Prosecutor of the Russian Federation.

909. The higher prosecutor shall make one of the following decisions within ten days of the receipt of the relevant materials: either dismiss the petition of the investigator or quash the decision of the subordinate prosecutor. In the latter case, the higher prosecutor confirms the indictment and files it to the court.

910. An appeal against the prosecutor's decision to the higher prosecutor suspends its execution (Article 221, paragraph 5 UPKR).

911. After the confirmation of the indictment, the prosecutor files the indictment to the court (Article 222, paragraph 1 UPKR). The prosecutor shall notify the

1057. *See* more in Barabash, Priroda rossijskogo ugolovnogo processa, 2005, pp. 3–257.

accused, his/her legal counsel, the victim, the civil claimant (party),[1058] the civil defendant and/or their representatives about filing the indictment to the court and explain to them their right to lodge a petition for holding a preliminary hearing (Chapter 15 UPKR).

4. Inquiry

912. As described above, **inquiry** *(дознание)*[1059] is the second form of the preliminary investigation (Articles 223–226.9 UPKR). With regard to the inquiry, the general rules for conducting investigative activities in the pretrial investigation[1060] are applicable to the same extent with the exemptions of specific rules provided for by Chapter 32 UPKR for this form of investigation (Article 223, paragraph 1 UPKR). The differences between the two forms of the preliminary investigation are explained in this chapter, e.g., an inquiry has shorter deadlines compared to the pretrial investigation and only applicable for minor crimes.

913. Under the investigative jurisdiction of the inquiry, bodies fall minor crimes, such as intentional bodily harm of average gravity, Article 112 UKR, (Articles 150, paragraph 3, 151, 223, paragraph 2 UPKR UPKR). To recall, while the pretrial investigation (the first form) is conducted by investigating bodies or investigators, the inquiry is conducted by **inquiry bodies or inquirers** *(дознаватели)*.[1061]

a. Deadlines for the Inquiry

914. The inquiry shall be completed within thirty days after the day when the criminal proceedings were initiated. The term may be extended by the prosecutor by up to thirty days (Article 223, paragraph 3, UPKR).

b. Decisions Made During the Inquiry

915. The inquiry can be suspended by the inquirer based on the same grounds that are stipulated for the suspension of the pretrial investigation (Article 223, paragraph 1 UPKR).[1062]

916. **Suspended** inquiry can be reopened by order of the public prosecutor or the head of the inquiry units (Articles 211, 223, paragraph 3.1. UPKR).

1058. On the legal position of the victim and the civil party (civil claimant), *see* paras. 944–960.

1059. Paramonova, National characteristics, fundamental principles, and history of criminal law in Russia, 2014, pp. 185–186.

1060. For the pre-trial investigation, *see* paras. 866–911.

1061. For the different types of investigating bodies, *see* above General Introduction, §2, III, paras. 43–47.

1062. For the pre-trial investigation, *see* paras. 866–911.

917. The public prosecutor and the head of the inquiry unit have the power to recognize the decision regarding suspension of the inquiry as illegal or unreasonable: the prosecutor in the case of illegal or unreasonable suspension, and the head of the inquiry unit in the case of unreasonable grounds for suspension (Article 223 paragraph 3 UPKR). In this case, the prosecutor or the chief of the inquiry unit is obliged to pass a motivated resolution on the suspension. Both are competent on an equal basis to quash the decision regarding the unreasonable suspension (Article 223, paragraph 3.1 UPKR). However, in the case of expiration of the deadlines for the inquiry (Article 223, paragraph 3 UPKR), the period of inquiry can be prolonged by the prosecutor up to 10 days on the basis of a request from the head of the inquiry unit (Article 223, paragraph 3.2 UPKR). The prosecutor, no later than five days from the receipt of the case file, makes a decision on quashing a suspension and is obliged to send his/her reasoned resolution to the chief of the inquiry body. In this resolution, the prosecutor has to set out specific circumstances that have to be inquired.

918. In certain cases that include forensic investigation, the inquiry period can be extended by the district or city prosecutors and by (equal to them) military prosecutors and their deputies for up to 6 months (Article 223, paragraph 4 UPKR).

919. The inquiry procedure can be **terminated** by the head of the group of inquirers if any of the grounds for the termination of the criminal proceedings are present (Articles 24–28.1, 223, paragraph 1, 223.2, paragraphs 3 and 4 UPKR). The investigation of a criminal case, due to its complexity, can be entrusted to a group of inquires instead of one. The head of the group of inquirers is appointed by the head of the inquiry body. The grounds are the same as for the termination of the criminal procedure within the pretrial investigation (Article 223, paragraph 1 UPKR).[1063] The decision on termination can be overruled by the prosecutor according to the procedure applicable to the pretrial investigation.

c. Closing the Inquiry. Prosecutor´s Decisions on the Indictment and Filing the Indictment to the Court

920. After the inquiry has been completed, the inquirer shall draft the indictment and file it to the prosecutor (Article 225, paragraph 1 UPKR). The inquiry is considered closed once the indictment has been filed to the court or terminated.

921. The accused and his/her defense counsel inspect all the materials of the criminal case and the content of the indictment, which is noted in the protocol of the inspection of the criminal case materials. The victim and his/her representative can inspect the materials of the case and the indictment upon their request (Article 225, paragraphs 2, 3 UPKR).

1063. For the pre-trial investigation, *see* paras. 866–911.

922. The indictment shall be approved by the head of the inquiry body. After the approval, the criminal case materials, together with the indictment, shall be forwarded to the prosecutor (Article 225, paragraph 4 UPKR).

923. According to Article 226, paragraph 1 UPKR, the public prosecutor considers the criminal case and the indictment and shall take within two days, one of the following decisions:

– approval of the indictment and filing the criminal case to the court;
– return of the criminal case for carrying out an additional inquiry (which can last a maximum of ten days) or for the new drafting of the indictment (which has to be finished within three days;
– termination of the criminal case on the grounds that are provided for by Articles 24–28.1 UPKR; The grounds are the same as for the termination of the criminal procedure within the pretrial investigation (Article 223, paragraph 1 UPKR);
– directing the criminal case for the conducting pretrial investigation (instead of continuing the preliminary investigation in its second form - inquiry).

924. By the approval of the indictment, the public prosecutor, before filing the case to the court, has the right with his/her resolution to remove allegations or to requalify the charges into less grave ones (Article 226, paragraph 2 UPKR). A copy of the indictment with all annexes shall be handed to the accused, to his/her defense counsel and to the victim (Article 226, paragraph 3 UPKR).

925. According to Article 226, paragraph 4 UPKR, the decision of the prosecutor to return the criminal case for carrying out an additional inquiry or for the new drafting of the indictment can be appealed by the inquirer with the consent of the head of the inquiry body to a higher prosecutor within 48 hours as of the receipt of the criminal case by the inquirer. The higher prosecutor is obliged to make one of the following decisions within three days as of the receipt of the relevant materials:

– dismissal of the request of the inquirer;
– quashing the decision of the subordinate prosecutor. In this case, the higher prosecutor approves the indictment and files it to the court.

926. The appeal of the prosecutor´s decision suspends its execution (Article 226, paragraph 5 UPKR).

III. The Trial

927. Investigating judges do not exist in the Russian criminal procedural system. The inquiry in court, as an inherent part of the trial, will be discussed below in connection with the trial.[1064]

1064. On the trial, *see* paras. 1068–1191.

§7. The Legal Position of the Accused and the Victim

I. The Legal Position of the Suspect and Accused

A. Definitions

928. The Russian criminal procedure uses the word **'suspect'** (*подозреваемый*) to designate the person against whom the criminal investigation has been opened or the person who was detained according to Articles 91–92 UPKR, e.g., he/she was caught red-handed (Article 46, paragraph 1 UPKR). A suspect is also considered a person with respect to whom a coercive measure was applied before bringing charges (Article 100 UPKR) as well as a person who was notified according to Article 223.1 UPKR (i.e., within the inquiry as a form of investigation) of suspicion of committing a crime, (Article 46, paragraph 1 UPKR).

929. The suspect may be a participant of the criminal proceedings *only in the stage of the preliminary investigation* in contrast to an accused.

930. **Accused** (*обвиняемый*) is considered to be a person with respect to whom in the course of the preliminary investigation the investigator or inquirer has issued a decision on bringing him/her to the criminal proceedings in the capacity of the accused (Article 171 UPKR) as well as a person against whom the indictment has been submitted to the court (Article 47 UPKR).

931. "Accused" is a generic term for three legal status of the accused. The accused, on whose criminal case is appointed the trial, is called the **defendant** (*подсудимый*). The accused, with respect to whom a verdict of guilty is passed, is called the **convict** (*осужденный*). The accused, with respect to whom the verdict of not guilty is passed, shall be seen as **acquitted** (*оправданный*) (Article 47, paragraph 2 UPKR).

B. The Rights and Obligations of the Suspect

932. The rights of the suspect are based on the **principles of criminal procedure** that are underpinned by the constitutional provisions.[1065]

933. One of the essential rights of the suspect is the **right to know about the charges** that have been brought up against him/her and to get a copy of the decision to initiate criminal proceedings, a copy of the protocol of detention, or a copy of the decision to apply coercive measures against him/her.

1065. On the principles of the criminal procedure, *see* Part II, Chapter 1, §3, paras. 814–827.

934. The suspect is considered innocent until his/her guilt is proved by a court verdict (**presumption of innocence**, Article 49 Constitution). The burden of proving the charge lies on the prosecution.

935. The suspect that has been detained has to be interrogated within 24 hours, as of the time of his/her actual detention (Article 46, paragraph 2 UPKR). Among other grounds, the suspect can be detained due to the presence of one of the following grounds (Article 91 UPKR): a person is caught red-handed when committing the crime or immediately after committing it; the victims or the witnesses point to the person as the perpetrator of the crime; on this person or in his/her clothes, near him/her or in his/her dwelling the undoubted traces of the crime are found.

936. Among the inevitable rights of the suspect is the **right to a phone call** to his/her relatives or close persons to inform them about the detention and his/her location (Article 46, paragraph 3 UPKR).

937. Other rights of the suspect are the following ones:

- the **right to give explanations and submit evidence** concerning the suspicion brought against him/her or to refuse to testify against him-/herself. If the suspect agrees to testify, he/she has to be warned by the investigator/inquirer that his/her evidence may be used as proof in a criminal case against him/her unless the evidence is inadmissible (Article 75 UPKR);
- the **right to legal assistance**. It includes, first, using the legal advice of the defense counsel from the moment of his/her detention or initiation of the criminal case and, second, the right to have private and confidential communication with the defense counsel;
- the **right to submit petitions and recusals,** e.g., to judges, prosecutors, investigators in the cases of a possible conflict of interests;
- the right to give testimony and explanations in his/her **native language** or the language he/she speaks;
- the right to use the **interpreter's services free of charge**;
- the right to inspect the protocols of **investigative activities** carried out with his/her participation and to submit comments on them;
- the right to take part with the approval of the investigator or inquirer in the investigative activities carried out at his/her own petition, at the petition of his/her defense counsel;
- the **right to lodge complaints** against the actions (ommissions) and decisions of the inquirer, of the head of the inquiry unit, of the head of the body of inquiry, of the investigator, of the prosecutor or of the court;
- the right to defend him- or herself using **any other means and ways not prohibited by the law** (Article 46, paragraph 4 UPKR).

938. Along with these rights, the suspect also has **obligations**. The suspect who is summoned for interrogation by the inquirer or investigator is obliged to come at the appointed time or has to notify the inquirer/investigator in advance about the reasons for his/her being unable to come. Otherwise, coercive procedural measures can be applied (Articles 111, 188, paragraph 3 UPKR). The suspect cannot interfere in the normal course of investigation with unlawful methods. Otherwise, he/she may be subjected to stricter coercive measures.

C. Rights and Obligations of the Accused (Defendant, Convict, Acquitted)

939. The rights of the accused are based as well on the **principles of criminal procedure** that are underpinned by the constitutional provisions.[1066,1067]

940. By virtue of Article 49 Constitution, the accused is regarded as innocent until his/her guilt is proved as provided by the Federal Law and established by a court verdict (**presumption of innocence**). The accused is not obliged to prove his or her innocence. The burden of proving the charge lies on the prosecution. A verdict of guilt cannot be based on assumptions, and all doubts concerning the guilt of the accused must be interpreted in the accused's favor. One of the essential rights of the accused is the right to defend his/her rights and legitimate interests and the right to have adequate time and opportunity to prepare the line of his/her defense (Article 47, paragraph 3 UPKR).[1068]

941. The accused possesses moreover all the rights the suspect does (Article 46 UPKR), including the right to legal assistance, also free of charge, the right to private and confidential communication with his/her defense counsel without limiting the number and duration of the meetings (Article 47, paragraph 4 UPKR).

942. Besides, the Code of Criminal Procedure in compliance with the Constitution provides for additional rights of the accused (Article 47, paragraph 4 UPKR):

- the right to **inspect all materials of the criminal case** after the preliminary investigation has been completed, including the **right to copy** from the criminal case any information and in any volume;
- the right to object to the termination of the criminal proceedings;
- the right to **participate in trial proceedings** in the courts of the first, the second and the appeals instances;
- the right to **read the protocols** of the court sessions and to submit comments on them;
- the right to **file complaints and appeals** against the sentence, the ruling or the resolution of the court, including the right to receive the copies of the decisions he/she complains and appeals against;
- the right to take part in the examination of the questions involving the execution of the sentence;
- the right to defend him- or herself while resorting to any other means and ways that are not prohibited by the law.

1066. For the difference in legal status of the suspect and accused, *see* paras. 928–943.
1067. On the principles of the criminal procedure, *see* Part II, Chapter 1, §3, paras. 814–827.
1068. Chelcov-Bebutov, Kurs ugolovno-processualnogo prava, p. 78.

943. Besides, participation in the criminal proceedings of the defense counsel or legal representative of the accused does not serve as any ground for restricting any rights of the accused (Article 47, paragraph 5 UPKR).[1069]

II. The Legal Position of the Victim and the Civil Party (Civil Claimant)

A. General Rights and Duties of the Victim

944. In the Russian criminal procedure, the victim is "a natural person, upon whom a physical, property or moral damage was inflicted by the crime as well as a legal entity if its property or/and business reputation were damaged by the crime" (Article 42, paragraph 1 UPKR). The decision on recognizing a person to be a victim is formalized by the resolution of the inquirer, investigator or of the court at the stage of initiating a criminal case or immediately after receiving the information about the victim.

945. The victim can perform as a private prosecuting party (Article 43 UPKR), as a civil party (Article 44 UPKR) and as a witness (Article 42, paragraph 2 UPKR). The scope of the rights and the possible claims vary accordingly, depending on the procedural position. These positions can overlap in a concrete case.

946. In general, the victim is **entitled** (Article 42, paragraph 2 UPKR):

- to know the charges of the accused;
- to be informed by the investigative authorities and/or prosecutor about his/her rights and obligations;
- to participate in the procedural actions and to be informed about their progress, such as taking part in trial proceedings;
- to support the prosecution;
- to submit evidence;
- to inspect the documents;
- to make motions/objections;
- to lodge claims, appeal;
- to have other rights, such as the right to have a representative free of charge or to use interpreter´s services free of charge;
- to be informed on the process/any changes in the execution of the sentence;
- other means and ways that are not prohibited by the law.

947. The victim has certain **obligations** in the criminal procedure (Article 42, paragraph 5 UPKR). It is prohibited for the victim to ignore the summons of the inquirer, investigator, prosecutor or of the court; to give false evidence; to refuse to testify (excluding the case of testifying against him-/herself, his/her relatives or against close persons); to refuse to participate in certain procedural actions, e.g., giving a sample of his/her handwriting for comparative analysis; to disclose the data

1069. Smirnov/ Kalinowski, Ugolovnij process: uchebnik, 2015, pp. 45.

of the preliminary investigation if he/she was warned about it in advance. The obligation to appear or a monetary penalty serves as sanctions (Article 111, paragraph 2 UPKR); in certain cases, also criminal punishment (Articles 307, 308, 310 UKR).[1070]

B. Victim as a Private Prosecuting Party

948. As discussed above,[1071] the Russian criminal procedure is based on the principle of mandatory prosecution (Article 21 UPKR). All the crimes have to be prosecuted in compliance with the principle of mandatory prosecution unless otherwise stated with regard to concrete crimes (Article 20, paragraph 5 UPKR). The idea behind this rule is that in the case of the commission of offenses with grave consequences, the state has to prevent serious social danger by regulating, balancing private and social interests and prosecuting such behavior.

949. However, there are minor exceptions to this rule, such as so-called **private prosecution** and **private-public prosecution cases** in which the victim has suffered only a slight injury (e.g., Article 115 UKR), and prosecution may only be initiated upon application by the victim or his/her legal representative. (Article 20 UPKR).[1072]

950. To the private prosecution cases belong, for instance, intentional bodily harm of small gravity (Article 115 UKR) or battery (Article 116 UKR). Private prosecution is subject to termination in the case of reconciliation of the victim with the accused. Reconciliation is admissible until the court departs to the consultation room for a passing sentence (Article 20, paragraph 2 UPKR).

951. The private-public prosecution cases constitute more serious crimes than the private prosecution ones. These are, for example, rape (Article 131, paragraph1 UKR) or violent sexual actions (Article 132, paragraph 1 UKR), both without aggravating circumstances. With regard to this group of offenses, the prosecution may only be commenced upon the application of the victim or his/her legal representative. However, as a rule, it is not subject to termination of criminal proceedings in the case of the victim's reconciliation with the accused (Article 20, paragraph 3 UPKR).

952. Another criminal procedural provision that emphasizes the principle of mandatory prosecution reads as follows: the head of the investigative body, the investigator and the inquirer with the consent of the public prosecutor can initiate criminal proceedings for any offense, including crimes of the private or private-public prosecution. The precondition for it is that the offense is committed against

1070. Lebedev, Nauchno-prakticheskij kommentarij k UPKR, 2016, pp. 230.
1071. On the principles of the criminal procedure, *see* Part II, Chapter 1, §3, paras. 814–827.
1072. Radchenko, Kommentarij k UPKR, p. 84; Paramonova, National characteristics, fundamental principles, and history of criminal law in Russia, 2014, pp. 175–200.

a person who, due to his/her dependent or helpless condition or for other reasons, cannot defend his/her rights (Article 20, paragraph 4 UPKR).

953. The victim, as a prosecuting party, possesses the rights of the victim. He/she is additionally entitled to modify the charges against the accused if it does not worsen the situation of the accused and does not infringe his/her right to defense and to drop the charges. In the latter case, if it is allowed by the provisions, criminal proceedings are terminated (Article 20, paragraphs 2, 3 UPKR). The prosecuting party has the right to enforce and support the civil claim.

C. The Civil Party

954. The civil party (or civil claimant) is the victim enforcing a civil claim in criminal proceedings against the defendant (Article 44 UPKR). The so-called **civil claimant (*гражданский истец*)** is considered a natural or a legal person, who (which) has filed a claim that relates to the consequences or damages caused by the offense. Terms "civil party" and "civil claimant" are synonyms. There must be sufficient grounds to presume that the damage was inflicted upon the victim as a result of the committed crime (Article 44, paragraph 1 UPKR). The civil claimant may enforce a civil claim for compensation of the material and moral damages. The amount of the material and moral damages is determined according to the rules of the Civil Code of the Russian Federation (Articles 151 and 1064–1101).

955. A civil claim may be filed after the institution of criminal proceedings and up to the end of the trial proceedings in a Court of First Instance. The civil claimant is exempted from paying the state fee (Article 44, paragraph 2 UPKR).

956. In the cases when persons cannot defend their rights and lawful interests themselves, such as minors, persons recognized as legally incapable, or as restricted in their legal capacity or for some other reasons, a civil claim may be lodged by their legal representatives or by the prosecutor. If the damage caused is related to the interests of the state, the prosecutor is entitled to take action as a civil party (Article 44, paragraph 3 UPKR).

957. Before the judgment on the case is made, the civil party can renounce the civil claim at any time. The renouncement of the civil claim entails the termination of the proceedings on it (Article 44, paragraph 5 UPKR).

958. The civil party in the criminal procedure has all **rights** and **obligations** that the victim is entitled to (Articles 42, paragraph 2, 44, paragraph 4 UPKR).

959. In particular, the civil party has the right to be informed by the investigative authorities and/or prosecutor about his/her rights and obligations; the right to participate in the procedural actions; the right to submit evidence; the right to make motions/objections; the right to lodge claims, appeal and others. Additionally, the civil party is entitled to support the civil claim in the procedure (Article 44, paragraph 4 UPKR).

960. The obligations of the civil party are stipulated in the general obligations of the victim (Article 42, paragraph 5 UPKR). For example, the civil claimant is bound by the obligation not to disclose the data of the preliminary investigation if he/she was warned about it in advance (Article 44, paragraph 6 UPKR).

§8. The Rules of Evidence

I. Basics

961. Russian law belongs to the continental legal system,[1073] which determines the main features of the rules of evidence in the criminal procedural law. In contrast to the common law criminal procedure, the pursuit of finding the truth regarding a particular case based on the evidence presented is considered a goal of the criminal procedure. The criminal responsibility of a person is based upon the factual truth and cannot be the result of the better/worse legal bargaining.[1074] It explains, for example, a restrictive and cautious approach to the application of plea bargaining[1075] in the Russian criminal procedure.[1076] The court is given the role of the final evaluation of the evidence that was obtained and evaluated at all stages of the criminal procedure.[1077]

962. The process of **proving (*доказывание*)** (Article 85 UPKR) consists of the collection, verification and evaluation of the evidence for the purpose of disclosing the circumstances of the committed crime. The circumstances are stipulated in Article 73 UPKR and are subject to proof during the criminal proceedings:[1078]

- the event of the crime (time, place, mode and the other circumstances of committing the crime);
- the culpability of the person in committing the crime;
- the form of his/her guilt and the motives;
- the circumstances characterizing the personality of the accused;
- the character and the scale of the damage caused by the crime;
- the circumstances releasing/excluding the criminal responsibility as well as punishability of the act;

1073. On classifications and techniques of criminal law, *see* General Introduction, paras. 182–193.
1074. For the more detailed information on the plea bargaining in Russia, *see* Paramonova, Revista Penal 2012, 264–268; Poznyshev, Russkij ugolovnij prozess, pp. 29–30; Petrukhin, Reforma ugolovnogo prozessa, p. 26. For plea bargaining, *see* paras. 114, 810, 961, 1273–1278.
1075. For the special criminal procedures, *see* p. 276.
1076. *See* Paramonova, Revista Penal 2012, 264–268.
1077. For the stages of the penal process, *see* paras. 858–865.
1078. Barabash, Priroda rossijskogo ugolovnogo processa, 2005, pp. 115; Bozhjev, Ugolovnij process, p. 16.

- the mitigating and aggravating circumstances;
- the circumstances confirming that the property that is subject to confiscation has been obtained as a result of committing the crime or used (or intended for use) as a weapon/ means for committing a crime;
- the circumstances that contributed to the commission of an offense.

963. **Collection of evidence** (Article 86 UPKR) is conducted in the course of the criminal proceedings by the inquirer, the investigator, the prosecutor and the court through conducting procedural actions.

964. As mentioned above, the suspect, the accused, the victim, the civil claimant (party),[1079] the civil defendant and their representatives, as well as the defense counsel and civil claimant´s counsel, have the right to collect and submit evidence. For instance, the defense counsel can obtain on demand the relevant documents from the state authorities, which are obliged to provide them (Article 86, paragraphs 2, 3 UPKR).

965. **Verification of evidence** is conducted by the investigating authorities and by the court through comparing it with other evidence related to the criminal case, by verifying the sources of information, by obtaining other evidence that confirms or negate the evidence that has been verified (Article 87 UPKR).

966. According to the rules of **evaluation** of evidence, the obtained evidence (only those that have been already verified) shall be **evaluated** from the point of view of its referability to the case, admissibility and reliability. The sufficiency of the evidence for the resolution of the criminal case is examined based on all collected evidence (Article 88 UPKR).

967. According to Article 88 paragraph 2 UPKR, if the evidence is recognized by the court, the prosecutor, the investigator or the inquirer as **inadmissible**,[1080] it leads to the exclusion of evidence (Articles 88, 75 paragraph 2 UPKR). According to Article 75, paragraph 1 UPKR, evidence obtained in violation of the legal provisions of the Code of Criminal Procedure is deemed to be inadmissible. The evidence that has been recognized as inadmissible cannot be used in the criminal proceedings, e.g., the results of illegally conducted investigative activities cannot be included in the indictment or a testimony of the victim based on a rumor (Articles 73 paragraph 2, 88, 89, paragraph 3 UPKR). Another important rule of evidence is the **collateral estoppel** (*преюдиция*) (Article 90 UPKR). According to this rule, the circumstances established by a sentence or by any other court decision made within civil or administrative proceedings, which have come into legal force, have a prejudicial effect. It means that they shall be recognized by the court, by the prosecutor, by the investigator and by the inquirer without any additional verification, e.g., the property of a house was recognized by a decision of a civil court.

1079. On the legal position of the victim and the civil party (civil claimant), *see* paras. 944–960.
1080. For inadmissible evidence, *see* para. 1029.

II. The Principles of Evidentiary Law

968. The major principle of evidentiary law is determined by the main goal of the criminal procedure, which is, traditionally, the pursuit of objective truth.[1081] The process of introducing and examining evidence is underpinned by the **principle of comprehensiveness, completeness,** and **objectivity** of the investigation of the factual circumstances (Articles 73, 6 UPKR).[1082] It is invoked to serve the main goal of the pursuit of objective truth to the full.

969. The principles of the Russian criminal procedure discussed above cover the principles that concern the law of evidence.[1083] This way, the basic principles of the criminal procedure, principles concerning due process and procedural safeguards, principles concerning the judiciary and the administration of criminal justice as well as other principles of criminal justice are fully applicable to the field of evidentiary law.

970. For instance, **respect for the person's honor and dignity** is one of the fundamental principles of the criminal procedure and forms the base of the evidentiary law in criminal procedure.[1084] It prohibits violence, torture, and other kinds of cruel or humiliating treatment in criminal proceedings, including illegal and inhuman methods of obtaining evidence in the criminal procedure (Article 21 Const., Article 9 UPKR, Article 302 UKR). With regard to the proof collected in the criminal procedure, a violation of this principle leads to the recognition of the evidence as inadmissible, hence, to its exclusion from the procedure (Article 75, 89 UPKR).

971. The violation of the principle of the **protection of the rights and lawful interests of a person in criminal proceedings** can as well lead to the inadmissibility of evidence in the criminal procedure, for example, if the court, prosecutor, investigator, or inquirer fails to explain to the participants in the criminal proceedings their rights, responsibilities, and liabilities or fails to guarantee the possibility of exercising these rights (Article 45 Const., Articles 11 and 6, paragraph 1 UPKR), e.g., the right of the accused to refuse to testify against him- or herself or his or her spouse or close relatives or persons.

972. Other basic principles, such as the **principle of justice** as well as the **principle of legality in the criminal procedure**, are applicable regarding evidentiary law. An inherent precondition for the imposition of a just punishment on a guilty person (Article 6 UPKR) is compliance with the criminal procedural provisions. They are binding upon all state authorities, in particular upon the court, prosecutor,

1081. Paramonova/Bogush, ZStW 125 (2013), 722–724; Poznyshev, Russkij ugolovnij prozess, pp. 29–30; Petrukhin, Reforma ugolovnogo prozessa, p. 26.
1082. Golovko, Al'ternativy ugolovnomu presledovaniyu v sovremennom prave, pp. 182–187; Paramonova/Bogush, ZStW, 125 (2013), 703–728.
1083. On the principles of the criminal procedure, *see* Part II, Chapter 1, §3, paras. 814–827.
1084. On the principles of the criminal procedure, *see* Part II, Chapter 1, §3, paras. 814–827.

investigator, and inquirer (Article 7 UPKR).[1085] Evidence obtained in violation of provisions of the Code of Criminal Procedure is inadmissible[1086] (Article 7, paragraph 4 UPKR).[1087]

973. Among the maxims concerning due process and procedural safeguards, the principles, such as the **principle of integrity of personality** (Article 22 Const. and Article 10 UPKR) and the **principle of a reasonable time period for criminal proceedings** (Article 6.1 UPKR), are required to be observed obtaining evidence in the criminal procedure.[1088]

974. According to the **principle of the presumption of innocence** as set out in Article 49 Const. and Article 14 UPKR, the suspect or accused[1089] is regarded as innocent until guilt has been proved, and he/she is not obliged to prove his or her own innocence. Instead, according to the **ex officio principle**, the burden of proving the charge as well as refuting the arguments and evidence introduced by the suspect or accused[1090] is on the prosecution. The suspect or accused has the right to introduce evidence and to use any means not prohibited by law to establish his or her innocence (Articles 46 and 47 UPKR). Moreover, one of the key procedural safeguards—the ***'in dubio pro reo'*** principle, which derives from the presumption of innocence—states that any uncertainty of the evidence may not be contemplated to the detriment of the defendant.

975. Another key principle regarding the evidentiary law is the **principle of the free assessment of evidence** (Article 17 UPKR), which could be classified as a principle concerning the judiciary and the administration of criminal justice as well as a procedural safeguard.[1091] In compliance with this principle, prosecutors, investigative authorities, as well as judges and jurors must assess the evidence in accordance with their inner convictions, based on the aggregate of the evidence presented in the given criminal case. In so doing, they must rely on the law and on their conscience. No evidence may be regarded as possessing force established in advance.

976. Among other principles of criminal justice that directly relate to the evidence in the criminal procedure is the **principle of immediacy with respect to evidence** (Article 240 UPKR). It is embodied in the requirement that all evidence is subject to direct examination as well as in the provision that a sentence can only be based on evidence that has been presented and argued in open court. This principle underpins another significant safeguard, namely, the right of the suspect (Article 46,

1085. For the principle of legality, *see* Part I, Chapter 1, paras. 197–226.
1086. For inadmissible evidence, *see* para. 1029.
1087. Paramonova, National characteristics, fundamental principles, and history of criminal law in Russia, 2014, pp. 175–292.
1088. For principles concerning due process and procedural safeguards, *see* paras. 822–827.
1089. For the difference in legal status of the suspect and accused, *see* paras. 928–943.
1090. For the difference in legal status of the suspect and accused, *see* paras. 928–943.
1091. On the principles of the criminal procedure, *see* Part II, Chapter 1, §3, paras. 814–827.

paragraph 4 UPKR), accused (Article 47, paragraph 4 UPKR), the victim (Article 42, paragraph 2 UPKR), and other participants in the criminal process to present evidence (Article 74 UPKR).

III. The Means of Proof

977. According to the Russian procedural law, evidence in the criminal case is all information on the basis of which the court, the prosecutor, the investigator and the inquirer decide over the existence or the absence of the circumstances that are subject to proving in the course of the proceedings on the criminal case. Other circumstances of relevance to the criminal case are seen as evidence in the criminal case.[1092]

978. The list of admissible means of proof is given by the Code of Criminal Procedure (Article 74 UPKR): testimony of the suspect (Article 76 UPKR); testimony of the accused (Article 77 UPKR); testimony of the victim (Article 78 UPKR); testimony of the witness (Article 79 UPKR); expert evidence (Article 80 UPKR); specialist evidence (Article 80 UPKR); physical evidence in different forms, including documents (Articles 81, 82 UPKR); records of the investigative and the judicial actions (Article 83 UPKR); other documents (Article 84 UPKR).

979. The interrogation of the suspect, the accused,[1093] as well as the victim and the witness, is conducted in compliance with the same basic rules stipulated in the Code of Criminal Procedure (Articles 187–190 UPKR). Besides, all participants of the criminal proceedings, including the aforementioned, give evidence in accordance with their rights and obligations.[1094]

980. With regard to the place and the time of interrogation, it is performed at the place where the preliminary investigation is conducted, with some exceptions, when it can be carried out at the place of location of the interrogated person. An interrogation shall not be conducted for more than four hours in a row. In total, an interrogation in the course of one day cannot exceed eight hours; on the ground of medical condition, the length can be reduced (Article 187 UPKR).

981. It is obligatory to keep a record (protocol of interrogation) of every interrogation. In the protocol of interrogation shall be named all the persons who have participated in the interrogation. Each of them is obliged to sign the protocol, as well as all the addenda and the specifications made in it. The refusal or impossibility (with the reason) to sign the protocol is noted in the protocol (Article 190 UPKR).

1092. Lebedev, Nauchno-prakticheskij kommentarij k UPKR, 2016, pp. 56.
1093. For the difference in legal status of the suspect and accused, *see* paras. 928–943.
1094. On the legal status of the suspect and the accused, *see* Part II, Chapter 1, §6.

982. The person under interrogation has the right to make use of documents and notes. At the initiative of the investigator as well as at the request of the interrogated person, during interrogation, photographing, audio and/or video recording, filming may be carried out. These materials are attached to the criminal file; the parties may have copies of them. The materials shall be sealed after completing the preliminary investigation (Article 189, paragraphs 3, 4 UPKR).

983. According to the procedure for summoning to an interrogation (Article 188 UPKR), the witness and the victim are summoned by a writ, in which it shall be laid down who and in what capacity is summoned, to whom and at what address, the date and the hour appointed for the appearance at the interrogation, and the consequences of the failure to appear without a serious reason. In certain cases of violation of these rules, it leads to criminal responsibility, such as in the case of refusal of a witness or a victim to testify, when their consent to testify is not obligatory (Article 308 UPK).

A. Testimony of the Suspect and the Accused

984. The rules of the testimony of the suspect and the accused[1095] are laid down in Articles 76, 77, 173, 174, 187–190 and 275 UPKR.

985. Testimonies of the accused—are oral statements of the accused that have been taken during the interrogations held in the pretrial and trial criminal proceedings on the charges brought against him/her and on the circumstances of the committed criminal offense. The statement has to be placed in record in accordance with the procedural legal provisions (Articles 47, 77, 187–190, 275 UPKR).[1096]

986. The statement of the accused has a dual nature: on the one hand, it is a source of evidence; on the other hand, it is the means of defense of the accused against the accusation brought against him/her.[1097]

987. The suspect and the accused give evidence in accordance with their rights and obligations.[1098] For instance, the accused shall be interrogated immediately after being charged (Article 173, paragraph 1 UPKR). In compliance with the rules of evidentiary law, the investigator/inquirer is obliged to keep a record (protocol of an interrogation of the accused) at every interrogation (Article 174, paragraph 1 UPKR). The protocol contains, besides investigative information a detailed data on the person of the accused, such as name, citizenship, criminal record etc. (Article 174, paragraph 2 UPKR).

1095. For the difference in legal status of the suspect and accused, *see* paras. 928–943.
1096. Radchenko, Kommentarij k UPKR, p. 124.
1097. Radchenko, Kommentarij k UPKR, p. 124.
1098. On the legal status of the suspect and the accused, *see* paras. 928–943 .

988. The statement of the accused is no primary evidence due to the principle of the free assessment of evidence[1099] (Article 17 UPKR): No evidence may be regarded as having force established in advance. Consequently, it is only one among others. Therefore, the admission by the accused of his/her guilt in committing the crime can serve as the basis for the charges, however, only under the circumstance that his/her culpability is confirmed by the aggregate of all evidence existing on the criminal case (Article 77, paragraph 2 UPKR).

B. Testimony of the Witness and the Victim

989. The rules applicable to the statement of a witness and of a victim are stipulated in Articles 78, 79, 187–191, 277, 278 UPKR.

990. Testimony of the witness and the victim is an oral statement on the circumstances relevant to the investigation and resolution of the criminal case that has been taken during the interrogation in compliance with the procedural rules (Articles 56, 79, 187–191, 277, 278 UPKR).

991. The witness as well as the victim may be interrogated about any kind of circumstances that are subject to proof during the criminal proceedings and any other circumstances related to the criminal case. This way, the witness can be asked about the personality of the accused and of the victim as well as about his/her relationships with them and other witnesses (Articles 79, paragraph 2, 278 UPKR). The victim may be interrogated about any circumstances, including about his/her relationships with the suspect or with the accused[1100] (Articles 78, paragraph 2, 277 UPKR).

992. The **testimony of the witness** should contain specific information on the circumstances of the case. Assumptions and conjectures have no evidentiary value. The information cannot serve as evidence if the witness does not indicate the source of his/her knowledge.[1101]

993. The witness can give evidence about the circumstances that he/she observed, perceived in-person/directly, as well as on the circumstances that he/she got to know from the words of others.

994. Moreover, a person can be summoned and interrogated in the capacity of a witness only by the officials that have the competence to carry out criminal proceedings. No other public or private institutions or organizations are vested with

1099. For the principle of the free assessment of evidence, *see* para. 975.
1100. For the difference in legal status of the suspect and accused, *see* paras. 928–943.
1101. Radchenko, Kommentarij k UPKR, pp. 125–126.

such power.[1102] In accordance with Article 55, paragraph 4 UPKR, the witness is entitled to use the service of a legal counsel during the interrogation. (Article 189, paragraph 5 UPKR).

995. A witness has the right to give evidence without compulsion. It is forbidden to obtain testimony by violence, threats or other illegal measures. An official who allows such abuse can be prosecuted under Article 302 UPK (coercion to testify).

996. For the protection of the witness, his/her relatives and close persons, the court can decide not to disclose the real identity of the witness and can interrogate the witness under conditions excluding the visual observation of the witness by other participants of the proceedings (Article 278, paragraph 5 UPKR).

997. A witness has the right not to testify against him- or herself, his/her spouse, close relatives and close persons, as defined in Article 51 Const., Articles 5, paragraph 1, 56, paragraph 4 UPKR. With the consent of a witness to give evidence, he/she shall be warned by the investigative authorities that the information presented can be used as evidence in the criminal proceedings on the case, including in the event of his/her subsequent refusal to acknowledge the testimony.

998. The procedural rules of interrogation of the victim and the witness are the same, but there are exceptions due to the status of the victim.

999. "To testify" is not only the duty of the **victim** but also his/her right: the interrogation may be conducted on the initiative of the investigating authorities, the prosecutor and the court or upon the initiative of the victim. The victim is an equal party in the criminal proceedings (Article 244 UPKR). This means that he/she, unlike witnesses, cannot only communicate certain facts he/she has a knowledge of but also has the right to assess others evidence collected on the case, e.g., he/she can file petitions on the exclusion of certain proofs from the list of evidence (Article 235 UPKR).

1000. The victim—like the witness—is subject to rules on witness immunity, i.e., the right not to testify against him- or herself, relatives and close persons (Article 51 Const., Article 42, paragraph 2 UPKR).

1001. Just like other evidence, the statement of the witness and the victim cannot be regarded as primary evidence and is evidence, among others, due to the principle of the free assessment of evidence[1103] (Article 17 UPKR). When evaluating the testimony of the victim, it is taken into account that he/she is a party of the process and interested in a certain outcome of the proceedings of the criminal case. The

1102. Radchenko, Kommentarij k UPKR, pp. 125–126; Smirnov/ Kalinowski, Ugolovnij process: uchebnik, 2015, pp. 3.

1103. For the principle of the free assessment of evidence, *see* para. 975.

outcome of the case, in particular the culpability of the accused, has to be confirmed by the aggregate of all evidence existing on the criminal case (Article 77, paragraph 2 UPKR).

1002. In accordance with Article 307 UKR, the witness and the victim can be punished for a criminal offense in case of giving a false statement. A translator can also be criminally charged for giving deliberately false translation.

C. Expert and Specialist Opinion

1003. Expert and specialist opinion is another means of proof (Article 80 UPKR).

1004. **Expert opinion** (*заключение эксперта*) is a conclusion done in a written form by a person having specific knowledge and designated to conduct a forensic examination. His statement contains the conclusions of his study on the issues/questions raised before him, whether by the investigating authorities, the court or the parties (Articles 80, paragraph 1, 283 UPKR).

1005. 'Specific knowledge' is considered such knowledge that goes beyond general education and life experience, for which it is required to possess special theoretical and practical training and professional skills. The knowledge can relate to any area: science, technology, arts, and crafts.[1104]

1006. Article 196 UPKR provides for a number of cases in which an expert opinion is obligatory:

- the cause of death;
- the nature and degree of harm caused to health;
- mental or physical condition of the suspect, the accused, when there is doubt on his/her sanity or ability to defend his/her rights and legitimate interests in the criminal proceedings;
- the mental state of the suspect, the accused of the age of over 18 years, who has been accused of a crime against the sexual integrity of a minor (who has not attained the age of 14 years), to address the question of the presence or absence of the disorder of sexual preference (pedophilia);
- mental or physical condition of the suspect, the accused, when there is reason to believe that he/she is a drug addict;
- mental or physical condition of the victim, where there is doubt as to his/her ability to perceive the circumstances relevant to the criminal case adequately and to give evidence;
- the age of the suspect, the victim, when it is relevant for the criminal case and the documents proving his/her age are missing or raise doubt.

1104. Radchenko, Kommentarij k UPKR, p. 127; Smirnov/ Kalinowski, Ugolovnij process: uchebnik, 2015, pp. 3.

1007. The expert is giving his/her opinion on his/her own behalf, based on his/her inner conviction formed as a result of research conducted by him/her. The expert bears personal responsibility for it.

1008. The expert opinion shall be subject to verification and evaluation on a general basis with other evidence (Article 88 UPKR). It does not have a predetermined strength or any advantages over other evidence.

1009. In accordance with Article 17 UPKR, an expert opinion is not binding on the inquirer, investigator, prosecutor and the court. However, they are required to motivate their disagreement in an official form in the decision on the request of new or additional expertise (i.e., expert testimony) in the indictment, in the verdict or in the decision of the higher court. Any party, including the inquirer, investigator, prosecutor, and the court, as well as the suspect, accused, defense counsel, civil party, and witness, may ask for additional or new expertise (Article 206 UPKR).

1010. In case of doubt on the coherence of the expert opinion or due to the presence of contradictions in the conclusions of the expert or experts, the inquirer, investigator, prosecutor or the court may request second expertise. It shall be conducted by another expert or other experts (Article 207, paragraph 2 UPKR).

1011. There is also an option of an additional expert opinion, which is assigned to the same or other expert(s). It is carried out in the case of insufficient clarity or completeness of the conclusions of the expert as well as in the case of the emergence of new issues in relation to the previously investigated circumstances (Article 207, paragraph 1 UPKR).

1012. An expert can also be asked to give an oral statement, e.g., in the trial proceedings, regarding his/her expert opinion. For instance, an expert can be asked to clarify the application of expert research methods, to explain the level of modern achievements in the field of science, technology, arts or crafts, to give more information on expert competences in certain fields as well as on the reasons, why any contradictions between the experts are possible (Articles 80, paragraph 2; 166, 167, 205, 282 UPKR).

1013. **Specialist opinion** (*заключение специалиста*) is a conclusion done in a written form by a person having specific knowledge in certain fields. The statement contains the results of the study performed by the specialist on the issues/questions raised before him/her by the parties of the criminal proceedings (Article 80, paragraph 3 UPKR).

1014. The major difference between the specialist opinion and the expert opinion is that obtaining of specialist opinion can only be initiated by the parties of the criminal proceedings from the side of the prosecution (victim, civil claimant and their representatives) and from the side of the defense (accused, suspect, civil defendant, their representatives, defense counsel).

1015. In this respect, the interested parties of the criminal proceedings independently find a specialist, determine the degree of his/her professional competence and formulate their questions to find out his/her opinion. They may provide at the disposal of the specialist the copies of the procedural documents related to the criminal case as well as any other materials received within their capacity during the proceedings (Article 86, paragraphs 2, 3 UPKR).

1016. The results of the study conducted by the specialist, however, can serve as a basis for the appointment of an expert to conduct a forensic examination.

1017. The inquiry officer, investigator, prosecutor and the court shall consider and evaluate the specialist opinion along with other collected evidence in the criminal case without giving it a priority (Article 17 UPKR).

1018. The expert, as well as the specialist, commit a criminal offense they can be punished for in case of giving knowingly false testimony (Article 307 UKR).

D. Physical Evidence and Documents

1019. **Physical evidence** (*вещественные доказательства*) are any objects of the material world which were obtained and enclosed to the criminal case in accordance with the law and that have a capacity to preserve information relevant to the criminal case (Articles 81, 82 UPKR). In accordance with Article 81 UPKR, physical evidence are:

- items which served as tools, equipment, or other means of committing a crime or which preserved traces of the crime;
- items at which the criminal acts were aimed, e.g., money, valuables and other property obtained from the commission of the offense;
- other items and documents that can serve as a means to detect the crime and to establish the circumstances of the criminal case.

1020. Physical evidence shall be kept with the materials of the criminal case until the final judgment on the case comes into force or till the expiry of the term for lodging an appeal against the resolution on the termination of the criminal case. All disputes about the right of property of the material evidence shall be settled in civil proceedings (Article 82, paragraph 1 UPKR). For instance, money, valuables, and other property obtained from the commission of the crime shall be returned to its legal owner (Article 81, paragraph3 UPKR).

1021. The tools, equipment or other means belonging to the accused that were used for committing a crime shall be confiscated, given to appropriate institutions or shall be destroyed, e.g., items prohibited for circulation such as weapons, drugs and other intoxicating substances (Article 81, paragraph3 UPKR).

1022. In order for an object of the material world to gain the status of physical evidence in the criminal case, it has to fulfill the following requirements (Article 81 UPKR): (1) a document which records the origin of the object (the discovery, acquisition), such as an inspection protocol of the place of occurrence, a search or seizure protocol, etc.; (2) a document that indicates its individual and distinctive features, such as an inspection protocol of the detected object; (3) the decision (ruling) of the court for recognition of the concrete item as physical evidence.

1023. Where necessary, the detection, seizure and inspection of such items, valuables and documents are captured with the help of photos or video recording.

1024. **Documents** are admitted as evidence if the information contained in them is important to establish the circumstances that are subject to be proved in the case (Articles 84, 73 UPKR).

1025. Records and protocols of the investigative and the judicial actions are admissible as evidence if they comply with the requirements established by this Code of Criminal Procedure (Article 83 UPKR).

1026. It is important to distinguish the documents as an independent form of evidence, e.g., a sales agreement that determines the ownership, must be distinguished from the documents as physical evidence (e.g., paper with fingerprints or with blood marks: it might be that the content of the document is not relevant for the case but the marks on the paper of the document). For instance, in the case where the documents are counterfeited, have erasures or any other marks, e.g., fingerprints, which determine the features of the physical evidence (Article 81 UPKR), they shall be treated and be in compliance with the rules governing the procedure of physical evidence (Articles 81, 82 UPKR).

IV. Inadmissibility of Evidence

1027. Using evidence in the criminal proceedings that have been obtained in violation of the rules of evidentiary law can lead to serious infringements of several principles of the criminal procedure, including the maxim of the protection of the rights and lawful interests of a person in criminal proceedings as well as the principle of legality.[1105]

1028. The concept of admissibility of evidence in the criminal procedure is based on the principle of legality.[1106]

1029. According to Article 75, paragraph 1 UPKR, evidence obtained in violation of the legal provisions of the Code of Criminal Procedure is deemed to be inadmissible, i.e., such evidence has no legal force and cannot be the legal basis for the

1105. On the principles of the criminal procedure, *see* Part II, Chapter 1, §3.
1106. On the principles of the criminal procedure, *see* Part II, Chapter 1, §3.

criminal charges. In the Code of Criminal Procedure, there are no exceptions to the evidence obtained illegally that can be used as admissible evidence. Hence, it cannot be used to prove the circumstances which form the subject of proof (Article 73 UPKR). Article 75 UPKR gives some examples of inadmissible evidence that includes, for instance, the testimony of the suspect or accused obtained in the absence of the defense counsel or testimony of the victim or witness based on a rumor or assumption (Article 73, paragraph 2 UPRK).

1030. When determining whether evidence is admissible in the criminal procedure or not, both the content of the evidentiary information and its procedural form have to be taken into consideration. This is due to the fact that no information can have evidentiary value without a legally admissible procedural form. Vice versa, it is also true: the proper procedural form alone cannot replace the obligatory content element of the evidence.[1107]

1031. In accordance with the rules of evidentiary law regarding the **content** of evidence, as discussed above, the obtained evidence shall be evaluated from the point of view of its referability to the case and reliability. The sufficiency of the evidence for the resolution of the criminal case is examined based on all collected evidence (Article 88 UPKR).[1108]

1032. With regard to its procedural **form**, the evidence must meet the following mandatory requirements:

(1) it shall be derived from the activities of the state officials and bodies that are authorized to obtain such evidence, e.g., investigator, prosecutor;
(2) it shall be derived from the source provided by the law, such as protocols of interrogation or testimonies of the witnesses (Article 74, paragraph 2 UPKR). This way, anonymous declarations, rumors, speculations, the information obtained as a result of the use of illicit investigative activities cannot serve as evidence in the criminal case. For instance, the testimony of the victim or of the witness based on guessing, a supposition or a rumor, as well as the testimony of the witness, who cannot indicate the source of his/her knowledge, are not admissible (Article 75, paragraph 2 UPKR);
(3) it shall be obtained according to the procedure established by the legal provisions. The evidentiary material is inadmissible if the information has been obtained from a legitimate source but in violation of the procedure.[1109] For instance, the testimony of the accused given during the pretrial proceedings in the absence of his/her defense counsel is inadmissible. Another example is the case when the evidence has been obtained through the use of threats, intimidation, deception or other unlawful means of obtaining evidence;

1107. Radchenko, Kommentarij k UPKR, p. 137; Smirnov/ Kalinowski, Ugolovnij process: uchebnik, 2015, pp. 150.
1108. On the rules of evidence, *see* Part II, Chapter 1, paras. 961–967.
1109. Radchenko, Kommentarij k UPKR, pp. 121; Smirnov/ Kalinowski, Ugolovnij process: uchebnik, 2015, pp. 150.

(4) it shall be documented in the manner provided by the criminal procedural law. For instance, if someone is testifying within the criminal proceedings, it requires that a person has the status of a participant of the process, e.g., the status of a witness. Certain items, objects and documents, if they are used as evidential information in the case, must be described and documented in accordance with the prescribed procedure, e.g., in the pertinent protocols.

Chapter 2. Powers, Rights and Duties in the Pretrial Proceedings

§1. The Coercive Measures of the Criminal Procedure

1033. This chapter analyses the coercive measures applicable during the criminal procedure. Special attention is devoted to pretrial detention as the most intrusive pretrial coercive measures.

1034. The powers, duties and rights of the public prosecutor and the investigating authorities will be outlined in the legal framework of the particular coercive measures.

I. Introductory Remarks

1035. Three chapters of the Code of Criminal Procedure (12–14) regulate the application of coercive measures.

1036. **Coercive measures** (*меры принуждения*) are procedural means of compulsory nature provided for by the criminal procedural law that are applied in criminal proceedings by the authorized state officials and bodies to the suspects and accused[1110] (e.g., house arrest, Article 107 UPKR) and other participants of the criminal proceedings (e.g., obligation to appear regarding a witness, Article 111 UPKR) in order to protect the rights and legal interests of others as well as to guarantee the investigation of the criminal case based on the legal and motivated decisions (Articles 97, 111 UPKR).[1111]

1037. The list of coercive measures is exhaustive and defines the only possible legal forms of coercion in the pretrial proceedings, e.g., house arrest, Article 107 UPKR (Articles 91–118 UPKR). The measures can only be applied if the grounds laid down in the law are present, e.g., the danger that an accused flees (Article 91, paragraph 1 UPKR).

1038. The measures are imposed according to the following principle: if the conditions of more coercive measures are fulfilled for the same purpose, the milder coercive measure (which presupposes fewer restrictions for a person) shall be applied over a stricter one, e.g., recognizance not to leave over pretrial detention.

1110. For the difference in legal status of the suspect and accused, *see* paras. 928–943.

1111. Radchenko, Kommentarij k UPKR, p. 150; Barabash, Priroda rossijskogo ugolovnogo processa, 2005, p. 56.

A. General Rules for Conducting Investigative Activities in the Preliminary Investigation (Pretrial Investigation and Inquiry)

1039. The essence of the preliminary investigation is the clearance of crime. It requires that investigating bodies take all necessary legal measures in order to substantiate the facts and circumstances of the committed crime. Such measures are primarily **investigative activities** (*следственные действия*) that are stipulated in the criminal procedural provisions (Article 164 UPKR, Chapters 24–27 UPKR).[1112] These rules apply to both forms of the preliminary investigation: inquiry and investigation, however, with some exceptions to the inquiry that were discussed above (Article 223, paragraph 1 UPKR).[1113]

1040. All investigative activities can be divided into two groups. The first group of activities can be carried out on the ground of the **investigator's resolution** (*постановление следователя*) (Article 164, paragraph 1 UPKR): an **external examination of a corpse** (*осмотр трупа*) and **exhumation** (*эксгумация*) (Article 178 UPKR); **inspection**, i.e., exposure of the specific features and traces of a crime (*освидетельствование*) (Article 179, paragraph 3 UPKR); **personal search** (*обыск*) (Article 182 UPKR); **seize of certain objects and documents of importance for the criminal case** (*выемка*) (Article 183 UPKR).

1041. Activities that are categorized as the second group are conducted only by virtue of **court decision** (*судебное решение*) (Article 164, paragraph 2 UPKR). In compliance with Articles 23, paragraph 2, 25, 35, paragraph 3 of the Constitution, these activities are provided for by Articles 29, paragraph 2, items 4–9 and 11 UPKR. They are the following ones: inspection of the dwelling in the absence of the consent of the persons residing there (*осмотр жилища*); **search and/or seizure in the dwelling** (*обыск/ выемка в жилище*); seizure of the pledged or deposited item at a **pawnshop** (*выемка заложенной или сданной на хранение в ломбард вещи*); **personal search** (*личный обыск*); **seizure of the objects and the documents**, containing state secret information or other secrets protected by the Federal Law as well as information on the deposits and the accounts in banks and other credit institutions (*выемка предметов и документов*); **putting arrest on the correspondence, permit of its inspection and seizure at postal offices** (*наложение ареста на корреспонденцию, разрешение на ее осмотр и выемка в учреждениях связи*); **putting arrest on property** (*наложение ареста на имущество*); **control and recording of telephone and other conversations** (*контроль и запись телефонных и иных переговоров*).[1114]

1112. For coercive measures of the criminal procedure, *see* Part II, Chapter 2, §1, paras. 1033–1066.
1113. On the inquiry, *see* paras. 912–926.
1114. For coercive measures of the criminal procedure, *see* Part II, Chapter 2, §1, paras. 1033–1066.

1042. The procedure of obtaining **court permission to conduct an investigative activity** requires that an investigator with the consent of the head of the investigative body (in the case of inquiry, an inquirer with the consent of the prosecutor) lodges a request before a court for the pertinent investigative activity (Articles 165, 476 UPKR).

1043. The request shall be subject to consideration no later than 24 hours from the moment when the request came in by a judge at the place where the preliminary investigation or the investigative activity is conducted (Article 165, paragraph 2 UPKR). The public prosecutor, investigator, head of the investigative body (if necessary) and inquirer have the right to participate in the court session regarding the request (Article 165, paragraph 3 UPKR).

1044. Having considered the request for permission to conduct an investigative activity, the judge passes a resolution on permitting the performance of the investigative action or on the refusal to conduct such. The motives for the refusal shall be indicated (Article 165, paragraph 4 UPKR).

1045. In exceptional cases, when an inspection of the dwelling, search and/or seizure in the dwelling, personal search, seizure of the pledged or deposited item at a pawnshop, as well as putting arrest on the property (Article 104.1 UPKR) cannot be delayed, these investigative actions may be conducted on the ground of the investigator's or inquirer's resolution, without obtaining a judicial decision. However, in this case, the investigator or inquirer is obliged, within 24 hours, from the moment of starting the investigative action, to notify the judge and the public prosecutor about it (Article 165, paragraph 5 UPKR). Having received this notification, the judge shall be obliged to verify the legality of the conducted investigative action no later than 24 hours from the moment when the request came in (Article 165, paragraph 2 UPKR). As a result, the judge is obliged to pass a resolution on its legality or illegality. If the judge recognizes the performed investigative action as illegal, all proofs obtained in the course of such investigative action shall be recognized as inadmissible in compliance with Article 75 UPKR (Article 165, paragraph 5 UPKR).

1046. In accordance with Article 164, paragraph 3 UPKR, investigative activities shall be carried out during the daytime. **Conducting investigative activities at night** (from 10 pm till 6 am) time is inadmissible with the exception of urgent cases, for example, in the case of homicide when it is necessary to conduct urgent investigative measures to secure evidence.

1047. **Time-frames for conducting investigative activities** are provided for by the Code of Criminal Procedure.[1115] For instance, the interrogation of the suspect shall be conducted no later than 24 hours from the date of pronouncement of the decision to initiate a criminal case or as of the time of his/her actual detention (Articles 46, paragraph 2, 91 UPKR). The decision to initiate a criminal case can be

1115. For the detailed information on particular investigative activities, *see* paras. 1060–1123.

made without a suspect. The suspect becomes an accused after being charged. The accused shall be interrogated immediately after being charged (Article 173, paragraph 1 UPKR). At the beginning of the interrogation, the investigator finds out from the accused whether he/she pleads guilty, whether he/she wants to testify on the merits of the charges and in which language. If the accused refuses to testify, the investigator makes a note in the protocol of interrogation. Repeated interrogation of the accused on the same charge if he/she refused to testify at the first interrogation can be carried out only at the request of the accused (Article 173, paragraph 2, 4 UPKR).

1048. The **application of violence, threats and other illegal actions in conducting investigative activities** shall be prohibited (Article 164, paragraph 4 UPKR). The Criminal Code criminalizes several types of conduct with this regard, e.g., obtaining evidence by compulsion (Article 302 UKR), knowingly false testimony, opinion of an expert or specialist, or mistranslation (Article 307 UKR). Moreover, creation of a threat to the life and health of the participants of the investigative activities is not allowed (Article 164, paragraph 4 UPKR). For example, custody of detainees under conditions and in premises that are not adapted for temporary isolation is prohibited within the criminal proceedings.

1049. It is the obligation of the investigator/inquirer to explain to the participants of the criminal proceedings (including suspect, accused,[1116] civil party (claimant),[1117] victim, expert, specialist,[1118] translator) their **rights and responsibilities**. For instance, about the right not to testify against oneself, one's spouse, or close relatives (Article 51, paragraph 1 Const.) or about responsibility for giving false testimony (Article 307 UKR). Another obligation of theirs is to verify the identity of the participants of the criminal proceedings as well as to explain the procedure of conducting an investigative activity (Article 164, paragraph 5 UPKR). For instance, that an investigative activity may involve the application of technical devices and methods for the detection, fixation and seizure of the traces and evidence of the committed crime, such as photo, video, audio devices (Article 164, paragraph 6 UPKR).

1050. A **protocol of investigative action** prepared by the investigator or inquirer shall be compiled in the course of conducting an investigative activity as well as directly after its completion (Articles 164, paragraph 6, 166 UPKR). This is a document that records the contents of investigative action and its results. It certifies its conduction and includes the following information: place, date, starting and ending time with precision of up to a minute; position, name and initials of the person who has compiled the protocol; the name of each person who participated in the investigative activity, and if necessary, their addresses and other identifying information (Article 166, paragraph 3 UPKR).

1116. For the difference in legal status of the suspect and accused, *see* paras. 928–943.
1117. On the legal position of the victim and the civil party (civil claimant), *see* paras. 944–960.
1118. For the difference in legal status of the expert and the specialist, *see* paras. 1003–1018.

1051. The protocol contains factual data on which the circumstances of a crime are established. It serves as the most reliable means of securing the progress and results of the investigative process. One of the preconditions for evidence to be recognized as legal evidence is that evidence shall be documented in a protocol of the investigative action (Articles 74, 74, 166 UPKR). Protocols allow monitoring compliance with the procedural rules. According to these documents, the prosecutor, judge and court can control upon legality and quality of the preliminary investigation and inquiry.

1052. The protocol has to be signed by the investigator/inquirer and the persons who participated in the investigative activity (Article 166, paragraph 7 UPKR).

1053. Investigator may involve a **specialist or expert** (*эксперт*) in the investigative action to assist them in finding, securing and seizing objects and documents (Article 168 UPKR). Criminal procedural provisions provide for certain cases when the involvement of an expert is mandatory, for example, the participation of a forensic medical expert in the exhumation and examination of the corpse (Article 178 UPKR).

1054. The law provides for the participation of **interpreters** (*переводчик*) involved in the preliminary investigation (Articles 59, 169 UPKR). If an accused or another participant of the investigative procedure does not have sufficient command of the language in which the criminal proceedings are conducted, the investigator or inquirer is obliged to ensure the participation of an interpreter. The participation of an interpreter is also mandatory in the case if any participant of the criminal procedure does not have sufficient command of the language but nonetheless expressed the unwillingness of having an interpreter. (Articles 169, paragraph 1, 59 UPKR).

1055. For conducting such investigative actions as search, e.g., of a dwelling (Article 182 UPKR), seizure of electronic storage devices (Article 183, paragraph 3.1. UPKR), personal search (Article 184 UPKR), presenting for identification, e.g., of an object or of a corpse (Article 193 UPKR), the participation of at least two **attesting witnesses** (*понятые*) is necessary (Article 170 UPKR). An attesting witness is a person who is not interested in the outcome of a criminal case; he/she is called by the inquirer or investigator to certify the fact of an investigative measure, its progress and results, e.g., a neighbor or any random person who happens to be around while an investigative measure takes place. Certain persons are not allowed to be attesting witnesses, such as minors or close relatives of the participants of the criminal procedure (Article 60, paragraph 2 UPRK). In a locality that is difficult to access and if there are no proper communication facilities, as well as in the cases when the conduction of an investigative action is connected with danger for the life and health of people, it may be carried out without the participation of attesting witnesses. If so, technical devices shall be applied for documenting its course and results. This information is stipulated in the protocol of an investigative activity (Article 170, paragraph 3 UPKR).

II. The Powers and Duties of the Police in the Preliminary Investigation

1056. The main burden of internal investigation lies on investigators and inquirers of the domestic affairs body—police. The scope of the official duties of the police[1119] (investigators and inquirers of the domestic affairs body), including coercive measures they are authorized to conduct, in addition to the Code of Criminal Procedure, is regulated by the special Federal Law on the Police.[1120] This law cannot contradict the provisions of the Code of Criminal Procedure; it describes the competencies of the police in a more detailed way. Police interventions, including various types of coercive measures, circumstances, and prerequisites for the use of physical force, special means, and weapons, are regulated in this Federal Law. For instance, with regard to the police interventions, the law requires that it must be necessary and proportional. This rule applies to all police activities, in particular to coercive measures and acts.

1057. Chapter 4 OtP provides a list of the types of coercive measures that police officers are authorized to take as well as the limits within which they must be taken, e.g., the performance of some procedural actions requires a prosecutor's or court's authorization. They are the following: detention; entry into residential and other premises and territories; cordoning off (blocking) of territories, dwellings, buildings, and other objects; and the establishment and maintenance of databases on citizens (Articles 14–17 OtP). For instance, due to the right to liberty and personal inviolability, the police can detain only those persons who satisfy criteria established in the law on the Police (e.g., persons suspected of committing a crime or persons who have escaped from custody) and cannot hold them for longer than 48 hours (Article 14, paragraph 1 and 2 OtP).

1058. When carrying out official duties, particularly coercive measures, the police must follow the principles determined by the law, including the following: the principle of maintenance and respect for human rights (Article 5 OtP); the principle of legality,[1121] which requires that duties be carried out in strict accordance with the law (Article 6 OtP); impartiality (Article 7 OtP); and the principle of openness and publicness (Article 8 OtP). In compliance with the Constitution (Articles 2, 17, and 18) and the Criminal Code (Article 7), the principle of maintenance and respect of human rights prohibits the use of violence or other cruel, inhuman, or degrading treatment (Article 5, paragraph 3 OtP). Police officers are obliged to exercise restraint with respect to acts that intentionally inflict pain, physical or mental suffering to a person.

1059. The use of weapons by police officers is legitimate but is restricted to cases provided for by provisions of the law on the Police, for example, for the

1119. For the overview of the investigating authorities, *see* paras. 43–47.
1120. Federal Law on the Police, Feb. 7, 2011, N 3-FZ.
1121. For the principle of legality, *see* Part I, Chapter 1, paras. 197–226.

protection of other persons or themselves from assault if the assault is associated with violence that is dangerous to life or health, as well as for the release of hostages (Article 23, paragraph 1 OtP).

III. Classification of Coercive Measures

1060. All **coercive measures** (*меры принуждения*) in the criminal procedure can be divided into several types depending on the major aim of the pertinent measure.

1061. The first group refers to the measures that **restrict the right to personal freedom**, such as detention (Article 108 UPKR), house arrest (Article 107 UPKR), recognizance not to leave and behave in a proper way (Article 102 UPKR), supervision of accused by the command of a military unit (Article 104 UPKR), supervision of a juvenile accused (Article 105 UPKR).

1062. Other measures can be classified as **restraining constitutional rights by search and seizure.** Among later ones are the following: search (Article 182 UPKR), personal search (Article 184 UPKR), seizure (Article 183 UPKR), search and seizure of postal and telegraph messages (Article 185 UPKR), search and seizure of electronic data (Articles 182, paragraph 9.1, 183, paragraph 3.1 UPKR), monitoring and recording of conversations (Article 186 UPKR), obtaining information about connections between subscribers and (or) the subscriber units (Article 186.1 UPKR); freezing of property (Article 115 UPKR); temporary dismissal from the post (Article 114).

1063. The third type of coercive measure is applied for **securing the order of the proceedings**, such as the obligation to appear to a procedural activity (Article 112 UPKR), forcible bringing to court (Article 113 UPK), disciplinary fine (Article 117 UPKR). These measures, besides a suspect and accused,[1122] can also be applied to other participants of the criminal proceedings, for example, to the witness, victim or translator (Article 111 UPKR).

1064. There are other coercive measures, such as bail (Article 106 UPKR) and personal guarantee (Article 103 UPKR).

1065. Pretrial restrictions or **measures of restriction or prevention** (*меры пресечения*) is a special type of coercive or compulsory measures in the Russian criminal procedure, Article 98 UPKR. They primarily aim at the prevention of committing new criminal actions by the suspects and accused during the preliminary investigation.

1122. For the difference in legal status of the suspect and accused, *see* paras. 928–943.

1066. Measures of restriction are divided into two groups based on the specific characteristics of an individual on whom they are imposed: general and special measures. To the general pretrial restrictions—which can be applied to any suspect or accused—belong the following ones: recognizance not to leave, house arrest, personal guarantee, bail, and detention. Among the special measures—that can be imposed only on the individuals with certain additional characteristics—are the following: supervision of suspect or accused by the command of a military unit (Article 104 UPKR) and supervision of a juvenile suspect or accused by his/her parents, by *in loco parentis*, other trustworthy persons or by the officials of the specialized children's institution (Article 105 UPKR).

IV. Powers to Deprive Personal Freedom

1067. In Russia, everyone shall have the right to freedom and personal immunity, which are given by the Constitution, Article 22 Const.

1068. In compliance with Article 55, paragraphs 2, 3 Const., in the Russian Federation, no laws shall be adopted canceling or derogating human rights and freedoms. The rights and freedoms of man and citizen may be limited by the Federal Law only to such an extent to which it is necessary for the protection of the fundamental principles of the constitutional system, morality, health, the rights and lawful interests of other people, for ensuring the defense of the country and security of the state.

1069. Coercive measures that restrict the right to personal freedom can be conducted only on the grounds defined in the law and on the basis of legal proceedings (Article 22, paragraph 2 Const., Article 7 UPKR). Arrest, taking into custody and detention shall be allowed only by a court decision. Without the court's decision, a person may be detained for a term more than 48 hours (Article 22, paragraph 2 Const.).

1070. Detention is discussed in a more detailed way later in this chapter.[1123]

A. House Arrest

1071. The main limitation associated with the use of such measure of restriction as house arrest (Article 107 UPKR) lies in the fact that the accused or the suspect is not free to move, i.e., his/her freedom to leave the place of his/her permanent or temporary residence (apartment, house, villa, etc.) is deprived.

1072. There can be imposed other restrictions in addition to the main limitation, such as prohibition to communicate with certain people, prohibition to send and

1123. For pre-trial detention, *see* paras. 1049–1167.

receive correspondence, prohibition to use any means of communication, e.g., telephone, internet (Article 107, paragraph 7 UPKR).

1073. By the imposition of the measure, the court selects the pertinent scope of restrictions taking into account the personality of the suspect/accused,[1124] the facts of the case, age, health, marital status, and other relevant circumstances, as well as the severity of the charges (Article 107, paragraphs 7, 8 UPKR). In some cases, only certain additional restriction(s) of the available ones within this measure is imposed, for instance, if the complete isolation of a person is not justified. However, in the case when the prohibition against using the means of communication has been imposed, the suspect or accused cannot be limited in his/her right to call emergency services, e.g., medical, law enforcement etc. On each of such calls, the suspect/accused shall inform the supervisory authority (Article 107, paragraph 8 UPKR).

1074. The house arrest can be imposed only by a court decision (Article 107, paragraph 1 UPKR). The request on the application of a preventive measure in the form of house arrest can be initiated by a prosecutor or investigator. The term of the house arrest (its maximum term as well) is counted as the term of detention/custody (Articles 107, paragraph 2.1, 109 UPKR).

B. Recognizance Not to Leave

1075. The pretrial restriction 'recognizance not to leave and behave in a proper way', Article 102 UPKR, consists in assuming in writing an obligation of the suspect or of the accused:

- to not leave the place of his permanent or temporary residence without the permission of the inquirer, of the investigator, of the public prosecutor or of the court;
- to come at the appointed time on the summons of the inquirer, of the investigator and of the public prosecutor, as well as to the court;
- to not interfere with the proceedings on the criminal case in any other way.

1076. The accused (the suspect) is warned that in the case of violation of the obligations imposed on him/her with this measure, a stricter pretrial restriction can be applied.

C. Supervision of the Accused by the Command of a Military Unit

1077. As pointed out above, this pretrial restriction belongs to the so-called special measures that can be imposed only on the subjects with certain characteristics.

1124. For the difference in legal status of the suspect and accused, *see* paras. 928–943.

1078. The supervision of the accused by the command of a military unit (Article 104 UPKR) can be called as de facto "recognizance not to leave and behave in a proper way" for the military servicemen (women) (Article 104, paragraph 1 UPKR). It applies only to soldiers and citizens on military reserve duty. On them can be imposed restrictions stipulated by the Charter of the Armed Forces of the Russian Federation, such as a temporary ban on the right to carry weapons, the prohibition on leaving the military unit, the ban on work outside the military unit, the ban on guard duty and other responsible duties etc.[1125]

1079. The goal of the measure coincides with the aim of the "recognizance not to leave." This is to ensure the attendance of the suspect/accused[1126] at the appointed time on the summons of the inquirer, investigator, public prosecutor, as well as to the court. The measure is also invoked to ensure that the suspect/accused does not hinder the proceedings on the criminal case in any other way.

1080. The imposition of the supervision of the accused by the command of a military unit shall be permitted only with the consent of the suspect/accused (Article 104, paragraph 2 UPKR). However, the consent of the military unit for the execution of this measure is not required.

D. Supervision of a Juvenile Accused

1081. This coercive measure—supervision of a juvenile accused (Article 105 UPKR)—belongs to the group of the "special measures" and can be imposed only on the juvenile suspects/accused.[1127]

1082. Supervision of juvenile suspect/accused presupposes that his/her lawful behavior, which is embodied in the compliance of the goal of the pretrial restriction 'recognizance not to leave and behave in a proper way' (Article 102 UPKR), is guaranteed.

1083. The guarantors of the realization of the ensuring the attendance of the juvenile suspect/accused at the appointed time on the summons of the inquirer, investigator, public prosecutor, court and the fact that the suspect/accused does not hinder the criminal proceedings are defined by the law. These can be the parents of the juvenile, his/her *in loco parentis*, other trustworthy persons or the officials of the specialized children's institution. They give a written obligation to fulfill their

1125. Instructions for the Inquiry Bodies of the Armed Forces of the Russian Federation, approved by the Chief Military Prosecutor and entered into force by order of the Minister of Defense of the Russian Federation, N 275, Aug. 18, 1994; Barabash, Priroda rossijskogo ugolovnogo processa, 2005, p. 156; Radchenko, Kommentarij k UPKR, p. 150.

1126. For the difference in legal status of the suspect and accused, *see* paras. 928–943.

1127. For the difference in legal status of the suspect and accused, *see* paras. 928–943.

duties. They are warned as well about the responsibility in the case of the failure to fulfill their duties, e.g., disciplinary fine (Articles 105, paragraph 2, 103, paragraph 4 UPKR).

1084. The measure is applied upon the request or with the consent of the parents, of *in loco parentis* or other trustworthy persons. The consent of the officials of the specialized children's institutions is not required. They are entitled to take the measures of supervision in accordance with the internal rules of the institution, such as entrust the supervision of the juvenile to one of the teachers, put limitations on the accused regarding his/her leave of the institution as well as on the meetings with others, etc.

V. Powers of Search and Seizure

1085. Other measures can be classified as **restraining constitutional rights by search and seizure.** Among later ones are the following: search (Article 182 UPKR), personal search (Article 184 UPKR), seizure (Article 183 UPKR), search and seizure of postal and telegraph messages (Article 185 UPKR), search and seizure of electronic data (Articles 182, paragraph 9.1 and183, paragraph 3.1 UPKR), monitoring and recording of conversations (Article 186 UPKR), obtaining information about connections between subscribers and (or) the subscriber units (Article 186.1 UPKR); freezing of property (Article 115 UPKR); temporary dismissal from the post (Article 114).

1086. No laws shall be adopted canceling or derogating human rights and freedoms, Article 55, paragraphs 2, 3 Const. The rights and freedoms of man and citizen may be limited by the Federal Law only. The measures that restrain constitutional rights by search and seizure shall be based on the law and allowed by a court decision. Hence, all the investigative measures below require a prior written decision, except for personal search.[1128]

A. Search and Seizure of Evidence

1087. Legal ground for conducting a **search** is considered the existence of sufficient information to believe that in a place, e.g., dwelling, can be kept the means and tools used for committing a crime as well as other objects, documents and valuables which may prove to be of importance to the criminal case (Article 182 UPKR).[1129] The search may also be aimed at finding the wanted persons and the corpses (Article 182, paragraph 16 UPKR).

1088. A search in dwellings as a coercive measure can be conducted only on the ground of a judicial decision (Articles 182, paragraph 3, 165 UPKR).

1128. *For personal search, see* paras. 1098–1101.
1129. Decision of the Constitutional Court of the Russian Federation N 33-P, Dec. 17, 2015.

1089. Before the start of the search and seizure of the evidence, the investigator is obliged to present the court´s decision permitting the search and seizure as well as has an obligation to suggest the person give out voluntarily the items that may be of importance for the criminal case (Article 183, paragraph 5 UPKR). In the case, when the objects are given out voluntarily, and there are no grounds for an apprehension that they may be concealed, the investigator has the right not to perform the search and seizure of the evidence (Articles 182, paragraphs 4, 5, 183, paragraph 5 UPKR).

1090. While carrying out the search, the objects and the documents which are of illegal possession, e.g., a weapon without permission, are seized in any case (Article 182, paragraph 9 UPKR).

1091. The seized objects, documents and valuables shall be presented to the attesting witnesses and to the other persons present at the search. Some items, if necessary, shall be packed and sealed at the scene of the search. It has to be certified with the signatures of the persons present.

1092. According to Article 183, paragraph 3 UPKR, the seizure of the objects and documents which contain state secrets or other kinds of secrets information protected by the Federal Law, such as information on the deposits and the bank accounts, is permitted only on the ground of the judicial decision

1093. When a search is conducted, a defense counsel, as well as a lawyer of the person whose premises are searched, are entitled to be present. (Article 182, paragraphs 10, 11 UPKR).

1094. In the search protocol, besides the place and all the circumstances of the conducting a search shall be documented, all the seized objects, documents and valuables must be listed, with a precise indication of their quantity, weight, individual features and, if possible, their cost (Article 182, paragraph 13 UPKR).

1095. The investigator has certain rights and obligations while conducting the search.

1096. When conducting a search, any premises may be opened if the owner refuses to open them voluntarily. In this case, the investigator has to ensure that no unnecessary damage is done to the property. The investigator shall take all measures to prevent the disclosure of the circumstances of the private life, family secrets of the person, in whose dwelling the search was performed, as well as of the circumstances of the private lives of other persons exposed during the search (Article 182, paragraph 7 UPKR).

1097. The investigator has the right to put certain limitations on other persons participating in the conduction of this coercive measure; such as the right to prohibit the persons present at the place of the search to leave this place and/or to communicate with one another or with the other persons until the end of the search (Article 182, paragraph 8 UPKR).

B. Personal Search

1098. Personal search is conducted according to the general rules of the search (Articles 182, 184 UPKR).

1099. A personal search is conducted if there are reasons to believe that a person possesses any means and/or tools used for committing a crime as well as other objects, documents and valuables, which may prove to be of importance to the criminal case (Article 184 UPKR).

1100. The personal search is performed on the basis of the resolution of the investigator (Article 182, paragraph 2 UPKR). However, the personal search may be carried out in the absence of the resolution, if the person is put into custody, and also if there are sufficient grounds to believe that the person is in possession of any objects relevant to the criminal case (Article 184, paragraph 2 UPKR).

1101. The personal search may be conducted only by a person of the same sex and in the presence of the attesting witnesses and of the specialists of the same sex if they are taking part in the pertinent investigative action (Article 184, paragraph 3 UPKR).

C. Seizure and Copying of Electronic Data

1102. Until 2018, the general rules of the search and seizure of evidence were applicable to the search and seizure of electronic data.[1130] In 2018, Article 164.1 UPKR that regulates the withdrawal of electronic information carriers and copying information from them in the criminal proceedings was introduced to the Code of Criminal Procedure by the new Federal Law.[1131] Seizure and copying of electronic data are carried out by investigating authorities; however, service/telecommunication providers and other non-state actors have an obligation to collaborate.

1103. According to Article 164.1 UPKR, the seizure of electronic information carriers is not allowed, except when:

1130. Federal Law, Jul. 28, 2012, N 143-FZ.
1131. Federal Law, Dec. 27, 2018, N 533-FZ.

- the seizure of electronic storage media is based on a court decision or;
- there is a court decision on a forensic examination in relation to electronic storage media or;
- electronic information carriers contain information that can be used to commit new crimes or copying of which—according to a specialist—may lead to its loss or change.

1104. Electronic storage media are seized during investigative proceedings with the participation of a specialist. Information can be copied upon the request of the legal owner of the information. Information is copied (unless the copying is prohibited due to the possibility of the loss of information) to other electronic storage media provided by the legal owner of the seized electronic storage media or by the owner of the information contained therein. The legal owner of the information gets a copy of the data.

1105. The investigator is entitled to copy the information contained in the electronic information carrier. Electronic media containing information copied from other electronic media during the investigation are attached to the protocol (Article 164.1 paragraph 3 UPKR).

1106. With regard to the localization of data, the extension of searches on servers outside of Russia is possible only if jurisdiction is justified through one of the principles governing the exercise of extraterritorial criminal jurisdiction:[1132] the nationality principle, the protective principle, the universality principle, and the patronizing principle.[1133] For instance, the application of Russian criminal law can be justified through the protective principle (Article 12, paragraph 3 UKR) that aims to protect domestic interests that can be injured by foreign nationals outside the territory of the Russian Federation by means of national regulations.[1134] If the content is prohibited in other countries, these countries can legitimately claim their jurisdiction based, e.g., on the territoriality or protective principle.[1135]

1132. For the extraterritorial jurisdiction, *see* paras. 282–303; Paramonova, Extraterritorial jurisdiction in Russia. In: Sieber, U. / Forster, S. / Jarvers, K. (ed(s).): National Criminal Law in a Comparative Legal Context. Volume 2.1: General limitations on the application of criminal law. Berlin, Duncker & Humblot, 2011, p. 299.
1133. For the overview of the principles governing the exercise of criminal jurisdiction, *see* paras. 263–303; Kruglikov, Kommentarii k Ugolovnomu Kodeksu RF, pp. 28–31; Naumov, Rossiiskoe ugolovnoe pravo, p. 231.
1134. Paramonova, Extraterritorial jurisdiction in Russia. In: Sieber, U. / Forster, S. / Jarvers, K. (ed(s).): National Criminal Law in a Comparative Legal Context. Volume 2.1: General limitations on the application of criminal law. Berlin, Duncker & Humblot, 2011, p. 308.
1135. Paramonova, Challenges for Criminal Law and International Criminal Law in Cyberspace. In: Justice Report. Canadian Criminal Justice Association, 2014, Issue/Volume 29, N 4, pp. 26–29; Paramonova, Internationales Strafrecht im Cyberspace: Strafrechtliche Analyse der Rechtslage in Deutschland, Russland und den USA (Criminal Jurisdiction in Cyberspace: Legal Situation in Germany, Russia and the USA). Wiesbaden / Berlin, Springer-Verlag, 2013, pp. 128–158.

D. Seizure and Inspection of Postal and Telegraph Dispatches

1107. If there are sufficient grounds to suppose that objects, documents or information of importance for the criminal case may be contained in postal parcels or in other mail and telegraph dispatches, or in telegrams or radiograms, they may be put under arrest, seized and/or inspected (Article 185, paragraph 1 UPKR).

1108. The conduction of this coercive measure is possible only on the ground of a court decision. The copy of this decision is immediately directed to the postal/telegraph offices that are obliged to keep the correspondence and immediately inform the investigator upon its arrival (Articles 185, paragraphs 2, 4, 165 UPKR). If necessary, the investigator can invite a specialist as well as an interpreter for taking part in the examination and in the seizure of the postal and telegraph dispatches (Article 185, paragraph 5 UPKR).

1109. The arrest of the postal and telegraph dispatches can be canceled by the investigator with obligatory notification of the court, which has taken the decision on the arrest, and the prosecutor, if the measure is no longer needed. However, it cannot be canceled before the end of the preliminary investigation of the criminal case (Article 185, paragraph 6 UPKR).

E. Monitoring and Recording of Conversations

1110. If there are sufficient grounds to suppose that telephone and other conversations of the suspect, the accused, or other persons may contain essential information for the criminal case, monitoring and recording of the conversations can be permitted on the ground of a court decision (Articles 186, paragraph 1, 165 UPKR). This coercive measure is not applicable with regard to the cases that involve crimes of small gravity, such as destruction or damage of property by negligence.[1136]

1111. In compliance with the legal provisions, monitoring and recording of conversations are carried out strictly by investigating authorities; however, service/telecommunication providers and other non-state actors have an obligation to collaborate, if necessary. The monitoring and recording of the telephone (including internet communication, e.g., VoIP) and other conversations are admissible in the case of the threat of the use of violence, extortion or other criminal actions with respect to the victim, the witness or to their close relatives or persons. The measure is imposed upon a written request of the pertinent persons and on the ground of a court decision (Article 186, paragraph 2 UPKR).

1112. The measure can be imposed for a term of up to six months. Its performance is ended by the resolution of the investigator when the conduction of the

1136. For the categories of crimes, *see* paras. 34, 638–646.

monitoring and recording is no longer needed. It cannot be terminated before the preliminary investigation has been completed (Article 186, paragraph 5 UPKR).

F. Obtaining Information about Connections Between Subscribers and (or) the Subscriber Units

1113. The coercive measure "production order about connections between subscribers and (or) the subscriber units" (Article 186.1 UPKR) is imposed according to the same rules as the monitoring and recording of the telephone and other conversations (Article 186 UPKR). The obligation to provide this information has all types of organizations (state and non-state) that provide any type of communication services, including service/telecommunication providers etc.

1114. The measure can be imposed for a term of a maximum of six months and only on the ground of the judicial decision. The organization of the communication services is obliged to provide the investigator with the required information on the connections between subscribers as it becomes available, but not less than once a week (Article 186.1, paragraph 4 UPKR). The investigator is allowed to involve the specialist to interpret the information.

1115. The conduction of the measure is ended by the resolution of the investigator when its performance is no longer necessary. It cannot be terminated before the preliminary investigation has been completed (Article 186, paragraph 5 UPKR).

G. Temporary Dismissal from the Post

1116. The coercive measure as 'temporary dismissal from the post' (Article 114 UPKR) can be imposed on the suspect/accused[1137] if it is necessary for the investigation, e.g., to preserve evidence. The measure can be required, for example, if the accused can manipulate the documents that serve as evidentiary information if he/she continues to work at his/her current post.

1117. The request for the imposition of such a measure can be lodged by the inquirer or the investigator before the court. The judge shall pass a decision on it within 48 hours from the moment of the arrival of the request (Article 114, paragraph 2 UPKR).

1118. The temporary dismissal of the suspect/accused from the post is canceled by the resolution of the inquirer or the investigator when the application of this measure is no longer necessary (Article 114, paragraph 4 UPKR).

1137. For the difference in legal status of the suspect and accused, *see* paras. 928–943.

H. Freezing of Property (Arrest of Property)

1119. To ensure the execution of the civil suit and possible proprietary recoverables, such as fines, penalties, for instance, confiscation of property (Article 104.1 UKR) freezing of property of a suspect, accused or of persons legally bearing material responsibility for their actions (Article 115, paragraph 1 UPKR). An investigator with the consent of the head of the investigative body or an inquirer with the consent of the prosecutor is entitled to request the imposition of this pretrial coercive measure before the court.

1120. This coercive measure consists of the temporary seizure of property from its owner or possessor with the prohibition to dispose and use the property (Article 115, paragraph 2 UPKR).

1121. When deciding on the seizure of property, the court must indicate the specific factual circumstances that justify the imposition of the limits related to possession, use and disposal of the property that has been frozen. The court is obliged to specify the time period for the freezing of property (Article 115, paragraph 1, 3 UPKR).

1122. The freezing of property may be imposed on the property of other persons besides property of a suspect, accused or of persons legally bearing material responsibility for them. It is possible in the case when there are reasonable grounds to believe that the property was obtained as a result of the criminal actions of the suspect or accused. Other 'reasonable grounds' in this case can be that the property was used as a weapon or as other means to commit a crime as well as it was used for financing terrorism, or extremist activity (extremism), or for financing illegal activities of organized criminal groups, illegal armed formations, criminal organizations, Article 115, paragraph 3 UPKR.

1123. Freezing of property cannot be imposed on the property that is in accordance with the Civil Procedure Code of the Russian Federation cannot be seized, e.g., things of the first necessity (Article 115, paragraph 4 UPKR).

VI. Coercive Measures Securing the Order of the Proceedings

1124. Among the coercive measures that are applied for **securing the order of the proceedings** are the following ones: the obligation to appear to a procedural activity (Article 112 UPKR), the forcible bringing to court (Article 113 UPK), and the disciplinary fine (Article 117 UPKR).

1125. If necessary, from the suspect and the accused,[1138] as well as from the victim or the witness, may be taken an **obligation to appear** (Article 112, paragraph

1138. For the difference in legal status of the suspect and accused, *see* paras. 928–943.

1 UPKR). It consists of a written commitment of the person to appear upon the summons of the inquirer, the investigator, or to the court. The person is also obliged in the case of the change of the place of residence to immediately inform the pertinent state bodies about the change.

1126. In the case of the violation of the rules of the imposed measure, the person bears responsibility unless there are serious reasons interfering with the appearance in response to the summons at the fixed time. For instance, if he/she fails to appear at the summons without serious reasons, the suspect and the accused, as well as the victim and the witness, may be brought forcibly to the court or to any other investigating body (Article 113, paragraph 1 UPKR).

1127. A **forcible bringing** consists of taking the person under coercion to the inquirer, the investigator, or to the court. There are, however, exceptions to the rule. A forcible bringing cannot be carried out at night time unless it is urgent, and the matter cannot be delayed (Article 113, paragraph 5 UPKR). The minors under 14 years of age, pregnant women, and sick persons who cannot leave the place of their stay due to the poor health condition are not subject to a forcible bringing (Article 113, paragraph 6 UPKR).

1128. Another coercive measure that can be imposed on the participants of the criminal proceedings in the case of noncompliance with their procedural obligations and also in the case of their disorderly conduct in the courtroom is a **disciplinary fine** (Article 117).

VII. Miscellaneous

1129. There are other coercive measures, such as bail (Article 106 UPKR) and personal guarantee (Article 103 UPKR).

A. Bail

1130. Bail is a pretrial measure of restriction that is applied to the suspect or accused on the ground of the court decision for the purpose of preventing him/her from committing new crimes as well as for the fulfillment by the suspect/accused of his/her obligations during the criminal proceedings, e.g., appear upon the summons of the inquirer, investigator, public prosecutor, or to the court.

1131. Bail as a coercive measure is applied to the suspect or the accused by the court. The suspect, the accused or another person or entity are entitled to request the application of bail before the court (Article 106, paragraph 2 UPKR).

1132. Bail as a restrictive measure is possible only on a voluntary basis. The pledgor is entitled to refuse the application of the measure under certain conditions, for example, his/her exceptional difficult financial circumstances. If the bail is imposed instead of the previously applied measure of restriction, the latter is valid until the bail has been deposited/pledged. This way, if the bail is imposed instead of detention or house arrest, the suspect (accused) shall remain in custody or under house arrest until the bail has been deposited. The court, in its decision or ruling on the application of the bail, sets a deadline for its deposition (Article 106, paragraphs 7, 8 UPKR).

1133. Bail is executed through deposing money (or other legal valuable assets) on the bank account of the body that requested the coercive measure. At the phase of the preliminary investigation, the money/values shall be transferred to the account of the inquiry or investigating body that is in charge of the criminal case, and at the stage of judicial proceedings—to the account of the court (Article 106, paragraphs 1, 2 UPKR).

1134. If the deposit is paid by the person who is not a suspect or accused in the case, such a person must be informed about the criminal charges of the suspect/accused as well as about the legal consequences and penalties that occur in the event of violating the rules of the pretrial restriction by the suspect/accused (Article 106, paragraph 6 UPKR).

1135. The type and amount of the bail are determined by the court with regard to the severity of the offense, personal data of the suspect/accused as well as with regard to the financial status of the pledgor. The Code of Criminal Procedure provides for several limitations regarding the size of the imposed bail as a pretrial restriction for certain crimes. Thus, regarding criminal cases involving grave crimes, the amount of bail may not be less than RUB 5,000, which is about USD 89,000 (Article 106 paragraph 3 UPKR.).[1139]

1136. The bail is classified as one of the riskiest and strictest measures because there is a high risk of the loss of the property belonging to the pledgor. The deposit can be forfeited to the state on the ground of the court´s judgment in the case of violation of the bail conditions by the suspect/accused (Articles 106, paragraph 4, 118, 106, paragraph 9 UPKR). In all other cases, the bail has to be returned to the pledgor on the basis of the judicial decision. If the criminal proceedings on the case have been terminated, the bail must be returned to the pledgor upon the ruling of the investigator or inquirer (Article 106, paragraph 10 UPKR).

B. Personal Guarantee

1137. The coercive measure that ensures the fulfillment by the suspect/accused of his/her obligations during the criminal proceedings, e.g., appear upon the summons of the inquirer, investigator, public prosecutor, or to the court, is a personal guarantee. It requires a written form and shall be given by a person worthy of trust (Article 103 UPKR).

1139. For the categories of crimes, *see* paras 34, 638–646.

1138. This pretrial restriction can be imposed only with the consent of the suspect/accused upon request of one or several guarantors.

1139. The guarantors are warned about the responsibility in the form of the fine if the suspect/accused does not fulfill the obligations imposed on him/her (Article 103, paragraph 4 UPKR).

§2. Powers, Rights and Duties within the Framework of the Pretrial Detention

I. Introductory Remarks and Influence of the ECtHR

1140. The Russian Constitution entitles the court to decide on the imposition of all the measures that **deprive personal freedom, including pretrial** detention of suspects and accused[1140] in committing crimes (Article 22, paragraph 2 Const.). This position corresponds to Article 5, paragraph 4 of the ECHR.

1141. Previously, the imposition of such pretrial restrictions as arrest and detention were upon the discretion of the prosecutor, who in most cases made the decision in absentia, i.e., in the absence of a person who has been arrested/detained. The prosecutor was obliged to interrogate only some categories of persons, e.g., juveniles.

1142. The judicial procedure that was introduced with regard to the imposition of the measures that deprive personal freedom was aimed at the adoption of the lawful mechanism for legal and just decisions. The provision of the Constitution (Article 22) became effective after the criminal procedure legislation was amended in conformity with the international law norms. According to the amended version of the Code of Criminal Procedure (Article 29, paragraph 2 UPKR),[1141] only the court, including the stage of the pretrial proceedings, is entitled to make decisions on conducting measures of restriction in the form of detention as well as on its extension.

1143. The imposition of the pretrial detention as a restrictive measure in the preliminary investigation that has, first, a preventive goal in hindering the accused to commit new criminal acts, second, aims at maintaining evidence, third, ensure the attendance of the accused at the procedure.

1144. Since Russia's accession to the Council of Europe and recognition of the jurisdiction of the ECtHR in 1998, the Court has delivered more than 600 judgments finding inhuman and degrading treatment of individuals in Russia's restricted-access detention facilities, among them pretrial detention facilities.

1140. For the difference in legal status of the suspect and accused, *see* paras. 928–943.
1141. Federal Law Dec. 18, 2001, N 174-FZ.

1145. The judgment in *Kalashnikov v. Russia*[1142] of July 2002 was the first judgment against Russia concerning detention conditions in pretrial detention centers (SIZOs), followed by more than 200 similar cases, which now form the *Kalashnikov* group of cases, pending implementation before the Committee of Ministers. The judgments in the *Kalashnikov* group of cases address the problems of cell overcrowding in SIZOs and inadequate detention conditions, such as a lack of separation between the sanitary and living areas, limited access to natural light, and problems with water, heating and ventilation.[1143]

1146. In January 2012, the Court also issued a pilot judgment in *Ananyev and others v. Russia.*[1144] There, the ECtHR separately addressed the excessive recourse to detention on remand as a preventive measure and the need to take steps at the domestic level to ensure that remand in custody be used only as an exceptional measure. It stated the need for a domestic remedy for appealing detention conditions and obtaining compensation. The Court also noted that the award of compensation should not be conditional on the claimant's ability to prove the fault of officials or bodies and the unlawfulness of their actions.[1145]

1147. Over the years, Russia has, in turn, made substantial efforts to improve pretrial detention conditions.[1146] In particular, the extent of SIZOs overcrowding has tangibly decreased. Although certain facilities continue to fall short of the minimum standard of floor space per person, the nightmarish situation of the 1990s is now mostly a thing of the past. However, a number of problems persist. Still common is the use of unsuitable cells at police stations for prolonged and overnight detention. Many temporary detention wards at all police stations are not designed for overnight detention; rooms for detainees are equipped with narrow wooden benches, which serve as beds for persons detained overnight; mattresses are generally unavailable. This problem has become particularly relevant in recent years due to a growing number of arrests of peaceful protesters.

1148. The lack of proper detention conditions at police stations has repeatedly been challenged in Russian courts, and a few cases have been taken to the Court. In particular, the cases of *Kalmykova and others v. Russia*[1147] that have been added to *Kapustin v. Russia*[1148] and 18 other applications.

1142. *Kalashnikov v. Russia*, July 15, 2002, App. No. 47095/99.
1143. Taubina, Natalia, How do European Court Judgements influence detention conditions in Russia? Dec., 2017: http://www.einnetwork.org/ein-voices.
1144. *Ananyev and others v. Russia,* Jan. 2012, App. No. 42525/07 and 60800/08.
1145. Taubina, Natalia, How do European Court Judgements influence detention conditions in Russia? Dec., 2017: http://www.einnetwork.org/ein-voices.
1146. Interim report/Plan of action on execution of pilot judgment Ananyev and others v. Russia; Russian NGO Shadow Report on the Observance of the Convention against Torture and Other Cruel, Inhuman or Degrading Treatment or Punishment by the Russian Federation for the period from 2006 to 2012.
1147. *Kalmykova and others v. Russia,* Nov. 1, 2015, App. No. 56516/15.
1148. *Kapustin v. Russia*, June 30, 2017, App. No. 36801/09.

II. The Conditions for the Pretrial Detention

1149. The pretrial detention as a measure of restriction (Article 108 UPKR) is applied only on the ground of judicial decision to the suspect/accused of committing crimes, for which the envisaged criminal punishment in the form of imprisonment exceeds the term of three years.

1150. In exceptional cases, the pretrial detention may be imposed on the suspect or accused of committing a crime that is punishable by imprisonment for up to three years if one of the following requirements is fulfilled:

- the suspect/accused does not have a permanent residence on the territory of the Russian Federation;
- the identity of the suspect/accused has not been established;
- the suspect/accused violated the previously imposed pretrial restriction;
- the suspect/accused escaped from the investigating bodies or the court.

1151. The imposition of this pretrial restriction is legal only if the court justifies the impossibility to apply a different milder coercive measure. This way, the court, in its decision, is obliged to outline concrete factual circumstances that served as the grounds for the judgment. Such circumstances cannot be the information that has not been proved during the trial proceedings on the imposition of this measure, in particular the results of the investigative activities that were obtained in violation of the evidentiary law (Article 89 UPKR).[1149]

1152. Detention as a preventive measure cannot be applied in respect of the suspect or accused of committing certain economic and tax crimes that did not include any elements of physical violence, such as fraud, forgery, illegal entrepreneurship, etc. However, in this case, four exceptional conditions for the pretrial detention mentioned above shall be absent (Article 108, paragraph 1.1 UPKR).

1153. With regard to juveniles, the pretrial detention can be chosen as a measure of restriction if he/she is suspected or accused of committing a grave or especially grave crime, e.g., murder. In exceptional cases, this preventive measure may also be imposed on the juvenile when a crime of medium gravity has been committed (Article 108, paragraph 2 UPKR).[1150]

III. The Procedure of Imposition and Decisions Made Regarding the Pretrial Detention

1154. The request for the imposition of the pretrial detention is lodged with the court by the investigator with the consent of the head of the investigative body or by the inquirer with the consent of the prosecutor (Article 108, paragraph 3 UPKR).

1149. On the rules of evidence, *see* Part II, Chapter 1, paras. 961–967.
1150. For the categories of crimes, *see* paras. 34, 638–646.

The request shall contain the reasons and the grounds that prove the necessity of the pretrial detention as well as the grounds of the impossibility to choose a different restriction measure.

1155. In some urgent cases that are stipulated in Articles 91 and 92 UPKR, such as when a person was caught red-handed or when the victims or witnesses point out the person who has committed a crime, the request must be filed to the judge no later than 8 hours before the expiration of the period of detention, which cannot last more than 48 hours (Articles 94, paragraph 2, 108, paragraph 3 UPKR).

1156. The decision on the imposition of the pretrial detention is considered by a single judge of the district court or a military court of a corresponding level with the obligatory participation of the suspect or accused, the public prosecutor, and defense counsel (Article 108, paragraph 4 UPKR). The legal representative of a juvenile suspect or accused, the head of the investigating body, the investigator, and the inquirer are entitled to participate in the court session.

1157. The absence of the participants of the court proceedings that were notified of the court hearing without a serious reason is not an obstacle for consideration of the application, except in cases of absence of the accused. The imposition of pretrial detention in the absence of the accused is allowed only in the case if the accused is on the international wanted list (Article 108, paragraph 5 UPKR).

1158. Having considered the petition, the judge makes one of the following decisions:

- imposition on the suspect or the accused the coercive measure in the form of detention;
- dismissal of the application;
- extension of the period of detention.

1159. The **imposition** of the measure shall occur immediately. The judicial decision is sent to the person who initiated the request, to the prosecutor, to the suspect/ accused and to the victim (Article 108 p. 8 UPKR).

1160. In the case of detention of the accused/suspect, the person in charge of the criminal case (investigator or inquirer) is obliged to inform immediately about the place of detention of the suspect or accused or its change any of his/her close relatives. If the accused/suspect does not have such, then other relatives shall be informed. If a soldier or a police officer has been detained, the information about their place of detention additionally has to be provided to the command of the military unit or to the head of the pertinent body of internal affairs, accordingly (Article 108, paragraph 12 UPKR).

1161. In the case of **dismissal** of the application, the judge is entitled on his/her own initiative to choose detention as a pretrial restriction if the grounds provided for in Article 97 UPKR are present, such as the danger that the accused evades preliminary investigation or/and trial proceedings or he/she may threaten the witness or other participants of the criminal proceedings.

1162. If the application was dismissed, a repeated request on the imposition of the pretrial detention regarding the same person and within the same criminal case is possible only in the event of the newly discovered circumstances justifying the necessity of the person´s detention (Article 108, paragraph 9 UPKR).[1151]

1163. If detention was considered legal and justified, its **extension** can be imposed by the court. However, the period of extension cannot exceed 72 hours from the moment of passing a judgment on the request of one of the parties on the submission of additional evidence on whether the pretrial detention is justified or not (Article 108, paragraph 7 UPKR).

1164. It is prohibited to give the powers to decide on the imposition of pretrial detention as a coercive measure to the same judge on a permanent basis. These powers are shared between the judges in accordance with the principle of the jurisdiction of the pertinent criminal cases (Article 108, paragraph 13 UPKR).

IV. The Review of the Pretrial Detention and its Termination

1165. The judicial decision on the imposition of the pretrial detention or a dismissal of the request can be appealed according to the rules of appeal (Article 389.3 UPKR). The court´s ruling can be appealed within three days after the decision has been passed.[1152] The court of appeal shall decide on the complaint not later than three days from the date of its entry.

1166. The decision of the court of appeal to abolish the decision of the judge on the imposition of the pretrial detention has to be executed immediately. The decision of the court of appeal may be challenged in the court of cassation (Chapter 47.1 UPKR).[1153]

1167. The **termination** of the pretrial detention occurs on the same grounds as the termination of the investigation, such as noninvolvement of the suspect or accused in the committing crime (Article 27, paragraph 1 UPKR), absence of the event of a crime (Article 24, paragraph 1 UPKR), termination of the criminal proceedings in connection with the parties' reconciliation (Article 25 UPKR) and others.[1154]

1151. Decision of the Constitutional Court of the Russian Federation N 4-P, Mar. 22, 2005.
1152. For the Legal Remedies, *see* Chapter 3. The Trial, §4 Legal Remedies.
1153. For the Legal Remedies, *see* Chapter 3. The Trial, §4 Legal Remedies.
1154. For the termination of the investigation, *see*, *see* paras. 898–926

Chapter 3. The Trial

1168. As discussed above, Russian criminal procedure is divided into three main stages: pretrial stage (that includes the initiation of a criminal case and a preliminary investigation in one of the forms: pretrial investigation or inquiry), the court procedure or the **trial** (*судебное производство*), and the execution of sentence.

1169. The trial is the central stage of the criminal procedure, which consists of three substages: the preparatory stage of the trial, the trial investigation, and the stage of appeal.

1170. This chapter addresses the preparatory stage of the trial (Chapters 33 and 34 UPKR) and the trial investigation, where evidence obtained in the preliminary investigation are examined (Chapters 35–42 UPKR). A further part of the chapter is devoted to the legal remedies (Chapters 43–45 UPKR). Some special procedures of the court are outlined, e.g., court procedure if there is a plea bargaining agreement.

§1. The Preparatory Stage of the Trial

1171. The trial stage of the criminal proceedings can be launched by filing the indictment to the court. After receiving the indictment, the court launches the preparatory stage of the trial (Chapters 33 and 34 UPKR).

1172. The preparation of the trial investigation marks the first substage of the trial proceedings. The purpose of the preparatory part is to ensure that the trial investigation is carried out in strict accordance with the law, without any long delays, and provides the preconditions to the court, in compliance with the principle of immediacy with respect to evidence (Article 240 UPKR) of the direct investigation of the evidence and establishing the facts of the case (Article 227 UPKR).

1173. Preparation of the trial is conducted by the sentencing court. The questions that have to be decided at the preparatory stage do not require the examination of evidence but determine the further procedural movement of the criminal case.

1174. According to Article 228 UPKR, during the preparation of the trial, the following questions shall be clarified by the presiding judge with respect to every of the accused:

(1) whether the criminal case is within the jurisdiction of the court;
(2) whether the copies of the indictment have been received by all the participants;
(3) whether the selected coercive measure is subject to cancellation or to a change as well as whether the duration of the house arrest or the detention is subject to an extension;
(4) whether the lodged requests and complaints are subject to satisfaction;

(5) whether the measures have been taken to ensure the execution of the penalty in the form of a fine;
(6) whether measures have been taken for the compensation of the damage caused by the committing a crime, for the confiscation of the property, if applicable;
(7) the question of the extension of the freezing of property as a coercive measure has to be clarified;
(8) whether there are grounds for conducting a preliminary hearing (Article 229 UPKR).

1175. After consideration of the abovementioned questions, the court is entitled to take one of the following **decisions** upon the received case (Article 227, paragraph 1 UPKR):

- on transfer the criminal case to a competent jurisdiction;
- on the scheduling of a **preliminary hearing** (*предварительное слушание*, Article 229 UPKR);
- on the scheduling the first **court hearing/trial investigation** (*назначение судебного заседания или разбирательства*, Article 231 UPKR).

1176. The deadlines for making the decisions by the court at the preparatory stage are stipulated by the law. It shall be taken within a time term of not later than thirty days after the day of receiving the case at the court. With respect to an accused who is held in detention, the judge is obliged to take the decision within a shorter term—not later than fourteen days upon arrival of the case (Article 227, paragraph 3 UPKR). Copies of the judicial decision have to be sent out by the judge to the accused, to the victim and to the public prosecutor (Article 227, paragraph 4 UPKR).

1177. The sentencing court is entitled, whether upon the request of one of the parties or on its own initiative, to schedule a **preliminary hearing** if the grounds stipulated in Article 229 UPKR are present. Normally, these are the grounds that require additional attention and consideration of the court. These can be the following ones:

- if there is a request filed by one of the parties on the exclusion of evidence after reviewing the case file or upon the receipt of the copy of the indictment (Article 229, paragraphs 2, 3 UPKR);
- if there are grounds for the return of the criminal file to the prosecutor, when, e.g., an indictment was prepared with the violation of the criminal procedural provisions, such as the defendant was not informed about his/her rights (Article 237, paragraphs 1, 5 UPKR);
- if there are grounds for suspension or termination of the criminal proceedings;
- if the party has requested a procedure of investigating a case involving a defendant located outside the territory of the Russian Federation and (or) refuses to appear in court;
- if it has to be decided on the examination of the criminal case by jury and other grounds.

1178. As a result of the preliminary hearings, the court is entitled to transfer the criminal case to a competent jurisdiction (Article 236, paragraph 1 UPKR), to return the criminal case to the prosecutor (Article 237 UPKR), to suspend the criminal proceedings (Article 238 UPKR), to terminate the criminal proceedings (Article 239 UPKR), to join two and more criminal cases in one trial investigation (Article 239.2 UPKR), to separate a criminal case into different trial investigations (Article 239. 1 UPKR). At this point, the court can also schedule the court hearing/trial investigation (Article 236, paragraph 1 UPKR).

1179. Hence, the court can schedule the court hearings whether without the preliminary hearing or after the issues that were considered within the preliminary hearings have been clarified (Articles 229, 231, 236, paragraph 1 UPKR).

1180. The parties shall be notified of the place, date and time of the first court hearing; however, not later than five days before they start. After the court hearing has been scheduled, the defendant is not entitled to file certain requests, such as on the consideration of the criminal case by jury (the questing that has to be decided during the preliminary hearing session) or request to hold a preliminary hearing (Article 231, paragraphs 4, 5 UPKR).

§2. The Trial Investigation in the Courts of First Instance

1181. The **trial investigation** or **court hearings** (*судебное разбирательство*) is the second substage of the trial, after the preparatory and before the appeal procedure (Chapters 35–39 UPKR).

1182. The trial investigation is an essential part of the criminal procedure due to the fact that the central question of whether the defendant is guilty or not in committing a crime has to be decided. At this stage, the principle of immediacy with respect to evidence (Article 240 UPKR) is realized. The factual truth regarding the relevant criminal case is established in the decision of the court that is based on the directly examined evidence (Article 227 UPKR).

1183. The Court of First Instance considers the case on merits. The court decides—among others—on the following key issues: (1) whether it is proved that the offense of the commission of which the defendant is charged has taken place; (2) whether it is proved that the offense was committed by the defendant; (3) whether the committed act is a crime and, if so, under which provisions of the Criminal Code of the Russian Federation it is criminalized; (4) whether the defendant is guilty of the committing a crime; (5) whether the defendant is subject to punishment for the committed crime; (6) whether there are circumstances mitigating or aggravating punishment; (7) which punishment should be imposed on the defendant, and also on other issues of importance for the case that allows the proper consideration of the criminal case.

I. General Requirements for the Trial

A. Basic Principles of the Trial

1184. All principles of the criminal procedure, including basic principles of criminal procedure, such as respect for the person's honor and dignity, the principle of justice, the principle of legality in the criminal trial, are fully applicable with regard to the trial investigation. The principles concerning due process safeguards—the right to qualified legal assistance, the presumption of innocence, the right to appeal, the principle of a reasonable time period for criminal proceedings, the right to interpreter's services free of charge—also belong to the key procedural maxims regulating trial investigation.

1185. Nonetheless, with regard to the trial stage, the principles concerning the judiciary and criminal justice administration are put under particular scrutiny. They form the base for the **general requirements for the trial investigation** (*общие условия судебного разбирательства*, Chapter 35 UPKR).[1155] These are the following procedural safeguards.

1186. The **principle of orality of criminal court proceedings** (*устность судебного разбирательства*, Article 240 UPKR) requires trials to be conducted orally rather than according to written materials. The court must hear the testimony of defendants, victims, and witnesses, as well as the conclusions of experts, and must examine evidence and read protocols and other documents aloud in open court.

1187. The requirement that all evidence be subject to direct examination as well as the provision that a sentence can only be based on evidence that has been presented and argued in open court reveal another principle of criminal proceedings: the **principle of immediacy with respect to evidence** (*непосредственность исследования доказательств*, Article 240 UPKR). This principle underpins another significant safeguard, namely, the right of the suspect (Article 46, paragraph 4 UPKR), the accused (Article 47, paragraph 4 UPKR), the victim (Article 42, paragraph 2 UPKR), and other participants in the criminal process to present evidence (Article 74 UPKR).

1188. The **principle of openness and transparency of criminal court proceedings** *(гласность судебного разбирательства)* provided for in Article 241 UPKR guarantees the right to an open, public trial. Judicial proceedings may be conducted in camera only if, under the circumstances surrounding a particular case, one or more of the items listed in Article 241 UPKR call for the exclusion of the public. These items include, for example, the security of the participants in the

1155. Paramonova, National characteristics, fundamental principles, and history of criminal law in Russia, 2014, pp. 175–292; for the classification of the principles of the criminal procedure, *see* Part II, Chapter 1, §3.

criminal process, their (close) relatives, or other close persons (Article 241, paragraph 2, No. 4 UPKR) or if the defendant is under the age of 16 (Article 241, paragraph 2, No. 2 UPKR).[1156]

1189. The **principle of invariability of the court composition** *(неизменность состава суда)* requires that a criminal case be dealt with from beginning to end by the same judge(s). Where a replacement is necessary, the proceedings must be started anew (Article 242 UPKR).

1190. With regard to the form of procedure, the Code of Criminal Procedure is a compromise between new liberal ideas that reflect the principle of adversarial procedure proclaimed by the Constitution, on the one hand, and the inquisitorial model of criminal procedure that dates from the Code of Criminal Procedure of the RSFSR 1960, on the other.[1157] According to the current Code, the **principle of adversarial procedure** *(принцип состязательности)* applies to both the investigative and the court stages of the proceedings (Article 15 UPKR). It also provides for the rule of equality of arms, namely, that prosecution and defense enjoy equal rights before the court (Articles 15, paragraph 4, 244 UPKR). In practice, however, the Code of Criminal Procedure represents a "neo-inquisitorial" model of criminal procedure: investigative authorities are given priority over the defense; the accused, the victims, and witnesses are more "objects of investigation" than independent participants in the criminal proceedings.[1158]

1191. According to the Constitution, the **principle of judicial independence** is directly applicable to the trial investigation stage: "Judges shall be independent and are bound only by the Constitution and the Federal Law" (Article 120, paragraph 1 Const.). It also requires that judges, jurors, as well as prosecutors, investigators, and inquirers, must rely on the law and their own consciences. They are obliged to assess the evidence in accordance with their "inner conviction" and based on the aggregate of the evidence presented in the case. In compliance with the **principle of free evaluation of evidence**, no aspect of evidence can be regarded, in advance of the proceedings, as having any predetermined force (Article 17 UPKR).

B. Parties or Participants of the Trial

1192. The procedural rights and obligations of the parties in the trial depend on their role in the criminal procedure. The participants of the trial investigation whether belong to the party of the prosecution or defense, excluding experts and specialists that give an expert opinion based on the objective analysis of certain issues in specific areas.

1156. *See* Part I, Chapter 7, §6, paras. 765–767.
1157. Code of Criminal Procedure of the RSFSR, Oct. 23, 1960: Svod Zakonov RSFSR vol. 8. Art. 613 (Ugolovno-prozessual´nij Kodeks RSFSR).
1158. Paramonova/Bogush, ZStW 125 (2013), 703–728; Paramonova, National characteristics, fundamental principles, and history of criminal law in Russia, 2014, pp. 175–292.

1193. The court is an independent judicial body that is invoked to decide on the case in accordance with the principle of judicial independence and impartiality. Law prohibits the judges from favoring any of the parties in the court proceedings. This way, the principle of the equality of rights of the prosecution and defense before the court is emphasized (Articles 15, paragraph 4 and 244 UPKR).[1159]

– Prosecutor

1194. In compliance with the principle of mandatory prosecution (Article 21 UPKR), the criminal procedure law establishes mandatory participation of the prosecutor in the criminal trial, except for the private prosecution cases (Article 20, paragraphs 1 and 2 UPKR).

The failure of the prosecutor to appear in the trial entails the postponing of the court proceedings. In the criminal cases of the private prosecution, the victim has the role of the prosecutor in the case.

In the court proceedings, the state prosecutor is entitled to present evidence and participate in their investigation, to present the charges to the court. The prosecutor expresses his/her proposals to the court on the application of the criminal law and on the imposition of the criminal punishment (type, amount) to the defendant (Article 246, paragraph 5 UPKR). The prosecutor is obliged to support the civil suit presented in a criminal case if it is required for the protection of the rights of certain persons, e.g., of minors, of public or state interests (Article 246, paragraph 6 UPKR).[1160]

Based on an objective study of all the materials of the case during the trial, the prosecutor may decide to dismiss the charges at any time prior to the passing of the sentence.

Thus, the public prosecutor can change the charges toward mitigation, for example, by exclusion from the application of the criminal law qualifying circumstances that aggravate the punishment, e.g., murder committed with particular cruelty (Article 246, paragraph 8 UPKR);

If during the trial proceedings, the public prosecutor comes to the conclusion that the evidence does not confirm the charge brought against the defendant, the prosecutor can refuse to support the further prosecution and is obliged to outline the reasons to the court. Full or partial dismissal of the charges by the public prosecutor entails the termination of the criminal case or criminal prosecution in corresponding parts (Article 246, paragraph 7 UPKR).[1161]

– Defendant

1195. The participation of the defendant in the trial is his/her right and duty. Compliance with this rule is an essential guarantee of the constitutional right to a defense, which grants the defendant a possibility to appear in person before the court and give his/her explanations regarding the charges brought against him/her.

1159. Radchenko, Kommentarij k UPKR, pp. 267–268.
1160. Decision of the Constitutional Court of the Russian Federation N 18-P, Dec. 8, 2003.
1161. Decision of the Constitutional Court of the Russian Federation N 18-P, Dec. 8, 2003.

Therefore, the criminal procedural law requires obligatory participation of the defendant in the trial proceedings (Article 247 paragraph1 UPKR).

The court is obliged to postpone the trial if the defendant fails to appear at the court proceedings (Article 247, paragraph 2 UPKR). In the case, when the defendant does not attend the trial without a serious reason, e.g., poor health condition (Article 113, paragraph 6 UPKR), he/she can be subject to a forcible bringing to the trial hearings or the court is obliged to change the coercive measures of restriction in his/her respect, for instance, instead of such a coercive measure as bail court may apply house arrest or detention.[1162]

The trial in the absence of the accused is possible only in exceptional cases that are stipulated in the law. It is allowed when the case regards the crime of small or average gravity (Article 15 UKR), and there is an explicit request from the defendant for the consideration of the criminal case in his/her absence (Article 247, paragraph 4 UPKR). Another situation, when the court proceedings can be carried out in the absence of the defendant, including consideration of grave and especially grave crimes, is when the defendant is located outside of the territory of the Russian Federation and (or) refuses to appear in court (Article 247, paragraph 5 UPKR). It is only possible if the person has not been prosecuted on the territory of any foreign state for committing this crime in compliance with the double jeopardy prohibition.

– Defense Counsel

1196. Participation of defense counsel in the trial proceedings is one of the essential procedural safeguards that guarantees the implementation of the constitutional provisions granting everyone the right to qualified legal assistance (Article 48 Const.). The participation of the defense counsel is underpinned by the principle of justice as well as by the maxim of equality of the parties' rights in the trial proceedings (Article 123, paragraph 3 Const.).

The defense counsel participates in the examination of evidence, files requests, outlines his/her opinion before the court on the merits of the charges, on proved circumstances, on the circumstances mitigating punishment or justifying the defendant as well as on other matters arising in the course of the trial (Article 248, paragraph 1 UPKR).

If the defense counsel fails to appear at the trial proceedings and there is no possibility to replace him/her, the court hearings shall be postponed. However, the replacement of the defense counsel is allowed only with the consent of the defendant (Article 248, paragraph 2 UPKR).

In the case of the replacement of the defense counsel, the court provides time to the new defense counsel to review the case file and prepare for participation in the trial. In principle, the replacement of the defender does not entail the repetition of all procedural actions that have already been held during the trial investigation. Nonetheless, at the request of the defense counsel, the court may repeat the interrogations of witnesses, of victims, of experts or other court actions (Article 248, paragraph 3 UPKR).

1162. For the applicable coercive measures, *see* Part II, Chapter 2, §1, paras. 1033–1066.

Actions of the defense counsel in the court hearings should be aimed at clarifying the circumstances justifying the accused or mitigating his/her responsibility. The defense counsel is obliged to provide the defendant with legal assistance on all issues arising in the trial investigation, such as application of the law and the charges connected with it, about punishment, about the civil law consequences of the act, and others. Although the defense counsel evaluates evidence based on his/her inner conviction and guided by the law, he/she the right to express an opinion and to act only in the interests of the defendant.

– Civil Claimant (Party) and Civil Defendant

1197. Civil claimant (party),[1163] civil defendant and (or) their representatives are entitled to take part in the trial investigation (Article 250, paragraph 1 UPKR).

It is the right of the civil claimant to participate in the trial investigation.

1198. The court can consider the civil suit in the absence of the civil claimant in the following situations:

- if it is requested by a civil claimant him-, herself or by his/her representative;
- if a civil action is supported by the public prosecutor;
- if the defendant agrees fully with the presented civil claim.

1199. In all other cases, if the civil claimant/ his or her representative fails to appear at the trial, the court has the right to leave the civil action without consideration. In this case, however, the civil claimant retains the right to sue in civil proceedings (Article 250, paragraph 3 UPKR).

1200. Contrary to the civil claimant, the civil defendant is obliged to be present at the court proceedings if the court finds his/her presence necessary. Otherwise, the civil defendant may be subject to coercive procedural measures, such as forcible bringing to the court (Article 113 UPKR).

II. The Course of the Trial

1201. The scope of the trial proceedings is provided for by the law (Article 252 UPKR). The trial proceedings shall be conducted only in relation to the defendant and only on the charges against him/her. It means that it is allowed only within the framework of the accusation formulated in the indictment. This way, it is prohibited to conduct an evaluation of evidence on the involvement in the crime of other persons.

The judgment of the court cannot include assertions/statements on the commission of the crime by other persons rather than the defendant.

1163. On the legal position of the victim and the civil party (civil claimant), *see* paras. 944–960.

A. Preparation of the Court Session

1202. The procedure of the preparation of the court session is regulated by Chapter 36 UPKR.

1203. At the appointed time, the presiding judge opens the court hearing (Article 261 UPKR) and announces which criminal case is subject to consideration. All actions of the presiding judge in the preparatory part of the trial can be divided into four groups:

- opening the court hearing and checking the attendance of the participants of the trial;
- checking the legality of the participation of the parties and of other participants of the process in the trial proceedings;
- informing the persons participating in the proceedings about their rights;
- ensuring the possibility of considering the requests and petitions of the participants.

1204. The next step in the preparation of the court session is the report of the secretary of the court session on the attendance of the participants involved in the case and on their reasons for absence, Article 262 UPKR.

1205. Afterward, if there is an interpreter participating in the court proceedings, the presiding judge shall explain him/her his/her rights and duties, in particular, about the responsibility for the knowingly wrong interpretation (Article 263 UPKR). The participants of the court proceedings who do not speak or speak the language of the proceedings have the right to free assistance of an interpreter, Article 18 UPKR.

1206. Then, the presiding judge requests the witnesses to leave the courtroom. This is done in order to comply with the requirements of the law on the interrogation of witnesses separately (Article 278, paragraph 1 UPKR).

1207. After the witnesses have left the courtroom, the presiding judge establishes the identity of the defendant (Article 265 UPKR): the name, date and place of his/her birth, whether he/she speaks the language of the criminal proceedings, the place of the defendant's residence, place of employment, occupation, education, marital status and other data relating to his/her person as well as other information that can be relevant for the further court proceedings. For example, information on his/her disability or on the presence of minor children who need care. Afterward, all information obtained in preparation for the court hearings procedure must be compared with the information that was presented to the court in respect of the defendant by the preliminary investigating authorities.

1208. As next, the presiding judge announces the composition of the court, explaining who is a prosecutor, defender, victim, civil claimant (party), civil defendant or (and) their representatives, as well as the secretary of the court session, expert, specialist, and translator.

1209. As a general rule, recusations and challenges are requested at the preparatory stage of the trial; however, the law does not prohibit the possibility to declare such a request in the later stages of the trial proceedings.

1210. In accordance with the Code of Criminal Procedure, the presiding judge has an obligation to explain to the participants their rights and obligations and provide an order throughout the entire course of the trial. First of all, the presiding judge should clarify the rights of the accused (Article 267 UPKR). These rights that are set out in Article 47 UPKR were explained to the **accused** (***обвиняемый***) in the preliminary investigation. However, in the preparation of the court hearing, it is obligatory to explain them again to the **defendant** (***подсудимый***). The reason for this is the new legal status of the defendant; hence, new rights and obligations connected with it. At the stage of the trial, the defendant has, for instance, the right to participate in the trial proceedings in the Court of First Instance or the right to study the protocol of the court session.

1211. Then, the presiding judge shall inform the victim, civil claimant (party), civil defendant, experts and specialists of their rights and responsibilities (Articles 268–270 UPKR). For instance, to the victim, it is important to explain the possibility of reconciliation with the defendant since the court may terminate criminal proceedings on this ground under certain circumstances stipulated in Article 25 UPKR also at the stage of the trial investigation.[1164] It is possible, however, only with regard to the crimes of small or average gravity (Article 15 UKR).

1212. As the next step, the judge asks the parties whether they have any requests and (or) motions to summon new witnesses, experts, specialists, to request any (physical) evidence and (or) documents, or to exclude some evidence obtained in violation of the law, Article 271 UPKR.

1213. All motions must be resolved immediately after the application. Each motion and request has to be resolved on an individual basis. They cannot be resolved all at once within one procedural action. It is regarded as a grave violation of procedural order and of the rights of the trial participants (Article 271, paragraph 2 UPKR).

1214. The person whose motion/request was dismissed by the court is eligible to apply again with the same request at any other time of the trial proceedings. The motions/requests should be considered on a general basis (Article 271, paragraph 3 UPKR). However, all types of motions have to address the substance of the criminal case.

1164. For the grounds for the termination of the preliminary procedure, *see* paras. 898–900, 919.

1215. The court may not refuse to grant a motion on the interrogation of a witness or an expert in the court proceedings, who appeared in the court upon the initiative of the parties (Article 271, paragraph 4 UPKR).

1216. After the completion of the consideration of all issues that needed to be resolved in the preparatory part of the court proceedings, the presiding judge announces the beginning of the trial investigation.

B. Trial Investigation

1217. The **judicial** or **trial investigation** (*судебное следствие*, Chapter 37 UPKR) is the main part of the trial proceedings, during which a direct investigation of the evidence presented by the parties and the establishment of the factual circumstances of the crime takes place. Examination of the evidence in the judicial investigation makes it possible to evaluate them in terms of relevance, admissibility, reliability, and regarding all the presented evidence—in terms of sufficiency for the resolution of criminal proceedings (Article 88 UPKR).

1218. The judicial investigation is not a repetition of the preliminary investigation but an independent stage of the analysis and evaluation of evidence. The findings of the court may not coincide with the findings of the preliminary investigation. In court, the circumstances can be investigated, which were not the subject of a preliminary investigation (e.g., testimonies of additional witnesses, information that characterizes the defendant as a personality, expert reports, etc.).

1219. During the judicial investigation, all versions of the commission of the offense shall be considered, including the versions set out by the parties and that are different from the position of the public prosecutor.

1220. The main procedural actions of the trial investigation are interrogations (of defendant, victim and witnesses), reports of experts and (or) specialists, examination and disclosure of evidence, and others.

1221. The judicial investigation begins with a statement by the public prosecutor on the charges brought against the defendant. In cases of private prosecution (Article 20 UPKR), it begins with the statement of the private prosecutor.

1222. After the statement of the public prosecutor, the presiding judge addresses the defendant asking whether he/she understood the charges brought against him/her, whether he/she acknowledges his/her guilt and whether he/she that his/her defense counsel expresses his/her attitude to the charges brought (Article 273 UPKR).

1223. In accordance with the provisions of the Code of Criminal Procedure, the evidence can be presented to the court, the prosecution and the defense parties. The procedure is strictly regulated by the law (Article 274 UPKR).

1224. The **prosecution** is the first to provide evidence. The order, how the examination of evidence is done, is determined by the party.

1225. After examining the evidence submitted by the prosecution, the evidence presented by the **defense** shall be investigated. The order of submission and examination is also determined by the party. It should be borne in mind that the defendant has the right not to testify against him-, herself and his/her close relatives and close persons, Article 51 Const. Presentation of evidence proving the guilt of the defendant is the obligation of the prosecuting party in compliance with the ex officio principle (Article 49 Const., Article 14 UPKR).

1226. If the defendant agrees to testify, he/she is first interrogated by his/her defense counsel and by other participants of the defense party, then by the public prosecutor and the participants of the prosecuting party. The presiding judge may intervene in the questioning of the defendant when the questions are declined or irrelevant to the case.

1227. The court, during the interrogation of the defendant, should formulate questions in order to verify the evidence submitted by the parties.

1228. Testimony of **witness** is one of the main pieces of evidence in the criminal case, although it does not have any privileged position in front of the other evidence. According to Article 278, paragraph 1 UPKR, witnesses are interrogated separately and in the absence the witnesses that have not been interrogated. The reason for this rule is that the testimonies should be objective and should not depend on the testimonies of others. The witness is first questioned by the party, at the request of which it was called to the hearing. Then the other party can interrogate. The court asks questions to the witness after the interrogation by the parties.

1229. As for the **victim**, first, it has to be interrogated by the state prosecutor. The interrogation is carried out according to the rules of interrogation of the witnesses.

1230. The Code of Criminal Procedure provides for the possibility of interrogating witnesses and victims without disclosing their true identity by excluding the visual observation of the witness/victim by other participants in the proceedings. For this purpose, a separate room with the technical means of communication can be used for interrogation. These measures are taken when it is necessary to ensure the security of the witness/victim, his/her relatives, and his/her close persons.

1231. There are some special rules regarding the interrogation of **juvenile victims or witnesses**. In principle, the interrogation is carried out according to general rules; however, the law provides for some additional regulations aimed at the protection of their rights and legitimate interests.

1232. Thus, during the interrogation of the victim or witness under the age of 14 years, the participation of a teacher is obligatory. The teacher's participation regarding the victims and witnesses between the ages of 14 and 18 years occurs at the discretion of the court. The teacher´s role is to explain certain terms, definitions, concepts to the juvenile that cause him/her difficulty in understanding.

1233. Interrogation of a minor under the age of 14 years requires the participation of his/her legal representative: parents, *loco parentis,* and in their absence—close relatives or representatives of the children protection services. Parents that were deprived of their parental rights cannot be legal representatives in the court investigation.

1234. In general, the examination of evidence is conducted based on the principle of immediacy. Nonetheless, the **disclosure of evidence** (*оглашение показаний*) of the participant can take place at the request of a party or on upon the initiative of the court only when certain requirements are satisfied.

1235. Regarding the disclosure of evidence of victim or witness, these are the following cases: the death of the victim or witness; serious illness, which prevents appearance in court; the refusal of a victim or witness who is a foreign citizen to appear at court hearings; a natural disaster or other extraordinary circumstances that prevent appearance in court, Article 281, paragraph 2 UPKR.

1236. Disclosure of evidence of the defendant is also possible, for instance, when the testimony given during the trial investigation differs significantly from the information that has been given by the defendant in the course of the preliminary investigation or during the preliminary hearing (Article 276, paragraph 1 UPKR).

1237. In the course of the trial investigation, there can also be conducted interrogations of **experts and specialists**. The party, on whose initiative the expert/specialist was called, questions first (Articles 282, 283 UPKR).

1238. Inspection of **physical evidence** must be organized in such a way that they are not damaged or destroyed. The subject to inspection may be evidence obtained in the preliminary investigation as well as submitted by the parties during the trial investigation.

1239. If there is a need in the examination of evidence, which cannot be delivered to the court, e.g., due to their size, the inspection can be conducted by the court on their location (for instance, car, boat, etc.), Article 284 UPKR.

1240. **Documents** presented by the parties or requested by the court at the judicial investigation are investigated and included in the criminal case upon the ruling of the court, Articles 285, 286 UPKR.

1241. During the trial investigation, the investigative **experiment**, Article 181 UPKR, or **identification of a person or object** in accordance with the requirements of Article 193 UPKR and other procedural actions can be carried out on the basis of a court ruling, Articles 288–290 UPKR.

1242. The **final stage** of judicial investigation is a decisive phase of the investigation, Article 291 UPKR. This stage is characterized by the fact that all the evidence in the case has been fully investigated, and the parties are no longer submitting any other evidence relevant to the case. The presiding judge shall ask the parties whether they wish to complete a judicial investigation. If additional motions and requests appear, the court shall discuss them and take appropriate procedural action. In the case when additional relevant materials must be examined, the court continues the judicial investigation.

1243. After resolving all the petitions, motions and requests, the presiding judge announces that the judicial investigation is completed.

C. Oral Court Hearings

1244. **Oral court hearings** or **pleadings in court** (*прения сторон*, Chapter 38 UPKR), and the **last plea** or **final statement of defendant** (*последнее слово подсудимого*) is the last stage in the trial proceedings before issuing the judgment of the case.

1245. Pleadings consist of the speeches of the prosecutor and defense counsel (Article 292 UPKR) that are obliged to be present.

1246. Refusal of the prosecutor to participate in the oral court hearings constitutes a dismissal of charges; hence, the court must acquit the defendant. The absence of defense counsel is prohibited by the law. In exceptional cases, he/she must be replaced (Article 49, paragraph 7 UPKR).

1247. The **public prosecutor** in his/her speech must disclose the social danger of the committed crime, the harm caused by the crime; he/she analyzes the evidence examined at the court session and expresses his/her views on whether the charges were proved. The prosecutor gives his/her qualification of the criminal offense committed by the defendant, gives a description of the defendant's personality and expresses his/her views on the appropriate and fair punishment, taking into account all the aggravating and mitigating circumstances, as well as expresses his/her view on other issues that must be resolved by the court, e.g., civil action or compensation of moral damage.

1248. **Defense counsel** should focus his/her speech on the circumstances that deny the accusation or at least raise some doubts on the charges brought against the defendant. Particular attention should be given to the characteristics of the personality of the defendant. The defense counsel can offer a different legal opinion regarding the qualification of the actions of the defendant. In general, the counsel must have a clear, consistent position on the case. In any instance, he/she is obliged to put forward the position most favorable for the defendant.

1249. The victim and his/her representative have the right to participate in the pleadings in court. The victim's refusal to participate in the hearings, however, does not imply any limitation of his/her right to a fair trial (Article 292, paragraph 2 UPKR). The civil claimant (party), civil defendant and their representatives are also entitled to participate in the pleadings.

1250. The sequence of the participants' pleadings is determined by the court. Thus, it is obligatory that the prosecutor is the first one, and the defendant and his/her counsel speak as the last ones in the oral hearings (Article 292, paragraph 3 UPKR).

1251. As already mentioned, the verdict cannot be based on the evidence, which was investigated in the court (principle of immediacy of examination of evidence). This way, it is not allowed for the participants of the pleadings to refer to any information that has not been examined in the trial, or it was classified as inadmissible evidence (Article 75 UPKR) by the court.

1252. The court may not limit the duration of the pleadings of the parties. Nonetheless, the presiding judge has the right to stop the person if his/her refers to the circumstances not related to the criminal case as well as to inadmissible evidence (Article 292 paragraph 5 UPKR).

1253. After the oral court hearings, the presiding judge gives the defendant the opportunity of the **final statement** (Article 293 UPKR). This court action is aimed at giving the defendant the last possibility to address the court regarding the case.

1254. While pronouncing the last plea, any questions to the defendant are not allowed. The final statement is not an obligation of the defendant.

1255. After hearing the last plea of the defendant, the court retires to the room for issuing a judgment (Article 293 UPKR). The presiding judge declares the time for the announcement of the judgment (Article 295 UPKR). At the declared time, it must be announced. If for some reason, the court failed to meet the deadline, the clerk of the court shall inform the participants about the new time of the announcement of judgment.

III. The Judgement of the Case

1256. The court renders a judgment in the name of the Russian Federation (Article 296 UPKR). The court judgment shall be lawful, reasonable and fair, which includes making a decision in accordance with the legal provisions and correct application of the criminal law (Article 297 UPKR).[1165]

1165. Smirnov/ Kalinowski, Ugolovnij process: uchebnik, 2015, pp. 505–736.

1257. The court makes a decision concerning the charges of two types: either acquitting or convicting the defendant (Article 302 UPKR).

1258. The judgment of **acquittal** is rendered by the court in the following cases:

- event of crime has not been established;
- the defendant was not involved in the crime;
- the defendant´s act does not constitute a crime;
- the jury passed a verdict of acquittal regarding the defendant.[1166]

1259. The judgment based on any of the abovementioned grounds has as a legal consequence for the defendant that he/she is not guilty in the committed crime and is subject to rehabilitation (Chapter 18 UPKR, Article 302, paragraphs 2, 3 UPKR).

1260. As regards **conviction**, it cannot be based on assumptions but on the profound analysis of the aggregate of the evidence examined by the court that confirmed the guilt of the defendant (Article 302, paragraph 4 UPKR). While rendering a judgment of conviction, the court shall outline a form of the imposed criminal punishment, its term, as well as the beginning of the execution of the sentence.

1261. The major questions upon which the court has to decide are the following ones (Article 299 UPKR):

- whether it is proved that there has been an act, in the commission of which the defendant is charged;
- whether it is proved that the offense has been committed by the defendant;
- whether the act is criminalized and if so, under which provision;
- whether the defendant is guilty of the crime;
- whether the defendant is a subject to punishment for his/her crime;
- whether there are circumstances mitigating or aggravating punishment.

1262. To other questions that have to be considered by the court belong, for instance, the question, whether the defendant needs drug treatment and (or) medical and (or) social rehabilitation (Article 72.1 UPKR) or the question on the kind of correctional facility for the execution of sentence (Article 299, paragraph 1 UPKR).

1263. After resolving the above-listed issues, the court proceeds to the drafting of the sentence (Article 303 UPKR). It is drafted in the language in which the trial was conducted. If in the course of the trial, the information on the victims, witnesses or other participants' identities were not disclosed, the court in the judgment refers to the nicknames of such persons (Article 303, paragraph 5 UPKR).

1264. The judgment consists of the introductory part (Article 304 UPKR), descriptive-reasoning part (Articles 305, 307 UPKR) and conclusion (Articles 306, 308 UPKR).

1166. For the verdict of the jurors, *see* paras. 1280–1302.

1265. The **introductory part** contains all formal information, such as the date and place of a verdict, the name of the court, of all participants, the defendant´s identity information, etc.

1266. The **descriptive-reasoning part** of the verdict shall contain the substance of the charges; the circumstances of the criminal case, established by the court; the grounds for acquittal/conviction of the defendant and the evidence supporting the decision; the reasons for which the court rejects the evidence presented by the prosecution (in the case of acquittal); the reasons for the decision in respect of a civil action. In the judgment of acquittal, the formulations that can raise doubt on the innocence of the acquitted are not permitted (Article 305, paragraph 2 UPKR).

1267. As regards the judgment of conviction, it shall contain a description of the criminal act with the location, time and method of its commission, the form of guilt, motives, goals and consequences of the crime, as well as information on the circumstances aggravating or mitigating punishment (Article 307 UPKR).

1268. The **conclusion** of the judgment provides an overview of the most important decisions that the court has substantiated in the descriptive-reasoning part. Thus, it stipulates, in short, whether the defendant was acquitted or found guilty. If found guilty, the article of the Criminal Code that criminalizes the act has to be laid down in the judgment. Additionally, the information on the execution of the sentence shall be provided, such as the type and term of the punishment, the part of the suspended punishment, of the punishment that has to be served, the information on probation, on the types of additional punishment, etc. (Article 308 UPKR).

1269. Within five days from the date of the announcement of the judgment, the copies of the judgment shall be handed to the convicted or acquitted, to his/her defense counsel and the prosecutor. The copies must be sent to the victim, civil claimant (party), civil defendant and their representatives. At the request of these participants, the copies are also sent within five days after the announcement of the judgment (Article 312 UPKR).

§3. Some Special Procedures of the Court

1270. Besides the ordinary trial procedure, criminal procedural law provides for the special procedures of the court (Chapters 40–42 UPKR).

There are four types of special procedures that are possible in Russian criminal procedure:

- special judicial procedure with the consent of the accused with the charges against him/her (Chapter 40 UPKR);

- special judicial procedure with the pretrial agreement on cooperation between prosecution and defense (Chapter 40.1. UPKR)—an *analog* of *plea bargaining*;[1167]
- trial proceedings at the magistrate courts regarding private prosecution cases (Chapter 41 UPKR);
- trial proceedings with juries (Chapter 42 UPKR).

1271. In contrast to the previous Criminal Procedure Code, the current Code, 2001, introduced the concept of the differentiation of the forms of judicial proceedings. The severity of the crime served as a basis: the more socially dangerous and serious the act, the more complicated the trial proceedings, and vice versa. On the one hand, the court proceedings are the most complicated for a number of particularly serious crimes, where a defendant has the right to have his/her case tried by a jury; on the other hand, the procedure can be simplified for sentencing in the cases of less significant crimes, e.g., special judicial procedure with the consent of the accused with the charges against him/her (Chapter 40 UPKR).[1168]

I. Judicial Procedure with the Consent of the Accused with the Charges Against Him/Her

1272. Judicial procedure for rendering a judgment with the consent of the accused with the charges against him/her is a simplified form of the court proceedings, which excludes fully or partially the direct examination of evidence in the criminal cases involving crimes with a maximum penalty of ten years' imprisonment (Article 314 UPKR). In spite of the fact that the principle of immediacy of the examination of evidence in the court proceedings is not applicable to this procedure, it is carried out with strict maintenance of the rights of participants in criminal proceedings.

This way, if an ordinary trial procedure consists of the following required elements—preparatory stage, judicial investigation, pleadings in the court, the final statement of the defendant as well as of the announcement of the judgment, the simplified form of the court proceedings does not contain the central and most cumbersome part—judicial investigation.

The grounds and procedure for the special simplified judicial procedure are regulated by Chapter 40 UPKR. In accordance with its provisions, if the accused has agreed with the charges against him/her, he/she is entitled to apply for the simplified judicial procedure that excludes trial investigation.

However, for the application of this special judicial procedure, besides the consent of the defendant, certain conditions have to be fulfilled (Article 314 UPKR). First, the state or the private prosecutor and the victim must agree with an application of the procedure and second, the maximum penalty for the crime with which

---

1167. Federal Law on Changes to Code of Criminal Procedure, Jun. 29, 2009, N 141-FZ; Paramonova, Svetlana: Recent Reforms of Criminal and Criminal Procedural Law in Russia. In: Revista Penal, 2012, N 30, pp. 264–268.

1168. Radchenko, Kommentarij k UPKR, p. 303.

a defendant is charged cannot exceed ten years of imprisonment. The court within the simplified procedure is also obliged to assure that the defendant understands the nature and consequences of the application of his/her request regarding the special judicial procedure and the motion on the application of the special procedure was lodged voluntarily and after consultations with the defense counsel (Article 314, paragraph 2 UPKR). Any coercion (physical or psychological) from the side of the state officials toward the defendant on the application of the simplified judicial procedure without the consent of the defendant as well toward the defense counsel is unacceptable. All violations of the abovementioned rules lead that the case is considered within an ordinary procedure.

The criminal procedural law does not provide for the possibility of applying the simplified trial procedure with regard to juvenile defendants (Article 420, paragraph 2 UPKR).

Legal qualification of the crime should meet the actual circumstances of the case that are underpinned by the legally collected evidence. It cannot be a result of cooperation between the defense and the prosecution.

In any case, the final decision on the possible application of a special judicial procedure is made by the court while scheduling the first court session (Article 228, paragraph 4 UPKR).

II. Judicial Procedure with the Pretrial Agreement (Plea Bargaining)

1273. The special judicial procedure is stipulated by the criminal procedural law if there was a cooperation agreement concluded between prosecution and defense at the stage of the preliminary investigation—an analog of so-called *plea bargaining* in the Russian criminal procedure.[1169]

1274. With the introduction by the Federal Law, 2009 (Chapter 40.1 UKR) of the **plea-bargaining** within the preliminary investigation and trial stage, the hybrid model of the Russian criminal procedure gained certain features of adversariality.[1170] This institute, however, belongs to one of the most controversial issues. Due to the particular social danger of the criminal conduct and of its consequences, the criminal responsibility of a person must be based upon the factual truth and cannot be the outcome of a better legal deal (Article 6 UPKR).[1171] Therefore, the Russian criminal procedure characteristically has a cautious approach toward the application of plea bargaining, both at the preliminary and the trial investigation stages.

1169. For the more detailed information on the plea bargaining in Russia, *see* Paramonova, : Recent Reforms of Criminal and Criminal Procedural Law in Russia. In: Revista Penal, 2012, N 30, pp. 264–268; Poznyshev, Russkij ugolovnij prozess, pp. 29–30; Petrukhin, Reforma ugolovnogo prozessa, p. 26. For plea bargaining, *see* paras. 114, 810, 961, 1273–1278.

1170. Federal Law on Amendments of the Criminal Code, Jun. 29, 2009, N 141-FZ.

1171. For the more detailed information on the plea bargaining in Russia, *see* Paramonova, Revista Penal 2012, 264–268; Poznyshev, Russkij ugolovnij prozess, pp. 29–30; Petrukhin, Reforma ugolovnogo prozessa, p. 26. For plea bargaining, *see* paras. 114, 810, 961, 1273–1278.

1275. The suspect or accused[1172] has the right to lodge a motion to the prosecutor on the conclusion of the pretrial agreement on cooperation from the start of the criminal prosecution till the ending of the preliminary investigation (Article 317.1, paragraph 2 UPKR). The prosecutor, in the case of confirmation of the indictment, renders a resolution on the permission of the special judicial procedure that considers the pretrial agreement (Article 317.5, paragraph 1 UPKR).

1276. This institute is not intended for a mass application and primarily aims at the investigation of organized crime. In principle, it gives law enforcement agencies the possibility of attracting the suspect or accused of cooperating at the stage of investigation under the terms of a significant reduction of criminal punishment. With plea bargaining, the investigating authorities guarantee the suspect/accused the state protection measures provided by the law for victims, witnesses and other participants of the criminal proceedings (Article 317.9 UPKR).

1277. The special judicial procedure with the consideration of the pretrial agreement is applicable when the court comes to the conclusion that the following requirements have been satisfied (Article 317.6, paragraph 2 UPKR):

(1) the public prosecutor confirmed the active participation of the accused in the detection and investigation of the crime, in exposing and prosecuting others involved in the crime, as well as in contributing to search of the property obtained by crime;
(2) a pretrial agreement on cooperation was signed voluntarily and with the assistance of the defense counsel.

In the case when the court does not find that the abovementioned requirements were met, the trial proceedings are held in an ordinary procedure (Article 317.6, paragraph 3 UPKR).

1278. In terms of the reduction of punishment, there cannot be any guarantees given by the investigating authorities or prosecutor. Only in the case when the court decides to apply the procedure and take into consideration the pretrial agreement, the imposed punishment cannot exceed half of the maximum sentence possible for this crime (Article 317.7, paragraph 5 UPKR). However, this rule with the imposition of the punishment is only applicable when the crime was committed under the mitigating circumstances, and there were no aggravating circumstances involved (Article 62, paragraph 2 UKR).

III. Trial Proceedings at the Magistrate Courts

1279. The special position of the **magistrate courts** (*мировые суды*) in the criminal proceedings is primarily determined by its right to initiate criminal proceedings (Chapter 41 UPKR, Article 318, paragraph 1 UPKR). This right does not

1172. For the difference in legal status of the suspect and accused, *see* paras. 928–943.

extend to all crimes within the jurisdiction of the magistrate courts, but only regarding the so-called private prosecution cases, in which the victim has suffered only a slight injury. To those belong the following ones: intentional bodily harm of small gravity (Article 115 UKR), battery (Art 116.1 UKR), and slander (Article 128.1 UPKR) (Article 20, paragraphs 1 and 2 UPKR).

The magistrate court is obliged to initiate criminal proceedings only at the request of the victim. However, if the harm is caused to a minor or mentally ill person, a criminal case may be initiated at the request of his/her legal representative, and in the case of the victim's death—at the request of his/her close relatives (Article 318, paragraph 2 UPKR).

The criminal proceedings are considered to be initiated with the filing of the relevant application to the judge. The person that has filed the application to the court becomes a private prosecutor.

The consideration of the private prosecution cases by the magistrate courts is conducted within the adversarial procedure. The burden of proof lies on the victim and is carried out by him/her directly in the trial hearing. The judge is only entitled to support the adversarial procedure, ensuring the collection of such evidence, which cannot be obtained by the parties themselves (Article 319 UPKR).

In exceptional situations, the criminal proceedings on the cases of the private prosecution may be instituted by the public prosecutor. In this case, the victim's application is not required. The prosecutor may initiate criminal proceedings in the case of the death of the victim or when the victim, due to his/her helpless state or due to other reasons, is unable to defend his/her rights. In such cases, the prosecutor, in the instance of initiating criminal proceedings, must direct the case to the preliminary investigating authorities, i.e., to investigator or body of inquiry. Subsequently, the magistrate courts consider these cases by the rules of the public prosecution cases, however, with the right of reconciliation of the victim and defendant (Article 25 UPKR).

IV. Jury Trial

1280. In Russia, a jury system was introduced in 1864 by the judicial reform of Czar *Alexander II.*[1173]

1281. The institute functioned until the end of 1917 and was reintroduced in the country by the Federal Law in 1993.[1174]

1282. The Russian judicial system provides for the opportunity of a **jury trial** ***(суд с участием присяжных заседателей)*** with a professional judge as a chairman in criminal cases involving grave crimes against life.

1173. For historical details, *see* General Introduction, paras. 86–87.
1174. For the development of the jury trial, *see* Paramonova, Znachenie suda prizyazhnich, Novosibirsk, NGU, 2011, p. 165–168: http://www.philosophy.nsc.ru/youngcons/mol/2011.pdf; Federal Law, July 16, 1993. For the jury trials, *see* paras. 1280–1302.

1283. In the past, for the crimes for which the death penalty was applicable as an exclusive form of punishment, the accused had the right to have his/her case examined by jury trial (Article 20, paragraph 2 Const.). Capital punishment has not been carried out in Russia since 1996. On November 19, 2009, the Constitutional Court of the Russian Federation issued a decision,[1175] according to which the death penalty cannot be applied even after the expiration of the moratorium on capital punishment on January 1, 2010, which had been proclaimed by a previous decision of the Constitutional Court (February 2, 1999).[1176]

1284. The imposition of the moratorium was based on the violation of Article 20 Const. Article 20 of the Russian Constitution guarantees jury trial for all cases carrying a possible death sentence. In 1999, the Constitutional Court, considering Article 20 in conjunction with Article 19 (the principle of equality in rights and freedoms), decided that jury trial would be required in every region of the country in order to provide to all citizens, and across the entire territory of the Russian Federation, the equal right to have their case examined with the participation of jurors. On January 1, 2010, a jury trial was finally implemented in the last Russian region that did not have at that moment jury trials established—Chechen Republic. According to the Constitutional Court's 1999 decision, formal obstacles to the application of capital punishment would no longer have existed after that date.[1177]

1285. Nonetheless, the decision of the Constitutional Court of 2009[1178] stated a refusal to impose capital punishment on the territory of the Russian Federation, basing its decision on the necessity to comply with international obligations (Protocol No. 6 to the ECHR in conjunction with Article 18 of the Vienna Convention on the Law of Treaties), as well as on the fact that, according to the Constitution of the Russian Federation, the death penalty is a measure of a temporary character. Besides, the Court emphasized a "legitimate constitutional regime"[1179] that has developed firm guarantees of non-application of the death penalty.[1180]

1286. In principle, jury trials are conducted according to the general rules of the court proceedings, however, with the peculiarities stipulated by Chapter 42 UPKR (Article 324 UPKR).

1175. Decision of November 19, 2009. N 1344-O-P: http://www.ksrf.ru/Docs/Pages/default.aspx (official Website of the Constitutional Court of the Russian Federation).

1176. Decision of the Constitutional Court of the Russian Federation "On the explanation of the clause 5 of the decision of the Constitutional Court of the Russian Federation" from February 2, 1999 N 3-П.

1177. Paramonova, Svetlana: Towards universal abolition of the death penalty. In: Luis Arroyo / Paloma Biglino / William Schabas (Hrsg.): Russia's Constitutional Court and the death penalty. Valencia, tirant la blanch, 2010, S. 167–177.

1178. Decision of November 19, 2009. N 1344-O-P: http://www.ksrf.ru/Docs/Pages/default.aspx (official Website of the Constitutional Court of the Russian Federation).

1179. Decision of November 19, 2009. N 1344-O-P http://www.ksrf.ru/Docs/Pages/default.aspx (official Website of the Constitutional Court of the Russian Federation).

1180. Paramonova, Svetlana: Towards universal abolition of the death penalty. In: Luis Arroyo / Paloma Biglino / William Schabas (Hrsg.): Russia´s Constitutional Court and the death penalty. Valencia, tirant la blanch, 2010, S. 167–177.

1287. At present, ten citizens are randomly selected as jurors from the lists available at the court (Article 328, paragraph 1 UPKR). The jury panel in a criminal case at the present time is made up of eight **jurors**. Two additional jurors take part in the examination of the criminal case as reserve jurors (Article 328 UPKR).

1288. The new amendment of 2016 (a legislative initiative of the judge of the Constitutional Court) aimed at the expansion of the kinds of criminal cases that could be considered by a jury while reducing the number of jurors from twelve to eight people. The ultimate purpose of the amendment of the Code of Criminal Procedure was to make the procedure less complicated and to provide more accused with the right to a jury trial.[1181]

1289. At present, a defendant has the right that his/her case, if it involves grave crimes against life, is examined with the participation of jurors (Article 20, paragraph 2 Const.). For the realization of the right, the defendant (if several—at least one) has to lodge a motion on requesting his/her case tried with a jury at the preliminary hearings of the preparatory stage of the court proceedings (Article 325, paragraph 2 UPKR). The ruling of the court at the preliminary hearings on the composition of the trial with juries is final. The subsequent refusal of the defendant to change the procedure is not accepted. (Article 325, paragraph 5 UPKR).

1290. The court proceedings with the participation of jurors consist of the same stages as the ordinary trial proceedings, including the preparatory stage, judicial investigation, pleadings in the court, the final statement of the defendant as well as the announcement of the judgment. However, the jury trial proceedings contain additional elements.

1291. Thus, at the preparatory stage, the **formation of the jurors** is conducted, which takes place in a closed court hearing (Article 328, paragraph 3 UPKR). At this stage, the presiding professional judge informs the parties as well as the jurors about their rights and obligations. For instance, the parties are entitled to challenge the jurors, and the defendant, his/her defense counsel and the prosecutor can make use of their right to an unmotivated objection to a juror twice.

1292. The presiding judge informs the jury about their rights, obligations and challenges that they might face during the trial (Article 328, paragraph 2 UPKR). In particular, they have the right to participate in the examination of all the circumstances of the criminal case, right to ask the presiding judge to explain the meaning of the legal provisions relating to the criminal case (Article 333 UPKR). Jurors, however, may not be absent from the courtroom during the hearing of the criminal case, express their opinion on this criminal case before the discussions on the verdict, or to discuss with persons who are not participants of the court proceedings and the circumstances of the criminal case (Article 333, paragraph 2 UPKR).

1181. Golubkova, Mariya/Kozlova, Natalya. Bud´te sudimi, Rossijskaya Gazeta 25.02.2016: http://rg.ru/2016/02/25/ks-rf-rasshiril-polnomochiia-prisiazhnyh-i-razreshil-im-sudit-zhenshchin.html.

According to Article 333, paragraph 3 UPKR, the failure to appear in court without a reasonable excuse a juror may be subject to a disciplinary fine (Article 118 UPKR).

1293. Before the beginning of the court hearings, the jurors are obliged to an **oathtaking** (Article 332 UPKR). This procedural action, for instance, is not a part of ordinary court proceedings. The text of the oath reads as follows: "While taking responsibilities of being a juror, I solemnly swear to perform them honestly and impartially, to take into account all of the evidence examined in the court both incriminating and justifying the defendant, to consider the criminal case upon my inner conscience, not to justify the guilty and not to convict the innocent, as it ought to be for a free citizen and a just person."

1294. The difference from the ordinary court proceedings is that the jury shall retire to the deliberation room to reach a verdict after the **jury instructions** or summing given by the presiding judge and not after the final statement of the defendant (Article 341 UPKR.).

1295. When giving the jury instructions, it is prohibited for the presiding judge to express in any form his/her views on matters put before the jury, e.g., the question of the guilt of the defendant. In the instructions, he/she explains the contents of the charges; the content of the criminal law provisions that are applicable in the case; sets out the position of the public prosecutor and defense, however, not expressing his/her attitude toward any of the positions; explains to the jury the basic rules of evaluation of evidence; gives further information on the procedure. The main rule that the judge has to comply with is that while explaining the rules, presenting positions of the parties and recalling the evidence examined in the court both incriminating and justifying the defendant, it is not allowed to express his/her opinion on the evidence by drawing conclusions from them (Article 340 UPKR).

1296. After the jury instructions have been given, the jury shall retire to the **deliberation room** to reach a verdict. Presence in the deliberation room of other persons except for the jury is not allowed (Article 341 UPKR).

1297. Regarding each crime and each defendant, the jurors are obliged to answer the following **questions** (Article 339 UPKR):

(1) whether it has been proved that the act took place;
(2) whether it has been proved that the act was committed by the defendant;
(3) whether the defendant is guilty of committing the act.

1298. The jurors in the discussion of the issues put before them should endeavor to adopt a unanimous decision. If the jurors failed to reach a consensus after three hours of discussion, the decision is taken by the majority vote (Article 343 UPKR).

1299. Before the final judgment is announced, the **verdict of juries** should be announced, Article 343 UPKR.

1300. According to Article 348, paragraph 1 UPKR, a non-guilty verdict passed by the jurors is binding upon the judge and leads to an acquittal. A guilty verdict, in principle, is binding upon the judge (Article 348, paragraph 2 UPKR). However, is not considered binding if, for example, an act committed by a defendant cannot be qualified as a crime or in the case, when the presiding judge acknowledges that there are sufficient grounds for the decision of acquittal due to the fact that it has not been proved that the act took place or it has not been proved that the defendant participated in committing of the offense (Article 348, paragraphs 4, 5 UPKR).

1301. Article 350 UPKR provides for the types of decisions that can be taken by the presiding judge that are considered to be **final judgments** in the Court of First Instance:

(1) the decision to terminate criminal proceedings (Article 254 UPKR);
(2) the acquittal—when the jury gave a negative answer to at least one of the three questions (Article 339 UPKR) or the presiding judge recognized the absence of the criminal conduct in the committed act;
(3) conviction;
(4) decision on the dissolution of the jury and forwarding the case for a new consideration with a different composition of the court (Article 348, paragraph 5 UPKR).

1302. The judgment can be appealed (Article 351, paragraph 4 UPKR).

§4. The Legal Remedies

I. Overview: Reform of Judicial Remedies

1303. The **reform of judicial remedies** of 2016 is one of the measures undertaken in response to the case law of the ECtHR.[1182] It began in 2010, and the latest amendments were introduced by the Federal Law in 2016.[1183] The reform has changed the system of legal remedies in criminal cases fundamentally.[1184]

1304. The previous model of judicial remedies basically foresaw two instances: **cassation** ***(кассация)***, in which decisions of lower instance courts that had not yet entered into force were examined, and **supervision procedure** ***(надзор)***, which applied to judgments that had already entered into force. The **appeal procedure** ***(апелляция)*** that presupposed consideration of the case on its merits applied only to decisions of the magistrate courts.

1182. *See* Ryabykh v. Russia, Jul. 24, 2003, App. No. 52854/99; Smarygin v. Russia, Dec. 1, 2005, App. No. 73203/01; Federal Law, Dec. 29, 2010, N 433-FZ. Paramonova, KritVj 2013, 207.
1183. Federal Law, Jul. 6, 2016, N 375-FZ.
1184. For a detailed analysis of the reform, *see* Paramonova/Bogush, ZStW 125 (2013), 703–728.

1305. According to the previous model that was in force till July 2016, in compliance with Articles 354, 355 UPKR (no longer in force), only the decisions of magistrate courts could be appealed on the merits. The only courts with jurisdiction over appeals were the district courts: they reviewed the sentences of the magistrate courts. This situation resulted in a paradox: only minor cases heard by magistrate courts (those involving offenses subject to a maximum of three years' imprisonment) were eligible for appeal and (if necessary) cassation. For more serious crimes, there was only the cassation procedure (revision of the decision on formal grounds).

1306. Under that model, regional courts and the Judicial Panel for criminal cases of the Supreme Court served as courts of cassation (formerly second instance courts that basically reviewed decisions on formal grounds, e.g., violation of the procedural provisions). They were abolished with the reform.[1185]

1307. The fact that the appeals procedure (review on the merits) was only open to decisions of the magistrate courts was criticized both in practice (including by the ECtHR[1186]) and in the literature.[1187] This criticism led to the abovementioned reform.[1188]

1308. Under the current (reformed) model of judicial remedies, the **first instance courts** examine the case on the merits (Articles 5, paragraphs 52 and 227–314 UPKR). Decisions of all lower instance courts (not only magistrate courts) that have not yet entered into force are reexamined by the second instance courts, namely, the **Courts of Appeal** ***(апелляция)***. These courts reconsider the merits of the case (Articles 5, paragraph 53 and 389.1–389.36 UPKR). The **cassation courts** (*кассация*) examine the legality of the sentences, rulings or orders of the court that had already entered into force (Articles 401.1–401.17 UPKR).

1309. In addition, the Presidium of the Supreme Court can reexamine decisions that have already entered into force by means of the judicial **supervision procedure** (***надзор***, Articles 412.1–412.13 UPKR). Articles 413–419 UPKR provide for the **procedure of resumption of proceedings in a criminal case due to new or newly-revealed circumstances** ***(возобновление производства ввиду новых или вновь открывшихся обстоятельств)***.[1189]

1310. After exhausting "all domestic judicial remedies," it is possible to direct a complaint to the **ECtHR** (Articles 45, 46 Const.).

1185. Federal Law, Dec. 29, 2010, N 433-FZ.
1186. *See* Ryabykh v. Russia, Jul. 24, 2003; Smarygin v. Russia, Dec. 1, 2005.
1187. Golovko, O rossijskoj sudebnoj reforme.
1188. Federal Law, Dec. 29, 2010, N 433-FZ.
1189. Paramonova, KritVj 2013, 207.

1311. The latest amendments, which entered into force in 2016, created a model of judicial remedies with a strong non-formalistic procedure of judicial remedies.[1190]

II. Appeal Procedure

1312. According to the reformed model of the legal remedies, decisions of all lower instance courts, including magistrate courts that have not yet entered into force, can be reexamined by the second instance courts—the **Courts of Appeal** *(апелляция)*.

1313. The courts of appeal **consider cases on their merits**, i.e., verifying the legality, reasonableness and justice of the first instance courts´ decisions (Articles 5, paragraph 53, 389.1–389.36 UPKR). This way, the trial proceedings in the Court of Appeal are conducted with all the rules of the ordinary trial procedure (Chapters 35–39 UPKR), having a preparatory stage, judicial investigation, pleadings in the court, etc. (Article 389.13 UPKR). However, there are certain special regulations that have to be followed.

1314. The **right to file an appeal** to the second instance court belongs to the convict, the acquitted, their defense counsels and legal representatives, as well as to the public prosecutor and (or) higher prosecutor, the victim, the private prosecutor, their legal representatives, and other persons to the extent to which the appealed judgment affects their rights and legitimate interests (Article 389.1 UPKR).

1315. Together with the appeal of the final judgment of the first instance court, any types of court decisions, such as rulings or (and) orders on the procedure for the examination of evidence, on the acceptance or dismissal of the requests/motions of the participants of the proceedings and other court decisions during the trial can be appealed (Article 389.2, paragraph 2 UPKR).

1316. The appeal has to be submitted to the respective **courts**, which are the following (Article 389.3 UPKR):

(1) an appeal on the judgments or other decisions of the magistrate courts is filed to the district courts;
(2) an appeal on the judgments or other decisions of the district courts and of military presidial courts is filed to the Judicial Board on criminal cases of the Supreme Court of the entities of the Russian Federation as well as to the military (naval) district courts accordingly;
(3) an appeal on the interim decision of the Supreme Court of any entity of the Russian Federation or of the military (naval) district courts—to the judicial board on criminal cases of the respective court;

1190. *Ibid.*

(4) an appeal on the judgment or on any other final decision of the Supreme Court of the entity of the Russian Federation or of the military (naval) district courts is filed to the Judicial Board on criminal cases of the Supreme Court and to the Judicial board on the military affairs of the Supreme Court, respectively;
(5) an appeal on the judgment of the judge of the Supreme Court of the Russian Federation—to the Appeals Panel of the Supreme Court of the Russian Federation.

1317. The **deadlines** for filing an appeal are stipulated by Article 389.4 UPKR. An appeal filed on the final court judgment or other decision of the court may be submitted within ten days from the day of adjudication of the decision by the first instance court. During this period, the materials of the case must be stored in the court. The appeals that were filed with missed deadlines are left without consideration (Article 389.4, paragraph 3 UPKR). Unless the requester has an admissible excuse, e.g., illness. (Article 389.5 UPKR)

1318. With regard to the **examination of evidence** during the trial investigation stage, there are some special rules. For example, that the evidence which had not been investigated by the Court of First Instance (new evidence) is accepted by the Court of Appeal, only if the person who made the request on the examination of the new evidence, including testimonies of new witnesses, proves the impossibility of the submission of this evidence to the trial court due to the reasons beyond his/her control, and the Court of Appeal recognizes these reasons as justifiable reasons (Article 389.13, paragraph 6.1 UPKR).

1319. Regarding the witnesses that had been already interrogated in the trial court, the court of appeal can interrogate them if it finds it is necessary (Article 389.13, paragraph 5 UPKR).

1320. The **grounds for cancellation or modification of the judgment** by the court of appeal are as follows, Article 389.15 UPKR:

(1) discrepancy of the court´s conclusions set out in the judgment with the factual circumstances of the criminal case established by the Court of First Instance;
(2) a serious breach of the criminal procedure law;
(3) incorrect application of the criminal law;
(4) injustice of the sentence;
(5) the circumstances of Article 237, paragraph 1 have been identified, such as that new consequences of the act have been discovered that require more serious criminal charges
(6) identification of evidence of noncompliance with the conditions and obligations under the pretrial agreement on cooperation by the defendant.

1321. The **scope of review on appeal** is regulated by the following rules (Article 389.19 UPKR):

1322. The Court of Appeal is not bound by the arguments presented in the appeal that has been filed and has the right to conduct the trial proceedings, including the court investigation, on a full scale.

1323. If an appeal has been brought by only one of the convicts, although there we several persons convicted in the case, the court is entitled to consider the appeal regarding all the convicts. Decisions of the court of appeal are obligatory for the first instance court and the prosecutor (Article 389.19, paragraph 3 UPKR).

1324. It is important to mention that the Court of Appeal is prohibited from predetermining certain issues in the case when a judgment or other court decision was quashed and the criminal case was returned for a new trial or to the prosecutor. In this case, the Court of Appeal cannot predetermine 1) whether the charges were proved or unproved; 2) the accuracy or inaccuracy of the evidence; 3) the prevalence of one piece of evidence over the other; and 4) the form and term of punishment.

1325. As a result of the appeal procedure, the court takes one of the following **decisions** (Article 389.20 UPKR):

- to retain the judgment or any other decision in force;
- to quash the conviction or any other decision and to acquit;
- to quash the conviction and to convict (e.g., on a different ground);
- to quash the sentence or other court's decision and to transfer the materials of the criminal case for the new trial proceedings in the Court of First Instance;
- to quash the acquittal or any other decision of the first instance court and acquit (e.g., on a different ground);
- to quash the judgment or any other decision of the first instance court and to return the case to the prosecutor;
- to quash the judgment or any other decision of the first instance court and to terminate the criminal proceedings;
- to change the judgment or any other decision of the first instance court;
- to terminate the appeal proceedings.

1326. All decisions of the courts of appeal may be appealed to a higher court (Article 389.35 UPKR, Chapters 47.1 and 48.1 UPKR).

III. Cassation

1327. The **cassation courts** (***кассация***) examine the legality of the sentences, rulings or orders of the court that—in contrast to the courts of appeal—had already entered into force (Articles 401.1–401.17 UPKR). While the courts of appeal consider a case on its merits (examining legality, reasonableness and justice), the cassation courts review the decisions solely on its legality, i.e., its compliance with the legal provisions.

1328. The **right to file a cassation** has the convict, the acquitted, their defense counsels and legal representatives, as well as the public prosecutor and (or) higher prosecutor, the victim, the private prosecutor, their legal representatives, and other persons to the extent to which the reviewed judgment affects their rights and legitimate interests (Article 401.1 UPKR).

1329. Regarding the cassation, this right is also given to the prosecutors of the entities of the Russian Federation as well as to the Prosecutor General of the Russian Federation and his/her deputies.

1330. A cassation claim has to be submitted directly to the **court of cassation authorized** in accordance with Article 401.3. UPKR to review the judgment. The procedure of submission of the claim is the following:

(1) cassation claims on the decisions of the magistrate courts, decisions of the district court as well as on interim judicial decisions of the Supreme Courts of the entities of the Russian Federation (when they serve as the courts of the first instance) are filed to the presidium of the Supreme Court of the respective entity.
(2) claims on the decisions of the presidiums of the Supreme Court of the entities of the Russian Federation are subject to the cassation consideration at the Judicial Division for Criminal Cases of the Supreme Court of the Russian Federation;
(3) cassation claims on the decisions of the military presidial courts and on the intermediate judgments of the military district (naval) courts as Courts of First Instance are filed to the presidium of the military district (naval) court;
(4) cassation claims on the decisions of the Presidium of the military district (naval) court are filed to the Military Panel of the Supreme Court.

1331. The revision of the decisions within the cassation procedure that entails the **deterioration** of the situation of the convicted, acquitted as well as of the person with regard to whom criminal proceedings were terminated (*reformatio in peius*), e.g., requalification of the act as a more serious crime, is only allowed in a period not exceeding one year from the date of their entry into force (Article 401.6 UPKR). Additionally, at least one of the following requirements has to be fulfilled:

- if during the trial proceedings took place such violations of the law that affected the outcome of the case and distorted the very essence of justice and the meaning of the judgment as an act of justice or
- if the information of the noncompliance of the person with the conditions and obligations of pretrial agreement on cooperation has been identified.

1332. The scope of the rights of the cassation court on reviewing a claim is stipulated in Article 401.16 UPKR:

1333. The court is not bound by the arguments of the cassation complaint has the right to verify all the actions in the entire criminal proceedings. The court of cassation can mitigate the punishment or qualify a committed act as a less serious crime.

1334. In the case where there were several persons convicted, and the cassation complaint was brought by only one of them, the court is entitled to review the proceedings in respect of all of the convicts.

1335. However, in the case if quashing or changing the sentence worsens their position, it is not permitted to apply the cassation decision with regard to those who have not filed the claim.

1336. The decisions of the cassation court are binding for the lower courts if the case has to be reconsidered by the lower court.

1337. The court of cassation, with the exception of the Supreme Court, considers the claim within the **period** not exceeding one month from the date of its receipt. In the Supreme Court, the term for consideration of the cassation claims is two months starting from the date of their receipt (Article 401.9 UPKR).

1338. The **final judgments** of the courts of cassation are the following (Article 401.14 UPKR):

- to retain the judgment or any other decision in force;
- to quash the conviction or other further decisions and to terminate criminal proceedings;
- to quash the conviction and all further decisions and pass a criminal case for a new trial or to return the case to the prosecutor;
- to quash the judgment of the Court of Appeal and pass a criminal case for new consideration by the Court of Appeal;
- to quash the decision of the court of cassation and pass a criminal case for new consideration by the court of cassation;
- to change the judgment or any other decision.

1339. The submission of the repeated or new cassation complaints filed on the same or other legal grounds, or by the same or other persons is not allowed if they are filed to the same court of cassation and if this complaint has been already considered earlier by this court in respect of the same person(s) (Article 401.17 UPKR).

IV. Supervision Procedure

1340. The Presidium of the Supreme Court can reexamine decisions that have already entered into force by means of the judicial **supervision procedure** (*надзор*, Articles 412.1–412.13 UPKR), reviewing the decisions on its legality.

1341. According to Article 412.1 UPKR, the following decisions can be **subject to judicial supervision**:

(1) the court decisions of the Supreme Courts of the entities of the Russian Federation (courts of republics, courts of autonomous regions, of federal cities etc.) adjudicated by these courts in the first instance, if these decisions were subject to appeal before the Supreme Court of the Russian Federation;
(2) judicial decisions of the military district (naval) courts adjudicated by these courts in the first instance, if such decisions were subject to appeal before the Supreme Court of the Russian Federation;
(3) judgments of the Appeal Panel, of the Judicial Panel for Criminal Cases and the Military Panel of the Supreme Court of the Russian Federation adjudicated by them in the appeal procedure;
(4) rulings of the Judicial Panel for Criminal Cases and of Military Panel of the Supreme Court of the Russian Federation passed by them in the appeal procedure;
(5) rulings of the Supreme Court of the Russian Federation.

1342. The **time period** for the consideration of a supervisory complaint by the Presidium of the Supreme Court is one month from the date of its receipt (Article 412.6 UPKR).

1343. The **grounds for quashing or modification of the judgments** under the supervisory procedure (Article 412.9 UPKR) can be significant violations of criminal law and (or) the law of criminal procedure that influenced the outcome of the case or the identification of evidence of noncompliance with the conditions and obligations under the pretrial agreement of cooperation.

1344. In principle, the **scope of the rights** of the Presidium of the Supreme Court (Article 412.12 UPKR) includes the verification of the correct application of the criminal and criminal procedural law by the lower courts that dealt with the case only within the supervisory complaint. However, in some cases, e.g., if some violations of the criminal (procedural) law took place that was not mentioned in the complaint, the Presidium of the Supreme Court is entitled to go beyond the arguments of the supervisory complaint and consider the case also in respect of persons who did not file the complaint.

1345. The reexamination of the decisions within the supervision procedure cannot result in the *reformatio in peius*, i.e., deterioration of the situation of the convicted, acquitted as well as of the person with regard to whom criminal proceedings were terminated (Article 412.9 UPKR). The exceptions to this rule are the same as in cassation and regulated with the same provisions (Article 401.6 UPKR).

1346. The Presidium of the Supreme Court, in the case of quashing of the court decision, may not establish or consider the facts that were not examined or were dismissed by the Court of First or Appellate Instances as proved. The Presidium cannot predetermine the reliability or unreliability of the evidence, the superiority of one evidence over the other or determine, which judicial decision should be made in the new proceedings (Article 412.12, paragraph 3 UPKR).

1347. The decisions of the Presidium of the Supreme Court are binding on the court that is entitled to reconsider the case (Article 412.12, paragraph 2 UPKR).

1348. As a result of the judicial supervision procedure, the Presidium of the Supreme Court can make one of the **following decisions** (Article 412.11 UPKR):

- to retain the judgment or any other decision in force;
- to quash the conviction or other further decisions and to terminate criminal proceedings;
- to quash the conviction and all further decisions and return a criminal case for a new trial to the court of the first instance;
- to quash the judgment of the court of appeal and pass a criminal case for new consideration by the court of appeal;
- to quash the decision of the court of cassation and pass a criminal case for new consideration by the court of cassation;
- to quash the conviction and all further decisions and return a criminal case to the prosecutor;
- to amend the judgment or any other decision.
- to leave the complaint without consideration on its merits, if certain procedures of the application were not observed, e.g., the deadline to file a supervisory complaint was missed (Article 412.4 UPKR).

1349. The decision of the Presidium of the Supreme Court **comes into force** from the moment of its announcement (Article 412.13 UPKR).

1350. After exhausting “all domestic judicial remedies,” it is possible to direct a complaint to the ECtHR (Articles 45, 46 Const.).[1191]

V. Resumption of Proceedings due to New or Newly-Revealed Circumstances

1351. Chapter 49 of the Code of Criminal Procedure provides for the **procedure of resumption of proceedings in a criminal case due to new or newly-revealed circumstances** (*возобновление производства ввиду новых или вновь открывшихся обстоятельств*, Articles 413–419 UPKR).[1192]

1352. The sentences, rulings, and other court decisions entered into force may be quashed, and the criminal case re-opened because of new or newly-revealed circumstances (Article 413 UPKR).

1191. Paramonova, KritVj 2013, 207.
1192. Paramonova, KritVj 2013, 207.

1353. There are two groups of circumstances that can serve as the grounds for the resumption of proceedings due to the new or newly-revealed facts.

1354. The first group consists of the **newly-revealed circumstances** (*вновь открывшиеся обстоятельства*) that existed at the time when the court sentence entered into force, but they were not known to the court. They are the following ones (Article 413, paragraph 3 UPKR):

- the entry into force of an illegal, unreasonable or unjust judgment due to the deliberate falsity of the testimony of a victim or witness, or of an expert opinion, due to a forgery of evidence, protocols and/or of investigative and judicial actions, of other documents as well as due to the knowingly incorrect translation;
- the entry into force of an illegal, unreasonable or unjust judgment due to the criminal actions of an investigator, inquirer or prosecutor;
- the entry into force of an illegal, unreasonable or unjust judgment due to the criminal acts of a judge who considered the criminal case.

1355. The second group of circumstances represents **new circumstances** (*новые обстоятельства*). They are characterized as circumstances not known to the court at the time of adjudication. These are circumstances that exclude the criminality and punishability of an act or confirm the occurrence of the new socially dangerous consequences of the crime during the consideration of the criminal case by the court or after the adjudication. In the latter case, the circumstances serve as the basis for bringing new charges against the convict of committing a more serious crime.

1356. The list of the circumstances that can be considered as "new" is not exhaustive. Among such circumstances can be the following ones (Article 413, paragraph 4 UPKR):

- recognition by the Constitutional Court of the Russian Federation the law that has been applied by the court in the criminal case unconstitutional;
- recognition by the ECtHR the violation of the provisions of the European Convention on the Protection of Human Rights in consideration of the criminal case by the Russian court. The violation is whether related to the application of the Federal Law that is not in compliance with the provisions of the European Convention on the Protection of Human Rights or to other violations of the provisions of the Convention.
- the occurrence of the new socially dangerous consequences of the crime during the consideration of the criminal case by the court or after the adjudication that serves as the basis for bringing new charges against the convict of committing a more serious crime.
- other new circumstances.

1357. The resumption of proceedings in a criminal case due to new or newly-revealed circumstances that are in favor of the convict is not limited by any deadlines (Article 414 UPKR). The death of the convicted person is not an obstacle for the resumption of criminal proceedings on this ground if the purpose is the rehabilitation of his/her good name.

1358. The right to initiate a procedure of resumption of proceedings in a criminal case due to new or newly-revealed circumstances belongs to the prosecutor, except in some cases when the review of the decisions is conducted by the Presidium of the Supreme Court of the Russian Federation (Article 415 UPKR). The new or newly-revealed facts may be reported by private persons and by officials as well as the information obtained during the preliminary and trial investigation of other criminal cases can be used.

1359. Having considered the conclusion of the prosecutor on the resumption of proceedings in a criminal case due to new or newly-revealed circumstances, the court shall make one of the following decisions (Article 418 UPKR):

- quashing the sentence and other court decisions and passing the criminal case for conducting new trial proceedings;
- quashing the sentence and further court decisions and returning the criminal case to the prosecutor;
- quashing the sentence and other court decisions and terminating criminal proceedings;
- dismissal of the conclusion of the prosecutor.

1360. The trial proceedings on the criminal case after the quashing the previous judicial decisions because of the new or newly-revealed circumstances, as well as the appeal of the new court decisions, are conducted according to the general rules of criminal procedure (Article 419 UPKR).

Part III. Execution and Extinction of Sanctions

Chapter 1. Correctional Law as Branch of Law and its Sources

1361. **Correctional law** *(уголовно-исполнительное право)*, or the **law on the execution of criminal sanctions**, regulates the legal status of prisoners and addresses questions pertaining to the execution and service of sentences as well as of other measures of the criminal-law nature.

1362. Correctional law represents a self-contained branch of law. Substantive criminal law cannot be implemented without criminal procedural and correctional law. The latter, likewise, is not of use without substantive criminal law. For instance, substantive criminal law determines the grounds of release from criminal responsibility, whereas the proceedings of such release are the domain of criminal procedural and correctional law (Articles 75 UKR, 28 UPKR and Chapter 21 UIKR).

1363. In the broadest sense, the category "criminal law" encompasses all criminal law related areas: substantive criminal law, criminal procedure, and correctional law. Some scholars consider criminal procedural and correctional law as sub-branches of a superordinate criminal law; nonetheless, according to the prevailing opinion, they are independent branches of law. This is because these branches of law have subject-matter, methods, and functions that are different from criminal law.[1193]

1364. The legal sources of the criminal correctional law constitute a diversified system consisting of the following several levels:

(1) **International legal provisions on human rights** (*международные правовые акты в области прав человека*);
(2) **Constitution of the Russian Federation** (*Конституция РФ*);
(3) **Legislative acts governing correctional law** (*уголовно-исполнительное законодательство*);

1193. For the methodology of distinguishing between the branches of law, *see* Part I, Chapter 7, §3, paras. 685–699; Sucharev, Kommentarij k UPK RF, p. 16; Matuzov, Teoriya gosudarstva i prava, p. 233.

(4) **Non-legislative acts or normative legal acts** *(нормативные правовые акты)*:
- normative legal acts of the President (*нормативные правовые акты Президента РФ*);
- regulations enacted by the Government (*нормативные правовые акты Правительства РФ*);
- interministerial normative legal acts (*межведомственные нормативные правовые акты*);
- ministerial normative legal acts (*ведомственные нормативные правовые акты*);
- decisions of the highest courts concerning execution of criminal penalties.

(1) **International Legal Provisions on Human Rights** is one of the primary sources of law for the standards and rules laid down in the Russian penalty enforcement law. First, legal provisions stipulated in the international treaties, e.g., in such as ECHR, which is binding for Russia, contain the basic human rights and international standard minimum rules for the treatment of different categories of convicts. Article 17, paragraph 1 Constitution recognizes and guarantees human rights and freedoms in accordance with universally recognized principles and norms of international law. Second, national laws are required to conform to the norms and general principles of international law, which are a “component part” of the Russian legal system (Article 15, paragraph 4 Const.).[1194]

The sources-of-law hierarchy is controversial with regard to some norms of international treaties.[1195] However, it is not the case in terms of rights and freedoms that are provided for, e.g., by the ECHR and the protocols thereto.[1196] Since the ECHR and the additional protocols (nos. 1, 2, 4, 7, 9, 10, and 11) were ratified by the Russian Federation, their rules can be directly enforced on Russian territory.[1197] In terms of prisoners, the following fundamental rights are of special significance: protection of human dignity (Article 21, paragraph 1 Const.); prohibition of torture, violence, and other severe or humiliating treatment or punishment; prohibition of medical, scientific, and other experiments without the free consent of a person (Article 21, paragraph 2 Const., Article 3 ECHR); and prohibition of unlawful arrest, detention, and keeping in custody (Article 22, paragraph 2 Const., Article 5 ECHR).

The same applies to the rules of the International Covenant on Civil and Political Rights of 1966 (ICCPR) as well as to those of the International Covenant on Economic, Social and Cultural Rights of 1966 (ICESCR). Both covenants were ratified in 1973.[1198] The fact that these rules can be directly

1194. For the sources of criminal law, *see* General Introduction, §5, I and II, paras. 116–181.
1195. For international sources of criminal law, *see* General Introduction, §5, paras. 116–144.
1196. Ivanenko, Pravovedenie, N 3, 2010, 152–153; Baglaj, Konstituzionnoe pravo RF, p. 178.
1197. Art. 1 Federal Law on Ratification of the ECHR, Mar. 30, 1998, N 54-FZ; http://www.echr.ru/convention/protocols.htm [last visited Dec. 18, 2019]; for the sources of criminal law, *see* General Introduction, §5, I and II, paras. 116–181.
1198. For international sources of criminal law, *see* General Introduction, §5, paras. 116–144; UN Treaties, http://treaties.un.org/ [last visited Dec. 18, 2019].

enforced in domestic courts can be concluded on the basis of prevailing scholarship and legal practice.[1199] With regard to prisoners, some civil, economic and cultural rights are applicable in a confined mode.

(2) **Constitution of the Russian Federation**:

The Constitution of the Russian Federation, for the first time, enshrined the priority of the human rights and freedoms, their recognition, supervision and protection as the responsibility of the State (Article 2). Chapter II of the Constitution (Articles 17–64), entitled "Rights and Freedoms of Man and Citizen," is completely devoted to human and civil rights and freedoms. These rights and freedoms are "inalienable and shall be enjoyed by everyone from birth" (Article 17 Const.). Everyone, including convicts, is free to protect his or her rights and freedom by all means not prohibited by law (Article 45, paragraph 2 Const.).

Constitution provides for a group of rights and freedoms that are not subject to limitation, the so-called fundamental rights and freedoms (Article 56, paragraph 3 Const.). These rights that are laid down in Articles 20, 21, 23, paragraph 1, 24, 28, 34, paragraph 1, 40, paragraph 1, as well as in Articles 46–54 Const. cannot be abolished or suspended. Among them are, for instance, protection of human dignity or prohibition of torture and violence.

By virtue of Article 18 Const., human rights and freedoms shall have direct effect, determine the meaning, content and application of laws, the activities of the legislative and executive authorities and be guaranteed by the judiciary. These provisions fully apply to persons serving criminal sentences. Therefore, in terms of sources of the **correctional law**, constitutional provisions that enshrine the rights and freedoms of convicts are of primary importance.

(3) **Legislative Acts Governing Correctional Law** (***уголовно-исполнительное законодательство***): According to the constitutional norm, Article 71 item "o" Const., correctional law lies within the exclusive jurisdiction of the Russian Federation, which means that this criminal law-related area can be regulated solely by the federal legislative (Federal Laws) and non-legislative acts.

Criminal enforcement legislation of the Russian Federation consists of the Correctional Code of the Russian Federation (UIKR) and other Federal Laws, Article 2, paragraph 1 UIKR. The Criminal Code and the Code of Criminal Procedure of the Russian Federation belong to the basic Federal Laws that are the main sources of criminal law in its broadest sense, hence, of the correctional law.

Among others, the following specific Federal Laws constitute the system of the correctional law sources, such as Federal Law on institutions and bodies executing criminal penalties in the form of deprivation of freedom.[1200] It defines the principles, objectives and legal bases of activity of the correctional system and its organizational structure as well as organizational, legal bases of activity of institutions executing punishment. The law establishes the rights

1199. Resolution of the Supreme Court RF, Sep. 29, 1994; Resolution of the Supreme Court RF, Nov. 18, 1999 N 79; Gaverdovskij, Implementaziya norm mezhdunarodnogo prava, pp. 47–48; Gavrilov, MZMP, N 4, 1995, 24–37; Baglaj, Konstituzionnoe pravo RF, p. 178.

1200. Federal Law, July 21, 1993, N5473-1.

and obligations of the staff of the correctional system, their legal and social guarantees. Another Federal Law on Enforcement Proceedings,[1201] in addition to the Correctional Code, establishes the procedure for the execution of criminal penalties in the form of a fine. The law of 2008 is devoted to public control over the rights of prisoners in the correctional institutions.[1202]

(4) **Non-legislative Acts or Normative Legal Acts** (*нормативные правовые акты*):

Various aspects of the execution of criminal punishment, as well as of the other criminal law-related measures in a detailed way, are regulated by the non-legislative acts. They are enacted on the ground of and in the realization of the Federal Laws. These subordinate norms are divided into the following groups: **normative legal acts of the President** (*нормативные правовые акты Президента РФ*); **regulations enacted by the Government** (*нормативные правовые акты Правительства РФ*); **interministerial normative legal acts** (*межведомственные нормативные правовые акты*) and **ministerial normative legal acts** (*ведомственные нормативные правовые акты*). For instance, a decree of the Russian Government "On the medical examination of convicts submitted to the release from punishment due to illness"[1203] is aimed at the implementation of Article 175 UIKR (the procedure for application to the release from serving a sentence or replacing the unserved part of the punishment with a milder punishment). To the ministerial normative legal acts belong, for example, "Rules of Internal Order for Corrective-Educational Colonies of the Correctional System of the Ministry of Justice of the Russia Federation."

(5) **Case Law of the Highest Judicial Bodies** (*решения высших судебных инстанций*):

Case law is not recognized as official source of criminal law.[1204] Although decisions, resolutions *(постановления Пленума Верховного Суда РФ)*, reviews of judicial practice of the Supreme Court *(обзоры судебной практики Верховного Суда РФ)* and of other highest courts of the Russian Federation, play a significant role in shaping a standardized application of law concerning correctional law.[1205] Decisions of the highest courts concerning execution of criminal penalties are of the great importance in setting standards and regulating execution of criminal punishments. For example, the Constitutional Court of the Russian Federation (*Конституционный Суд Российской Федерации*)

1201. Federal Law on Enforcement Proceedings, July 21, 1997, N119-FZ.
1202. Federal Law, on Public Control over the Rights of Prisoners in the Correctional Institutions Jun. 10, 2008 N 76-FZ.
1203. Decree of the Russian Government on the medical examination of convicts submitted to the release from punishment due to illness, February 6, 2004, N54.
1204. Kropachev, Ugolovnoe pravo Rossii, p. 69; Lebedev, Kommentarij k UK RF, p. 29; Kuznezova, Uchenie o prestuplenii, p. 67.
1205. For the sources of criminal law, *see* General Introduction, §5, I and II, paras. 116–181.

which has a monopoly over the interpretation of the Constitution, constituted a turning point with regard to the abolition of capital punishment.[1206]

1206. Paramonova, in: Arroyo/Biglino/Schabas (eds.), Towards Universal Abolition of the Death Penalty, pp. 168–175.

Chapter 2. General Principles Concerning the Execution of Penalties

1365. General principles of the criminal enforcement law are basic legal ideas of the state policy concerning the execution of criminal punishment and regulation of social relations in this area. These principles are stipulated in the Correctional Code of the Russian Federation, Article 8 UIKR. This system of rules is based on the principles of substantive criminal law, such as the principle of justice, the principle of humanity and others.[1207]

1366. Russian law on the execution of criminal sanctions is based on the following guidelines that are divided into two major groups.

1367. On the one hand, this branch of law is governed by a number of **general legal principles** (*общеправовые принципы*): The **principle of legality** (*принцип законности*), the **principle of humanity** (*принцип гуманизма*), the **principle of democratism** (*принцип демократизма*), and the **principle of equality** of convicts before the law (*принцип равенства осужденных перед законом*).

1368. On the other hand, it is characterized by a number of **branch-specific maxims** (*отраслевые принципы*) are the following ones: the **principle of differentiation and individualization in terms of execution of punishment** (*принцип дифференциации и индивидуализации исполнения наказаний*) and the **principle of the rational use of coercive measures alongside with the means of reformation and stimulation of convicts in their law-abiding behavior** (*принцип рационального применения мер принуждения, средств исправления осужденных и.*

1369. **The principle of legality** (the rule of law) is a key principle in the Russian legal system, in general, and in the correctional law, in particular (Article 54, paragraph 2 Const., Article 3 UKR, Article 8 UIKR, Article 7 ECHR).[1208] It is expressed, first, in the rule of law, i.e., in the supremacy of the laws over the non-legislative acts (Article 4, paragraph 2 Const.). Second, the principle of legality, enshrined in the Constitution, is binding upon all state authorities: legislative, executive, and judicial.[1209]

1370. The principle "the bodies of the State authority, the bodies of local self-government, officials, private citizens and their associations shall be obliged to observe the Constitution of the Russian Federation and laws" extends to all branches of the law and is regulated by appropriate legal provisions. This maxim is equally applicable within the criminal law-related areas, such as the law on the

1207. On the principles of criminal law, *see* Part I, Chapter 1, paras. 194–196, and on the principles of the criminal procedure, *see* Part II, Chapter 1, §3, paras. 814–827.
1208. On the principles of criminal law, *see* Part I, Chapter 1, paras. 194–196, and on the principles of the criminal procedure, *see* Part II, Chapter 1, §3, paras. 814–827.
1209. Paramonova, Principle of legality in Russia, 2011, p. 107.

execution of criminal sanctions (Articles 2 UIKR, 8 UIKR). In the context of criminal enforcement, the principle of legality determines the unconditional observation and subordination of all convicts, personnel of the state bodies executing criminal penalties and other state and public organizations. The principle of legality also means observation of the freedoms and legitimate interests of convicts by all state authorities (Articles 12–15 UIKR)

1371. Of particular importance is the binding force on the legislative level of the rights, freedoms and legitimate interests of convicts (Articles 12–15 UIKR), which creates a guarantee of their realization in the process of executing criminal penalties.

1372. The **principle of humanity** is another general legal principle that governs the law on the execution of criminal sanctions. It is laid down in the legal (national and international) provisions binding on Russia, such as in the International Covenant on Civil and Political Rights of 1966 (Articles 7, 10) and the ECHR (Article 3). In accordance with the international rules and Article 8 UIKR, all persons deprived of their liberty shall have the right to humane treatment and respect as it is inherent to the dignity of the human being. The importance of this principle increases due to the fact that the convicts are less than other citizens protected from the arbitrariness of the state in the face of the staff of institutions and bodies executing criminal punishment. The convicts are more likely to be subject to torture, cruel, inhuman or degrading treatment. This behavior is explicitly prohibited by the Correctional Code, and humane treatment, in particular, by the staff of correctional facilities, is safeguarded by Article 12 UIKR (basic guarantees and individual rights of the convicts).

1373. In accordance with the Universal Declaration of Human Rights (Article 6) and the International Covenant on Civil and Political Rights (Article 16), Russian correctional law recognizes the **principle of democratism**. The principle is understood as the recognition of the legal capacity of the convicts: “everyone has the right to recognition everywhere as a person before the law.” Article 10 UIKR establishes that by the execution of criminal punishment, convicts possess the rights and freedoms that are guaranteed to Russian citizens, although with the restrictions stipulated by the criminal, correctional and other relevant laws.

1374. The **principle of equality of convicts before the law** is based upon the constitutional maxim of equality before the law and court (Article 19, paragraph 1 Const.) and equality of human and civil rights and freedoms regardless of sex, race, nationality, language, origin, property and official status, place of residence, religion, convictions, membership in public associations, or of other circumstances (Article 19, paragraph 2 Const., Article 14 ECHR). In the field of the law on the execution of criminal sanctions, it means that all prisoners, who are serving a certain kind of punishment under corresponding conditions, have the same legal status regardless of race, ethnicity, material and social status, religion. The differences in their legal status, however, are determined due to such characteristics as gender, age, health status, the behavior of the convicted person while serving a sentence.

1375. As the principle of equality of convicts, the **principle of differentiation and individualization with regard to the execution of punishment** is the component part of the principle of justice.[1210]

1376. Differentiation regarding the execution of criminal sanctions involves the classification of convicted prisoners into groups on the criminal-law and penitentiary grounds. It means that to the different categories of the convicts, depending on the nature and degree of social danger of their crimes, the form of guilt, the presence of recidivism, and their behavior during the serving punishment, different correctional tools and in various amounts are applicable. For example, all persons sentenced to imprisonment are serving their sentences in different types of correctional institutions under different conditions (Articles 74, 78 UIKR).[1211]

1377. Thanks to this principle, in addition to the group factors, individual characteristics of the convicted person are taken into account, such as socio-demographic and moral-psychological characteristics of the personality of each convicted person. The staff of the correctional bodies, especially psychologists and teachers, have the goal to reveal, stimulate and develop positive personality traits and neutralize the negative ones. Ideally, one of the main goals of criminal punishment shall be achieved—the reformation of a convicted person (Article 43 UKR).

1378. The principle of the rational use of coercive measures alongside with the means of reformation and stimulation of convicts in their law-abiding behavior is a maxim directed at the achievement of the balance between two in many aspects opposing methods: On the one hand, the use of coercive measures and, on the other hand, stimulation of the positive, law-abiding behavior of the person sentenced to criminal penalty.

1379. This principle develops the ideas of the differentiation and individualization of punishment through being guidance to the staff of correctional bodies in the comprehensive and balanced implementation of different types of punishment on an individual basis (Articles 9, paragraph 3, 11, paragraph 6 UIKR).

1380. On the one hand, rational use of coercive measures holds the infliction of responsibility on the convicted person for violation of the internal rules and requirements of the correctional facilities. When imposing different types of sanctions and of other coercive measures applicable with regard to such violation, the personality of the convict and his/her previous behavior, the nature of the offense as well as circumstances of its commission shall be taken into consideration (Articles 9, paragraph 3, 29, 32, 46, 58, 59, 71, 102, 115, 117, 136, 138 UIKR).

1381. On the other hand, when carrying out official duties, particularly coercive measures of any kind, the staff of correctional facilities must follow the principles

1210. On the principles of criminal law, *see* Part I, Chapter 1, paras. 194–196, and on the principles of the criminal procedure, *see* Part II, Chapter 1, §3, paras. 814–827.
1211. For types of correctional facilities, *see* paras. 57–59, 1388.

determined by the law, including the principle of legality, the principle of humanity, impartiality, the principle of maintenance and respect for human rights that prohibits the use of violence or other cruel, inhuman, or degrading treatment like the principle of humanity, etc.[1212]

1382. In the law on the execution of criminal sanctions, a special place is given to the legal incentives since their use entails for the convicted favorable legal consequences. Various forms of such legal incentives applicable to the convict in accordance with the type of penalty he/she is serving are provided by the Correctional Code (e.g., Articles 45, 57, 71, 113, 134 UIKR), such as the permission to spend holidays outside of the territory of the municipality (Article 57 UIKR).

1383. The result of the well-balanced implementation of both opposing components of the principle is, if not a reformation, at least a law-abiding behavior of the convict in the future.

1212. On the principles of criminal law, *see* Part I, Chapter 1, paras. 194–196, and on the principles of the criminal procedure, *see* Part II, Chapter 1, §3, paras. 814–827.

Chapter 3. The Prison System

§1. Organizational Structure

I. Prison Administration

1384. **Federal Correctional Service of Russia** (*Федеральная служба исполнения наказаний*, hereinafter FPS)[1213]—is a federal executive prison authority responsible for security and maintenance of prisons in Russia. It performs law enforcement functions and the functions of control and supervision in the penitentiary sphere. The prison administration and the institutions of the FPS are parts of the organizational structure of the Ministry of Justice.

1385. As already mentioned above, penitentiary legislation lies within the exclusive jurisdiction of the Russian State (Article 71 item. "o" Const.). All federal entities shall follow the Federal Laws and non-legislative acts in this area.

1386. The Federal Law on institutions and bodies executing criminal penalties in the form of deprivation of freedom[1214] *inter alia* defines the organizational structure of the correctional institutions. According to Article 5 of this Law, the Russian correctional system consists of the federal executive body authorized to enforce or execute criminal sanctions (i.e., Federal Correctional Service), territorial correctional bodies, as well as correctional institutions. Moreover, the system includes detention centers, enterprises that are specially designed for the operation of the correctional system, medical, educational and other institutions.

1387. **Territorial bodies of the correctional system** (*территориальные органы УИС*) are General Directorates of the Federal Correctional Service in 85 entities of the Federation, e.g., General Directorate of the Federal Correctional Service of Krasnoyarsk Region. They are established by the FPS in order to manage and control the subordinated institutions executing punishment, as well as special units for correctional escort.

1388. The **correctional institutions** (*учреждения, исполняющие наказания*) are provided for by Article 16 UIKR. For the enforcement of custodial types of punishment, there are the following types of correctional facilities: arrest houses (Articles 67–72 UIKR); correctional prison camps (Article 74, paragraph 1 UIKR); prisons (Article 74, paragraph 7 UIKR); specialized facilities in prison camps and prisons for medical treatment during incarceration (Article 74, paragraph 8 UIKR); and educational juvenile correctional facilities designed for juveniles ages 14 to 18 (Article 74, paragraph 9 UIKR).

1213. Decree of the President of the Russian Federation from 13.10.2004, N 1314 "On the Federal Correctional Service."
1214. Federal Law, Jul. 21, 1993, N 5473-1.

II. Types of Correctional Facilities

1389. The prison system in terms of types of correctional facilities has already been described above in the General Introduction (*supra*, § 1, III.D.).[1215]

§2. The Correctional Regime

I. Introduction

1390. The **correctional regime** (*режим в исправительных учреждениях*) and its basic requirements are stipulated inArticle 82 UIKR. It is defined as an order established by the legal provisions for execution and serving of imprisonment, which provides security and isolation of convicts, the constant supervision of them, the performance of their duties, the realization of their rights and legitimate interests, the personal security of convicts and the staff, the separation of different categories of convicts, the consideration of various conditions of detention, depending on the type of correctional institution assigned by the court as well as relevant changes of such conditions.

1391. The rules and standards relating directly to the regime of execution and serving of a sentence in the form of imprisonment are provided for by the Chapter 12 UIKR. They are specified in the ministerial normative legal acts, such as "Internal Regulations of Correctional Institutions"[1216] and "Internal Regulations of Educational Juvenile Correctional Facilities".[1217]

II. Aspects of Living Conditions

1392. Living conditions in a correctional facility fully depends on the type of correctional regime of the correctional facility. Within a correctional prison camp, convicts can serve their punishment under conditions of a general, light or strict regime. For the persons serving their sentence in prison, there are two types of regimes: general and strict (Article 87 UIKR).

A. Social and Health Care: Education

1393. The Correctional Code establishes the obligation of the administration of the correctional facilities not only to provide health and social care but also to provide proper education.

1215. *See* paras. 57–59.

1216. "Internal Regulations of Correctional Institutions" approved by the order of the Ministry of Justice, November 3, 2005 No. 205.

1217. "Internal Regulations of Educational Juvenile Correctional Facilities" approved by the order of the Ministry of Justice, October 6, 2006 No. 311.

1394. In the correctional facilities, general high school **education** is obligatory for the convicts under the age of 30 years. Convicts also have an opportunity to obtain vocational education or qualified training in various professions, e.g., carpenter. For exams, the convicts are released from work in accordance with Russian labor legislation. Obtaining by a convict any kind of education is encouraged and taken into account in determining the extent of his/her reformation (Articles 108, 112 UIKR). Moreover, taking into account the existing capacity of the correctional institution, the administration is obliged to provide assistance to prisoners in receiving higher education (Article 108 UIKR).

1395. There are obligatory **state social insurance** and **pension security** for persons sentenced to imprisonment (Article 98 UIKR).

1396. Thus, persons sentenced to deprivation of freedom involved in the work are subject to obligatory state social insurance. Convicts have the right to a state pension in old age, to disability pensions, to the pensions in the case of loss of a breadwinner, and in other cases.

1397. Convicted women are provided with **maternity benefits**. These allowances are paid regardless of the performance of the work duties by a woman and of other circumstances. In the correctional facilities, where women with children serve their sentences, child care centers can be organized. They may be allowed to live together with their children. The convicted pregnant women, women during childbirth and women in the postpartum period shall receive specialized medical care (Article 100 UIKR).

The **health care** system in the correctional field consists of medical institutions (hospitals, specialized psychiatric and tuberculosis hospitals), medical units, and correctional treatment facilities for the in- and outpatient treatment of convicts suffering from the open forms of tuberculosis, alcoholism or drug addiction. The aim of this system is to ensure health, hygiene, and appropriate alimentation of the convicts through proper medical and sanitary care (Article 101 UIKR).

Prison authorities are responsible for the fulfillment of the established sanitary and epidemiological requirements to ensure the protection of the health of convicts, such as through organizing and conducting regular health surveillance, conducting medical and sanitation inspections, providing conditions for rehabilitation measures, e.g., for people with disabilities. In cases of refusal of a convict on food intake and the occurrence of a threat to his/her life, a convict may be forced to food intake for medical reasons (Article 101, paragraphs 3, 4 UIKR).

B. Communications

1398. Persons sentenced to deprivation of freedom are entitled to short **visits** lasting four hours and long visits lasting three days on the territory of the correctional institution. Short visits are granted to relatives or other persons in the presence of a representative of the administration of the correctional institution. Long visits are provided with the right to live together with the husband (wife), parents, children, adoptive parents, adopted children, siblings, grandparents, grandchildren, and with the permission of the chief of the prison—with other persons (Article 89 UIKR). In some cases, e.g., due to exceptional family reasons, a convict can be granted a long visit with living outside the prison for five days. In this case, the head of the correctional institution determines the location of the visit. Convicted persons at their request are allowed to replace a long meeting with a short-term visit and a short-term or long meeting with a telephone conversation.

1399. For legal assistance, convicts are granted **private, confidential meetings with lawyers** or other persons entitled to legal assistance, without limiting their number. Each meeting can last up to four hours.

1400. Persons sentenced to deprivation of freedom shall have the right to make **telephone calls**. In the absence of the technical capabilities in a correctional facility, the prison administration may limit the number of telephone conversations to six per year. The duration of each call should not exceed 15 minutes. Upon arrival at the prison, as well as under the exceptional personal circumstances of the convict, the prison administration provides the opportunity to convict to make a phone call at his/her request (Article 92 UIKR).

1401. Convicts are allowed to send and receive at their own expense letters, postcards and telegrams without limitation of their number. However, all **correspondence** is censored by the prison authorities, except for certain cases, such as proposals, applications, petitions and complaints addressed to the President of the Russian Federation, to the chambers of the Federal Assembly of the Russian Federation, to the Government of Russian Federation, to the legislative or law enforcement regional state bodies, to the court, etc. (Article 15, paragraph 4 UIKR). Additionally, correspondence of the convict with his/her lawyer or other person providing legal assistance on the legal grounds cannot be censored. An exception to this case is the situation when the prison administration has reliable data on that the correspondence contains information aimed at initiating, planning, or organizing a crime organization (Article 91 UIKR).

C. Work

1402. Every person sentenced to imprisonment shall be obliged to work in places and jobs determined by the administration of correctional institutions. The prison administration has an obligation to involve convicts in work based on their gender, age, professional capabilities, health status, and, if possible, their professional specialization, as well as on the basis of the availability of jobs (Article 103 UIKR).

1403. Prisoners are assigned to work to the centers for labor adaptation of convicts, to the so-called labor workshops of the correctional institutions, to the federal or regional state enterprises, e.g., unitary enterprises that cooperate with the correctional facilities, and private organizations. The working centers or any other organizations where the convicts are assigned to work can be located on the territory of correctional institutions and (or) outside. The only condition that has to be fulfilled is ensuring adequate protection and isolation of prisoners.

1404. Refusal to work is considered to be a malicious violation of the correctional order and may result in the application of disciplinary penalties and liability for damage (Article 103, paragraph 6 UIKR).

1405. Article 103, paragraph 2 UIKR provides for special rules concerning labor for different categories of convicts. Thus, convicted men older than 60 years and convicted women older than 55 years, as well as prisoners who belong to the first or second group of disabilities, can be assigned to work solely at their request. Juvenile convicts cannot be assigned to certain heavy types of work. Thereby, the legal provisions of labor and social law of the Russian Federation are taken into consideration, such as social protection of vulnerable groups of society, e.g., disabled persons.

D. Incentive and Disciplinary Measures

1406. For good behavior, a conscientious attitude to work, education, and active participation in educational activities, the following **incentive measures** (***меры поощрения***) may be applied to the convict: acknowledgment (e.g., a positive note in the convict´s file that has to be considered by any further evaluation), awarding with a gift, cash prize, authorization for additional packages or transfer, granting an additional short-term and long-term leave from prison, early withdrawal of the previously imposed disciplinary measures, and others (Article 113 UIKR).

1407. Additional incentive measures can be applied depending on the type of correctional facility. For example, to the convicted person serving a sentence in settlement prison camps (correctional facilities with a least strict regime), permission to spend weekends and holidays outside the prison camp can be granted (Article 113, paragraph 2 UIKR).

1408. In general, for the further reformation effect, a positively characterized convict may be recommended to the replacement of the unserved part of the punishment with a milder form of punishment.[1218]

1409. Article 115 UIKR provide for the **disciplinary measures** (***меры взыскания***) that are applicable to persons sentenced to imprisonment. For violation of the correctional order, the following measures may be applied to the

1218. For the replacement of the unserved part of the punishment with a milder form of punishment, *see* para. 1364.

convicts: reprimand, a disciplinary fine of up to RUB 200, placement in a punishment cell for up to fifteen days, and others.

1410. Following the principle of differentiation and individualization of execution of criminal punishment, there are differences in the kinds of disciplinary measures that can be imposed on men and women. Another factor influencing the imposition of such measures is the gravity of a committed crime that determines the type of correctional regime.

1411. This way, men who maliciously and repeatedly have violated the rules of the correctional regime can be placed in single cell-type rooms for up to one year. In contrast, for women, the maximum period of this disciplinary measure cannot exceed three months.

1412. However, to the convicts serving imprisonment in settlement prison camps, such disciplinary measures as isolation in single cell-type rooms are not applicable (Article 115, paragraph 3 UIKR).

E. Leave from Prison

1413. Persons sentenced to deprivation of freedom may be permitted leave from prison. There are two types of leave from prison: short-term and long-term leave (Article 97 UIKR).

1414. **Short-term leave** (*краткосрочные выезды*) is granted due to exceptional personal circumstances, such as death or serious illness of a close relative, a natural disaster that has caused significant material damage to the convicted person or his/her family as well as due to the necessity to resolve the employment and accommodation questions before being released. The leave may last up to seven days. Thereby, the time needed to travel is not counted. To convicted women with children, leave can be granted for a period of up to fifteen days. An application for a short-term leave due to exceptional personal circumstances should be considered for one day.

1415. **Long-term leave** (*длительный выезды*) can be granted for the period of annual paid leave according to the labor law.

1416. The permission for the leave from prisons of any kind is given by the chief of the correctional institution, who shall take into account the nature and gravity of the crime, the served period, personality and behavior of the convict.

1417. Leave from prison is not allowed in some cases. These are, for example, the following situations: convicts that serve their punishment for especially dangerous recidivism, convicts sentenced to life imprisonment, prisoners with an open form of tuberculosis, convicts that have not undergone a full course of treatment of venereal disease, alcoholism, and drug addiction.

1418. Additionally, convicted persons suffering from mental disorders that do not exclude responsibilities, convicts who need home health care, as well as juvenile offenders may get permission for the leave from prison only if they are accompanied by a relative or another person (Article 97, paragraph 4 UIKR).

1419. The time during which the convicted person is permitted to leave prison is included in the term of punishment (Article 97, paragraph 7 UIKR).

F. Other

1420. Persons sentenced to imprisonment can buy **food and articles of daily necessity** on the money they earned while serving their sentences, on the pensions, social benefits and cash transfers they receive. These funds are credited to the personal accounts of convicts (Article 88 UIKR).

1421. The prison administration shall provide the convicts with **clothing** (Article 82 UIKR). The type of clothing allowed is determined by the "Internal Regulations of Correctional Institutions."

1422. Convicts are allowed to receive **parcels, packages, and postal packets**; they are subject to inspection. Packages with medicines and medical supplies obtained in accordance with a medical opinion are not included in the number of parcels and packages. With the permission of the administration of the prison, convicts may also send parcels and packages (Article 90 UIKR). They are also entitled to receive **cash transfers** as well as transfer money to close relatives and other persons (Article 91 UIKR).

1423. Convicted persons serving their imprisonment in the locked premises, such as punitive isolators, disciplinary isolators, cell-type rooms, single cell-type rooms, if they do not work in the open air, have the right to **walk** and to be in the open air. Depending on the correctional regime of the type of correctional facility and the behavior of the convicted person, the walk can last from one up to two hours (Articles 93,118 UIKR). The walks for the convicts are held in the daytime on the specially equipped territory of the correctional institution. If the internal regulations of correctional institutions have been violated, walks can be terminated prematurely.

1424. Convicted persons, except for those on whom certain disciplinary measures were imposed, e.g., punitive isolators, are allowed to watch **television** in their free time from work, except for the time for a night rest. Convicts may buy their own televisions and radios at their own expenses through the trade network or receive them from their relatives and other persons (Article 94 UIKR).

1425. In the libraries of the correctional facilities, convicts have at their disposal **books**, newspapers, and magazines. Additionally, they are allowed to purchase or receive in parcels and packages writing materials, and different types of literature, as well as, without limitation, subscribe to newspapers and magazines at their own expense. However, it is prohibited to receive, to purchase, to store, and to distribute materials advocating war, inciting national and religious hatred, the cult of violence or cruelty, pornographic publications (Article 95 UIKR).

§3. Legal Status of Prisoners: Complaints Procedure

1426. The basic rights and obligations of convicts—as described above—are stipulated in a large number of provisions that form the base for the legal status of prisoners.[1219] The legal status of prisoners is determined through the **principle of the prohibition of the limitation of the so-called fundamental rights and freedoms** (Article 56, paragraph 3 Const.). These rights cannot be abolished or suspended. According to Article 56, paragraph 3 Const., these fundamental rights and freedoms are provided for in Articles 20, 21, 23, paragraph 1, 24, 28, 34, paragraph 1, 40, paragraph 1, as well as in Articles 46–54 Const.: the right to life (Article 20 Const., Article 2 ECHR); protection of human dignity (Article 21, paragraph 1 Const.); prohibition of torture, violence, and other severe or humiliating treatment or punishment; prohibition of medical, scientific, and other experiments without the free consent of a person (Article 21, paragraph 2 Const., Article 3 ECHR).

1427. On the other hand, due to the special legal status of the prisoners in terms of a number of the justified restrictions imposed on them by society, the **principle of the limitation of human rights and freedoms** to the extent necessary for the protection of the fundamental principles of the constitutional system, morality, health, the rights and lawful interests of other people, and for ensuring the defense of the country and security of the state (Article 55, paragraph 3 Const.) is applicable. These are, for instance, the right to freedom and personal inviolability or right to privacy of correspondence, telephone conversations, postal, telegraph, and other messages. The limitation can be imposed solely by Federal Law.

1428. The Correctional Code is one of the Federal Laws that provides for additional rights and obligations of convicts and imposes limitations[1220] on the human rights and freedoms of prisoners—that are seen in the correctional regime based on this constitutional mechanism.

1429. Chapter 2 of the Correctional Code is devoted to the legal status of prisoners. Basic rights of convicts are enshrined in Article12 UIKR.

1430. Convicted persons have the right to receive information about their rights and obligations, about the procedure and conditions of serving a penalty assigned by the court. The administration of the correctional institution is obliged to provide a convict with this information, as well as to acquaint him/her with the changes of internal rules and penal conditions.

1219. For the sources of correctional law, *see* Part III, Chapter 1, para. 1364.
1220. For the correctional regime, *see* Part III, Chapter 3, §2, paras. 1390–1425.

1431. Convicted persons have the right to courteous treatment by prison staff. Coercive measures may not be applied except for cases provided for by law. Inhuman or degrading treatment, as well as medical, scientific, and other experiments without free consent of a convict, are explicitly prohibited by the UIKR in accordance with the Constitution and the ECHR (Article 12, paragraphs 2, 3 UIKR).

1432. Another important right is the right to make proposals, complaints, applications, and petitions that can be addressed to the institution or body carrying out the punishment, to courts, to prosecutor's offices, to international bodies for the protection of human rights and freedoms, to public authorities and local governments, including various representatives of the state, such as Ombudsman of the Russian Federation for the human rights or the Commissioner of the President of the Russian Federation on the children's rights as well as to different nongovernmental monitoring commissions and associations. (Article 12, paragraph 4 UIKR). The convicts have the right to complain and handle correspondence in their native language or any other language they speak.

1433. Besides, persons serving sentences have the right to health protection, including the right to (specialized) health care in the outpatient or inpatient setting. Prisoners are also entitled to psychological assistance provided by the staff of the psychological service of the correctional institution, however, only with their consent.

1434. The right to social security, including pensions and social benefits, is guaranteed to the convicts in accordance with the Russian legislation.

1435. To obtain legal aid, convicts can use the services of attorneys and other persons entitled to such assistance. Foreign citizens serving custodial penalties in Russia have the right to maintain contact with the diplomatic missions and consular offices of their countries in the Russian Federation (Article 12, paragraph 9 UIKR).

1436. Besides, in the correctional institutions, the right of convicted persons to personal security shall be maintained. If needed, the head of the institution is obliged to transfer a convict to a safe place or undertake other measures to eliminate the threat to his/her personal security (Article 13 UIKR).

1437. In the correctional institutions, freedom of conscience and freedom of religion of convicts is guaranteed. According to Article 14 UIKR, they have the right to profess any religion or to profess no religion, to freely choose, possess and disseminate religious beliefs and to act in accordance with them.

1438. Realizing their right to complain, convicts may submit proposals, applications, petitions and complaints in accordance with the Federal Law on the Procedure of Consideration of Applications and Complaints of Citizens of the Russian Federation[1221] (Article 15 UIKR).

1439. There are **two complaints procedures** that are distinguished by means of the type of punishment served (Article 15, paragraph 3 UIKR).

1440. The first complaints procedure presupposes that persons sentenced to arrest, detention in a disciplinary military unit, or imprisonment may complain through the institutions and bodies enforcing punishment. These complaints within one working day are transferred to operators for delivery. This correspondence cannot be censored by the prison authorities (Article 15, paragraph 4 UIKR).

1441. According to the second complaints procedure, convicts sentenced to any other types of punishment send their proposals, applications, petitions and complaints on their own.

1442. Bodies and officials to whom proposals, applications and complaints are addressed must consider them within the established by law terms and bring decisions to the attention of the convicts. In accordance with Article 12 of the Federal Law on the Procedure of Consideration of Applications and Complaints of Citizens of the Russian Federation, they must be considered within 30 days from the date of registration of the written request.

§4. Judicial Control and Supervision over the Enforcement of Criminal Sanctions

1443. The activities and decisions of the institutions and bodies enforcing penalties underlie several types of control.

1444. First, there is **judicial control** (*судебный контроль*) over the enforcement of criminal sanctions. The prison inmate has a right to appeal the decision of the correctional institution imposing any type of measures on him/her (Article 20 UIKR).

1445. Second, over the activities of institutions and bodies executing punishment, **institutional control** (*ведомственный контроль*) is carried out by the higher authorities and their officials, for instance, Federal Correctional Service controls their regional General Directorates in 85 entities of the Federation (Article 21 UIKR).

1221. Federal Law on the Procedure of Consideration of Applications and Complaints of Citizens of the Russian Federation, 2 May 2006, N 59-FZ.

1446. Third, the **public prosecutor's supervision** (*прокурорский надзор*, Article 22 UIKR) is carried out over observance of the laws by correctional institutions. It is exercised by the General Prosecutor of the Russian Federation and subordinate prosecutors, in accordance with the Federal Law on Prosecutor's Office of the Russian Federation.[1222]

1447. Fourth, there is a **public control** (*общественный контроль*) over ensuring human rights in detention centers, prisons and disciplinary military units. In compliance with the Federal Law on Public Control over Ensuring Human Rights in Places of Detention,[1223] the public control is carried out by regional public monitoring commissions.

§5. Grounds for Relief from Serving Criminal Punishment

I. Conditional Early Release from Serving Punishment

1448. A person serving punishment in a disciplinary military unit or in the form of compulsory labor or deprivation of freedom may be eligible for conditional early release if the court decides a full serving of the sentence is not needed for his or her reformation. The person may be fully or partially released from serving an additional penalty (Article 79, paragraph 1 UKR).[1224]

1449. Conditional early release may only be ordered if a number of requirements have been satisfied. Among these is the actual serving of a predefined portion of the sentence, the duration of which depends on the severity of the offense. For instance, at least one-third of a sentence for a commission of a crime of small or average gravity and at least half of a sentence for a grave crime must actually be served (Article 79, paragraph 3 UKR). However, the actual term of deprivation of freedom actually served cannot be less than six months (Article 79, paragraph 4 UKR). With regard to persons who are serving a life sentence, the term of imprisonment actually served cannot be less than twenty-five years (Article 79, paragraph 5 UKR). When considering an application for conditional release, the court takes into account the behavior of the person, his or her attitude to studying and work throughout the period of serving a sentence (including his or her disciplinary record with incentives and penalties), the person's attitude toward the crime he or she committed, partial or full compensation of the damage to the victim, as well as the report of the prison administration about the appropriateness of conditional release (Article 79, paragraph 4.1 UKR).[1225]

1222. For the prosecuting authorities, *see* General Introduction, §2, III, B, paras. 48–51.
1223. Federal Law on Public Control over Ensuring Human Rights in Places of Detention, June 10 2008, N 76-FZ.
1224. Lebedev, Kommentarii k UK RF, pp. 185–189; Naumov, Rossiiskoe ugolovnoe pravo, pp. 592–598; Zhuravlev, Ugolovnoe pravo, pp. 247–250.
1225. Komissarov/Krilova/Tyazhkova, Ugolovnoe pravo RF, pp. 714–724.

II. Replacement of Unserved Term of Punishment with Milder Punishment

1450. With regard to a person serving punishment in a disciplinary military unit or in the form of compulsory labor or deprivation of freedom, the court can decide to replace the unserved term of punishment with a milder punishment. The person may be fully or partially released from serving an additional penalty (Article 80 UKR).[1226] Under the law, a predefined portion of the sentence, the duration of which depends on the severity of the offense, must actually be served. For instance, at least one-third of a sentence for a commission of a crime of small or average gravity and at least half of a sentence for a grave crime must actually be served (Article 80, paragraph 2 UKR).

1451. As far as the replacement of the remaining term of punishment is concerned, the court may choose any milder type of punishment that is provided for in Article 44 UKR (Article 80, paragraph 3 UKR).[1227] Furthermore, the court must consider the behavior of a convict, his or her attitude to studying and work throughout the period of serving a sentence, his or her disciplinary record with incentives and penalties, the attitude of the convicted person to his or her crime, and whether partial or full compensation of the damage to the victim has been made (Article 80, paragraph 4 UKR).

III. Release from Punishment due to a Change of Situation

1452. A first-time offender who has committed a crime of small or average gravity must be released from serving punishment if the court determines that the offender or his or her crime has ceased to be regarded as socially dangerous due to a change of situation (Article 80.1 UKR). The circumstances that characterize the "changed situation" may have to do with the offender or with the offense: for example, death of a close person, a serious disease of the offender, the birth of a child, etc.[1228]

IV. Release from Punishment due to Illness

1453. An additional ground for relief from criminal punishment is an illness. Relief in this context may be granted if, after the commission of a crime, a person becomes mentally ill and is consequently deprived of the possibility of realizing the actual nature and social danger of his or her acts or of controlling them (Article 81 UKR). The court may impose compulsory medical measures upon such persons

1226. Lebedev, Kommentarii k UK RF, pp. 189–190; Naumov, Rossiiskoe ugolovnoe pravo, p. 627; Zhuravlev, Ugolovnoe pravo, pp. 250–251.
1227. Komissarov/Krilova/Tyazhkova, Ugolovnoe pravo RF, pp. 740–745.
1228. Lebedev, Kommentarii k UK RF, pp. 190–192; Naumov, Rossiiskoe ugolovnoe pravo, pp. 627–628.

(Article 81, paragraph 1 UKR).[1229] In addition, Article 81 UKR extends to persons who, after the commission of a crime, contract a grave illness other than a mental illness that prevents them from serving their sentence (Article 81, paragraph 2 UKR). However, if a person who has been released from serving punishment because of illness on the basis of either of these grounds recovers, his or her criminal responsibility will be re-assessed unless the period of limitation has expired (Article 81, paragraph 4 UKR).[1230]

V. Suspension of Serving Punishment with a Possible Full or Partial Release for Pregnant Women and Women and Men with Children

1454. Pregnant women and women and men with children may be relieved from criminal punishment (Article 82 UKR). In this context, the court, as a first step, can suspend the actual serving of punishment (Article 82, paragraph 1 UKR); however, under certain conditions, convicts may be fully or partially released from serving their sentences (Article 82, paragraph 4 UKR).[1231] The court may suspend the actual serving of punishment for pregnant women and for women and men with a child under the age of 14 until the child reaches the age of 14. However, this provision does not apply to persons who have committed certain crimes, such as offenses against the sexual integrity of minors or crimes connected with terrorist activity (Article 82, paragraph 1 UKR).

1455. Hence, the convicts may be fully or partially released from serving their sentences. In order to do this, the court will take into consideration the behavior of the convict during the time of the suspension of the punishment based on a report of the authority responsible for his or her supervision (Article 82, paragraph 4 UKR).

1229. Naumov, Rossiiskoe ugolovnoe pravo, pp. 628–629; Zhuravlev, Ugolovnoe pravo, pp. 252–254.
1230. Komissarov/Krilova/Tyazhkova, Ugolovnoe pravo RF, pp. 725–732.
1231. Lebedev, Kommentarii k UK RF, pp. 194–197.

Chapter 4. Extinction of Sanctions or Sentences

§1. Pardon

1456. **Pardon**—also referred to as **clemency** *(помилование)*—is an act undertaken by the president of the Russian Federation with respect to an individually defined person or group of persons. Although an act of clemency is a nonjudicial decision, it is binding on the relevant law enforcement agencies.[1232] The purpose of the institution of pardon is to implement the principle of humanism and compassion in criminal policy and laws.[1233]

1457. According to Article 85 UKR (Pardon):[1234]

(1) A pardon shall be granted by the President of the Russian Federation with respect to an individually determined person.
(2) A person who has been convicted for the commission of a crime may be released from the further serving of his or her sentence, or the imposed punishment may be reduced or replaced with a milder punishment by an act of pardon. The criminal record may be removed from a person who has served punishment by an act of pardon.

1458. Through an act of pardon, a person convicted of a crime may be released from the further serving of his or her sentence, or the imposed punishment may be reduced or replaced with a milder punishment. Typically, an act of pardon does not expunge the criminal record. As a result, legal provisions regarding recidivism are applicable, as these norms apply to offenders who have a criminal record (Article 18, paragraph 1 UKR). It should be noted, however, that the criminal record of a person who has already served his or her punishment may be expunged at the discretion of the court (Article 85, paragraph 2 UKR).[1235]

1459. The act of pardon is an exceptional measure at the discretion of the president of Russia. The law does not establish any specific conditions for the granting of a pardon: there are no restrictions on particular groups of persons or on the nature and degree of the social danger of their crimes, nor are there any explicit restrictions with regard to any particular types of offenses.[1236] A pardon can be granted with respect to any convict, regardless of the length of the sentence he or she has served. However, the application of this institution in practice shows that factors

1232. Komissarov/Krilova/Tyazhkova, Ugolovnoe pravo RF, p. 752; Naumov, Rossiiskoe ugolovnoe pravo, pp. 638–640.
1233. Paramonova, Grounds for excluding criminal liability in Russia, 2016, pp. 344–346; Revin, Ugolovnoe pravo Rossii.
1234. Translations of the provisions of the Criminal Code in this chapter are based on Butler, The Criminal Code of the Russian Federation.
1235. Zhuravlev, Ugolovnoe pravo, pp. 261–262.
1236. Naumov, Rossiiskoe ugolovnoe pravo, p. 638; Zhuravlev, Ugolovnoe pravo, p. 261.

influencing the decision to grant pardon include the conduct of the convicted person while serving his or her sentence, the nature and seriousness of the offense, as well as the personality of the offender.[1237]

1460. According to the Constitution of the Russian Federation, convicted persons have the right to petition for a pardon against a final judgment (Article 50, paragraph 3 Const.). Detailed regulation of the procedure of consideration of such petitions is provided by the Decree of the President of the Russian Federation on Clemency Commissions on the Territory of the Russian Federation.[1238] The provisions of the Decree require that the petition be in writing, that it be registered by the authority executing punishment (e.g., by the prison authority), and that it be sent to the clemency commission. Within thirty days, the commission must present the petition to the chief of the highest executive authority of the entity of the federation (e.g., the president of the republic or governor of the region). The latter is obliged to direct it (within fifteen days) to the president of the Russian Federation. The president, in turn, must make a decision in the form of a decree within two days. If the petition is rejected, the convict has the right to reapply after one year.[1239]

1461. An act of pardon is a ground for terminating, reducing, or replacing the criminal punishment.[1240] It does not have a retroactive impact. Rather, it is prospective: it terminates the serving of criminal punishment beginning at the time it is granted.[1241]

§2. Amnesty

I. General Requirements for an Amnesty

1462. One of the instruments for terminating criminal liability and punishment is **amnesty** *(амнистия)*, which derives from the Greek *amnestia*: forgetting, forgiveness. As the instrument of pardon, amnesty is a means of implementing the principle of humanism in criminal policy and criminal laws.[1242]

1463. Article 84 UKR (Amnesty) sets:

(1) An amnesty shall be declared by the State Duma of the Federal Assembly of the Russian Federation with regard to a group of persons whose members are not individually determined.

1237. Lebedev, Kommentarii k UK RF, pp. 201–202; Revin, Ugolovnoe pravo Rossii.
1238. Decree of the President of the Russian Federation "On Clemency Commissions on the Territory of the Russian Federation," Dec. 28, 2001, N 1500.
1239. Komissarov/Krilova/Tyazhkova, Ugolovnoe pravo RF, pp. 752–759.
1240. Naumov, Rossiiskoe ugolovnoe pravo, pp. 633–634, 638; Zhuravlev, Ugolovnoe pravo, p. 261.
1241. Paramonova, Grounds for excluding criminal liability in Russia, 2016, pp.344–345.
1242. Lebedev, Kommentarii k UK RF, pp. 199–201; Komissarov/Krilova/Tyazhkova, Ugolovnoe pravo RF, p. 745; Revin, Ugolovnoe pravo Rossii; Zhuravlev, Ugolovnoe pravo, pp. 257–261.

(2) Persons who have committed crimes may be relieved from criminal responsibility by an act of amnesty. Persons convicted for the commission of crimes may be relieved from punishment, or the punishment imposed on them may be reduced or replaced by a milder type of punishment, or such persons may be relieved from additional types of punishment. With regard to persons who have served punishment, the conviction may be expunged from the record by an act of amnesty.

1464. An act of amnesty has the force of law since it is adopted by the Chamber of the supreme legislative body of the country: the State Duma of the Russian Federation (Article 103, paragraph 1 Const.). Offenders cannot apply for an amnesty. As a rule, amnesties are timed to coincide with certain important dates or (historical) events or anniversaries.[1243] An example is the resolution of the State Duma on Amnesty in Connection with the 100th Anniversary of the Establishment of the State Duma in Russia.[1244] Sometimes the adoption of an amnesty act is determined by major changes in economic, social, or political systems, such as the resolution of the State Duma on the Declaration of Political and Economic Amnesty.[1245]

1465. In general, there are no explicit restrictions with regard to the types of offenses that can be the subject of an amnesty. An amnesty extends to a group of persons whose members are not individually determined.[1246] The scope of its application depends on the conditions provided in the individual act. The following are typical criteria used to define the groups of persons to be amnestied: the seriousness of the offense, gender, age, the existence of a disability, whether state awards (such as medals or titles) have been presented, the existence of a certain legal status (e.g., a veteran of World War II), the presence of young children, pregnancy, and the form of culpability.[1247] An example of how these criteria may be applied can be seen in the Resolution of the State Duma on Amnesty in Connection with the 20th Anniversary of the Adoption of the Constitution of the Russian Federation,[1248] which defined the persons to which it applied, among other criteria, as women with children younger than 18 years of age on the day the act of amnesty entered into force.[1249]

1243. Naumov, Rossiiskoe ugolovnoe pravo, p. 633.

1244. Resolution of the State Duma on Amnesty in Connection with the 100th Anniversary of the Establishment of the State Duma in Russia, Apr. 19, 2006, N 3043-IV GD.

1245. Resolution of the State Duma on the Declaration of Political and Economic Amnesty, Feb. 24, 1994, N 65-1 GD.

1246. Naumov, Rossiiskoe ugolovnoe pravo, p. 633.

1247. For forms of culpability, *see* paras. 194–195, 388, 425; Zhuravlev, Ugolovnoe pravo, pp. 259–260.

1248. Resolution of the State Duma "On Amnesty in Connection with the 20th Anniversary of the Adoption of the Constitution of the Russian Federation," Dec. 18, 2013, N 3503-6 DGP.

1249. Paramonova, Grounds for excluding criminal liability in Russia, 2016, pp.346.

II. Types of Amnesty

1466. In accordance with the law (Article 84, paragraph 2 UKR and Article 27 of the Code of Criminal Procedure of the Russian Federation, *Ugolovno prozessual'nij Kodeks RF*, UPKR),[1250] there are three main types of amnesty, each of which addresses a different group of persons. The first type targets persons who have committed crimes but have not yet been convicted. These persons may be relieved from criminal responsibility by an act of amnesty. Persons who have been convicted of crimes are targeted by the second type. They may be relieved by an amnesty from serving criminal punishment, the punishment imposed on them may be reduced or replaced by a milder type of punishment, or they may be relieved from additional types of punishment. The third type targets persons who have served punishment. Their convictions may be expunged from the record by an act of amnesty.[1251]

III. Scope of Application of the Amnesty Act

1467. The scope of application is regulated by the particular act of amnesty. Among other things, the act specifies the procedure by which it is to be applied, the law enforcement powers with regard to its implementation, and its (time/space) limits.[1252]

1468. The final decision on the application or non-application of an amnesty to an individual person depends largely on the discretion of the body charged with carrying it out. For example, if the person is already serving a sentence, the final decision—one that reflects an evaluation of the prisoner's behavior—will be made by the prison authorities.

1469. As a rule, an act of amnesty extends to offenders who have committed crimes prior to the adoption of the act. In exceptional cases, the application of such an act may be extended to crimes committed within a certain time after its entry into force. This will only be the case, however, if an offender fulfills conditions specified in the act, such as providing a full confession.[1253]

1470. An amnesty does not decriminalize offenses that are mentioned in it. Rather, it terminates criminal liability and (or) punishment or mitigates punishment with respect to certain categories of persons (Article 84, paragraph 2 UKR). Furthermore, a person released from punishment due to an amnesty is not automatically considered not to have a record of conviction (Article 86, paragraph 2 UKR). Instead, an individual act of amnesty may contain special rules for the expunging of criminal records with regard to certain categories of persons.

1250. Dec. 18. 2001, N 174-FZ.
1251. Naumov, Rossiiskoe ugolovnoe pravo, pp. 633–634.
1252. Zhuravlev, Ugolovnoe pravo, p. 257.
1253. Revin, Ugolovnoe pravo Rossii.

1471. Offenses committed by persons whose criminal liability has been terminated (the first type of amnesty) or whose conviction has been expunged from the record (third type) may not be taken into consideration with respect to the issue of recidivism (Article 18, paragraph 1 UKR in conjunction with Article 86, paragraphs 2 and 6 UKR). On the other hand, legal provisions regarding recidivism are applicable to persons whose criminal punishment (but not criminal liability) has been terminated, reduced, or replaced by a milder type of punishment or who have been relieved from additional types of punishment (second type).

1472. In general, legal provisions that address recidivism apply only to offenders who have a criminal record (Article 18, paragraph 1 UKR). The expunging of criminal liability annuls all legal consequences related to the record of the conviction (Article 86, paragraphs 2 and 6 UKR). Nevertheless, acts of amnesty can contain special rules that reflect, for example, the fact that an individual has previously committed an intentional crime.[1254] For instance, the resolution of the State Duma "On the Declaration of an Amnesty" stated that the amnesty does not apply to convicted persons who previously have been released from prison due to a pardon or an act of amnesty or who have repeatedly committed intentional crimes.[1255]

1473. Procedural questions relating to the expunging of criminal liability by an act of amnesty are regulated by law (Articles 27, 239, 302, paragraph 6 UPKR). When an amnesty is granted at the stage of the opening of a criminal investigation (pretrial proceeding), the investigation is terminated. Where criminal investigative proceedings have already commenced (pretrial proceeding), the case is dismissed (Articles 27, 239 UPKR).[1256] Where an amnesty is granted at the trial stage, the court decides the case in accordance with regular procedure. If the final decision is a guilty verdict, the court announces the verdict and orders relief from serving punishment at the same time (Article 302, paragraphs 5, 6 UPKR).[1257]

§3. Statute of Limitations

1474. Time limits for the prosecution of crimes and the execution of sentences are legal institutions that are considered part of substantive criminal law. The relevant legal provisions are found in the Criminal Code (Articles 78 and 83). The

1254. Revin, Ugolovnoe pravo Rossii.
1255. Resolution of the State Duma of "On Declaration of Amnesty" Dec. 24, 1997, N 2038-II GD.
1256. For the classification of the principles of the criminal procedure, *see* Part II, Chapter 1, §3, paras. 816–827.
1257. Komissarov/Krilova/Tyazhkova, Ugolovnoe pravo RF, pp. 745–752; Lebedev, Kommentarii k UK RF, pp. 199–201; Paramonova, Grounds for excluding criminal liability in Russia, 2016, pp.346–349.

existence of time limits is justified by the principle of humanity[1258] and legal certainty:[1259] the state is obliged to exercise justice within a reasonable and predictable period of time.[1260]

I. The Limitation Period for Prosecution of Crimes

1475. The **statute of limitations for criminal responsibility** ***(давность привлечения к уголовной ответственности)*** designates the period of time provided for by the criminal law after the expiration of which a person cannot be prosecuted for a crime he or she has committed.[1261] The time limit for prosecution depends on the category of crime.[1262] Accordingly, a person is relieved from criminal liability if the following time limits have expired: two years after the commission of a crime of small gravity, six years after the commission of a crime of average gravity, ten years after the commission of a grave crime, and fifteen years after the commission of an especially grave crime (Article 78, paragraph 1 UKR).[1263] Article 78 UKR (Release from Criminal Responsibility Due to Expiration of Statutes Limitation) states:

(1) A person shall be released from criminal responsibility if the following time limits have expired since the day of commission of a crime:
 (a) two years after the commission of a crime of small gravity;
 (b) six years after the commission of a crime of average gravity;
 (c) 10 years after the commission of a grave crime;
 (d) 15 years after the commission of an especially grave crime.
(2) The statute of limitations shall be calculated from the day of committing a crime to the time of the entry of a court's judgment into legal force. If a person commits a new crime, then the period of limitation for each crime shall be counted independently.
(3) The running of the statute of limitations shall be suspended if the person who has committed the crime evades the investigation or the trial. In this case, the running of the limitation period shall be reinstated from the moment of detention of the said person or his or her acknowledgment of guilt.
(4) The question of the application of the limitation period to a person who has committed a crime punishable with the death penalty or deprivation of freedom for a life-term shall be decided by the court. If the court does not consider it possible to release the said person from criminal responsibility due to

1258. On the principles of criminal law, *see* Part I, Chapter 1, paras. 194–196, and on the principles of the criminal procedure, *see* Part II, Chapter 1, §3, paras. 814–827.
1259. For the principle of legality, *see* Part I, Chapter 1, paras. 197–226.
1260. Naumov, Rossiiskoe ugolovnoe pravo, pp. 622–623; Paramonova, Grounds for excluding criminal liability in Russia, 2016, pp.349.
1261. Lebedev, Kommentarii k UK RF, pp. 183–185; Naumov, Rossiiskoe ugolovnoe pravo, pp. 614–616; Zhuravlev, Ugolovnoe pravo, pp. 243–245.
1262. On the categories of crimes, *see* paras. 34, 638–646.
1263. On the categories of crimes, *see* paras. 34, 638–646.

the expiry of the limitation period, then the death penalty or deprivation of freedom for the life-term shall not be applied.

(5) The statute of limitations shall not be applied to persons who have committed offenses under articles 205, 205.1, 205.3, 205.4, 205.5, third and fourth parts of article 206, part four of article 211, articles 353, 356, 357, 358 of this Code, as well as to persons who have committed offenses in connection with the terrorist crimes provided for in articles 277, 278, 279, and 360 of this Code.

1476. In order for the statute of limitations to apply, the following two requirements must be fulfilled: first, the expiration of the time limits provided for by the law (Article 78, paragraph 1 UKR); and second, the absence of circumstances that suspend the time limit (Article 78, paragraph 3 UKR). The limitation period begins the day of the crime is committed and runs until a judicial decision enters into force. For each crime a person commits, the statute of limitations is calculated independently (Article 78, paragraph 2 UKR). The running of the limitation period is suspended if the person evades investigation or trial (Article 78, paragraph 3 UKR). A person cannot be considered to be "evading investigation or trial" if he or she has committed a crime that law enforcement authorities are not aware of or if his or her involvement in the crime has not yet been established at the pretrial proceeding. "Evading investigation or trial" includes any acts undertaken in order to avoid criminal liability for the committed offense. If a person who has committed a crime is considered to be evading investigation or trial, the running of the period of limitations is suspended. The clock does not begin to run again until after the person has been detained or he or she has acknowledged guilt.[1264]

1477. For certain crimes, there are no time limits for prosecution (Article 78, paragraph 5 UKR). These include the following crimes against peace and security: planning, preparing, unleashing, or waging of aggressive war (Article 353 UKR); use of prohibited means and methods of warfare (Article 356 UKR); genocide (Article 357 UKR); ecocide (Article 358 UKR); and attacks on persons or institutions enjoying international protection (Article 360 UKR). Moreover, the statute of limitations is not applied to persons who have committed offenses criminalized by selected articles of the Criminal Code (Articles 205, 205.1, 205.3, 205.4, 205.5, 206, paragraphs 3 and 4, and 211, paragraph 4 UKR), nor is it applied to persons who have committed offenses in connection with the terrorist crimes provided for in selected articles of the Criminal Code (Articles 277–279 UKR).[1265]

II. The Limitation Period for the Execution of Sentences

1478. In legal practice, there are cases where, for various reasons (such as natural disasters, social upheavals, and war or other conflicts), sentences are not

1264. Naumov, Rossiiskoe ugolovnoe pravo, pp. 618–620; Zhuravlev, Ugolovnoe pravo, pp. 243–245.
1265. Komissarov/Krilova/Tyazhkova, Ugolovnoe pravo RF, pp. 693–700.

executed within a reasonable time. In compliance with the principles of humanity[1266] and certainty,[1267] this situation is dealt with according to the legal institution referred to as **release from serving punishment due to expiry of the limitation period of the court's sentence** (*освобождение от отбывания наказания в связи с истечением сроков давности обвинительного приговора*).[1268]

Article 83 UKR (Release from Serving Punishment Due Expiry of the Limitation Period of the Court's Sentence) provides:

(1) A person convicted for the commission of a crime shall be released from serving punishment if the court's sentence has not been enforced within the following time periods since the time of its entry into legal force:
(a) two years, in case of conviction for a crime of small gravity;
(b) six years, in case of conviction for a crime of average gravity;
(c) 10 years, in case of conviction for a grave crime;
(d) 15 years, in case of conviction for an especially grave crime.

(2) The running of the limitation period shall be suspended if the convicted person evades serving punishment. In this case, the running of the limitation period shall be reinstated from the moment of detention of the convicted person or the acknowledgment of his or her guilt. Periods of limitation that have expired due to/during the time of evasion by the convicted person of the serving of the punishment shall be subject to set-off.

(2.1.) The running of the periods of limitation shall be interrupted if a convicted person has been granted a suspension from serving punishment. In this case, the limitation period is reinstated from the time of the expiration of the time limits of the suspension of the serving of punishment, except for the case provided for by the third and the fourth paragraph of article 82 and the third paragraph of article 82.1 of this Code, or from the time of the abolition of the suspension of serving punishment.

(3) The question of the application of the limitation periods to a person sentenced to capital punishment or deprivation of freedom for a life-term shall be decided by the court. If the court does not consider that it is possible to apply the limitation periods, then these punishments shall be replaced with deprivation of freedom for a definite term.

(4) Statutes of limitation shall not be applicable to persons convicted for the commission of offenses provided for by articles 205, 205.1, 205.3, 205.4, 205.5, third and fourth parts of article 206, part four of article 211, articles 353, 356, 357 and 358 of this Code, as well as to persons convicted for the commission of offenses in connection with the terrorist crimes provided for in articles 277, 278, 279 and 360 of this Code.

1266. On the principles of criminal law, *see* Part I, Chapter 1, paras. 194–196, and on the principles of the criminal procedure, *see* Part II, Chapter 1, §3, paras. 814–827.

1267. For the principle of legality, *see* Part I, Chapter 1, paras. 197–226.

1268. Lebedev, Kommentarii k UK RF, pp. 197–199; Zhuravlev, Ugolovnoe pravo, pp. 255–257.

1479. The **statute of limitations for the execution of court sentence** ***(давностью исполне-ния обвинительного приговора)*** means the establishment by law of time limits, after whose expiration the guilty verdict cannot be enforced and the convict is released from serving his or her punishment. Following the expiration of the time limitation, no punishment imposed by a court judgment—neither main punishments nor additional punishments—may be enforced.[1269]

1480. The limitation period depends on the category of crime.[1270] If the following time limits regarding the execution of sentences have expired, the convicted person must be released from serving punishment: in cases involving crimes of small gravity, two years; in cases involving crimes of average gravity, six years; in cases involving grave crimes, ten years; and in cases involving especially grave crimes, fifteen years (Article 83 UKR).

1481. The limitation period is suspended if a convicted person evades serving a sentence by, for example, fleeing to a different city or country. The running of the limitation period is reinstated from the moment of detention of the convicted person or from the moment the convicted person gives him- or herself up (Article 83, paragraph 2 UKR).[1271]

1482. The expiration of the statute of limitations is an obligatory ground for release from serving criminal punishment, except for those sentenced to death[1272] or life imprisonment. In these two instances, release from serving punishment is at the discretion of the court (Article 83, paragraph 3 UKR). Even if a convicted person is released from serving criminal punishment on the ground of expiration of the statute of limitations for the execution of sentences, the offense still appears on the person's criminal record. Hence, it can still be taken into account with respect to the issue of recidivism (Article 18, paragraph 1 UKR), since expunging a criminal record occurs only after the expiration of certain periods of time provided for by the criminal law (Article 86, paragraph 3 UKR). Exceptions to this general rule whereby the record of conviction can be removed before these time limits expire include, for instance, an amnesty.

1483. In accordance with provisions of international law, Russian criminal law provides for the non-application of the statute of limitations of execution of sentences with regard to certain crimes. These include the following crimes against peace and security: planning, preparing, unleashing, or waging of aggressive war (Article 353 UKR); use of prohibited means and methods of warfare (Article 356 UKR); genocide (Article 357 UKR); ecocide (Article 358 UKR); and attacks on persons or institutions enjoying international protection (Article 360 UKR). Moreover,

1269. Naumov, Rossiiskoe ugolovnoe pravo, pp. 631–632.
1270. On the categories of crimes, *see* paras. 34, 638–646.
1271. Zhuravlev, Ugolovnoe pravo, pp. 255–257.
1272. On death penalty in Russia and the sanctioning system, *see* Part I. Chapter 7, paras. 723–724, 1283–1285; Paramonova, in: Arroyo/Biglino/Schabas (eds.), Towards Universal Abolition of the Death Penalty, pp. 167–175.

the statute of limitations is not applied to persons who have committed offenses criminalized by selected articles of the Criminal Code (Articles 205, 205.1, 205.3, 205.4, 205.5, 206, paragraphs 3 and 4, 211, paragraph 4 UKR), nor is it applied to persons who have committed offenses in connection with the terrorist crimes provided for in selected articles of the Criminal Code (Articles 277–279 UKR).[1273]

§4. Social Rehabilitation

1484. Social rehabilitation of persons, who have served their sentence, is an array of measures that are aimed, first, at prevention of the commission of further crimes, second, at including former convicts to a normal way of life in freedom through their employment, grating responsibility and strengthening their social positions.[1274]

1485. There are concrete obligations of the administration of institutions executing punishment to support the process of social rehabilitation.

1486. In order to enhance the rehabilitation process and preparation of the convict for release, **educational** work was carried out in the correctional institutions. It includes *inter alia* explanation of his/her rights, obligations, and certain social benefits.

1487. Besides, not later than two months before the expiration of the term of arrest or six months before the expiry of the term imprisonment, the administration of the institution carrying out the sentence notifies the local authorities and the federal **employment** service in the chosen place of residence of a convict of his/her release. Cooperating with the federal employment service, the prison administration informs it on the ability of a convict to work and on his/her professions.

1488. In respect of the convicted persons that underwent the treatment in the form of compulsory **medical** measures, the correctional institution delivers health records to the health authorities in the chosen place of residence of the convict to decide on his/her further treatment, if necessary. Further medical treatment is carried out with the consent of a former convict. If a person suffers from mental disorders, he/she can be treated in a stationary organization of social services (Article 180, paragraph 4 UIKR).

1489. This way, with regard to convicted of crimes against sexual inviolability and freedom, the institution carrying out the sentence is required to explain to the convict the right to the psychiatric examination on the presence or absence of the sexual preference disorders (pedophilia). Based on the results of this examination,

1273. Komissarov/Krilova/Tyazhkova, Ugolovnoe pravo RF, pp. 738–740.; Paramonova, Grounds for excluding criminal liability in Russia, 2016, pp.-349–353.

1274. Vasiliev, Legal psychology, pp. 1–10.

the convict may decide to undergo health treatment aimed at improving his/her mental state preventing him/her from committing new crimes.

1490. **Social services**, such as psychological help or visits of social workers, are also available to former convicts. For instance, prisoners who have the first or second grade of disability, as well as convicted men older than 60 years and women older than 55 years, have the right to social services. In this case, the correctional institution, upon the request of a convict, sends a notification to the authorities providing social services in the chosen place of residence (Article 180, paragraph 3 UIKR).

1491. An array of **one-time help measures** to the convicts after release is one of the aspects of rehabilitation. Former convicts are provided, for example, with free travel to the place of residence, seasonal clothes, food, and money necessary for the travel. Those who need health care are accompanied by relatives, other persons, or an employee of the correctional institution (Article 181 UIKR).

General Conclusion

1492. Russian law belongs to the continental or Romano-Germanic legal system. Throughout history, the systematization and codification of legislative acts has been a decisive feature in the development of Russian criminal (procedural) law.

1493. The main features of the continental legal system, which characterize contemporary Russian criminal law, are as follows: the distinction between private and public law; differentiation between constitutional, civil, administrative, criminal, civil procedural, and criminal procedural branches of law; vertical and horizontal separation of powers on the constitutional level; the stable hierarchy of the sources of law; and systematization and codification of legislative acts; and supremacy of law.[1275]

1494. The current Criminal Code of the Russian Federation was enacted in 1996 and entered into force in 1997. It became a model for most of the post-Soviet Republics. One of its main characteristics is the establishment of the new hierarchy of legally protected values in compliance with the Constitution 1993. Section VII UKR (crimes against the person), which includes crimes against life, physical integrity, and dignity of the person, begins the Special Part of the Criminal Code in a way that was unlike any of the previous criminal codes:[1276] all of them had given priority to crimes against public security and order.

1495. In accordance with the main purposes of the criminal law reform (namely, to bring about social changes that corresponded to the new reality, to eliminate the ideological and declarative nature of Soviet law, and to bring domestic criminal legislation into line with the norms of international law), "old" forms of behavior that no longer represented a social danger in the new political situation—entrepreneurship, for instance—were decriminalized. New forms of conduct such as cybercrime (Chapter 28)[1277] and economic crimes related to the market economy (section VIII) (e.g., unfair competition and money laundering) were criminalized. An entire section on international criminal law entitled "crimes against the peace and security of mankind" was introduced (section XII).

1275. Tichomirov, Kurs sravnitelnogo pravovedeniya, p. 124; Glendon et al., Comparative Legal Traditions, pp. 114–120; Paramonova, National characteristics, fundamental principles, and history of criminal law in Russia, 2014, pp. 200–202.

1276. Criminal Code RSFSR 1922; Criminal Code RSFSR 1926; Criminal Code RSFSR 1960.

1277. Paramonova, Internationales Strafrecht im Cyberspace, pp. 77–123.

1496. With regard to the definition of crime, the Criminal Code 1996 follows a formal-substantive concept. Accordingly, a criminal offense is a behavior that is illegal in its form and socially dangerous in its content (Article 14 UKR).[1278] The degree of social danger (dangerousness) is of practical importance: It determines the strict distinction between criminal, administrative, and civil offenses as well as the distinction between crime and an insignificant act that is deemed not to be criminal.[1279]

1497. The special features of the new Code of Criminal Procedure, which was adopted in 2001, are the expansion of judicial review of measures taken by investigative and prosecution authorities as well as the differentiation of procedural forms. The procedure of the Code of Criminal Procedure 2001 represents a "neo-inquisitorial" (mixed or hybrid) model of criminal procedure.[1280] On the one hand, the Code of Criminal Procedure declares the principle of adversarial procedure for both the investigation stage and the subsequent stage of court proceedings (Article 15 UPKR) as well as the rule of equality of arms—the prosecution and defense enjoy equal rights before the court (Articles 15, paragraph 4, 244 UPKR). On the other hand, due to the public interest of the state in criminal matters, investigation authorities as the state authority are given priority over the defense.[1281]

1498. The criminal law and criminal procedure of modern Russia have changed quite extensively in recent decades.[1282] For example, the 1996 Criminal Code has undergone more than 3,000 amendments between its enactment and the year 2015. The Code of Criminal Procedure has been changed equally extensively. Some of the modifications, as well as the tendencies associated with them, are controversial.[1283]

1499. These numerous changes were/are aimed, on the one hand, at adopting domestic criminal (procedural) legislation to the new social forms of conducts that became relevant after the collapse of the Soviet Union and, on the other hand, at bringing domestic criminal legislation in line with the norms of international law. While some modifications of the domestic criminal (procedural) law are questionable, e.g., some aspects of the liberalization of criminal punishment toward economic crime, a substantial part of the amendments can be regarded as positive, including those arising from the legislative obligations derived from the

1278. On the formal and substantive concepts of the criminal offense, *see* Part I, Chapter 3, §1, paras. 317–321; Kropachev/Volzhenkin/Orechova, Ugolovnoe pravo Rossii, p. 326.
1279. On the delimitation and classification of criminal law, on distinction between criminal, administrative, and civil offenses, on "social danger," *see* Paramonova, National characteristics, fundamental principles, and history of criminal law in Russia, 2014, pp. 175–280.
1280. Bozhjev, Ugolovnij process, p. 16; Paramonova/Bogush, ZStW 125 (2013), 703–728.
1281. On the principles of criminal law, *see* Part I, Chapter 1, paras. 194–196 and on the principles of the criminal procedure, *see* Part II, Chapter 1, §3, paras. 814–827.
1282. Paramonova, Revista Penal 2012, 264–268.
1283. Paramonova, National characteristics, fundamental principles, and history of criminal law in Russia, 2014, p. 280; Supreme Court of the Russian Federation, http://www.supcourt.ru/ [last visited Dec. 18, 2019].

international law. An example thereof is the profound reform of judicial remedies in 2016 that was undertaken in response to the case law of the ECtHR.[1284]

1284. *See* Ryabykh v. Russia, Jul. 24, 2003, App. No. 52854/99; Smarygin v. Russia, Dec. 1, 2005, App. No. 73203/01; Federal Law, Dec. 29, 2010, N 433-FZ. Paramonova, KritVj 2013, 207.

Selected Bibliography

Adel'chanyan, Robert, Уголовное право России. Практический курс: учебник (Russian criminal law. Practical course: Textbook). Moscow 2010.

Ambamlin, Valerij, Сокращение численности тюремного населения России—проблемное поле дискуссий (Reduction of the Prison Population of Russia—a Problematic Field of Discussions), http://www.prison.org/penal/human_prison/doc001.htm [last visited December 18, 2019].

Ambamlin, Valerij, Сокращение численности тюремного населения России—проблемное поле дискуссий (Reduction of the Prison Population of Russia—a Problematic Field of Discussions), http://www.prison.org/penal/human_prison/doc001.htm [last visited December 18, 2019].

Anganzanov, Oleg, Привлечение лица к уголовной ответственности после привлечения его к административной ответственности за то же правонарушение. Законность, N 2, 2009 (Imposition of Criminal Punishment after Imposition of Administrative Sanction for the Same Offense). Zakonnost', N 2, 2009, p. 56.

Bachin, Sergej, Международная составляющая правовой системы России. Правоведение, N 6, 2007 (The International Component of the Russian Legal System). Pravovedenie, N 6, 2007, p. 126.

Bachrach, Demýan/Krolis, Luydmila, Административная ответственность и финансовые санкции. Журнал российского права (Administrative Responsibility and Financial Sanctions). Zhurnal rossijskogo prava, N 8, 1997, p. 86.

Baglaj, Marat, Конституционное право Российской Федерации (Constitutional Law of the Russian Federation). Moscow 2007, pp. 127–154.

Baglaj, Marat, Конституционное право Российской Федерации (Constitutional Law of the Russian Federation). Moscow 2007, pp. 127–154, 178.

Barabash, Anatoliy, Природа российского уголовного процесса (Nature of the Russian Criminal Procedure), the criminal purpose. Saint Petersburg 2005, pp. 3—257.

Bazhanov M.I., Назначение наказания по совокупности преступлений и совокупности приговоров, Харьков, 1977 (Sentencing for Cumulative Crimes and Cumulative Sentences). Har'kov, 1977, p. 3.

Batichko, Vladimir, Уголовное право. Общая часть (Criminal Law of Russia. General Part). Moscow 2006, http://padabum.net/d.php?id=79703 [last visited December 18, 2019].

Selected Bibliography

ReBezlepkin, Boris, Комментарий к Уголовно-процессуальному Кодексу Российской Федерации (Commen-taries on the Code of Criminal Procedure of the Russian Federation). Moscow 2011, www.consultant.ru [last visited December 18, 2019].

Biryukov, Pavel, Международное право, 2002 (International Law). 3d ed. Moscow 2002, pp. 15–25.

Blagov, Evgenij, Квалификация покушения на преступление (Subsumption of attempted crime, 2005). Journal of Russian Law 2005 no. 8, 71–76.

Blum, Jerome, Lord and Peasant in Russia. Princeton 1961, pp. 420–425.

Bogush, Gleb, Criminal Law Reform in Russia. In: Rocco Alagna/Silvio Riondato (eds.), Studi sulla riforma penale post-socialista (Studies on Criminal Law Reform in the Post-Soviet Countries). Padova 2013, pp. 49–60.

Bogush, Gleb/Trikoz, Elena, (eds.), Международное правосудие: Современные проблемы. Институт права и публичной политики (International Justice: Contemporary Problems). Moscow 2009, pp. 15–95.

Boizov, Alexandr, Действие уголовного закона во времени и пространстве (Retrospective Action of Criminal Law in Time and Space). Saint Petersburg 1995, p. 73.

Bozhjev, Vyacheslav, Уголовный процесс (Criminal Procedure). Moscow 1997, p. 16.

Burchak, Fedor, Учение о соучастии по уголовному праву (Doctrine of complicity in criminal law). Kiev 1970.

Burov, Anton, Статус Постановлений Пленума Верховного Суда РФ (The Status of the Resolutions of the Supreme Court's Plenary Assembly), http://media-pravo.info/book/37 [last visited December 18, 2019].

Butler. William E. Criminal Code of the Russian Federation. Translated by Wildy, Simmonds and Hill Publishing Ltd, 4th edition, London 2004.

Cereteli, Tinatin Причинная связь в уголовном праве. Москва, 1963 (Causality in the Criminal Law). Moscow 1963, p. 131.*Butler. William E.* Criminal Code of the Russian Federation. Translated by Wildy, Simmonds and Hill Publishing Ltd, 4th edition, London 2004.

Chelcov-Bebutov, Michail, Курс уголовно-процессуального права. Очерки по истории суда и уголовного процесса (Course on Criminal Procedure. Essays on the History of the Court and Criminal Procedure). St. Petersburg 1995, p. 782.

Chernichenko, Stanislav, Вопрос о соотношении международного и внутригосударственного права как правовых систем. Правоведение, N 1, 2009 (To the Problem of the Interaction of International and Domestic Legal Systems). Pravovedenie, N 1, 2009, p. 18.

Chirkov, Aleksandr, Служащий как субъект преступлений, совершаемых с использованием служебного положения (The public servant as the subject of crimes committed by abusing an official position). Bulletin of the Immanuel Kant Baltic Federal University 9/2010, pp. 91–95, available at http://journals.kantiana.ru/ upload/iblock/e38/imgrhpdmnsaj.pdf [last visited December 18, 2019].

CIA World Factbook, https://www.cia.gov/library/publications/the-world-factbook/rankorder/2119rank.html [last visited December 18, 2019].

CIA World Factbook: Russia, https://www.cia.gov/library/publications/the-world-factbook/geos/rs.html [last visited December 18, 2019].

CIA World Factbook: Russia, https://www.cia.gov/library/publications/the-world-factbook/geos/rs.html.

Danilevskij, Nikolaj, Россия и Европа, 1869 (Russia and Europe), http://monarhiya.narod.ru/DNY/dny-list.htm [last visited December 18, 2019].

David, Rene/Brierly, John E.C., Major Legal Systems in the World Today: An Introduction to the Comparative Study of Law. London 1985, pp. 150–256.

Diyakov, Segeij, Комментарии к Уголовному Кодексу РФ (Commentaries on the Criminal Code of the Russian Federation). Moscow 2008, pp. 36–44.

Dolgova, Azaliya (ed.), Криминология (Criminology). Moscow 2007.

Dolgova, Azaliya (ed.), Криминология (Criminology). Moscow 2007.

Dostoevskij, Fedor, Дневник писателя (Diary of a Writer). St. Petersburg 2008, pp. 201–209, 215–225.

Durmanov, Nikolai, Понятие преступления (The Definition of the Criminal Act). Moscow 1948, pp. 259–260.

Embassy of the Russian Federation. General Information, http://www.russianembassy.org/page/general-information [last visited December 18, 2019].

Encyclopedia Britannica: Russia, http://www.britannica.com/EBchecked/topic/513251/Russia [last visited December 18, 2019].

Encyclopedia Britannica: Russia, http://www.britannica.com/EBchecked/topic/513251/Russia [last visited December 18, 2019].

Encyclopedia Britannica: Russian language, http://www.britannica.com/EBchecked/topic/513764/Russian-language [last visited December 18, 2019].

Federal Drug Control Service of the Russian Federation, http://fskn.gov.ru [last visited December 18, 2019].

Federal Security Service of the Russian Federation, http://www.fsb.ru [last visited December 18, 2019].

Federal State Statistics Service, FSSS (Федеральная Служба Государственной Статистики), http://www.gks.ru [last visited December 18, 2019].

Feldstein, Grigorij, Главные течения в истории науки уголовного права в России (Main Trends in the History of Russian Criminal Law). Yaroslavl' 1909, p. 568.

Filimonov, Vadim, Принципы уголовного права (Principles of the Criminal Law). Moscow 2002, pp. 1–131.

Foinitsky, I, Курс уголовного судопроизводства (Course on Criminal Procedure. Vol. 1.) Alpha, Saint Petersburg, 1996, pp. 1–552.

Gaverdovskij, Aleksej, Имплементация норм международного права (Implementation of the Norms of International Law). Kiev 1980, pp. 47–48.

Gavrilov, Vyacheslav, Международный механизм контроля за имплементацией универсальных актов о правах человека. Московский журнал международного права, N 4, 1995 (International Mechanism of the

Control of the Implementation of the Universal Documents on Human Rights). Moskovskij Zhurnal mezhdunarodnogo prava, MZMP, N 4, 1995, pp. 24–37.

Gavrilov, Vyacheslav, Понятие и взаимодействие международной и национальной правовых систем (Definition and Interaction of International and Domestic Legal Systems). Vladivostok 2005, p. 11.

Georgievskij, Eduard, К вопросу о генезисе и развитии общего понятия преступления и его признаков в уголовном праве России, Сибирский Юридический Вестник (To the question of the genesis and development of the general concept of the criminal offense and its indicators in Russian criminal law). Sibirskij Yuridicheskij Vestnik, 2000, No. 4.

Gernet, Michail, История царской тюрьмы: 1825–1870, Тома 1–5 (History of Czar's Prisons: 1825–1870, Vols. 1–5). Moscow 1946.

Glendon, Mary Ann/Gordon, Michael Wallace/Osakwe, Christopher, Comparative Legal Traditions. St. Paul, Minn., 1994, pp. 44–52, 395–436.

Golovko, Leonid, Альтернативы уголовному преследованию в современном праве (Alternatives to Prosecution in the Modern Law). St. Petersburg 2002.

Golovko, Leonid, Конституционный суд vs суд присяжных (Constitutional Court vs Jury Trial), http://taxpravo.ru/analitika/statya-70942-konstitutsionnyiy_sud_VS_sud_prisyajnyih [last visited December 18, 2019].

Golovko, Leonid, Конституционный суд vs суд присяжных (Constitutional Court vs Jury Trial), http://taxpravo.ru/analitika/statya-70942-konstitutsionnyiy_sud_VS_sud_prisyajnyih [last visited December 18, 2019].

Golovko, Leonid, Размышления о российской судебной реформе (Thoughts about Russian Judicial Reform), http://www.index.org.ru/nevol/2010-22/09-golovko.html [last visited December 18, 2019].

Golovko, Leonid, Соотношение уголовных преступлений и административных правонарушений в контексте концепции "criminal matter"—уголовной сферы (Correlation of crimes and administrative offenses in the context of the concept of "criminal matter"). International Justice 2013 no. 1 (5), 42–52.

Gontar', Igor', Преступление и состав преступления как явления и понятия в уголовном праве: Вопросы теории и правотворчества (The Criminal Offense and "Elements of Criminal Offense" as Phenomena and Definitions in the Criminal law). Vladivostok 1997, pp. 60–62.

Grigonis, Eduard, Исследование процесса принятия новых УК и УПК стран СНГ и Балтии, их общие и отличительные черты. Юрист, N 7, 2007 (The Analysis of the Process of Adoption of the New Criminal and Code of Criminal Procedure s in the CIS countries). Jurist, N 7, 2007, http://journal.zakon.kz/203493-issledovanie-processa-prinjatija-novykh.html [last visited December 18, 2019].

Hellmann, Uwe/Esakov, Gennady/Golovnenkov, Pavel, Определение субъекта преступных деяний в российском и немецком экономическом уголовном праве (Defining the subject of crime in Russian and German economic criminal law). Potsdam 2010.

Ignatov, Aleksei / Krasikov, Yurij, Курс российского уголовного права (Course of the Russian Criminal Law). Moscow 2001, pp. 3–4, 14–16, 47–609.

Iljin, Ivan/Ustinov, Vladimir/Novickij, Ivan/Gernet, Michail, Основы законоведения (Fundamentals of Jurisprudence). 4th ed. Moscow 1915, pp. 344–345.

Inogamova-Khegai, Lubmila/Cherebedov, Sergej, Квалификация преступлений с использованием служебного положения // Уголовное право (Qualification of the crimes committed by an abusing official position). Criminal Law 2008 no. 4, 25–30.

International Centre for Prison Studies (ICPS), http://www.prisonstudies.org/country/russian-federation [last visited December 18, 2019].

Ivanenko, Vitalij, Международные договоры и конституция в правовой системе России: "война верховенств" или мирное взаимодействие. Правоведение, N 3, 2010 (International Treaties and Constitution in the Context of Russian Legal System). Pravovedenie, N 3, 2010, pp. 135–161.

Ivliev, Grigorij, Суд и подсудность (Trial and Jurisdiction). Гражданин и право (Grazhdanin i pravo), 2002, N 9/10, pp. 68–73.

Ivliev, Grigorij, Суд и подсудность (Trial and Jurisdiction). Гражданин и право (Grazhdanin i pravo), 2002, N 9/10, pp. 68–73.

Kafarov, Timur, Проблемы рецидива в советском уголовном праве (Problems of Recidivism in Soviet Criminal Law). Baku 1972, pp. 8–9.

Kahn, Jeffrey, Russia's Hybrid Code of Criminal Procedure. Paper presented at the annual meeting of The Law and Society Association, TBA, Berlin, Germany, 23.06.2012, http://www.allacademic.com/meta/p177544_index .html [last visited December 18, 2019].

Karamzin, Nikolai (ed.), История государсива Российского в 12 томах (History of the Russian State in 12 Volumes). http://bibliotekar.ru/karamzin/index.htm. [last visited December 18, 2019].

Kelina, S., Ответственность юридических лиц в проекте нового УК Российской Федерации // Уголовное право. Сборник статей (Liability of legal persons in the new Draft of the Criminal Code of the Russian Federation). In: Criminal Law. Collection of articles. Moscow 1994, pp. 52–53.

Kenii K., Основы уголовного права / перевод с английского. Москва, 1949 (Bases of the Criminal Law / English translation). Moscow 1949, p. 139.

Kistyakovskij Andrej, Элементарный учебник общего уголовного права. Часть Общая. СПб., 1895 (Elementare Book of the General Criminal Law. General Part). 2nd ed. Saint Petersburg 1895, pp. 59–68.

Kistyakovskij, Alexander, Исследование о смертной казни (The Study of the Death Penalty). Kiev 1867.

Klepitsky Ivan, Система хозяйственных преступлений (The system of economic crimes). Moscow 2005.

Komissarov, Vladimir, Responsibility for Terrorism According to the Criminal Code of the Russian Federation, forthcoming (translated by Svetlana Paramonova).

Komissarov, Vladimir/Krilova, Natalya/Tyazhkova, Irina, Уголовное право Российской Федерации (Criminal Law of the Russian Federation). Moscow 2012, pp. 12–34, 48–49, 53, 60–61, 63–72, 88–149, 273–299.

Selected Bibliography

Koni, Anatolij, О праве необходимой обороны (On the Right of Self-defense). Moscow 1966.

Koni, Anatolij, Отцы и дети судебной реформы. 1864–1914 (Fathers and Sons of the Judicial Reform. 1864–1914). Moscow 1914, p. 352.

Konyachin, Vladimir, Международный договор как источник российского уголовного права. Уголовное право в XXI веке. Материалы международной научной конференции, МГУ (International Treaty as a Source of the Russian Criminal Law). Materials of the International Conference, MGU. Moscow 2002, pp. 152–159.

Korobeev, Alexandr (ed.), Полный курс уголовного права. Том 1 (A Course of Criminal Law, Vol. 1). St. Petersburg 2008, pp. 14–30, 84–99, 739–773.

Kozachenko, Ivan (ed.), Уголовное право. Общая часть (Criminal Law. General Part). Moscow 2006, p. 507, 720.

Kramer, Mark, Rights and Restraints in Russia's Criminal Justice System Preliminary Results of the New Code of Criminal Procedure, Harvard 2003, http://www.gwu.edu/~ieresgwu/assets/docs/ponars/pm_0289.pdf [last visited December 18, 2019].

Kramer, Mark, Rights and Restraints in Russia's Criminal Justice System Preliminary Results of the New Code of Criminal Procedure, Harvard 2003, http://www.gwu.edu/~ieresgwu/assets/docs/ponars/pm_0289.pdf [last visited December 18, 2019].*Krivochenko, L.*, Классификация преступлений (Classification of Crimes). Har'kov 1983, pp. 20–28.

Krivolapov Grigoriy, Множественность преступлений по советскому уголовному праву. Москва, 1974 (Multiplicity of Crimes under Soviet Criminal Law), Moscow, pp. 10–19.

Kropachev Nikolai (ed.), Уголовное право России. Общая часть. Санкт-Петербург, 2006 (Criminal law of Russia. General Part), Sankt-Petersburg, State University of Sankt-Petersburg, 2006, pp. 10–60, 67–69, 71–86, 230–269, 325–349, 364–375, 403–420, 482, 504–509, 511–515.

Kropachev, Nikolai/Volzhenkin, Boris/Orechov, Vladimir (eds.), Уголовное право России. Общая часть (Criminal Law of Russia. General Part). St. Petersburg 2006, pp. 15–62, 69, 117–121, 124–130, 141, 142, 150–159, 147–166, 171–172, 326, 375.

Kruglikov Lev, Комментарии к Уголовному Кодексу РФ. Москва, 2005, «Волтерс Клувер» (Commentaries on the Criminal Code of the Russian Federation). Moscow, Wolters Kluwers, 2005, pp. 10–13, 22–33, 33–36, 53–62, 523–531.

Kucherov, Samuel, The Organs of Soviet Administration of Justice: Their History and Operation. Leiden 1970, available at http://books.google.com/books?id=ssMUAAAAIAAJ&dq [last visited December 18, 2019].

Kucherov, Samuel, The Organs of Soviet Administration of Justice: Their History and Operation. Leiden 1970, available at http://books.google.com/books?id=ssMUAAAAIAAJ&dq [last visited December 18, 2019].

Kudryavcev, Sergej, Роль судебных и внесудебных органов в проведении репрессий, 2006 (The Role of Judicial and Non-judicial Bodies in Carrying out Repressions), http://yaroslavl.fsb.ru/book/gl46.html [last visited December 18, 2019].

Kudryavzev Vladimir, Уголовное право России. Общая часть. Москва, Юрист, 2004 (Criminal Law of Russia. General Part). Moscow 2004, p. 69–98, 192–236.

Kudryavzev, Vladimir/Eminov, Vladimir (eds.), Криминология (Criminology). Moscow 2005.

Kurskii, Dmitrij, Уголовный Кодекс 1922 г. Избранные статьи и речи (The Criminal Code of 1922. Selected Articles and Speeches). Moscow 1948, pp. 86–87.

Kuznecova Ninel', Tyazhkova Irina (ed.), Курс уголовного права. Общая часть. Том 1: Учение о преступлении, Москва, 2002 (Course of the Criminal Law. General Part. Vol. 1). Moscow 2002, pp. 1, 37, 65–68, 91–108, 219–263, 297–350, 413–416.

Kuznecova, Ninel' (ed.), Курс уголовного права. Том 1 (Course of the Criminal Law, Vol. 1). Moscow 2002, pp. 164–176, 213–220.

Kuznecova, Ninel', Преступление и преступность (Criminal Offense and criminality). Moscow 1969, pp. 72–80.

Kuznecova, Ninel', Ответственность за приготовление к преступлению и покушение на преступление (Responsibility for the preparation of a crime and attempted crime). Moscow 1958.

Kuznetsova, Ninel', Цели и механизм реформы Уголовного кодекса // Советское государство и право (The objectives and mechanism for the reform of the Criminal Code). Soviet State and Law 1992 no. 6, 82.

Latkin, Vasilij, Учебник истории русского права периода империи: XVIII und XIX. (Russian History Textbook, Empire Period: XVIII und XIX). Moscow 2004, pp. 2, 415.

Lebedev Vyacheslav, Комментарии к Уголовному Кодексу РФ, 3. издание Верховного Суда РФ, Юрайт, Москва, 2005 (Commentaries on the Criminal Code of the Russian Federation), Moscow, 3rd edition of the Supreme Court of the Russian Federation, URAIT, 2005, pp. 27–31, 39–61, 334.

Lebedev, Vyacheslav (ed.), Scientific-practical Commentaries to the Code of Criminal Procedure of the Russian Federation (Научно-практический комментарий к Уголовно-процессуальному кодексу Российской Федерации). Moscow 2014, pp. 5–1056.

Lebedev, Vyacheslav, Комментарии к Уголовному Кодексу РФ, 3. изд. Верховного Суда РФ (Commentaries on the Criminal Code of the Russian Federation, 13th edition of the Supreme Court of the Russian Federation). Moscow 2013, pp. 1–29.

Lopashenko, Natalya, Преступления в сфере экономики. Комментарий к УК РФ (Economic crimes. Commentary to the Criminal Code of the Russian Federation). Moscow 2006.

Lukashevich, Vladimir, Актуальные вопросы уголовного преследования (Relevant Issues of Criminal Prosecution in Russia), Правоведение (Pravovedenie), 2006, N 6, pp. 214–219.

Selected Bibliography

Lukashevich, Vladimir, Актуальные вопросы уголовного преследования (Relevant Issues of Criminal Prosecution in Russia), Правоведение (Pravovedenie), 2006, N 6, pp. 214–219.

Luneev, Viktor, Преступность XX века. Мировые, региональные и российские тенденции: Мировой криминологический анализ (20th Century Delinquency: World, Regional, and Russian Tendencies). Moscow 1997.

Luneev, Viktor, Преступность XX века. Мировые, региональные и российские тенденции: Мировой криминологический анализ (20th Century Delinquency: World, Regional, and Russian Tendencies). Moscow 1997, p. 180.

Malkov V.P., Timershin Kh.A., Множественность преступлений. Уфа, 1995 (Multiplicity of Crimes). Ufa, 1995, p. 7.

Malzev, Vasilij, Принципы уголовного права и их реализация в правоприменительной деятельности (The Principles of the Criminal Law and their Realization in Law-Enforcement Practice). St. Petersburg 2004, pp. 1–684.

Matuzov, Nikolaj/Mal'co, Aleksandr, Теория государства и права (Theory of State and Law). Moscow, 2004, pp. 90, 217–233, 371, 394–403, 403–410, 418.

Mayr, Walter, "The Cold War at the Arctic Circle," Spiegel N 8, 2006, available at http://www.spiegel.de/international/spiegel/vying-for-extreme-tourists-in-siberia-the-cold-war-at-the-arctic-circle-a-402570.html [last visited December 18, 2019].

Mayr, Walter, "The Cold War at the Arctic Circle," Spiegel N 8, 2006, available at http://www.spiegel.de/international/spiegel/vying-for-extreme-tourists-in-siberia-the-cold-war-at-the-arctic-circle-a-402570.html [last visited December 18, 2019].

Ministry of Economic Development of the Russian Federation (MINEC), Russian Federation — Key Geographical Data, http://www.economy.gov.ru/wps/wcm/connect/a27fe1004d750c86a0d0bdc05beb4f7e/facts_march2013_f.pdf?MOD=AJPERES [last visited December 18, 2019].

Ministry of Economic Development of the Russian Federation (MINEC), Russian Federation — Key Geographical Data, http://www.economy.gov.ru/wps/wcm/connect/a27fe1004d750c86a0d0bdc05beb4f7e/facts_march2013_f.pdf?MOD=AJPERES [last visited December 18, 2019].

Ministry of the Interior of the Russian Federation (MVD), http://www.mvd.ru [last visited December 18, 2019].

Ministry of the Interior of the Russian Federation (MVD), www.mvd.ru [last visited December 18, 2019].

Mizkevich, Alexandr, Уголовное наказание: понятие, цели и механизмы действия (Criminal Punishment: Definition, Goals, and Mechanisms of Realization). St. Petersburg 2005, pp. 1–329.

Mizkevich, Ludmila, О правовой природе и признаках органа государства. Споры с участием государственных органов (On the Legal Nature and Characteristics of Public Bodies. Disputes Involving Government Agencies). Moscow 2006, pp. 69–85.

Nabokov, Vladimir, К вопросу о будущей ориентации русской науки уголовного права. Право, N 44, 1995 (To the Question of the Future Prospective of the Russian Criminal Law). Pravo, N 44, 1915, p. 14.

Naumov, Aleksandr, Российское уголовное право. Общая часть (Russian criminal law. General Part, Vol. 1). 4th ed. Moscow 1997, pp. 223–255, 313–323, 331, 334, 364–403.

Naumov, Aleksandr, Российское уголовное право. Общая часть. Том 1 (Russian Criminal Law, Vol. 1). 5th ed. Moscow 2011, pp. 1–36, 155–157, 62–199, 200–214, 223–230, 270–291.

Neklyudov, Nikolaj, Уголовно-статистические этюды (Criminal Statistics Studies). St. Petersburg 1865, pp. 1–250.

Nikiforov, Aleksandr, Юридическое лицо как субъект преступления и уголовной ответственности (The legal person as the subject of crime and criminal liability). Moscow 2002.

Oreshkina, Tatyana, Причинение вреда при исполнении приказа или распоряжения (Damage Resulting from the Carrying out of an Order or Instruction) // Ugolovnoe pravo 2000, N 4, p. 24.

Ostroumov, Sergej, Преступность и ее причины в дореволюционной России (Criminality and Its Roots in Pre-revolutionary Russia): http://adhdportal.com/book_1663.html [last visited December 18, 2019].

Ostroumov, Sergej, Преступность и ее причины в дореволюционной России (Criminality and Its Roots in Pre-revolutionary Russia): http://adhdportal.com/book_1663.html [last visited December 18, 2019].

Panfilova, Elena. The Barometer of the World Corruption 2007 (Transparency International), http://www.transparency.org.ru/doc/2RUS_press_release_01000_248.pdf [last visited December 18, 2019].

Panov, Vladimir, Тихая реформа. Эксперт N 28, 2011 (The Silent Reform). Expert N 28, 2011, p. 762, http://expert.ru/expert/2011/28/tihaya-reforma/ [last visited December 18, 2019].

Paramonova, Criminal liability for crimes in legal entities in Russia. In: Sieber, U. / Jarvers, K. /Silverman, E. (ed(s).): Criminal liability for crimes in legal entities. Berlin, Duncker & Humblot, 2016, pp. 340–350.

Paramonova, Svetlana, Challenges for Criminal Law and International Criminal Law in Cyberspace. In: Justice Report. Canadian Criminal Justice Association, 2014, Issue/Volume 29, N 4, pp. 26–29.

Paramonova, *Svetlana,* Concept and systematization of the criminal offense in Russia. In: Sieber, U. / Forster, S. / Jarvers, K. (ed(s).): National Criminal Law in a Comparative Legal Context. Volume 3.1: Defining criminal conduct. Berlin, Duncker & Humblot, 2011, pp. 86–97.

Paramonova, *Svetlana,* Crimes against Traffic and Operation of Transport Safety in Russia. In: Revista Penal, 2012, Vol. 29, pp. 252–254.

Paramonova, *Svetlana*, Criminal Law and Medicine. Revista Penal 2014, pp. 267–270.

Paramonova, *Svetlana,* El Tribunal Constitucional de Rusia y su Decisión del Ano 2009 in: Hacia la Abolición Universal de la pena capital, *Arroyo, Luis/Biglino, Paloma/Schabas, William* (eds.), pp. 189–197, Valencia, 2010.

Selected Bibliography

Paramonova, Svetlana, El Tribunal Constitucional de Rusia y su Decisión del Ano 2009 in: Hacia la Abolición Universal de la pena capital, *Arroyo, Luis/Biglino, Paloma/Schabas, William* (eds.), pp. 189–197, Valencia, 2010.

Paramonova, Svetlana, Extraterritorial jurisdiction in Russia. In: Sieber, U. / Forster, S. / Jarvers, K. (ed(s).): National Criminal Law in a Comparative Legal Context. Volume 2.1: General limitations on the application of criminal law. Berlin, Duncker & Humblot, 2011, pp. 297–315.

Paramonova, Svetlana, Grounds for excluding criminal liability in Russia. In: Sieber, U. / Jarvers, K. /Silverman, E. (ed(s).): Grounds for excluding criminal liability. Berlin, Duncker & Humblot, 2016, pp.126–163, 343–357.

Paramonova, Svetlana, Internationales Strafrecht im Cyberspace. Strafrechtliche Analyse der Rechtslage in Deutschland, Russland und den USA (Criminal Jurisdiction in Cyberspace: Legal Situation in Germany, Russia, and the USA). Berlin 2013, pp. 77–123.

Paramonova, Svetlana, Money Laundering, Revista Penal, 2011, Issue 28, pp. 251–254.

Paramonova, Svetlana, National characteristics, fundamental principles, and history of criminal law in Russia. In: Sieber, U. / Jarvers, K. /Silverman, E. (ed(s).): National Criminal Law in a Comparative Legal Context. Volume 1.4: Introduction to National Systems. Berlin, Duncker & Humblot, 2014, pp. 175–292.

Paramonova, Svetlana, Objective aspects of the offense in Russia. In: Sieber, U. / Forster, S. / Jarvers, K. (ed(s).): National Criminal Law in a Comparative Legal Context. Volume 3.1: Defining criminal conduct. Berlin, Duncker & Humblot, 2011, p. 239–254.

Paramonova, Svetlana, Parties to crime in Russia. In: Sieber, U. / Jarvers, K. /Silverman, E. (eds.): Special forms of criminal liability. Berlin, Duncker & Humblot, 2015, pp. 185–207.

Paramonova, Svetlana, Principle of legality in Russia. In: Sieber, U. / Forster, S. / Jarvers, K. (ed(s).): National Criminal Law in a Comparative Legal Context. Volume 2.1: General limitations on the application of criminal law. Berlin, Duncker & Humblot, 2011, pp. 103–117.

Paramonova, Svetlana, Punishable conduct prior to the completion of an offense in Russia. In: Sieber, U. / Jarvers, K. /Silverman, E. (ed(s).): Special forms of criminal liability. Berlin, Duncker & Humblot, 2015, pp. 46–62.

Paramonova, Svetlana, Recent Reforms of the Russian Criminal and Criminal Procedural Law. Revista Penal, 2012, Issue 30, pp. 264–268.

Paramonova, Svetlana, Russia's Constitutional Court and the Death Penalty in: Towards Universal Abolition of the Death Penalty. *Arroyo, Luis/Biglino, Paloma/Schabas, William* (eds.), pp. 167–175, Valencia, 2010/2011.

Paramonova, Svetlana, Russian Tax Criminal Law. New Developments. In: Revista Penal, 2011, Vol. 27, pp. 255–260.

Paramonova, Svetlana, Status der Europäischen Konvention zum Schutze der Menschenrechte und Grundfreiheiten (EMRK) und der Rechtsprechung des Europäischen Gerichtshofs für Menschenrechte (EGMR) sowie deren Rolle bei der Gestaltung des russischen Strafverfahrens (The status of the ECHR and of the jurisprudence of the ECtHR. Their role in shaping Russian criminal procedure). KritV 2013, 188–211.

Paramonova, Svetlana, Subjective aspects of the offense in Russia. In: Sieber, U. / Forster, S. / Jarvers, K. (ed(s).): National Criminal Law in a Comparative Legal Context. Volume 3.1: Defining criminal conduct. Berlin, Duncker & Humblot, 2011, pp. 436–452.

Paramonova, Svetlana, The Principle of Universality and Extradition in Russia. Revista Penal, Issue 26, 2010, pp. 220–224.

Paramonova, Svetlana, Уголовная юрисдикция в Интернет-пространстве: территориальный принцип в российском и немецком законодательстве. Журнал зарубежного законодательства и сравнительного правоведения, Выпуск 4, 2009 (Criminal Jurisdiction in Cyberspace: Principle of Territoriality According to Russian and German Law). ZSP, 2009, Issue 4, pp. 77–87.

Paramonova, Svetlana/Bogush, Gleb, Neue Entwicklungen im Strafprozessrecht Russlands (New Developments of the Russian Criminal Procedural Law). Zeitschrift für die gesamte Strafrechtswissenschaft, ZStW / Criminal Jurisprudence Journal, 2014, Issue 125/3, pp. 703–728.

Petrukhin, Igor, Теоретические основы реформы уголовного процесса в России. Том 2 (Theoretical Basis of the Reform of Criminal Process in Russia, Vol. 2*).* Moscow 2005, p. 26.

Pikalov, Igor, Уголовный процесс Российской Федерации (Criminal Procedure of the Russian Federation), http://www.allpravo.ru/library [last visited December 18, 2019].

Piontkovkij, Andrej, Курс советского уголовного права. Том 2: Преступление (Treatise on Soviet Criminal Law, vol. 2: Crime). Moscow 1970.

Piontkovskij Aleksej, Советское уголовное право. Часть Общая. т. I. М-Л., 1928 (Soviet Criminal Law. General Part). Moscow-Leningrad., Vol. I. 1928, pp. 30, 241.

Polls: Полиция с народом и без, 2013 (Police with the people and without), http://www.gazeta.ru/comments/2013/ 03/07_a_5003313.shtml [last visited December 18, 2019].

Polls: Социологический опрос: 47% считают, что полиция не способна защитить их от преступников, 2014 (Sociological Polls: 47% believe that the police cannot protect them from criminals), http://publicverdict.ru/topics/index_d/11880.html [last visited December 18, 2019].

Polls: Социологический опрос: В России наблюдается устойчивое недоверие населения к правоохранительным органам (Polls: In Russia Is Observed a Stable Mistrust in Law-enforcement Bodies), http://www.kuban.aif.ru/society/news/17770 [last visited December 18, 2019].

Pomorski, Stanislaw. Modern Russian Criminal Procedure: The Adversarial Principle and Guilty Plea. Criminal Law Forum, Vol. 17, N 2, 2006, pp. 129–148.

Pozdnischev, Sergej, Основные начала науки уголовного права. Общая часть (Basics of the Criminal Law. General Part). Moscow 1912, pp. 320–325.

Pristavkin Anatolij. Death penalty in Russia, 2012, http://www.prison.org/english/rpsdea.htm [last visited December 18, 2019].

Prosecutor General's Office of the Russian Federation, http://www.genproc.gov.ru [last visited December 18, 2019].

Radchenko, Vladimir, Комментарии к Уголовно-процессуальному Кодексу Российской Федерации (The Commentaries on the Code of Criminal Procedure of the Russian Federation). Moscow 2007, www.consultant.ru [last visited December 18, 2019].

Ragog, Alexej (ed.), Уголовное право России. Общая часть (Russian Criminal Law. General Part), Moscow 2009.

Rambaud, Alfred. Russia. Ivan III, the Great, the Uniter of the Russian Land (1462–1505), Leonora B. Lang, tr., Vol. 1, New York, 1900, pp. 161–174.

Research Service "Sreda," http://sreda.org/arena [last visited December 18, 2019].

Revin, Valerij (ed.), Уголовное право России. Общая часть (Criminal law of Russia. General Part). 2d ed. Moscow 2010, http://book2.me/418-ugolovnoe-pravo-obschaya-chast.html [last visited December 18, 2019].

Rudnev, Vladimir, Необходимость участия народных заседателей в отправлении правосудия как гарантия реализации конституционных прав граждан (The Necessity of the Participation of Lay Judges in Administration of Justice), Адвокат (Advokat), 2005, N 8, pp. 39–42.

Rudnev, Vladimir, Необходимость участия народных заседателей в отправлении правосудия как гарантия реализации конституционных прав граждан (The Necessity of the Participation of Lay Judges in Administration of Justice), Адвокат (Advokat), 2005, N 8, pp. 39–42.

Russia's Economy under Vladimir Putin: Achievements and Failures. RIA Novosti, 2008, http://en.rian.ru/analysis/20080301/100381963.html [last visited December 18, 2019].

Schedrin, Nikolaj, Меры безопасности как средство предупреждения преступности (Security Measures as a Crime Prevention Tool). Yekaterinburg 2001, pp. 1–348.

Schjolberg, Stein. Cyberspace Treaty—a United Nations Convention or Protocol on Cybersecurity and Cybercrime, http://www.cybercrimelaw.net/documents/UN_12th_Crime_Congress.pdf [last visited December 18, 2019].

Sergeevskij, Nikolaj, Русское уголовное право. Часть общая (Russian Criminal Law. General Part). St. Petersburg 1905, pp. 10–13.

Shargorodskij, Michail, Предмет и система уголовного права. Советское уголовное право (The Subject-matter and the System of Criminal Law). Soviet Criminal Law, N 4, 1941, p. 41.

Shershenevich, Gabriel', Учебник русского гражданского права (Russian Civil Law). Moscow 1995, p. 546.

Shishko, Irina, Экономические правонарушения: вопросы юридической оценки и ответственности (Economic offenses: legal issues of qualification and liability). St. Petersburg 2004.

Shishov Oleg, Смертная казнь в России в XX веке (The Death Penalty in Russia in XX century), http://www.index.org.ru/journal/14/shishov1401.html [last visited December 18, 2019].

Shuster, Simon, Khodorkovsky Case: Russia's Courtroom of the Absurd, 2010, http://content.time.com/time/world/article/0,8599,2039824,00.html [last visited December 18, 2019].

Shuster, Simon, Khodorkovsky Case: Russia's Courtroom of the Absurd, 2010, http://content.time.com/time/world/article/0,8599,2039824,00.html [last visited December 18, 2019].

Smirnov A./ Kalinowski K., Criminal Procedure: Textbook (Уголовный процесс: учебник для вузов). 6th ed., Norma, Moscow, 2015, pp. 3 –736.

Smith, Gordon B., Reforming the Russian Legal System. Cambridge 1996, pp. 1–5, 10–11, 14, 27, 79–103.

Solodkin, Iosif, Очерки по истории русского уголовного права, XIX век (Essays on the History of Russian Criminal Law, XIX century). Leningrad 1961.

Solomon, Peter H. Jr. (ed.), Reforming Justice in Russia, 1864–1996. New York 1997, pp. 282–347.

Spasovich, Vladimir, Учебник уголовного права (Textbook for the Criminal Law). 1st ed. St. Petersburg 1863, pp. 60–65.

Sucharev, Alexandr, Комментарий к Уголовно-процессуальному кодексу РФ (Commentaries to the Code of Criminal Procedure of the Russian Federation). Moscow 2004, p. 16–18.

Sundurov, Fedor, Наказание и альтернативные меры в уголовном праве (Punishment and Alternative Measures in the Criminal Law). Kazan' 2005, pp. 32–36, 103.

Supreme Court of the Russian Federation, http://www.supcourt.ru [last visited December 18, 2019].

Sverchkov, Vladimir, Уголовное право. Общая и Особенная части (Criminal law. General and Special Parts). Moscow 2009.

Tagantsev Nikolaj, Русское уголовное право. Лекции. Часть общая (Russian Criminal Law. Lectures. General Part). Moscow 1994, p. 16.

Tagantsev, Nikolaj, Курс русского уголовного права. Часть Общая (Textbook for Russian Criminal Law. General Part). St. Petersburg 1874, pp. 5, 45–46.

Tagantsev, Nikolaj, Русское уголовное право. Лекции. Часть общая (Russian Criminal Law. Lectures. General Part). St. Petersburg 1888, pp. 141, 487–488.

Taubina, Natalia, How do European Court Judgements influence detention conditions in Russia?: http://www.einnetwork.org/ein-voices/2017/12/12/how-do-european-court-judgments-influence-detention-condi tions-in-russia.

The Nuremberg Trials: The Collection of Materials, vol. 1 (Нюрнбергский процесс: Сборник материалов, Том 1). «Государственное издательство юридической литературы». Moscow 1955.

Thoughts about Russian Judicial Reform (Размышления о российской судебной реформе), http://www.index.org.ru/nevol/2010-22/09-golovko.html [last visited December 18, 2019].

Tichomirov, Yurij, Курс сравнительного правоведения (Comparative Law). Moscow 1996, pp. 113–181.

Tichomirov, Yurij/Talapina, Elvira, Введение в российское право (Introduction to Russian Law). Moscow 2003, pp. 50–60.

Trainin, Aron, Общее учение о составе преступления (General Doctrine about the Elements of Crime). Moscow 1957, pp. 59–60.

Trajnin, Aron, Уголовное право. Общая часть (Textbook on the Criminal Law. General Part). Moscow 1929, p. 101. *Butler, William E.* Criminal Code of the Russian Federation. Translated by Wildy, Simmonds and Hill Publishing Ltd. 4th edition. London 2004.

United Nations Organization (UNO), www.un.org [last visited December 18, 2019].

Uss, Aleksandr, Социально-интегративная роль уголовного права (The Socio-integrative Role of the Criminal Law). Krasnoyarsk 1993, pp. 11–323.

Vasiliev, Vladislav, Юридическая психология. Учебник для вузов. Москва 1991 (Legal Psychology. Textbook for Universities). Moscow 1991.

Volzhenkin, Boris, Уголовная ответственность юридических лиц: Серия "Современные стандарты в уголовном праве и уголовном процессе" (Criminal liability of legal persons: issue "Modern Standards in Criminal Law and Criminal Procedure"). St. Petersburg 1998.

Walden, *Ian,* Crime and Security in Cyberspace, http://www.lawnet.lk/docs/articles/sri_lankan/HTML/CV47.html [last visited December 18, 2019].

World Prison Brief, http://www.prisonstudies.org/ [last visited December 18, 2019].

Worldpopulationreview, http://worldpopulationreview.com/countries/russia-population/ [last visited December 18, 2019].

Yakovlev, Alexandr, Теория криминологии и социальная практика (The Theory of Criminology and Social Practice). Moscow 1985, pp. 7–9.

Yakovlev, Boris/Burtsov, Aleksej, Концентрационные лагеря СССР (Concentration Camps in the USSR), http://javot.net/arhiv/8.htm [last visited December 18, 2019].

Yalbulganov, Alexandr, Финансовое право (Financial Law). Moscow 2001, p. 82.

Yeltsin, Boris, Биография Ельцина (Autobiography. Boris Yeltsin), http://www.bibliotekar.ru/boris-eltsin/5.htm [last visited December 18, 2019].

Yushkov Serafim (ed.), Памятники русского права. Вып. 1 (Monuments of Russian Law, Vol. 1). Moscow 1950, p. 79.

Zhalinskij, Alfred (ed.), Учебно-практический комментарий к Уголовному кодексу РФ (Commentaries on the Criminal Code). Moscow 2006.

Zhilzov, Sergej, Смертная казнь в древней Руси. Правоведение, 1997, N 4 (The Death Penalty in Ancient Rus'). Pravovedenie, 1997, N 4, p. 1.

Zhuravlev, Michail (ed.), Уголовное право. Общая и Особенная части (Criminal Law. General and Special Parts). Moscow 2004, pp. 3–11, 19–25, 60–63, 108–125, 187–189.

Zhuravlev, Michail/Nikulin, Sergej (eds.), Уголовное право. Общая и Особенная части (Criminal law: general and Special Parts). Moscow 2004.

Zimnenko, Bogdan, Международное право в судебной практике России: уголовное судопроизводство (International Law in Legal Practice of Russia: Criminal Justice), Российская юстиция (Rossijskaya Justiziya), 2003, N 10, pp. 10–13.

Index

The numbers here refer to paragraph numbers.

Index

Index

www.ingramcontent.com/pod-product-compliance
Ingram Content Group UK Ltd.
Pitfield, Milton Keynes, MK11 3LW, UK
UKHW020131290926
15471UKWH00003B/422

9 789403 531205